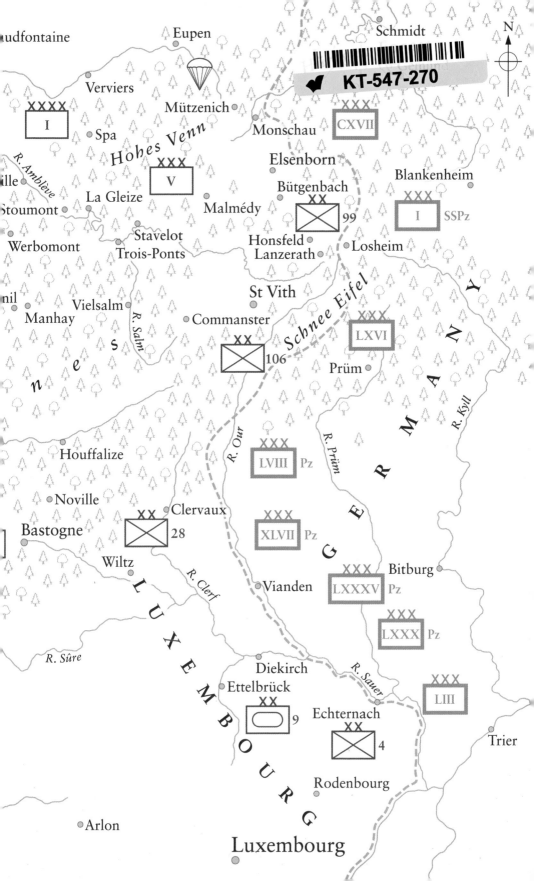

Ardennes 1944

By the Same Author

Inside the British Army
Crete: The Battle and the Resistance
Paris after the Liberation (*with Artemis Cooper*)
Stalingrad
Berlin: The Downfall 1945
The Mystery of Olga Chekhova
The Battle for Spain
D-Day
The Second World War

ARDENNES 1944

HITLER'S LAST GAMBLE

Antony Beevor

VIKING

an imprint of

PENGUIN BOOKS

VIKING

UK | USA | Canada | Ireland | Australia
India | New Zealand |South Africa

Viking is part of the Penguin Random House group of companies
whose addresses can be found at global.penguinrandomhouse.com.

First published 2015

001

Copyright © Ocito, 2015
Maps copyright © Jeff Edwards, 2015

The moral right of the copyright holders has been asserted

Typeset in Ehrhardt 11.75/14.5 pt by Palimpsest Book Production Limited,
Falkirk, Stirlingshire
Printed in Great Britain by Clays Ltd, St Ives plc

A CIP catalogue record for this book is available from the British Library

ISBN: 978–0–670–91864–5

For Adam Beevor

Contents

Contents

List of Illustrations

Illustration acknowledgements

The majority of the photographs come from The National Archives in the USA. Other photographs are from: 1, 13, 16, AKG Images; 5, Documentation Française; 11, Tank Museum; 12, Bundesarchiv, Koblenz; 6–7, 18, 20, 25–6, 30–32, 34, 36, 38–9, 41, 46–7, US Army (part of National Archives); 8, 23, 26, 40, Imperial War Museum, London; 10, Heinz Seidler, Bonn Bad Godersberg, reproduced from W. Goolrick and O. Tanner, *The Battle of the Bulge.*

List of Maps

Key to Military Symbols

Allied

XXXXX
`12AG` — 12th Army Group

XXXX
`1` — First US Army

XXX
`VII` — US VII Corps

XXX
`XXX` BR — British XXX Corps

XX
`101` — 101st Airborne Division

x
B `10` — Combat Command B of 10th Armored Division

III
335 `84` — 335th Infantry Regiment, 84th Division

German

XXXXX
`B` — Army Group B

XXXX
`5` Pz — Fifth Panzer Army

XX
`26VG` — 26th Volksgrenadier Division

XX
`LEHR` — Panzer Lehr Division

XX
`3FSJ` — 3rd Fallschirmjäger Division

III
115 `15Pzg` — 115th Panzergrenadier Regiment, 15th Panzergrenadier Division

III
Rcn `26VG` — Reconnaissance Battalion, 26th Volksgrenadier Division

Glossary

Abatis	Barriers across roads and tracks made by cutting down and dropping trees, which were often mined or booby-trapped.
Com Z	The Communications Zone commanded by General Lee responsible for all supplies and replacement soldiers.
Counter Intelligence Corps	The US Army equivalent of the British Field Security.
CSDIC	Combined Services Detailed Interrogation Centre included those holding pens and prison camps, such as Trent Park in England, where the conversation of German prisoners was secretly recorded by mainly German Jewish volunteers.
Dogface	US Army slang for an infantryman.
Doughboy	A term from the First World War for an ordinary American soldier.
G-2	Senior staff officer or staff for intelligence.
G-3	Senior staff officer or staff for operations.
Jabo	German abbreviation for fighter-bomber or *Jagdbomber*.
Kübelwagen	The German army's counterpart to the Jeep, it was made by Volkswagen and slightly larger and heavier.

Meat-chopper	US Army slang for anti-aircraft half-track mounting quadruple .50 machine guns when used against enemy infantry.
Meuse river	The French and English name for the river which German, Dutch and Flemish speakers called the Maas.
Non-battle casualties	Include the sick, those suffering from trench foot or frostbite, and neuropsychiatric or combat-fatigue breakdown.
Pozit fuses	These 'proximity' fuses for artillery shells, used for the first time in the Ardennes, exploded with devastating effect as air bursts above the enemy's heads.
PX	The Post Exchange, which sold items, including cigarettes, to US Army personnel.
Roer river	Rur river in German, but here for the sake of clarity given the Flemish/French/English name of Roer even on German territory.
SA	Sturmabteilung, the Nazi 'brownshirt' stormtroopers.
Schloss	German castle, or large country house.
Screaming meemies	The US Army slang for the German six-barrelled Nebelwerfer rocket launcher which made a terrifying sound.
SHAEF	Supreme Headquarters Allied Expeditionary Force. General Eisenhower's headquarters based at Versailles commanding the three army groups on the western front.
Trench foot	Trench foot was officially called 'immersion foot' in the US Army, but everyone continued to use the First World War term of 'trench foot'. It was a form of foot rot which was due to damp feet, a failure to change to dry socks and a lack of mobility. It could become gangrenous.
Ultra	The interception of German signals pre-

	pared on Enigma machines which were decoded at Bletchley Park.
Volksgrenadier	German infantry divisions reconstituted in the autumn of 1944 with a smaller establishment.
Wehrmachtführungsstab	The Wehrmacht operations staff led by Generaloberst Jodl.
Westwall	German name for the defence line on the Reich's western border which the Americans and British called the Siegfried Line.

Table of Military Ranks

American	British	German army	Waffen-SS
Private	Private/Trooper	Schütze/Kanonier/Jäger	Schütze
Private First Class		Oberschütze	Oberschütze
	Lance-Corporal	Gefreiter	Sturmmann
Corporal	Corporal	Obergefreiter	Rottenführer
Sergeant	Sergeant	Feldwebel/Wachtmeister	Oberscharführer
Staff Sergeant	Staff/Colour Sergeant	Oberfeldwebel	Hauptscharführer
Technical Sergeant	Regtl Quartermaster Sgt		
Master Sergeant	Coy/Sqn Sergeant Major	Stabsfeldwebel	Sturmscharführer
	Regimental Sergeant Major		
2nd Lieutenant	2nd Lieutenant	Leutnant	Untersturmführer
Lieutenant	Lieutenant	Oberleutnant	Obersturmführer
Captain	Captain	Hauptmann/Rittmeister	Hauptsturmführer
Major	Major	Major	Sturmbannführer
Lieutenant Colonel	Lieutenant Colonel	Oberstleutnant	Obersturmbannführer
Colonel	Colonel	Oberst	Standartenführer
Brigadier General	Brigadier *	Generalmajor	Oberführer
			Brigadeführer
Major General	Major General **	Generalleutnant	Gruppenführer

Lieutenant General	Lieutenant General	***	General der Infanterie/ Artillerie/Panzertruppe	Obergruppenführer/ General-der Waffen-SS
General	General	****	Generaloberst	Obergruppenführer
General of the Army	Field Marshal	*****	Generalfeldmarschall	

This can only be an approximate guide to equivalent ranks since each army has its own variations. Some ranks have been omitted in the interests of simplicity. In the British and US armies the following ranks command the following sub-units (below a battalion), units (battalion or regiment) and formations (brigade, division or corps).

Rank	British and Canadian army	US Army	Approx. number of men at full strength
Corporal	Section	Squad	8
2nd/Lieutenant	Platoon	Platoon	30
Captain/Major	Company	Company	120
Lieutenant Colonel	Battalion or Armoured Regiment	Battalion	700
Colonel		Regiment	2,400
Brigadier	Brigade	Combat command	2,400
Major General	Division	Division	10,000
Lieutenant General	Corps	Corps	30,000–40,000
General	Army	Army	70,000–150,000
Field Marshal/ General of the Army	Army Group	Army Group	200,000–350,000

I

Victory Fever

Early on 27 August 1944, General Dwight D. Eisenhower left Chartres to see the newly liberated Paris. 'It's Sunday,' the Supreme Allied Commander told General Omar Bradley, whom he took with him. 'Everyone will be sleeping late. We can do it without any fuss.' Yet the two generals were hardly inconspicuous as they bowled along towards the French capital on their supposedly 'informal visit'. The Supreme Commander's olive-drab Cadillac was escorted by two armoured cars, and a Jeep with a brigadier general leading the way.

When they reached the Porte d'Orléans, an even larger escort from the 38th Cavalry Reconnaissance Squadron awaited in review order under the orders of Major General Gerow. Leonard Gerow, an old friend of Eisenhower, still seethed with resentment because General Philippe Leclerc of the French 2nd Armoured Division had consistently disobeyed all his orders during the advance on Paris. The day before, Gerow, who considered himself the military governor of Paris, had forbidden Leclerc and his division to take part in General de Gaulle's procession from the Arc de Triomphe to Notre-Dame. He had told him instead to 'continue on present mission of clearing Paris and environs of enemy'. Leclerc had ignored Gerow throughout the liberation of the capital, but that morning he had sent part of his division north out of the city against German positions around Saint-Denis.

The streets of Paris were empty because the retreating Germans had seized almost every vehicle that could move. Even the Métro was unpredictable because of the feeble power supply; in fact the so-called 'City of

Light' was reduced to candles bought on the black market. Its beautiful buildings looked faded and tired, although they were mercifully intact. Hitler's order to reduce it to 'a field of rubble' had not been followed. In the immediate aftermath of joy, groups in the street still cheered every time they caught sight of an American soldier or vehicle. Yet it would not be long before the Parisians started muttering 'Pire que les boches' – 'Worse than the Boches'.

Despite Eisenhower's remark about going to Paris 'without any fuss', their visit had a definite purpose. They went to meet General Charles de Gaulle, the leader of the French provisional government which President Roosevelt refused to recognize. Eisenhower, a pragmatist, was prepared to ignore his President's firm instruction that United States forces in France were not there to install General de Gaulle in power. The Supreme Commander needed stability behind his front lines, and since de Gaulle was the only man likely to provide it, he was willing to support him.

Neither de Gaulle nor Eisenhower wanted the dangerous chaos of liberation to get out of hand, especially at a time of frenzied rumours, sudden panics, conspiracy theories and the ugly denunciations of alleged collaborators. Together with a comrade, the writer J. D. Salinger, a Counter Intelligence Corps staff sergeant with the 4th Infantry Division, had arrested a suspect in an action close to the Hôtel de Ville, only for the crowd to drag him away and beat him to death in front of their eyes. De Gaulle's triumphal procession the day before from the Arc de Triomphe to Notre-Dame had ended in wild fusillades within the cathedral itself. This incident convinced de Gaulle that he must disarm the Resistance and conscript its members into a regular French army. A request for 15,000 uniforms was passed that very afternoon to SHAEF – the Supreme Headquarters Allied Expeditionary Force.* Unfortunately, there were not enough small sizes because the average French male was distinctly shorter than his American contemporary.

De Gaulle's meeting with the two American generals took place in the ministry of war in the rue Saint-Dominique. This was where his short-lived ministerial career had begun in the tragic summer of 1940, and he had returned there to emphasize the impression of continuity.

* See Glossary.

His formula for erasing the shame of the Vichy regime was a majestically simple one: 'The Republic has never ceased to exist.' De Gaulle wanted Eisenhower to keep Leclerc's division in Paris to ensure law and order, but since some of Leclerc's units had now started to move out, he suggested that perhaps the Americans could impress the population with 'a show of force' to reassure them that the Germans would not be coming back. Why not march a whole division or even two through Paris on its way to the front? Eisenhower, thinking it slightly ironic that de Gaulle should be asking for American troops 'to establish his position firmly', turned to Bradley and asked what he thought. Bradley said that it would be perfectly possible to arrange within the next couple of days. So Eisenhower invited de Gaulle to take the salute, accompanied by General Bradley. He himself would stay away.

On their return to Chartres, Eisenhower invited General Sir Bernard Montgomery to join de Gaulle and Bradley for the parade, but he refused to come to Paris. Such a small but pertinent detail did not deter certain British newspapers from accusing the Americans of trying to hog all the glory for themselves. Inter-Allied relations were to be severely damaged by the compulsion in Fleet Street to see almost every decision by SHAEF as a slight to Montgomery and thus the British. This reflected the more widespread resentment that Britain was being sidelined. The Americans were now running the show and would claim the victory for themselves. Eisenhower's British deputy, Air Chief Marshal Sir Arthur Tedder, was alarmed by the prejudice of the English press: 'From what I heard at SHAEF, I could not help fearing that this process was sowing the seeds of a grave split between the Allies.'

The following evening the 28th Infantry Division, under its commander, Major General Norman D. Cota, moved from Versailles towards Paris in heavy rain. 'Dutch' Cota, who had shown extraordinary bravery and leadership on Omaha beach, had taken over command less than two weeks before, after a German sniper had killed his predecessor. The fighting in the heavy hedgerow country of Normandy had been slow and deadly during June and July, but the breakout led by General George S. Patton's Third Army at the beginning of August had produced a surge of optimism during the charge to the River Seine and Paris itself.

Showers had been set up for Cota's men in the Bois de Boulogne so that they could scrub themselves before the parade. The next morning, 29 August, the division set off up the Avenue Foch to the Arc de Triomphe, and then down the long vista of the Champs-Elysées. Helmeted infantry, with rifles slung and bayonets fixed, marched in full battle order. The mass of olive-drab, rank after rank twenty-four men abreast, stretched right across the broad avenue. Each man on his shoulder wore the divisional badge, the red 'Keystone' symbol of Pennsylvania, which the Germans had dubbed the 'bloody bucket' from its shape.

The French were amazed, both by the informality of American uniforms and by their seemingly limitless quantities of machinery. 'Une armée de mécanos,' the diarist Jean Galtier-Boissière remarked. On the Champs-Elysées that morning, the French crowds could not believe that a single infantry division could have so many vehicles: countless Jeeps, some with .50 machine guns mounted behind; scout-cars; the artillery, with their 155mm 'Long Tom' howitzers towed by tracked prime-movers; engineers; service units with small trucks and ten-tonners; M-4 Sherman tanks, and tank destroyers. This display made the Wehrmacht, the apparently invincible conqueror of France in 1940, appear bizarrely old-fashioned with its horse-drawn transport.

The saluting dais was on the Place de la Concorde. Army engineers had created it out of assault boats turned upside down and concealed by a long *tricolore* valance, while numerous Stars and Stripes fluttered in the breeze. In front the fifty-six-piece band, which had led the parade, played the division's march, 'Khaki Bill'. The French crowds watching the show may not have guessed, but all the soldiers knew that the 28th Division was headed against the German positions on the northern edge of the city. 'It was one of the most remarkable attack orders ever issued,' Bradley remarked later to his aide. 'I don't think many people realized the men were marching from parade into battle.'

On the Channel coast, the Canadian First Army had to capture the great port of Le Havre, while the Second British Army pushed north-east into the Pas de Calais towards some of the German V-weapon sites. Despite the exhaustion of tank drivers and a terrible storm on the night of 30–31 August, the Guards Armoured Division seized Amiens and the bridges over the Somme with the help of the French Resistance. General der Panzertruppe Heinrich Eberbach, the commander of the Fifth

Panzer Army, was taken unawares the next morning. The British advance then managed to drive a wedge between the remains of the Fifth Panzer Army and the Fifteenth Army, which had held the Pas de Calais. The Canadians, led by the Royal Regiment of Canada, the Royal Hamilton Light Infantry and the Essex Scottish, headed for Dieppe where they had suffered so grievously in the disastrous raid two years before.

Allied victory euphoria could not have been greater. The July bomb plot that summer against Hitler had encouraged the idea that disintegration had started, rather like in 1918, but in fact the failure of the assassination attempt had strengthened Nazi domination immeasurably. The G-2 intelligence department at SHAEF blithely claimed, 'The August battles have done it, and the enemy in the west has had it.' In London, the war cabinet believed it would all be over by Christmas, and set 31 December as the end of hostilities for planning purposes. Only Churchill remained wary of the German determination to fight on. In Washington a similar assumption allowed attention to turn increasingly to the still desperate fight against the Japanese in the Pacific. The US War Production Board began cancelling military contracts, including those for artillery shells.

Many Germans also thought the end had come. Oberstleutnant Fritz Fullriede in Utrecht wrote in his diary: 'The West Front is finished, the enemy is already in Belgium and on the German frontier; Romania, Bulgaria, Slovakia and Finland are pleading for peace. It is exactly like 1918.' In a Berlin railway station protesters had dared to put up a banner which read: 'We want peace at any price.' On the eastern front the Red Army had crushed Army Group Centre in Operation Bagration, which had taken them 500 kilometres forward to the gates of Warsaw and the River Vistula. In three months the Wehrmacht had lost 589,425 men on the eastern front and 156,726 in the west.

The dash to the Vistula had encouraged the brave but doomed Warsaw uprising of the Armia Krajowa. Stalin, not wanting an independent Poland, callously allowed the insurgents to be crushed by the Germans. East Prussia, with Hitler's headquarters at the Wolfsschanze near Rastenburg, was also threatened, and German armies were collapsing in the Balkans. Just two days before the liberation of Paris, Romania defected from the Axis as Soviet armies surged across its borders. On 30 August, the Red Army entered Bucharest and occupied the vital oilfields of

Ploeşti. The way lay open to the Hungarian plain and the River Danube stretched ahead into Austria and Germany itself.

In mid-August, General George Patton's Third Army charged from Normandy to the Seine. This coincided with the successful Operation Dragoon landings between Cannes and Toulon on the Mediterranean coast. The threat of being cut off prompted a massive German withdrawal right across the country. Members of the Vichy Milice who knew what awaited them at the hands of the Resistance also set out across hostile territory, in some cases for up to a thousand kilometres, to seek safety in Germany. Improvised 'march groups', a mixture of army, Luftwaffe, Kriegsmarine and non-combatant personnel from the Atlantic coast were ordered to escape east, while attempting to evade the French Resistance along the way. The Wehrmacht began to reinforce a salient around Dijon to receive almost a quarter of a million Germans. Another 51,000 soldiers were left trapped on the Atlantic coast and Mediterranean. Major ports were designated as 'fortresses' by the Führer even though there was no hope of ever relieving them. This denial of reality was described by one German general as being like a Catholic priest on Good Friday who sprinkles his plate of pork with holy water and says: 'You are fish.'

Hitler's paranoia had reached new heights in the wake of the 20 July bomb plot. In the Wolfsschanze in East Prussia, he went far beyond his earlier jibes that the German general staff was just 'a club of intellectuals'. 'Now I know why all my great plans in Russia had to fail in recent years,' he said. 'It was all treason! But for those traitors, we would have won long ago.' Hitler hated the July plotters, not just because of their treachery, but because of the damage they had done to the impression of German unity, and the effect this had on the Third Reich's allies and neutral states.

At the situation conference on 31 August, Hitler declared: 'There will be moments in which the tension between the Allies will become so great that the break will happen. Coalitions in world history have always been ruined at some point.' The propaganda minister Joseph Goebbels rapidly picked up on the Führer's line of thinking at a conference of ministers in Berlin soon afterwards. 'It is certain that the political conflicts will increase with the apparent approach of an Allied victory, and some day will cause cracks in the house of our enemies which no longer can be repaired.'

The chief of the general staff of the Luftwaffe, General der Flieger Werner Kreipe, noted in his diary on that last day of August: 'In the evening reports arrive of the collapse in the west.' A frenzy of activity continued through most of the night with 'orders, instructions, telephone conversations'. The next morning, Generalfeldmarschall Wilhelm Keitel, the chief of the Oberkommando der Wehrmacht (OKW), asked the Luftwaffe to transfer another 50,000 men to ground forces. On 2 September, Kreipe noted: 'Apparently disintegration has set in in the west, Jodl [chief of the Wehrmacht planning staff] surprisingly calm. The Finns detach themselves.' During that day's conference Hitler began insulting the Finnish leader, Marshal Mannerheim. He also became angry that Reichsmarschall Hermann Göring did not bother to turn up at such a critical moment and even suggested disbanding the Luftwaffe's squadrons and transferring flight crews to flak units.

With Red Army forces now on the East Prussian border, Hitler was afraid of a Soviet parachute operation to capture him. The Wolfsschanze had been turned into a fortress. 'By now a huge apparatus had been constructed,' wrote his secretary Traudl Junge. 'There were barriers and new guard posts everywhere, mines, tangles of barbed wire, watchtowers.'

Hitler wanted an officer whom he could trust to command the troops defending him. Oberst Otto Remer had brought the *Grossdeutschland* guard battalion in Berlin to defeat the plotters on 20 July, so on hearing of Remer's request to be posted back to a field command, Hitler summoned him to form a brigade to guard the Wolfsschanze. Initially based on the Berlin battalion and the *Hermann Göring* Flak-Regiment with eight batteries, Remer's brigade grew and grew. The *Führer Begleit*, or Führer Escort, Brigade was formed in September ready to defend the Wolfsschanze against 'an air landing of two to three airborne divisions'. What Remer himself called this 'unusual array' of combined arms was given absolute priority in weapons, equipment and 'experienced frontline soldiers' mostly from the *Grossdeutschland* Division.

The atmosphere in the Wolfsschanze was profoundly depressed. For some days Hitler retired to his bed and lay there listlessly while his secretaries were 'typing out whole reams of reports of losses' from both

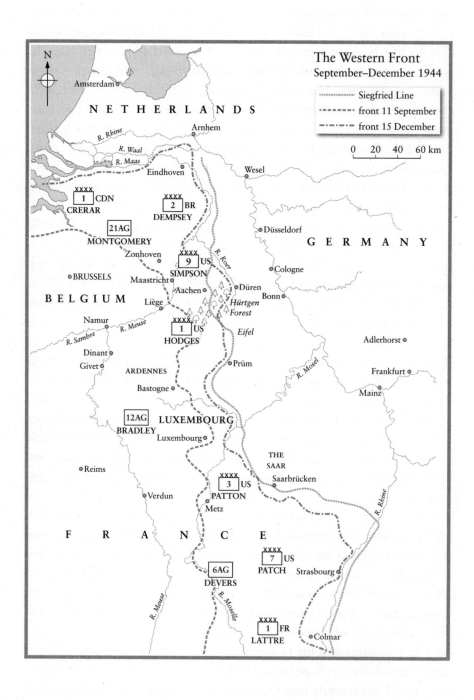

The Western Front
September–December 1944

········· Siegfried Line
– – – front 11 September
–·–·– front 15 December

0   20   40   60 km

N

NETHERLANDS

Amsterdam

R. Rhine

Arnhem

R. Waal
R. Maas

Eindhoven

Wesel

Düsseldorf

GERMANY

XXXX
1 CDN
CRERAR

XXXX
2 BR
DEMPSEY

21AG
MONTGOMERY

Zonhoven

XXXX
9 US
SIMPSON

R. Roer

Cologne

BRUSSELS

Maastricht

Aachen

Düren

Bonn

Hürtgen
Forest

BELGIUM

Liège

Namur

R. Meuse

XXXX
1 US
HODGES

Eifel

R. Sambre

Adlerhorst

Dinant
Givet

ARDENNES

Prüm

R. Mosel

Frankfurt

Bastogne

Mainz

12AG
BRADLEY

LUXEMBOURG

Luxembourg

Reims

THE
SAAR

Saarbrücken

XXXX
3 US
PATTON

Verdun

Metz

R. Rhine

F R A N C E

XXXX
7 US
PATCH

6AG
DEVERS

Strasbourg

R. Meuse

R. Moselle

XXXX
1 FR
LATTRE

Colmar

eastern and western fronts. Göring meanwhile was sulking on the Hohenzollern hunting estate of Rominten which he had appropriated in East Prussia. After the failure of his Luftwaffe in Normandy, he knew that he had been outmanoeuvred by his rivals at the Führer's court, especially the manipulative Martin Bormann who was eventually to prove his nemesis. His other opponent, Reichsführer-SS Heinrich Himmler, had been given command of the Ersatzheer – the Replacement Army – in whose headquarters the bomb plot had been hatched. And Goebbels appeared to have complete command of the home front, having been appointed Reich Plenipotentiary for the Total War Effort. But Bormann and the Gauleiters could still thwart almost any attempt to exert control over their fiefdoms.

Although most Germans had been shocked by the attempt on Hitler's life, a steep decline in morale soon followed as Soviet forces advanced to the borders of East Prussia. Women above all wanted the war to end and, as the security service of the SS reported, many had lost faith in the Führer. The more perceptive sensed that the war could not end while he remained alive.

Despite, or perhaps because of, the successes of that summer, rivalries were stirring in the highest echelons of the Allied command. Eisenhower, 'a military statesman rather than a warlord' as one observer put it, sought consensus, but to the resentment of Omar Bradley and the angry contempt of George Patton, he seemed bent on appeasing Montgomery and the British. The debate, which was to inflame relations throughout the rest of 1944 and into the new year, had begun on 19 August.

Montgomery had demanded that almost all Allied forces should advance under his command through Belgium and Holland into the industrial region of the Ruhr. After this proposal had been rejected, he wanted his own 21st Army Group, supported by General Courtney Hodges's First Army, to take this route. This would enable the Allies to capture the V-weapon launch sites bombarding London and take the deep-water port of Antwerp, which was vital to supply any further advances. Bradley and his two army commanders, Patton and Hodges, agreed that Antwerp must be secured, but they wanted to go east to the Saar, the shortest route into Germany. The American generals felt that their achievements in Operation Cobra, and the breakout all the way to the Seine led by Patton's Third Army, should give them the priority. Eisenhower, however, knew well that a single thrust, whether by the British in the north or by the Americans in the middle of the front, ran grave political dangers, even more than military ones. He would have the press and the politicians in either the United States or Great Britain exploding with outrage if their own army was halted because of supply problems while the other pushed on.

On 1 September, the announcement of the long-standing plan for Bradley, who had technically been Montgomery's subordinate, to assume command of the American 12th Army Group prompted the British press to feel aggrieved once again. Fleet Street saw the reorganization as a demotion for Montgomery because, with Eisenhower now based in France, he was no longer ground forces commander. This problem had been foreseen in London, so to calm things down Montgomery was promoted to field marshal (which in theory made him outrank Eisenhower, who had only four stars). Listening to the radio that morning, Patton was sickened when 'Ike said that Monty was the greatest living soldier and is now a Field Marshal.' No mention was made of what others had achieved. And after a meeting at Bradley's headquarters next day, Patton, who had led the charge across France, noted: 'Ike did not thank or congratulate any of us for what we have done.' Two days later his Third Army reached the River Meuse.

In any event, the headlong advance by the US First Army and the British Second Army to Belgium proved to be one of the most rapid in the whole war. It might have been even faster if they had not been delayed in every Belgian village and town by the local population greeting them with rapture. Lieutenant General Brian Horrocks, the commander of XXX Corps, remarked that 'what with champagne, flowers, crowds, and girls perched on the top of wireless trucks, it was difficult to get on with the war'. The Americans also found that their welcome in Belgium was far warmer and more enthusiastic than it had been in France. On 3 September, the Guards Armoured Division entered Brussels to the wildest scenes of jubilation ever.

The very next day, in a remarkable *coup de main*, Major General 'Pip' Roberts's 11th Armoured Division entered Antwerp. With the assistance of the Belgian Resistance, they seized the port before the Germans could destroy its installations. The 159th Infantry Brigade attacked the German headquarters in the park, and by 20.00 hours the commander of the German garrison had surrendered. His 6,000 men were marched off to be held in empty cages in the zoo, the animals having been eaten by a hungry population. 'The captives sat on the straw,' Martha Gellhorn observed, 'staring through the bars.' The fall of Antwerp shocked Führer headquarters. 'You had barely crossed the Somme,' General der Artillerie Walter Warlimont acknowledged to his Allied interrogators the following year, 'and suddenly one or two of your armoured divisions were at the gates of Antwerp. We had not expected any breakthrough so quickly and nothing was ready. When the news came it was a bitter surprise.'

The American First Army also moved fast to catch the retreating Germans. The reconnaissance battalion of the 2nd Armored Division, advancing well ahead of other troops, identified the enemy's route of withdrawal, then took up ambush positions with light tanks in a village or town just after dark. 'We would let a convoy get within [the] most effective range of our weapons before we opened fire. One light tank was used to tow knocked out vehicles into hiding among buildings in the town to prevent discovery by succeeding elements. This was kept up throughout the night.' One American tank commander calculated that from 18 August to 5 September his tank had done 563 miles 'with practically no maintenance'.

On the Franco-Belgian border, Bradley's forces had an even greater success than the British with a pincer movement meeting near Mons. Motorized units from three panzer divisions managed to break out just before the US 1st Infantry Division sealed the ring. The paratroopers of the 3rd and 6th Fallschirmjäger-Divisions were bitter that once again the Waffen-SS had saved themselves, leaving everybody else behind. The Americans had trapped the remnants of six divisions from Normandy, altogether more than 25,000 men. Until they surrendered they were sitting ducks. The 9th Infantry Division artillery reported: 'We employed our 155mm guns in a direct fire role against enemy troop columns, inflicting heavy casualties and contributing to the taking of 6,100 prisoners including three generals.'

Attacks by the Belgian Resistance in the Mons Pocket triggered the first of many reprisals, with sixty civilians killed and many houses set on fire. Groups of the Armée Secrète from the Mouvement National Belge, the Front de l'Indépendance and the Armée Blanche worked closely with the Americans in the mopping-up stage.* The German military command became angry and fearful of a mass rising as their forces retreated through Belgium to the safety of the Westwall, or Siegfried Line as the Allies called it. Young Belgians flocked to join in the attacks, with terrible consequences both at the time and later in December when the Ardennes offensive brought back German forces, longing for revenge.

On 1 September, in Jemelle, near Rochefort in the northern Ardennes, Maurice Delvenne watched the German withdrawal from Belgium with pleasure. 'The pace of the retreat by German armies accelerates and seems increasingly disorganized,' he wrote in his diary. 'Engineers, infantry, navy, Luftwaffe and artillery are all in the same truck. All of these men have obviously just been in the combat zone. They are dirty and haggard. Their greatest concern is to know how many kilometres still separate them from their homeland, and naturally we take a spiteful pleasure in exaggerating the distance.'

Two days later SS troops, some with bandaged heads, passed by Jemelle. 'Their looks are hard and they stare at people with hatred.' They were leaving a trail of destruction in their wake, by burning buildings, tearing down telegraph lines and driving stolen sheep and cattle before them. Farmers in the German-speaking eastern cantons of the Ardennes were ordered to move with their families and livestock back behind the Siegfried Line and into the Reich. News of the Allied bombing was enough to discourage them, but most simply did not want to leave their farms, so they hid with their livestock in the woods until the Germans had gone.

On 5 September, the exploits of young *résistants* provoked the retreating Germans into burning thirty-five houses beside the N4 highway from Marche-en-Famenne towards Bastogne, near the village of Bande. Far worse was to follow on Christmas Eve when the Germans returned in the Ardennes offensive. Ordinary people were terrified by the reprisals that followed Resistance attacks. At Buissonville on 6 September the

---

* The name L'Armée Blanche had nothing to do with the white armies of the Russian Civil War. It had evolved from the secret Belgian intelligence network established under German occupation during the First World War, which was called La Dame Blanche because of the legend that the Hohenzollern dynasty of the Kaiser would fall when the ghost of a white lady appeared.

Germans took revenge for an attack two days before. They set fire to twenty-two houses there and in the next-door village.

Further along the line of retreat, villagers and townsfolk turned out with Belgian, British and American flags to welcome their liberators. Sometimes they had to hide them quickly when yet another fleeing German detachment appeared in their main street. Back in Holland at Utrecht, Oberstleutnant Fritz Fullriede described 'a sad platoon of Dutch National Socialists being evacuated to Germany, to flee the wrath of the native Dutch. Lots of women and children.' These Dutch SS had been fighting at Hechtel over the Belgian border. They had escaped the encirclement by swimming a canal, but 'the wounded officers and men who wanted to give themselves up were for the most part – to the discredit of the British [who apparently stood by] – shot by the Belgians'. Both Dutch and Belgians had much to avenge after four years of occupation.

The German front in Belgium and Holland appeared completely broken. There was panic in the rear with chaotic scenes which prompted the LXXXIX Army Corps to speak in its war diary of 'a picture that is unworthy and disgraceful for the German army'. Feldjäger Streifengruppen, literally punishment groups, seized genuine stragglers and escorted them to a collection centre, or *Sammellager*. They were then sent back into the line under an officer, usually in batches of sixty. Near Liège, around a thousand men were marched to the front by officers with drawn pistols. Those suspected of desertion were court-martialled. If found guilty, they were sentenced either to death or to a Bewährungsbataillon (a so-called probation battalion, but in fact more of a punishment or Strafbataillon). Deserters who confessed, or who had put on civilian clothes, were executed on the spot.

Each Feldjäger wore a red armband with 'OKW Feldjäger' on it and possessed a special identity card with a green diagonal stripe which stated: 'He is entitled to make use of his weapon if disobeyed.' The Feldjäger were heavily indoctrinated. Once a week an officer lectured them on 'the world situation, the impossibility of destroying Germany, on the infallibility of the Führer and on underground factories which should help outwit the enemy'.

Generalfeldmarschall Walter Model's 'Appeal to the Soldiers of the

Army of the West' went unheeded when he called on them to hold on, to gain time for the Führer. The most ruthless measures were taken. Generalfeldmarschall Wilhelm Keitel ordered on 2 September that 'malingerers and cowardly shirkers, including officers' should be executed immediately. Model warned that he needed a minimum of ten infantry divisions and five panzer divisions if he were to prevent a breakthrough into northern Germany. No force of that magnitude was available.

The retreat in the north along the Channel coast had been much more orderly, mainly thanks to the delayed pursuit of the Canadians. General der Infanterie Gustav von Zangen had conducted the withdrawal of the Fifteenth Army from the Pas de Calais to northern Belgium in an impressive manner. Allied intelligence was severely mistaken when it stated that 'the only reinforcements known to be arriving in Holland are the demoralized and disorganized remnants of the Fifteenth Army now escaping from Belgium by way of the Dutch islands'.

The sudden seizure of Antwerp may have been a severe blow to the German high command, but over the following days, when the British Second Army failed to secure the north side of the Scheldt estuary, General von Zangen managed to establish defence lines. These included a twenty-kilometre-wide redoubt on the south side of the mouth of the Scheldt called the Breskens pocket, the South Beveland peninsula on the north side and the island of Walcheren. His force soon mustered 82,000 men and deployed some 530 guns which prevented any attempt by the Royal Navy to approach the heavily mined estuary.

Admiral Sir Bertram Ramsay, the Allied naval commander-in-chief, had told SHAEF and Montgomery that the Germans could block the Scheldt estuary with ease. And Admiral Sir Andrew Cunningham, the First Sea Lord, warned that Antwerp would be 'as much use to us as Timbuctoo' unless the approaches were cleared. General Horrocks, the corps commander, later admitted his own responsibility for the failure. 'Napoleon, no doubt, would have realized this,' he wrote, 'but I am afraid Horrocks didn't.' But it was not the fault of Horrocks, nor of Roberts, the commander of the 11th Armoured Division. The mistake lay with Montgomery, who was not interested in the estuary and thought that the Canadians could clear it later.

It was a massive error and led to a very nasty shock later, but in those days of euphoria generals who had served in the First World War convinced themselves that September 1944 was the equivalent of September 1918. 'Newspapers reported a 210-mile advance in six days and indicated that Allied forces were in Holland, Luxembourg, Saarbrücken, Brussels and Antwerp,' wrote the combat historian Forrest Pogue. 'The intelligence estimates all along the lines were marked by an almost hysterical optimism.' The eyes of senior officers were fixed on the Rhine, with the idea that the Allies could leap it in virtually one bound. This vision certainly beguiled Eisenhower, while Montgomery, for his own reasons, had become besotted with it.

2

Antwerp and the German Frontier

At the end of August, just when it seemed as if the German front was on the point of collapse, supply problems threatened to bring Eisenhower's armies to a halt. The French rail network had been largely destroyed by Allied bombing, so around 10,000 tons of fuel, rations and ammunition had to be hauled daily all the way from Normandy in the supply trucks of the US Army's 'Red Ball Express'. The distance from Cherbourg to the front in early September was close to 500 kilometres, which represented a three-day round trip. Liberated Paris alone needed an absolute minimum of 1,500 tons a day.

Only the wealth of American resources could have managed such a task, with some 7,000 trucks racing day and night along one-way routes, consuming almost 300,000 gallons of fuel a day. Altogether some 9,000 trucks were written off in the process. In a desperate attempt to keep up momentum in the dash across France, jerrycans had been delivered to front-line formations by the transport aircraft of IX Troop Carrier Command and even by bombers. But aircraft used up three gallons of aviation fuel for every two gallons of gasoline they delivered. Every aspect of the supply crisis underlined the urgent need to open the port of Antwerp, but Montgomery's focus was on crossing the Rhine.

On 3 September, Montgomery heard that, although a large part of the US First Army would support him in the north, it would not be under his command. Having thought that Eisenhower had agreed to a northern thrust under his sole control, he became exasperated when he heard that Patton's Third Army had not been brought to a halt as he had expected. Montgomery wrote to Field Marshal Sir Alan Brooke, the chief of the imperial general staff, in London on that fifth anniversary of Britain going to war. He revealed his intention to go all out for a Rhine crossing as soon as possible. He evidently felt that was the best way of forcing Eisenhower's hand to give his army group the bulk of the supplies and the command of Hodges's First Army.

Patton, instead of halting his army until the supply situation improved, had secretly stolen a march in his advance towards the Saar. 'In order to attack,' Patton explained in his diary, 'we first have to pretend to reconnoiter and then reinforce the reconnaissance and then finally attack. It is a very sad method of making war.' Patton was quite

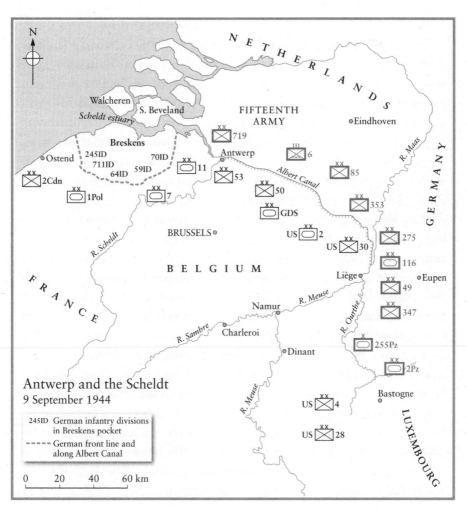

Antwerp and the Scheldt
9 September 1944

245ID German infantry divisions in Breskens pocket

German front line and along Albert Canal

0 20 40 60 km

shameless in getting his own way. Bomber pilots did not grumble when switched to a fuel run, because sometimes when they delivered supplies to Third Army divisions, a case of champagne would be brought to the pilot 'with [the] compliments of General Patton'. Patton could afford to be generous. He had somehow 'liberated' 50,000 cases.

Montgomery was so determined to mount the major strike in the north that he was prepared even to jeopardize the opening of the port of Antwerp for supplies. The new field marshal's operational outline of 3 September revealed that he had dropped the idea of diverting strong forces to clear the Scheldt estuary. This was why Roberts's 11th Armoured Division, on entering Antwerp, had received no orders to advance across the Albert Canal and round into the Beveland peninsula to the north-west where the Germans were starting to prepare positions.

Within the next few days the remnants of the German Fifteenth Army on both sides of the Scheldt started to become a formidable fighting force once more. The German army's extraordinary capacity to recover from disaster had been shown time and time again on the eastern front as well as in the west. Morale was bad, but the determination to fight on had not collapsed entirely. 'Even if all our allies abandon us, we must not lose courage,' an Unteroffizier wrote home. 'Once the Führer has his new weapons deployed, then the Final Victory will follow.'

While Eisenhower recognized the importance of securing the approaches to the port of Antwerp, he too was keen to get a bridgehead across the Rhine. In particular, he wanted to use the newly created First Allied Airborne Army in a major operation. His interest was shared by both General George C. Marshall, the chief of staff in Washington, and the US air force chief General 'Hap' Arnold. The great investment in time and effort building up the airborne arm had spurred on their desire to use it again at the first opportunity.

No fewer than nine plans for its deployment had been considered since the breakout in Normandy, but the speed of the Allied advance meant that every project had been overtaken before it could be launched. The exasperation of the paratroopers waiting on airfields can be imagined, as they repeatedly stood to, with aircraft and gliders packed, and then stood down again. General Patton boasted at a Third Army press conference: 'The damn airborne can't go fast enough to keep up with us.' He then added: 'That is off the record also.'

During the first week of September Field Marshal Montgomery began to look closely at the possibility of airborne drops to cross the Rhine at Arnhem. Operation Market Garden, to be launched on 17 September, was not merely ambitious. It was shockingly ill planned, with a minimal chance of success, and should never have been attempted. The drop zones, especially in the case of Arnhem, were too far from their bridge objectives to achieve surprise. Plans were not co-ordinated between the First Allied Airborne Army and the ground forces. The British XXX Corps was expected to charge up a single road for 104 kilometres to relieve the British airborne division at Arnhem, assuming it had secured the bridge there over the Neder Rijn, or lower Rhine. Worst of all, no allowance was made for anything to go wrong, including a change in the weather, which would prevent reinforcements from coming in rapidly.

The American 101st Airborne Division secured Eindhoven, and the 82nd Airborne eventually took Nijmegen and the bridge over the River Waal, only because Generalfeldmarschall Model refused to allow it to be blown up on the grounds that he might need it for a counter-offensive. But determined resistance and constant German flank attacks on the exposed road, soon known as 'Hell's Highway', seriously hampered the advance of the Guards Armoured Division.

Allied intelligence knew that the 9th SS Panzer-Division *Hohenstaufen* and the 10th SS Panzer-Division *Frundsberg* were in the area of Arnhem. But analysts made the fatal mistake of assuming that both formations were so run down after the retreat from France that they would not represent a serious threat. The German reaction to the drop of the British 1st Airborne Division was swift and brutal. Only a single battalion made it to the bridge, and even then it was trapped on the northern side. On 25 September, surviving paratroopers were evacuated across the river. Total Allied losses, British, American and Polish, exceeded 14,000 men. The whole operation did little to enhance American confidence in British leadership.

Allied excitement at the prospect of jumping the Rhine in almost one bound had distracted attention from the more mundane but essential task of securing a proper supply line. Admiral Sir Bertram Ramsay was livid that SHAEF, and especially Montgomery, had ignored his warnings to secure the Scheldt estuary and the approaches to Antwerp. Despite Eisenhower's urging to concentrate on the one major port captured with its dock facilities intact, Montgomery had insisted that the First Canadian Army should proceed with clearing the German garrisons holding out in Boulogne, Calais and Dunkirk. Yet none of these ports, which suffered from demolitions carried out by the defenders, would be navigable for some time.

Eisenhower, largely recovered from a knee injury, at last began to try to clarify Allied strategy. He set up a small advance headquarters near Reims, and on 20 September SHAEF took over the Trianon Palace Hotel at Versailles, an establishment of Belle Epoque grandeur. During the First World War, it had been the headquarters of the Inter-Allied Military Council. On 7 May 1919, Georges Clemenceau had dictated the conditions of the Treaty of Versailles in its main salon, several days before the document was signed in the Hall of Mirrors of the Château de Versailles.

Over the next two weeks, more departments moved into numerous buildings around it, including the huge stables. Soon some 1,800 properties around Versailles were commandeered to house 24,000 officers and men. In Paris, Lieutenant General John C. Lee, the American supply supremo of the Communications Zone, known as 'Com Z', took over 315 hotels and several thousand other buildings and apartments to house his senior officers in style. He also appropriated the Hôtel George V almost entirely for himself. The pompous and megalomaniac Lee even expected wounded soldiers to lie to attention in their hospital beds whenever he appeared on a tour of inspection in boots, spurs and riding whip, accompanied by a fawning staff.

Front-line divisions were outraged that the supply organization should concentrate on its own comforts before anything else, and French authorities complained that American demands were far greater than those of the Germans. One magazine said that SHAEF stood for the 'Societé des Hôteliers Américains en France'. Eisenhower was furious with Lee, who had blatantly contravened his instruction not to colonize Paris, but he never quite summoned up the determination to sack him. Even Patton, who loathed and despised Lee, never dared to cross him in case he retaliated by shutting down supplies to his Third Army.

The Supreme Commander also found that strategic issues had not been clarified, even after the great setback at Arnhem. Once Montgomery had an idea in his head, he could not let go. Ignoring the fact that his own forces had not opened Antwerp to ships and that his pet project of Market Garden had failed, he still argued that the bulk of supplies should be allotted to his army group for a strike into northern Germany. In a letter of 21 September, the day that the British parachute battalion was forced to surrender at Arnhem, Montgomery ticked off his Supreme Commander for not having stopped Patton in his tracks altogether. Significantly, even the Germans thought Montgomery was wrong. General Eberbach, whom the British had captured in Amiens, told fellow generals in Allied captivity: 'The whole point of their main effort is wrong. The traditional gateway is through the Saar.'

Patton argued that Montgomery's plan to lead a 'narrow front' with a 'single knife-like drive toward Berlin' was totally mistaken. Montgomery was far too cautious a commander for such a strategy and his northern route had to cross the main rivers of northern Europe at their widest. Bradley remarked that Montgomery's so-called 'dagger-thrust with the 21st Army Group at the heart of Germany' would probably be a 'butter-knife thrust'. Patton, who was struggling to take the fortified city of Metz, had been told to go over to the defensive, which did not improve his mood. But on 21 September, when Eisenhower referred to Montgomery as 'a clever son of a bitch', Patton was encouraged to believe that the Supreme Commander had at last started to see through the field marshal's manipulative ways. As part of his campaign to be appointed land forces commander, Montgomery had predicted that tight control of the campaign would wane once Eisenhower had assumed command. 'The problem was', as the historian John Buckley emphasized, 'that it was Monty himself as much as anyone, who worked to undermine his chief.'

Eisenhower tried to brush over the differences between Montgomery's proposal and his own strategy of advancing on both the Ruhr and the Saar at the same time. In fact he gave the impression that he supported Monty's single thrust, but just wanted to allow a little flexibility in the centre. This was a grave mistake. He needed to be explicit. Eisenhower knew that he could issue direct orders to Bradley and General Jacob L. Devers, the two American army group commanders, who were his subordinates. But he gave too much leeway to Montgomery because he was an ally and not part of the US Army chain of command. Eisenhower should have known by then that General Marshall in Washington would back him as Supreme Commander, and that Churchill no longer had any influence with President Roosevelt, especially when it came to military decisions. Eisenhower's reluctance to insist that the time for discussion was over and that his orders must be followed enabled Montgomery to keep questioning a strategy with which he disagreed, and chiselling at it constantly to get his own way. Montgomery had no idea of the tensions he was provoking in Anglo–American relations, which would come to a head in December and January.

The situation was not helped by Montgomery's failure to attend an important conference held by Eisenhower on 22 September at his headquarters in Versailles. In his stead, he sent his chief of staff Major General Francis de Guingand, known as 'Freddie', who was liked and trusted by all. American generals suspected that Montgomery did this on purpose so that he could wriggle out of agreements later. The conference focused on the strategy to be adopted as soon as the port of Antwerp was secured. Eisenhower accepted that the main thrust would be made by Montgomery's 21st Army Group, which was to envelop the Ruhr from the north. But at the same time he wanted Bradley's 12th Army Group to cross the Rhine in the region of Cologne and Bonn, to encircle the Ruhr from the south. Eisenhower set all this out in a letter to Montgomery two days later to ensure that there could be no doubt in the field marshal's mind.

Montgomery, having given the task of clearing the approaches to Antwerp to the First Canadian Army, seemed to pay little further attention in that direction. He was more interested in exploiting the Nijmegen salient seized during Operation Market Garden to attack towards the Reichswald, the forest just across the German border. But the Canadians, when they eventually finished in northern France and began the Scheldt operation in early October, found that German resistance was far stronger than imagined. They had a bitter fight on their hands, now that the remnants of the German Fifteenth Army had been given the time to escape and reinforce the island of Walcheren and the South Beveland peninsula.

Eisenhower, prompted by a report from the Royal Navy, was even more concerned at the slow progress. Montgomery became angrily defensive at any implication that he was not doing enough to open Antwerp and argued once more that the US First Army should be placed under his command, to speed the attack on the Ruhr. On 8 October, he again criticized Eisenhower's strategy, but this time to General Marshall himself who was visiting Eindhoven. It was a bad mistake. Even the supremely self-disciplined Marshall nearly lost his temper at this example of what he called Montgomery's 'overwhelming egotism'. The field marshal, devoid of any emotional intelligence, then renewed his onslaught on Eisenhower's command abilities with a paper entitled 'Notes on Command in Western Europe'. Montgomery was almost certainly sharper in his criticisms because of the heavy hints he had heard that his failure to secure the banks of the Scheldt was what had halted the advance of the Allied armies. He even implied that Market Garden had failed because he had not received sufficient support from SHAEF.

Eisenhower replied several days later with a powerful rebuttal which he had shown to Marshall for his approval. Neither his chief of staff General Walter Bedell Smith nor Marshall would let him soften the draft. Even the rhinoceros-hided Montgomery could not miss the import of one paragraph. 'If you, as the senior commander in this theater of one of the great Allies, feel that my conceptions and directives are such as to endanger the success of operations, it is our duty to refer the matter to higher authority for any action they may choose to take, however drastic.' Montgomery promptly climbed down. 'You will hear *no* more on the subject of command from me. I have given you my views and you have given your answer. That ends the matter . . . Your very devoted and loyal subordinate, Monty.' But for Montgomery, the matter would rumble on for the rest of his days.

The battle for the Scheldt approaches, which finally began on 2 October with a drive north and north-west from Antwerp, was conducted under heavy rain. It took the Canadians, with the support of the British I Corps on their right, two weeks to reach the base of the South Beveland peninsula and the rest of the month to clear it. Another force from II Canadian Corps meanwhile took most of October to clear the large pocket inside the Leopold Canal on the south side of the mouth of the Scheldt. To help take Walcheren, the RAF eventually agreed to bomb the dykes to flood most of the island and force the German garrison of more than 6,000 men out of their defensive positions. British commando forces from Ostend arrived in landing craft at the western tip and, despite heavy losses, met up with Canadian troops crossing from the captured southern enclave. On 3 November, the last German prisoners were rounded up, making a total of 40,000 Germans captured, but the Canadians and British had suffered 13,000 casualties in the Scheldt operation. Even so, the need to clear the German mines in the estuary meant that the first supply convoy did not enter the harbour of Antwerp until 28 November. That was eighty-five days after the 11th Armoured Division had taken the city by surprise.

The first American patrol crossed on to German soil from north-eastern Luxembourg on the afternoon of 11 September. From high ground, they sighted some concrete bunkers of the Siegfried Line. Many units from then on proclaimed their arrival on Nazi territory by symbolically urinating on the ground. The same day just north-west of Dijon, the French 2nd Armoured Division in Patton's XV Corps, the 2ème Division Blindée, met up with the 1st French Division of the Seventh Army coming up from the south of France. The Allies now had a solid line from the North Sea to Switzerland.

Patton took Nancy on 14 September, but his Third Army was blocked by the ancient fortifications of Metz and faced hard fighting to get across the Moselle. 'We took enough prisoners', reported an officer, 'to work on the river edge where the Germans were hitting our medics trying to get wounded back in assault boats. They shot and riddled wounded soldiers that could have pulled through. We made the prisoners expose themselves for this work and they even shot them. Finally, we said, "To hell with it," and shot the whole damned bunch.'

German divisions faced different handicaps. A regimental commander with the 17th SS Panzergrenadier-Division *Götz von Berlichingen* complained that his vehicles 'kept breaking down because the petrol was poor. There was water in it. That's the way we are supposed to fight a war! I had absolutely no artillery at all. You know, when our soldiers have to continually haul their own guns around then they soon say: "You can kiss my ass. I'd rather be taken prisoner."' Such sentiments were certainly not revealed to Führer headquarters. 'Relations between officers and men in the front line remain excellent and give no cause for alarm,' the German First Army reported to the OKW, and on balance that appeared to be true, to judge by letters home.

'The war has reached its climax,' an Obergefreiter wrote to his wife. 'I'm in the sector opposite my birthplace. As a result I can defend my homeland and you with more courage and determination . . . We must never contemplate the unthinkable possibility of defeat.' Others expressed disdain for their enemy. 'He doesn't attack without aircraft and tanks. He's too cowardly for that. He has every imaginable weapon at his disposal.' Another wrote: 'The American infantryman isn't worth a penny. They only operate with heavy weapons and as long as a German machine gun is still firing, the American soldier doesn't advance.' But Obergefreiter Riegler acknowledged that 'Whoever has air superiority is going to win this war, that's the truth.' And Obergefreiter Hoes was bitter about the lack of effect from the V-weapons. 'Why sacrifice more and more men? Allow more and more of our homeland to be destroyed? Why has there been no success with the V-weapons of which so much has been said?'

On 16 September, the day before Market Garden was launched, Hitler astonished his entourage at the Wolfsschanze when he summoned another meeting after the morning situation conference. Generaloberst Alfred Jodl was just speaking of the scarcity of heavy weapons, ammunition and tanks on the western front when, as General der Flieger Kreipe noted in his diary: 'Führer interrupts Jodl. Decision by the Führer, counter-attack from the Ardennes, objective Antwerp . . . Our attack group, thirty new Volksgrenadier divisions and new panzer divisions in addition to panzer divisions from the east. Attempt to break the boundary between the British and Americans, a new Dunkirk. Guderian [the army chief of staff responsible for the Russian front] protests because of the situation in the East. Jodl points to the superiority in the air and the expectation of parachute landings in Holland, Denmark and northern Germany. Hitler requests 1,500 fighter planes by 1 November! Offensive should be launched during the bad weather period, then the enemy cannot fly. Rundstedt is to take over the command. Preparations up to 1 November. The Führer again summarizes his decision in a long discourse. Binds us by obligation to maintain strict secrecy and asks us to employ few and reliable men . . . Briefed Göring who flies back to Karinhall at night. I am quite tired, headache.'

Guderian was dismayed by the plan because he knew that almost as soon as the ground froze hard enough to carry the Red Army's T-34 medium tanks, Stalin would launch a massive offensive against East Prussia and westward from the Soviet bridgeheads across the River Vistula. 'OKH [Army High Command] has serious doubts about the Ardennes plan,' Kreipe noted.

Hitler, having sacked Generalfeldmarschall Gerd von Rundstedt as commander-in-chief west during the battle for Normandy in July, recalled him in the same role. The 'old Prussian' was seen as the archetypal safe pair of hands. Hitler exploited him as a symbol of rectitude, having corrupted him with money and honours. Although Rundstedt still showed sound military judgement, he remained an alcoholic and had little to do with operational decisions. In December 1941 when Hitler had sacked him for the first time on health grounds, everyone thought that this was a pretence. In fact Rundstedt, exhausted and suffering from a grossly excessive consumption of brandy, had been screaming in his sleep at night, and sometimes had to be held down by his aides and given tranquillizers. That sacking had been sweetened by a 'birthday present' of 400,000 Reichsmarks. More recently, to the disgust of many traditional officers, Rundstedt had presided over Hitler's 'Court of Honour' to expel in disgrace any officer thought to have been connected with the July plot.

Ever since the failed assassination attempt, relations between the Nazi Party and the German army had deteriorated. A captain, whose wife was in Reutlingen east of Strasbourg, recounted: 'The [Nazi Party] Kreisleiter of Reutlingen told a women's meeting that the German army was just a crowd of low-down swine and that if it had not been for the SS and the *Hitler Jugend* Division, the war would have been over long ago. That German officers had slept with French girls and that when the English arrived they had been hauled out of bed, wearing only underpants, and that he despised every officer. Of course the women cried "Shame!" and my wife left the place amid a general uproar, yet she felt, perhaps naturally enough, not quite so sure of things after that denunciation.' The captain, when he heard of this from his wife, complained to his general. 'That's not the sort of thing to tell the people at home, even if it's partly true, for otherwise they will lose faith in the troops.' But his protest achieved little and must have been reported back. The local Nazis took their revenge against his family by billeting so many people on them that they had no room left to themselves.

Near Aachen, an Obersturmführer Woelky in the 1st SS Panzer-Division *Leibstandarte Adolf Hitler* was taken aback when German women started to object to the likelihood of fighting when they had hoped that the Americans would simply overrun the place. 'We have been lied to and cheated for five years, and promised a golden future, and what have we got?' the most outspoken of them railed. 'I just can't understand how there can be a single German soldier left who will fire another shot.' She was fortunate to have chosen Woelky for her outburst, because he must have been one of the very few in his division to have privately agreed that Germany could not hold out for long. And once the war is over, he thought cynically, 'They will start by re-educating us, the SS, to be democrats.'

3

The Battle for Aachen

On the northern flank of the US First Army the XIX Corps had secured Maastricht, but lacked ammunition and fuel to push on much further. V Corps, on the right flank of the US First Army, had meanwhile advanced into the Belgian and Luxembourg Ardennes. It included the 4th Infantry Division, which Ernest Hemingway had made his own, and the 28th Infantry Division, which had marched through Paris. The glow from that triumphant parade had gone. There seemed little glory in the slow, tedious and often dangerous reduction of the Siegfried Line. 'As we pass a pillbox,' wrote a soldier in the 30th Infantry Division, 'I see a GI sprawled pitifully on the ground, his face in the dirt – helmet on the ground near his head. Bulging from each hip pocket is a never-to-be-eaten K ration.'

Simply to blast a path through the concrete pyramids known as 'dragons' teeth', Sherman tanks needed to fire about fifty rounds. The Americans found that they first needed to infiltrate the area during the night to get troops in between the German mortar positions and the pillboxes. Assault teams of at least a dozen men, supported by tanks, tank destroyers or anti-tank guns, would take on each pillbox. The concrete was too strong to penetrate except by 155mm self-propelled guns, but tank destroyers firing armour-piercing rounds at the embrasures caused casualties from concussion. 'The wounded come out dazed and bleeding from the nose and mouth,' a US report stated. The Americans also used armour-piercing rounds on the steel doors, or pole or satchel charges containing at least thirty pounds of

TNT. 'If they still refuse to surrender, deafen them with a fragmentation grenade down the ventilation shaft,' the same report advised. And a white phosphorus grenade 'placed in the same air-shaft is found to be a great little reviser [of attitudes]'. They should then shout 'Kamerad?' and 'Wir schiessen nicht!' ('We won't shoot!'). 'If all this fails, call a tank to blast the rear of the pillbox or get a tank dozer to fill in the hole [and bury them].'

Soldiers were advised never to enter a pillbox; they should make the defenders come out. 'When the doors and ports had been blown in,' the 41st Armored Infantry Regiment with the 2nd Armored Division reported, 'and enemy automatic weapon fire silenced, the infantry moved to the blind side of the [pill]box and called for the occupants to come out. This was obeyed promptly. At one [pill]box, only 13 prisoners came out. A grenade was thrown through a blasted port and seven more emerged.'

If any German soldier called back to say that they could not move because they were wounded, the advice recommended another explosion. 'After a second charge of TNT, they somehow manage to walk out.' But the attackers should still throw in grenades or use a flame-thrower in case anyone was left hiding. Men had to be careful to watch for 'ointment box mines' which were very small, only two inches across and an inch deep. Finally, they needed to seal up the steel doors with blowtorches or a thermite grenade to prevent Germans from reoccupying the pillboxes. One unit had six pillboxes in its sector which had to be retaken three times. On one occasion, a whole platoon, exhausted and wet from the incessant rain, piled into a captured pillbox and fell asleep. A German patrol returned and the whole platoon was taken prisoner without a shot being fired.

In the centre of First Army, VII Corps advanced on the city of Aachen, the ancient capital of Charlemagne and *lieu sacré* of the Holy Roman Empire. The young commander of the corps, Major General J. Lawton Collins, was known to his troops as 'Lightning Joe' for his dynamism. With Aachen situated in a slight salient of German territory, the Siegfried Line ran round the west and southern side, with another line of fortifications behind the city. Collins wanted to avoid a house-to-house battle of attrition, so he decided to surround the city in the hope that the Germans might decide to pull out. But this reasoning failed to take into account Hitler's 'fortress' mentality and his obsessive refusal to give up towns, especially a place as historically significant as Aachen. Göring later said in a 1945 interrogation: 'The Führer wanted to defend Aachen to the last stone. He wanted to use it as an example for every other German city, and defend it, if necessary, until it was levelled to the ground.'

The sudden approach of American forces on 11 September triggered a panic. Nazi Party officials, Luftwaffe flak detachments, local functionaries, the police and troops fled east towards Cologne. According to the chief of staff of the German Seventh Army: 'The sight of the Luftwaffe and SS troops retreating, with the commanders leading the retreat, was very bad for morale. They simply got into their vehicles and took off. There was a riot in Aachen about it.'

Hitler ordered that the civilian population should be evacuated, forcibly if necessary. He suspected that they preferred an American occupation which would end the bombing. All those who did not leave would be considered traitors. But things did not turn out as he had expected. On 12 September, the 12th Volksgrenadier-Division was rushed to the sector, but the 116th Panzer-Division, which had retreated from Normandy, reached the city first. Its commander, Generalleutnant Gerhard Graf von Schwerin, promptly cancelled the Gauleiter's evacuation order. Schwerin was considered by colleagues to be too clever, and too contemptuous of the Nazis, for his own good. He had been sacked in Normandy for telling a corps commander what he thought of him, but then reinstated because he was such an effective leader. This perhaps encouraged him to think that he could get away with anything.

Schwerin first re-established order, with his panzergrenadiers instructed to shoot looters. He then sent an appeal to the American commander explaining that he had stopped the 'absurd' evacuation, and requested that the population be treated mercifully. Collins, however, carried on with his plan of encirclement. The 1st Infantry Division advanced from the south-east, with the 3rd Armored Division guarding its right flank. But the state of tank engines after the long advance from Normandy, and the shortage of every calibre of ammunition, greatly limited its striking power. The 1st Division was even short of rations. 'We were reduced to eating emergency D Rations – rock-hard chocolate bars full of artificial nutrients,' wrote Lieutenant Gardner Botsford. 'Three chocolate bars a day can make you very tired of chocolate bars.'

When it became clear to the Nazi authorities that Aachen was not immediately threatened, officials rushed back to restart the evacuation of civilians while a counter-attack was prepared from the north-east to prevent encirclement. News of Schwerin's letter leaked out, and the rash young general had to hide from arrest on charges of defeatism and even treason. Hitler, surprisingly, forgave him later. The forcible evacuation was carried out brutally. Most civilians wanted to stay. Wild rumours had spread of typhus in Cologne as a result of Allied bacteriological bombs. Many also believed that the Allies had bombs containing leprosy and plague bacilli.

'You should have seen how they treated their own German people in the evacuation areas,' Unteroffizier Huttary stated. 'They drove away cattle without giving any receipt for them. Then they made the owner himself go. The SA [Nazi Brownshirts] drove the cattle away in herds.' An engineer soldier called Bayer added: 'And when the houses were empty they looted them. They put up notices or announced that unrationed bread would be available at such and such a place from 2 to 4 o'clock. Then the women took up their places at the shop and when a queue had formed, trucks drove up and they were loaded into them. They picked up children on the street and threw them into the vehicles. Then they just took them out of the immediate danger zone, put them down on the road and left them to their fate.' Fear of a possible rising by foreign forced labourers prompted the SS to consider mass executions, but in the chaos nothing was done.

During the second half of September an intense debate had arisen, both in Washington and at SHAEF headquarters, over the wording the Supreme Commander should use when addressing the German people. If too conciliatory then the Germans would see it as a sign of weakness and be encouraged. If it sounded too harsh then it might persuade them to fight to the bitter end. On 28 September, SHAEF finally published Eisenhower's proclamation: 'The Allied Forces serving under my command have now entered Germany. We come as conquerors, but not as oppressors.' It went on to emphasize that they would 'obliterate Nazism and German militarism'.

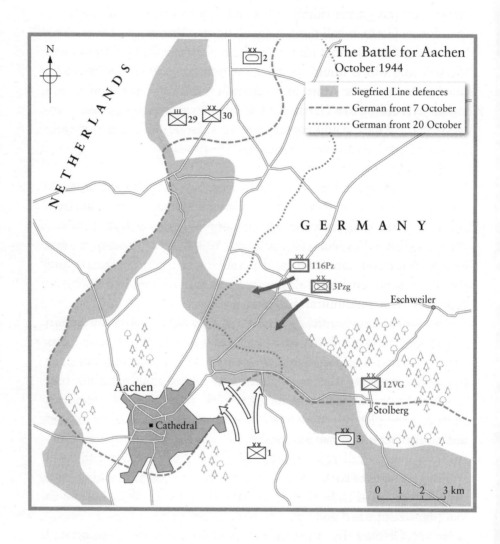

The Battle for Aachen
October 1944

Siegfried Line defences
German front 7 October
German front 20 October

The Nazi authorities soon countered with their own bizarre attempts at propaganda, even dropping leaflets by bomber over their own lines to strengthen the determination of their troops. One claimed that 'American officers [are] using riding whips on German women' and promised that 'Every German will fight in secret or openly to the last man.' The 'secret' fight was the first hint of Nazi plans for a resistance movement, the Werwolf, which would continue the fight and target Germans who collaborated with the Allies. But the leaflets did not succeed in raising morale. According to a German NCO, 'the troops were indignant, fearing that the Allies would capture one of these leaflets, and that their imminent captivity would be made most unpleasant'.

Early in October, the US Ninth Army took over the left flank of Bradley's 12th Army Group next to the British Second Army. This gave Hodges's First Army a greater density, especially round Aachen, where the 1st Infantry Division coming from the south-east worked its way towards the 30th Infantry Division advancing from the north to cut off the city entirely. By now the state of American vehicles had improved and supplies of ammunition had resumed.

The 12th Volksgrenadier-Division, recently arrived from the eastern front, faced the 1st Infantry Division near Stolberg. One of its officers wrote to a friend to say that their 'former proud regiment had been smashed completely at Mogilev'. Only six officers out of the whole regiment had survived and three of those were in hospital. The regiment had been completely rebuilt with new personnel and equipment and was now in action. It had suffered badly when thrown into a counterattack as soon as it detrained at the railhead. 'The Americans laid down artillery barrages of such intensity that many an old combat soldier from the East was dazed.' The writer himself was wounded with a hole in his foot 'the size of a fist' and was now lying in hospital.

On 11 October IX Tactical Air Command bombed and strafed Aachen for two days, and on 14 October the battle for the city began. Despite attempts by the Nazi authorities to evacuate its 160,000 civilians, some 40,000 remained. Women and old men were horrified to see German troops turning their houses into bunkers with reinforced concrete. The defending force of nearly 18,000 men was a very mixed collection under the command of Oberst Gerhard Wilck, with regular troops, Waffen-SS, Kriegsmarine sailors serving as infantry and low-quality fortress battalions. Before Aachen had been completely encircled on 16 October, the Germans rushed in a battalion of SS, the artillery of the 246th Infanterie-Division, the 219th Assault Gun Brigade and some combat engineers. Men from the fortress battalions were the most likely to surrender at the first opportunity, but Major Heimann of the 246th Infanterie-Division observed: 'I had the most excellent troops, half of whom were naval personnel intended for the U-Boat arm.' He also had 150 men from the SS *Leibstandarte Adolf Hitler*, but they wanted to pull out on their own. Heimann had to give them a severe warning that the Führer's order to hold the town to the last applied to them just as much as to everyone else.

The American attack began with two battalions from the 1st Division coming from the north and north-east, 'a job that should have been done by two regiments', as one of their officers complained later. The essential point was to make sure that adjacent companies remained in close contact to prevent the enemy slipping between them to attack from the flank or rear. 'To make sure that no individuals or small groups were overrun, we searched every room and closet of every building. In addition every sewer was blown in. This not only gave our fighting troops assurance that they would not be sniped at from the rear, but it enabled command and supply personnel to function more efficiently behind the lines.'

The 1st Division operated with tanks and tank destroyers well forward, each guarded by a squad of infantry against Germans with Panzerfaust rocket-propelled grenades. The M-4 Shermans mounted an extra .50 machine gun on the right front of the turret. This proved very useful in Aachen street fighting for suppressing fire from upper windows. Knowing that German soldiers moved from basement to basement, tank crews would first shoot into the cellar if possible with high-explosive shells from their main armament, then fire at the ground floor and work their way up the house. Others would deal with any Germans still sheltering in cellars by throwing in fragmentation and white phosphorus grenades. Flamethrowers often 'resulted in a quick enemy surrender'.

Bazookas or explosive charges were used to smash through walls from house to house, an activity which became known as 'mouse-holing'. It was safer to blast through a wall, which would shock anyone in the room beyond, than enter through the door. As soon as an opening into the next-door house had been made, one of the team would throw a hand grenade into the adjoining room, and they would rush in following the explosion. Soldiers carried armour-piercing rounds to shoot up through the ceiling or down through the floor. They then dashed to the top of the house and worked their way down, forcing the Germans into the cellar. When a whole block had been cleared, guards were posted to prevent Germans from sneaking back in. The Germans also used their Panzerfausts in a similar fashion. 'When attacked in this way,' a report admitted, 'American strong-point crews surrendered in most cases immediately, [once] deprived of sight due to dust clouds caused by explosions.'

The Americans soon found that mortar and longer-range artillery fire was uncertain and often dangerous to their own men in urban combat, so they insisted on direct fire wherever possible. In any case, fuses on American mortar rounds were so sensitive that they exploded as soon as they touched a roof, and did little damage to the inside of a building. But their artillery fire was so intense that Oberst Wilck, the commander of the German forces in the town, had to move his command post to an air-raid shelter. 'The few assault guns which we had just received were put out of action straight away,' Wilck recounted afterwards. 'You can't hold a town with just carbines!' The Germans in fact had more than carbines, and managed to use their heavy 120mm mortars very effectively.

Allied aircraft were closely managed by a ground controller, but it was impossible to identify specific points in the ruins, so 'no close-in bombing missions were undertaken'. In any case, the presence of friendly aircraft overhead certainly seemed to bolster the morale of the troops on the ground and kept German heads down. There were firm orders in place not to damage the cathedral, which was spared from ground fire. Even so, the destruction was so great that VII Corps could report that 'the flattened condition of the buildings' at least allowed 'actual physical contact [to] be maintained among adjacent units'.

'The operation was not unduly hurried,' VII Corps reported. 'It was realized that street fighting is a slow, tedious business which requires much physical exertion and time if buildings are searched thoroughly.' House clearing, the GIs had been told, meant firing constantly at every window until they were inside the house, then with one man ready with a grenade in his hand and two others covering him with rifles, or ideally Thompson sub-machine guns, they would go from room to room. But they soon found that they needed to mark houses occupied by their own troops. 'Numerous times we have had casualties by grenades thrown into buildings or shooting into them by our own troops after we had occupied the building.'

As the Red Army had discovered, heavy artillery at close range was the most cost-effective, as well as destructive, means of advance. The Americans in Aachen used 155mm self-propelled 'Long Toms' at ranges as close as 150 metres. Oberst Wilck admitted after his surrender that 'the direct fire of the 155mm self-propelled gun was very devastating and demoralizing. In one instance a shell completely pierced three houses before exploding in and wrecking the fourth house.'

'Civilians must be promptly and vigorously expelled from any area occupied by our troops,' one American officer in Aachen emphasized. 'Failure to do so costs lives.' Holding pens were constructed and guarded by MPs, but Collins's corps did not have enough trained interpreters or members of the Counter Intelligence Corps to filter out Nazi supporters, or interview the hundreds of foreign forced labourers. At one point during the battle, three small boys found a rifle. They fired at an American squad. A sergeant spotted them, ran over to grab the rifle off them and cuffed the boy who held it. This story somehow spread and was taken up as an example of heroism by German propaganda, which claimed with shameless exaggeration that 'they held up all the enemy troops there'. But as the diarist Victor Klemperer pointed out, the example was surely self-defeating. The Nazis now claimed to be using partisans, whom they had always condemned as 'terrorists'. It also underlined the weakness of German forces when, according to Nazi newspapers, 'Eisenhower is attacking with seven armies, with two million men (men not children!),' Klemperer emphasized.

On 16 October, the 30th and 1st Divisions finally met up north-east of Aachen, having suffered heavy casualties. Two days later, Himmler declared that 'Every German homestead will be defended to the last.'

But on 21 October Oberst Wilck surrendered with the remainder of his exhausted and hungry men. He was not a devotee of Hitler and knew that the killing went on because Hitler was living in his own fantasy world. 'Even the Führer's adjutant told me how the Führer is surrounded by lies,' he remarked in captivity. Knowing that it would please Hitler, Himmler would come in with a beaming face to say: '*Heil mein Führer*, I wish to report the establishment of a new division.'

One of Wilck's men later complained that the worst part of being taken prisoner was being marched through Aachen. 'The civilian population behaved worse than the French,' he said. 'They shouted abuse at us and the Americans had to intervene. We can't help it if their houses have been smashed to smithereens.' German women had soon emerged from cellars under the rubble to search for food. They could be seen butchering a fallen horse in the street hit by shellfire, and wheeling back turnips in little wooden baby carriages.

Goebbels tried to lessen the impact of the defeat. German propaganda assured the German people that 'the time gained at Aachen, Arnhem and Antwerp has made Fortress Germany impregnable. The Luftwaffe is being rejuvenated and Germany now has more artillery and tanks to throw into battle.'

The most frustrating delay for the Allies was their inability to use the port of Antwerp. This gave the Germans the breathing space they needed to rebuild and redeploy their armies for Hitler's new plan. But other factors also played a part. Encouraged by victory fever and the idea that the European war would be over by Christmas, American commanders in the Pacific had seized the chance to boost their own strengths. SHAEF suddenly woke up to the fact that the 'Germany first' policy, originally agreed in 1941, had slipped out of the window, resulting in alarming shortages of ammunition and men.

The Nazis, with Germany now threatened from the east, the southeast and the west, suffered their own internal tensions. On 15 October, Admiral Nikolaus Horthy, after secret negotiations with the Soviet Union, declared over the radio that Hungary was changing sides. The Germans knew of his betrayal. A commando led by SS-Obersturmbann-führer Otto Skorzeny, the enormous Austrian who had snatched Mussolini from the Gran Sasso, kidnapped Horthy's son as a hostage in a street ambush just before the broadcast.* Horthy himself was brought back to Germany and the government was handed over to the fascist and fiercely anti-semitic Arrow Cross.

In East Prussia, as the Red Army advanced on to German territory for the first time, the power struggle behind the scenes intensified. General der Flieger Kreipe, the chief of staff of the Luftwaffe, was now persona non grata in the Wolfsschanze. Keitel and even Hitler's Luftwaffe adjutant Oberst von Below turned their backs on him as a 'defeatist'. Göring decided to extend his deer hunt near by at Rominten, Kreipe noted in his diary, because 'he has to watch Himmler and Bormann a little closer. Himmler has now requested some squadrons for his SS.' This appears to have been Himmler's first attempt to increase his military empire beyond the ground forces of the Waffen-SS. Part of the power game around the Führer depended on the two gate-keepers: Bormann, who controlled access over anyone outside the Wehrmacht and SS, and Keitel. 'Before the Generals or anyone get to Adolf to make a report,' a captured general remarked to his companions, 'they are given detailed instructions by Keitel what they are to say, how they are to say it, and only then are they allowed into Adolf's presence.'

On an inspection of flak batteries nearer the front, Kreipe wrote on 18 October of the Red Army incursion: 'Fears in East Prussia, the first refugee treks to be seen, horrible.' Göring had to leave Rominten in a hurry, and Keitel tried to persuade Hitler to leave the Wolfsschanze, but he refused. A few days later, Kreipe visited the Panzer Corps *Hermann Göring* at Gumbinnen. 'Gumbinnen is on fire,' he noted. 'Columns of refugees. In Nemmersdorf, shot women and children have been nailed to barn doors.' Nemmersdorf was the site of an atrocity, which was almost certainly exaggerated in Nazi propaganda, and Kreipe had probably not visited the scene.

Also on 18 October, just as the battle for Aachen was coming to an end, Eisenhower, Bradley and Montgomery met in Brussels. Since the British and the Canadians were so involved clearing the Scheldt estuary,

---

* German army officers joked that Skorzeny had received the Knight's Cross of the Iron Cross for having freed Mussolini, but 'he would have been given the [even higher distinction of the] Oak Leaves if he had taken him back'.

Eisenhower decided that the US First Army should focus on obtaining a bridgehead across the Rhine south of Cologne, while the recently arrived Ninth Army protected its left flank. As might be imagined Montgomery was not pleased that the First Army was to be given priority, but he had been silenced for the moment after his climbdown. For the Americans, on the other hand, this strategy led to the plan to advance through the Hürtgen Forest. Neither the commanders nor the troops had any idea of the horrors that awaited them there.

4

Into the Winter of War

The brief Soviet rampage on to East Prussian territory in October prompted Goebbels to play up stories of rape, looting and destruction by the Red Army. He tried to invoke the idea of *Volksgemeinschaft*, or national solidarity, in the face of mortal danger. Yet on the western front Wehrmacht generals were shocked by reports of German soldiers looting German homes.

'The soldiers' behaviour today is unbelievable,' said a doctor with the 3rd Fallschirmjäger-Division. 'I was stationed in Düren and the soldiers there robbed their own people. They tore everything out of the cupboards . . . They were like wild animals.' Apparently this behaviour had started when the division was in Italy. And other formations which had looted during the retreat through France and Belgium did not change their habits when back on German soil. Their tattered uniforms had not been replaced, some 60 per cent of them were estimated to be infested with lice, and they were permanently hungry. Just behind the front line, there were reports of soldiers blinding horses so that they could be slaughtered and eaten.

This did not mean that they were reluctant to fight on, for the knowledge that the Red Army had reached the borders of the Reich had concentrated their minds. Significantly, a captured German army doctor called Dammann considered that 'German propaganda urging the men to save their Fatherland has helped to keep down the number of cases of combat exhaustion.'

Looting by German soldiers was not the only reason for relations between civilians and troops to deteriorate sharply in western Germany. Women wanted the fighting to end as quickly as possible. For them, East Prussia was very far away. 'You've no idea what morale is like at home,' an Obergefreiter told fellow prisoners. 'In the villages the women cursed and yelled: "Get out! We don't want to be shot to bits!"' A member of the 16th Fallschirmjäger-Regiment agreed. 'They called us "prolongers of the war", and that wasn't just in one place either, but in fifty towns and villages in the West.' An Unteroffizier Mükller said that in Heidelberg 'The mood there is shit, yet the hatred is not directed at the enemy, but against the German regime.' People were saying: 'If only the Allies would hurry up and come to end the war.' While most within the armed forces were still eager to believe in Hitler's promises of secret weapons, cynicism was much greater in civilian circles, except of course for the Party faithful and the desperate. In some places the unreliable V-1 flying bomb was already referred to as 'Versager-1', or 'No. 1 Dud'.

Goebbels seized every opportunity to make civilians in the west of Germany fear an Allied victory. The announcement in September of the plan by Henry Morgenthau, Roosevelt's secretary of the treasury, to turn Germany 'into a country primarily agricultural and pastoral in character' was disastrous. It enabled Goebbels to claim that 'every American soldier will bring Morgenthau along with him in his duffle bag' and Germany would be broken up. This idea clearly influenced Wehrmacht forces in the west. An officer taken prisoner was asked by his American interrogator whether he regretted the destruction of the Rhineland. 'Well, it probably won't be ours after the war,' he replied. 'Why not destroy it?'

The Nazi newspaper the *Völkischer Beobachter* warned: 'The German people must realize that we are engaged in a life and death struggle which imposes on every German the duty to do his utmost for the victorious conclusion of the war and the frustration of the plans of destruction planned by these cannibals.' The fact that Morgenthau was Jewish also played straight into the hands of the propaganda ministry and its conspiracy theories of a Jewish plot against Germany. The ministry tried to increase the effect with some dubious quotations from the British press, including 'Henningway' cited in the *Daily Mail* as saying: 'The power of Germany will have to be destroyed so thoroughly that Germany will never rise again to fight another battle. This goal can only be achieved by castration.'

After the presidential election in the United States, Goebbels said that President Roosevelt had been re-elected as 'generally expected', with the support of American Communists at Stalin's urging. Yet German propaganda also played a double game, encouraging the belief that the alliance of the Reich's enemies would soon fall apart. According to the US Counter Intelligence Corps, the Germans circulated leaflets showing 'Tommy and his Yankee pal regarding with disgust the spectacle of Russians taking over and policing Brussels, Berlin, etc.; the Teuton being apparently unable to get out of his head that when it comes to an abject fear of Bolshevism we're All Krauts Together'. Other leaflets tried to make the point that 'while Americans are being slaughtered by the thousand, Monty's troops are indulging in a "Dutch Holiday Slumber"'.

'German civilians don't know what to expect,' the Counter Intelligence Corps reported. 'They are torn between belief in the "terror" stories of German authorities and those which cross the lines, by rumor and Allied radio, about the fairness of our treatment of civilians in captured areas.' The Allies were of course helped by accounts which circulated within Germany of Nazi Party corruption at home and of the shameless looting in France by senior officials of the military administration. Gauleiters were amassing great wealth, and their children were allowed cars and petrol when even the heads of companies were rationed to forty litres a week.

The Counter Intelligence Corps admitted that it had crossed into German territory 'armed with a few directives, no precedents, uncertainty as to its potentialities, and [with an] uneasy expectation of partisan warfare'. Its priority was to seize Nazi Party records quickly, but its operatives found themselves overwhelmed by the numbers of 'suspicious civilians' arrested by American soldiers for screening along with the prisoners of war. German soldiers and civilians found it very easy to escape from American compounds. The other problem which the CIC faced was the number of Belgian and French Resistance members crossing into Germany to loot, or on 'intelligence missions of their own'.

In Aachen the Counter Intelligence Corps estimated that up to 30 per cent of the population had defied Nazi orders to evacuate the city. 'Don't kick them around,' was the CIC advice on treating Germans under American occupation, 'but don't let them fool you. The Germans are accustomed to taking orders, not complying with requests.' Many were indeed willing to denounce Nazis and to provide information, but it was often hard for Allied intelligence units to know exactly what to believe. Word had spread of the unrest in bomb-shattered Cologne, where police were engaged in running battles with the so-called 'Edelweiss Pirates': bands of dissident youth, plus an estimated 2,000 German deserters and absconded foreign workers sheltering in the ruins.

Allied bombing had not only flattened cities. Travel by train had become very difficult, if not impossible. German officers and soldiers who had finally obtained home leave found that almost all of their precious days were spent sitting in trains or waiting in stations. 'A Leutnant of ours went to Munich on leave [from Rheine near the Dutch border],' a Luftwaffe Unteroffizier Bock recounted. 'He was away ten days, but he only had one day at home.'

Hardly any soldier chose to go to Berlin on leave unless he had family or a sweetheart there. Everyone in the capital was exhausted from sleepless nights, as RAF Bomber Command fought its own 'Battle of Berlin', hammering the city night after night. 'What is cowardice?' ran a typical example of the city's gallows humour. 'When someone in Berlin volunteers for the Eastern Front.'

Visitors were often amazed how its inhabitants from all classes had adapted to the conditions. 'I am so accustomed now to living among these ruins,' wrote Missie Vassiltchikov in her diary, 'with the constant smell of gas in the air, mixed with the odour of rubble and rusty metal, and sometimes even the stench of putrefying flesh.' Apartments were particularly cold during that winter of fuel shortages. There was little glass available to repair windows and people opened their windows wide when the sirens sounded in the hope of saving any remaining panes from bomb blast.

During air raids, the packed cellars and concrete air-raid shelters shuddered and shook. The low-wattage bulbs flickered, dimmed still further, went out and then came back. Children screamed, many adults buried their heads between their knees. After the all-clear had finally sounded, many admitted to a curious exhilaration when they found themselves still alive. But some people stayed in the cellars even after the others had trooped off. It was warmer and less threatening there.

'Skin diseases', a doctor reported, 'have become very common both in the Army and at home, owing to the poor quality of the soap available, overcrowding in air-raid shelters and in those houses which are still standing, shortage of clothing, poor hygiene etc.' Workers in industrial areas were increasingly succumbing to diphtheria, and venereal diseases had spread, partly as a result of German troops returning from France, Belgium, the Balkans and Poland.

According to a court-martial judge, there were estimated to be 18,000 Wehrmacht deserters in Berlin. Many were hiding in huts on allotments. They no doubt subscribed to the German army joke: 'War is just like the picture-house: there's a lot going on up in the front, but the best seats are right at the back.' Ordinary Germans were at last ready to shelter deserters, usually sons or nephews but sometimes even strangers, at terrible risk to themselves. By the end of the year, the Wehrmacht had executed some 10,000 men, a figure which was to increase significantly in the final months of the war.

The families of deserters were also liable to severe penalties. 'During the night of 29–30 October', the commander of the 361st Volksgrenadier-Division announced in an order of the day, 'Soldat Wladislaus Schlachter of the 4th Company, 952nd Grenadier-Regiment, deserted to the enemy. The court martial assembled on the same day passed the death sentence on Schlachter. Thus he was expelled forever from the community of our people and may never return to his home. Most ruthless reprisals will be enacted against the members of his family, measures which are a necessity in this struggle for the survival of the German people.' Threats were also made against the families of prisoners of war who told their American captors too much.

The more prosperous classes increasingly feared the tens of thousands of foreign workers in and around the city. Some were volunteers, but most had been brought to Germany as forced labourers. The authorities were losing control of them. Barracks were often burned down, leaving the foreigners homeless. German shopkeepers would claim that gangs of them had broken in to their establishments and stolen supplies, when in fact they themselves had sold the missing items on the black market. Alongside food, cigarettes were the most sought-after commodity. In Berlin, according to one captured officer, a single English cigarette sold for five Reichsmarks, while a Camel went for twice as much. Real coffee was out of almost everyone's reach at 600 Reichsmarks a kilo. According to one officer, most of the black market in coffee was organized by the SS in Holland.

Coffee, because of its rarity, was the conspicuous consumption of choice for the Nazi hierarchy. A horrifying and bizarre conversation between two captured Kriegsmarine admirals was secretly recorded in their camp in England in 1945. Konteradmiral Engel told Vizeadmiral Utke about fellow admirals entertained by Arthur Greiser, the notorious Gauleiter of the Wartheland, who was later hanged by the Poles.

'Greiser boasted: "Do you know that the coffee you're drinking now, cost me 32,000 Jewish women?"'

'Where did they go?' Vizeadmiral Utke asked.

'"Into the incinerators probably," Greiser said to us at the time. "Let's hope we all get as easy a death as they had." That was the first thing he said. All the admirals sat around laughing themselves sick and thinking of the human suffering behind the coffee they were drinking.'

Following the Roman tradition of bread and circuses, the Nazi administration organized an ice show in the bomb-damaged Sportpalast to distract people from the shortage of rations. The Deutsches Frauenwerk welfare organization produced bakery booklets and brochures on how to save food. One was entitled 'Main meal without meat', which no doubt prompted another Berlin joke that the next one would be how to produce a main meal without food. A satirical song, sung to the tune of the Nazi anthem, the 'Horst Wessel Lied', went:

> The prices rise
> The shops are firmly shuttered
> Starvation marches
> With the German race
> Yet those who starve
> Are just the little comrades.
> While those above
> Can merely sympathize.

*

Leave was much easier for the Allied armies on the western front. The British and Canadians went to Brussels and the Americans to

Paris. Senior officers could always find a good excuse to visit SHAEF at Versailles or Com Z in the city itself. From mid-September, almost 10,000 American soldiers were arriving in Paris every day on seventy-two-hour passes. The priorities of what the poet-paratrooper Louis Simpson called 'the over-heated soul of the dogface fresh from his dugout' were predictable. Paris became known as 'the silver foxhole', and the term 'zig-zag' covered both drink and sex. Pigalle became known as 'Pig Alley' where prostitutes, both professional and amateur, charged anything up to 300 francs or five dollars.*

General Lee, the authoritarian commander of Com Z, was appalled by the informal and at times insulting behaviour of GIs on leave in Paris. He tried to instil some smartness by sending out officers from his headquarters to take the name of any soldier who failed to salute. The Avenue de Kléber soon became known as the 'Avenue de Salute' among frontline soldiers who resented the officers and MPs trying to make them behave.

GIs offset the expense of prostitutes and drink by buying cartons of Chesterfield, Lucky Strike and Camel cigarettes for fifty cents through the US Army's PX organization, then selling them for anything from fifteen to twenty dollars. French authorities complained in vain that US troops were exploiting their exemption from both import duties and exchange controls. American soldiers were able to make a killing at the expense of the French government by converting their pay in francs back into dollars at the official rate, then selling the dollars on the black market at a huge profit. Soldiers lured women with the offer of cigarettes, tinned ham, nylon stockings and other items posted from the States.

University graduates and anyone with a feel for European culture sympathized with the French and yearned, not just for carnal reasons, to see Paris, the intellectual capital of the world. But those with little knowledge of foreign countries tended to despise the French as losers who could not speak a proper language. They expected French girls and

---

* A private from a quartermaster company picked up, 'according to his VD contact form, nine different women in the vicinity of the same corner, took them to six different hotels, and actually managed seven sexual exposures', all within eight hours. The VD rate in the European Theater of Operations doubled during the year, with more than two-thirds of venereal infections acquired in France originating in Paris.

women alike to be ready to service the desires of their liberators. One of the very few phrases that many of them bothered to learn was 'Voulez-vous coucher avec moi?' The American embassy described US troops in Paris as 'ardent and often very enterprising' in the pursuit of women. In fact the lack of subtlety soon became counter-productive. Summoned in a café by a whistle and a proffered pack of Lucky Strike, one young woman earned the cheers of French onlookers by taking a cigarette from the GI, dropping it to the ground and grinding it under her foot. Young French males, unable to compete with American largesse, became increasingly bitter at what they saw as the presumption of their liberators. Mutual suspicion and resentment grew on both sides. 'The French, cynical before defeat; sullen after rescue,' wrote Louis Simpson. 'What do the sons of bitches want?'

If the black market in Berlin was flourishing, in Paris it became rampant when American deserters teamed up with local criminal gangs. The profits from stolen US Army gasoline were so large that even drug dealers were drawn to this new market. Up to half the jerrycans in continental Europe went missing. Increased criminal penalties, making the fuel more traceable by adding coloured dye, and numerous other attempts by the American authorities failed to dent a trade which made the supply situation at the front even worse. Paris soon became known as 'Chicago-sur-Seine'.

The most notorious racket that autumn was perpetrated by the railway battalion. These troops would stop the train on a bend so that the MPs guarding against theft at the end of the train could not see, then unload meat, coffee, cigarettes and canned goods to their confederates. A twenty-pound drum of coffee could go for $300 and a case of 10-in-1 rations for $100. Blankets and uniforms were also stolen from hospital trains. Some 180 officers and enlisted men were eventually charged and sentenced to terms of imprisonment ranging from three to fifty years. Altogether some 66 million packs of cigarettes disappeared in a single month.

French dislike for the 'new occupation' increased with the signs of American military privileges. White-helmeted American MPs directing traffic on the Place de la Concorde gave priority to US vehicles approaching the American embassy. Roosevelt had delayed recognition of the provisional government because he suspected that de Gaulle wanted to be a military dictator, but after much pressure from the State Department and Eisenhower, the President gave in. On Monday 23 October Jefferson Caffery, the US ambassador, Duff Cooper, the British ambassador, and Aleksandr Bogomolov, the Soviet representative, finally presented their letters of credence. De Gaulle invited Cooper and his wife to dinner that night, but he was still in such a bad mood that the British ambassador in his diary described the evening as an 'extremely frigid and dreary party, worse even than his entertainments usually are'.

Caffery was far more sympathetic towards the French than most of the senior officers at SHAEF, and as a result a number of them held him in contempt. He was an awkward man, both formal and ill at ease, and clearly did not enjoy diplomatic life. The Francophobe senior officers were determined to subordinate him to their own hierarchy and not allow any diplomatic independence. Caffery and Georges Bidault, the inexperienced French foreign minister, commiserated with each other over their difficulties. Bidault was constantly apologizing to Caffery and Cooper for de Gaulle's needless provocations. He even said to Caffery later that 'there is absolutely no one else in sight and that it must be admitted that de Gaulle loves France, even if he doesn't like Frenchmen'. Cooper's main problem was his old friend Winston Churchill. The Prime Minister wanted to visit SHAEF, without saying a word to de Gaulle beforehand, an act which would have been seen as an insult. Eventually, Churchill was persuaded to formalize his visit, and he walked down the Champs-Elysées with General de Gaulle, acclaimed by vast crowds. Their furious contretemps on the eve of D-Day was tactfully forgotten.

De Gaulle's displays of bad temper were due in part to the grave economic and political difficulties his government faced. Food and fuel supplies were uncertain, causing frequent protests. SHAEF estimated that 1,550,000 buildings had been destroyed during the war. Factories and mines were still not working properly, and the country's ports and transport system remained half paralysed after all the destruction from Allied bombing and German looting. De Gaulle also needed to deal with an embittered Resistance movement, which resented both its own loss of influence and the re-establishment of state power by the Gaullists returned from London. The French Communist Party and its supporters were the most vocal in their protests. Their hopes of carrying liberation into revolution had been thwarted, but they did not know that Stalin was totally opposed to the idea. He feared that the United States might cut off Lend-Lease support if there were disturbances in France behind Allied lines.

De Gaulle played his trump card towards the end of October. He would allow the French Communist Party leader Maurice Thorez to return to Paris from Moscow, but in return the two Communist ministers in his government would have to support his decree to abolish the 'patriotic militias' and force them to surrender their weapons. With uniforms and weapons provided by SHAEF, de Gaulle began to incorporate the patriotic militias into the regular French forces, sending the majority to General Jean-Marie de Lattre de Tassigny's First French Army advancing towards Strasbourg at the southernmost part of the Allied line.

One person who had no intention of surrendering his weapons was Ernest Hemingway, who had played at partisans around Rambouillet just before the liberation of Paris. At the beginning of October, Hemingway had to leave his roving court on the German frontier where the 22nd Infantry Regiment of the 4th Division had been breaching the Siegfried Line. After committing perjury to a court of inquiry into his illegal military activities at Rambouillet, he was acquitted and allowed to remain in France as an accredited war correspondent.

Although he took time and trouble in Paris to encourage the writing of Sergeant J. D. Salinger of the 4th Division, who had already started *Catcher in the Rye*, Hemingway remained an inveterate war tourist: he was after all the man who had coined the term 'whore de combat' during the Spanish Civil War. He returned to the Ritz in Paris to drink and sleep with Mary Welsh, the next Mrs Hemingway. Some time later, when drinking with Colonel 'Buck' Lanham, the commander of the 22nd Infantry Regiment, he seized a photograph of Mary's husband, threw it into the lavatory and fired a German machine pistol at it, with disastrous effects on the Ritz plumbing.

He also flirted paternally with Marlene Dietrich, who was in France entertaining American troops. One of Dietrich's 'ardent admirers' was General Patton, who gave her a set of pearl-handled pistols. Another was Jim Gavin of the 82nd Airborne, the extraordinarily young and good-looking paratrooper major general who became her lover. Gavin also later became the lover of Martha Gellhorn, the third Mrs Hemingway, who now could not stand the sight of 'Papa' any more. Paris was indeed a turbulent feast for the last year of the war.

Brussels was the leave centre for the First Canadian and the Second British Army. British officers used to say wistfully that, for someone who loves Paris, to go to Brussels was like having tea with the sister of the girl you love. The Belgian capital may not have been as riotous as Pigalle, but for their soldiers it offered the beer and women they so eagerly sought. And it too became a haven for deserters and black marketeers.

The political situation in Brussels was perhaps even more complicated than the one in Paris. Major General G. W. E. J. Erskine, the head of the SHAEF mission in Belgium, had tried to help the Belgian government of Hubert Pierlot re-establish order after its return from exile in London. The largely left-wing Resistance movements, rather like their counterparts in France, were hardly enthusiastic at being told what to do by conservative politicians who had spent the war years in the safety of London while they had suffered such dangers. Totalling some 30,000 members at the beginning of September, their numbers grew to 70,000. Those who had fought closely with British and American forces did not welcome the idea of being brigaded into the Belgian army and gendarmerie to act in a subordinate role.

General Eisenhower issued an order of the day on 29 September praising the work of the Resistance but also supporting the request of the Belgian government for them to hand over their arms and equipment and volunteer for military service in special battalions as auxiliaries. At a time of acute coal and food shortages when Belgium was short of manpower, this was greeted with a mixture of scorn and irritation. On 21 October, General Erskine pointed out to the Supreme Commander that the fractious members of the Resistance who refused to give up their weapons outnumbered the police and gendarmerie by more than ten to one. A breakdown in governmental control was a distinct possibility. Eisenhower then prompted the Belgian government to declare that the unauthorized possession of weapons in a combat zone was not permissible.

On 9 November Eisenhower made an official visit to the Belgian capital, where he addressed parliament. A few days later the Belgian ministry of national defence announced that all Resistance forces would be demobilized on 18 November. Two Communist ministers and a representative of the Resistance resigned from Pierlot's cabinet in protest. But General Erskine managed to convince them at a meeting later that SHAEF fully supported the government on this measure, and nobody should want to see clashes between the Resistance and Allied forces. Resistance groups backed down and agreed to hand over all weapons to the 'inter-Allied authorities'.

On 25 November, however, British troops and armoured vehicles were moved in to support police and gendarmerie facing a large demonstration in the government district of Brussels. Rather as was happening in Greece, this made it look as if the British had decided to maintain an unpopular government in power. Erskine was forced to justify his actions publicly, on the grounds that order had to be maintained behind the lines of a combat zone. However, until elections could be held, the military authorities had no option but to support governments which had survived in exile and were totally out of touch with all those who had suffered through a long occupation.

While American veterans of the fighting in Normandy had their seventy-two-hour passes back to Paris, a constant stream of replacements for those killed or wounded in action were sent forward from Cherbourg to holding camps. Most were teenagers freshly arrived from the United States, but there were many older men reassigned to infantry rifle platoons which had suffered about 80 per cent of the casualties, a far higher proportion than predicted.

Just about the only improvement that winter to the depressingly unimaginative system was to change the name 'replacements' to 're-inforcements' in an attempt to take away the idea that newcomers were just filling dead men's boots. This did little good. A regimental officer with the 28th Infantry Division said: 'We're still a first-class outfit, but not nearly as good as when we came across the beach [in Normandy]. We have a great deal more prodding to do now. The replacements, both officers and men, are green. They don't know how to take care of themselves. They become casualties very fast sometimes. They don't know their leaders and their buddies well, and it is hard to get them worked in as members of the team.' In one company twenty men reported sick, mostly with colds and trench foot, otherwise known as 'immersion foot'. All were new arrivals who had not been taught even the most basic rules of hygiene in the field, of which the most important was to change your socks. Their company commander admitted that he had lost twenty-six men to hospital in ten days because of trench foot. J. D. Salinger in the 4th Division was indeed fortunate to receive each week a pair of woollen socks knitted by his mother.

The Communications Zone personnel in charge showed little interest in the fate of their charges. For them, it was simply a question of processing the required numbers. Replacement depots were known as 'repple depples', and they resembled a gangmaster's collection point for casual labour. 'Each morning,' wrote a newcomer called Arthur Couch, 'some 1,000 men would stand outside a headquarters unit where someone would read out a list of some 100 or more soldiers' names who would go off in trucks to their division or regiment. The rest of us would go back to our tents until another name calling.' Young replacements had often been made even more apprehensive by wounded veterans returning from hospital to combat, who took pleasure in recounting weird and gruesome tales of fighting at the front.

Men often arrived with none of the training qualifications which their forms stated. Many could not swim. After losing a large number of men crossing the Moselle, a company commander in Patton's Third Army described the attack on Fort Driant with replacements for his casualties. 'We couldn't get the new untrained and inexperienced troops to move. We had to drag them up to the fort. The old men were tired and the new afraid and as green as grass. The three days we spent in the breach of the fort consisted in keeping the men in the lines. All the leaders were lost exposing themselves at the wrong time in order to get this accomplished. The new men seemed to lose all sense of reasoning. They left their rifles, flamethrowers, satchel charges and what not laying right where it was. I was disgusted and so damned mad I couldn't see straight. If it had not been for pre-planned defensive artillery fire [the Germans] would have shoved us clean out of the fort with the caliber of troops we had. Why? – The men wouldn't fight. Why wouldn't they fight? – They had not been trained nor disciplined to war.'

In all too many cases, replacements joined their platoon at night, not knowing where they were or even which unit they were with. They were often shunned by the survivors of the platoon they were joining who had lost close buddies. And because replacements were seen as clumsy and doomed, the veterans kept their distance. This became almost a self-fulfilling prophecy as badly led platoons would use the new arrivals for the most dangerous tasks rather than risk an experienced soldier. Many never survived the first forty-eight hours.

Replacements were sometimes treated little better than expendable slaves, and the whole system bred a cynicism which was deeply troubling. Martha Gellhorn, in her novel *Point of No Return*, repeats a clearly common piece of black humour: 'Sergeant Postalozzi says they ought to shoot the replacements at the repple depple and save trouble. He says it just wastes time carrying all them bodies back.'*

Only if a replacement was still alive after forty-eight hours at the front, did he stand a hope of surviving a little longer. One of Bradley's staff officers mused on the fate of a newly arrived 'doughboy'. 'His chances seem at their highest after he has been in the line – oh, perhaps a week. Then you know, sitting in a high headquarters, like an actuary behind an insurance desk, that the odds on his survival drop slowly but steadily and with mathematical certainty always down, down, down. The odds drop for every day he remains under fire until, if he's there long enough, he is the lone number on a roulette wheel which hasn't come up in a whole evening of play. And he knows it too.'

'I was lucky to be with old soldiers who wanted to help a new replacement to survive,' Arthur Couch wrote of his good fortune to be sent to the 1st Infantry Division. He was taught to fire a burst with the Browning Automatic Rifle, then immediately roll sideways to a new position because the Germans would direct all their fire back at any automatic weapon. Couch learned quickly, but he must have been in a minority. 'The quality of replacements has declined appreciably in recent weeks,' his division reported on 26 October. 'We receive too many men not physically fit for infantry combat. We have received some men forty-years-old who cannot take exposure to cold, mud, rain etc. Replacements are not sufficiently prepared mentally for combat. They have not been

---

* Hemingway repeated a very similar joke himself in *Across the River and into the Trees*, but after the bitterness of their marriage breakdown, neither would of course admit that they had heard it from the other.

impressed with the realities of war – as evidenced by one replacement inquiring if they were using live ammunition on the front.'

Front-line divisions were furious with the lack of training before their arrival. 'Replacements have 13 weeks basic training,' a sergeant in III Corps commented. 'They don't know [the] first thing about a machinegun, don't know how to reduce stoppage or get the gun in action quickly. They are good men but have not been trained. Up in the fight is no place to train them.' Another sergeant said that, in training back in the States, the raw recruits had been told that 'enemy weapons could be silenced and overcome by our weapons'. They arrived thinking the only danger was from small-arms fire. They had not imagined mines, mortars, artillery and tanks. In an attack, they bunched together, offering an easy target. When a rifle fired or a machine gun opened up, they would throw themselves flat on the ground, exposing themselves to mortar bursts, when the safest course was to rush forward.

The principle of 'marching fire', keeping up a steady volume at likely targets as they advanced, was something that few replacements seemed able to comprehend. 'The worst fault I have found', reported a company commander, 'has been the failure of men to fire weapons. I have seen them fired on and not fire back. They just took cover. When questioned, they said to fire would draw fire on themselves.' Paradoxically, when German soldiers tried to surrender, replacements were nearly always the first to try to shoot them down, which made them go to ground and fight on. Newcomers also needed to learn about German tricks which might throw them. 'Jerry puts mortar fire just behind our own artillery fire to make our troops believe that their own fire is falling short.' Experienced troops were well used to this, but replacements often panicked.

Divisions also despaired at the lack of preparation for officer and NCO replacements. They argued that officers needed to serve at the front before being given responsibility for men's lives. NCOs who arrived without any combat experience should be reduced in rank automatically before they arrive, and then be promoted again once they had proved they could do the job. 'We actually had a master sergeant sent to us,' one division reported. 'All he had done since being in the Army was paint a mural in the Pentagon. He is a good man but we have no job for him in grade.'

'My first contact with the enemy found me rather in a dazed frame of mind,' a young officer replacement admitted. 'I could not quite grasp the significance of what it was all about . . . It took me about four days to get where I did not think every shell that came over was for me.' He doubtless turned out to be a good platoon leader. But many, through no fault of their own, were utterly unsuited to the task. Some lieutenants were sent to tank battalions having never seen the inside of a tank. An infantry division was horrified to receive 'one group of officer replacements [who] had no experience as platoon leaders. They had been assistant special service officers, mess officers, etc.'

Commanders, in an attempt to galvanize their replacements, tried to stir up a hatred of the enemy. 'Before entering combat I have my leaders talk up German inhumanities,' stated a battalion commander with the 95th Division involved in the reduction of fortresses at Metz. 'Now that we have been in combat, we have lots of practical experience to draw on in this regard and it takes little urging to get the men ready to tear the Boche limb from limb. We avoid putting it on thick but merely try to point out that the German is a breed of vicious animal which will give us no quarter and must be exterminated.'

5

The Hürtgen Forest

Hemingway's friend and hero Colonel Buck Lanham of the 4th Division had soon found himself back in a world far removed from the comforts of the Ritz. At the end of October, General Eisenhower issued his orders for the autumn campaign. While the Canadian First Army finished securing the Scheldt estuary to open the port of Antwerp, the other six Allied armies under his command would advance to the Rhine with the industrial regions of the Ruhr and the Saar as their next objectives.

First Army's breaching of the Siegfried Line round Aachen put it no more than thirty kilometres from the Rhine, a tantalizingly small distance on the map. Some fifteen kilometres to the east lay the Roer river, which would have to be crossed first. The left wing of First Army, supported by the Ninth Army just to its north, would prepare to cross as soon as Collins's VII Corps and Gerow's V Corps secured the Hürtgen Forest and adjoining sectors.

Lieutenant General Courtney H. Hodges chose the old health resort of Spa for his headquarters. At the end of the First World War, Spa had been the base for Generalfeldmarschall Paul von Hindenburg and Kaiser Wilhelm II. There, in November 1918, the leadership of the Second Reich faced the sudden disintegration of their power as mutinies broke out back in Germany: the 'stab in the back' which Hitler was now obsessed with preventing twenty-six years later. Hodges took over the Grand Hôtel Britannique, while his operations staff set up their collapsible tables and situation maps under the chandeliers in the casino. The town's parks were packed with Jeeps and other military vehicles which had churned the grass into a mass of mud. The combat historian Forrest Pogue noted that, although less than thirty kilometres from the front line, nobody bothered to carry a weapon or wear field uniform.

First Army headquarters was not a happy place. It reeked of resentment and frustration at the slow progress during that stalemated autumn. Hodges, a strictly formal, colourless man with a clipped moustache, always held himself erect and seldom smiled. He had a southern drawl, was reluctant to take quick decisions and showed a lack of imagination for manoeuvre: he believed in simply going head-on at the enemy. More like a businessman in head office than a soldier, he hardly ever visited the front forward of a divisional command post. His decision to attack straight through the Hürtgen Forest as part of the plan to close with the Rhine led to the most gruesome part of the whole north-west Europe campaign.

South-east of Aachen, the Hürtgen Forest was a semi-mountainous expanse of deep pinewoods, with a few patches of oak and beech and some pasture on the ridges. Before the noise of war dominated its eerie peace, the only sounds were those of the wind in the trees and the mew of buzzards circling above. The forest, riven diagonally by ravines, had all too many vertiginous slopes. They were too steep for tanks and exhausting for heavily laden infantry, slipping and sliding amid the mud, rock and roots. The pine forest was so dense and so dark that it soon seemed cursed, as if in a sinister fairy-tale of witches and ogres. Men felt that they were intruders, and conversed in whispers as if the forest might be listening.

Tracks and firebreaks gave little sense of direction in this area of just under 150 square kilometres. There was little sign of human habitation except for a handful of villages, with woodcutters' houses and farms built in the local grey-brown stone at ground level, and timber-framed above. Piles of firewood were neatly stacked under shelters outside each dwelling.

After the initial forays into the edge of the forest by the 3rd Armored and the 1st Infantry Divisions in the second week of September, Hodges and his staff should have realized what they were asking their troops to take on. The subsequent experience of the 9th Infantry Division during the second half of September and October should have been a further warning. Progress had been good at first, advancing south-east towards the key town of Schmidt. Surprise was achieved because, in the words of the German divisional commander facing them, 'In general it was believed to be out of the question that in this extensive wooded area which was difficult to survey and had only a few roads, the Americans would try to fight their way to the Roer.' Once the German infantry were supported by their corps artillery, the forest fighting turned into a terrible battle of attrition.

The Germans brought in snipers to work from hides fixed high in the trees (closer to the ground there was little field of vision). They had been trained at Munsterlager in a *Scharfschutzen-Ausbildungskompanie*, or sniper-training company, where every day they had been subjected to half an hour of hate propaganda. 'This consisted of a kind of frenzied oration of the NCO instructors and usually took the following form:

'NCO: "Every shot must kill a Jewish Bolshevik."

'Chorus: "Every shot."

'NCO: "Kill the British Swine."

'Chorus: "Every shot must kill."'

The American 9th Infantry Division was attacking the sector held by the 275th Infanterie-Division led by Generalleutnant Hans Schmidt. Schmidt's regiments' command posts were log-huts in the forest. The division was only 6,500 strong with just six self-propelled assault guns. It had some soldiers with an idea of forest fighting, but others, such as the 20th Luftwaffe Festbataillon, had no infantry experience. One of its companies consisted of the Luftwaffe Interpreter School, which in Schmidt's view was 'absolutely unfit for employment at the front'. The following month 'almost the entire company went over to the enemy'. His troops were armed with a mixture of rifles, taken from foreign countries occupied earlier in the war.

Fighting in the Hürtgen Forest, Schmidt acknowledged, made 'the greatest demands on [the soldiers'] physical and psychological endurance'. They survived only because the Americans could not profit from their overwhelming superiority in tanks and airpower, and artillery observation was very difficult. But German supplies and rear-echelon personnel suffered badly from fighter-bomber attacks. The difficulties of bringing hot food forward meant that German troops received nothing but 'cold rations at irregular intervals.' Men in soaking uniforms had to remain in their foxholes for days in temperatures close to freezing.

On 8 October, the division was joined by Arbeitsbataillon 1412, consisting of old men. 'It was like a drop of water on a hot stove,' Schmidt commented. Virtually the whole battalion was annihilated in the course of a single day. An officer cadet battalion from the Luftwaffe was also torn to pieces. And on 9 October, when the division had already suffered 550 casualties 'without counting the great number of sick', a police battalion from Düren was thrown into the battle east of Wittscheide. The men, aged between forty-five and sixty, were still in their green police uniforms and had received no training since the First World War. 'The commitment of the old paterfamilias was painful,' Schmidt admitted. Casualties were so heavy that staff officers and training NCOs from the Feldersatzbataillon, their reserve and replacement unit, had to be sent forward to take command. Even badly needed signallers were sent in as infantrymen.

Only the very heavy rain on 10 October gave the 275th Division the chance to re-establish its line. Schmidt was impressed by the American 9th Infantry Division and even wondered whether it had received special training in forest warfare. That afternoon when his corps and army commanders paid a visit, they were so shaken by the condition of the division that they promised reinforcements.

Reinforcements did arrive, but to launch a counter-attack rather than strengthen the line. They consisted of a well-armed training regiment 2,000 strong, half of whom were officer candidates, commanded by Oberst Helmuth Wegelein. Hopes were high. The attack was launched at 07.00 hours on 12 October with heavy artillery support. But, to the despair of German officers, the advance became bogged down under very effective American fire. It appears that the battalion commanders of this elite training regiment became confused and the whole attack collapsed in chaos. A second attempt in the afternoon also failed. Training Regiment Wegelein lost 500 men in twelve hours, and Wegelein himself was killed the next day. On 14 October, the Germans were forced to pull back to reorganize, but as General Schmidt guessed with relief, the American 9th Division was also totally exhausted.

The 9th Division's painful and costly advance came to a halt on 16 October after it had suffered some 4,500 battle and non-battle casualties: one for every yard it had advanced. American army doctors, operating on both badly wounded GIs and German soldiers, had begun

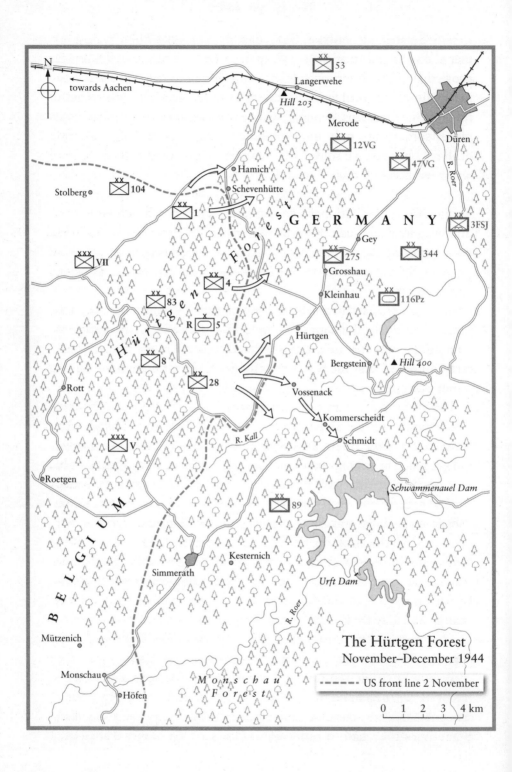

The Hürtgen Forest
November–December 1944

- - - - - US front line 2 November

0   1   2   3   4 km

towards Aachen

N

GERMANY

BELGIUM

Hürtgen Forest

Monschau Forest

Langerwehe
Hill 203
Merode
Düren
R. Roer
53
12VG
47VG
3FSJ
104
Stolberg
Hamich
Schevenhütte
1
Gey
275
344
VII
4
Grosshau
Kleinhau
116Pz
83
R 5
Hürtgen
8
Bergstein
Hill 400
Rott
28
Vossenack
V
Kommerscheidt
Schmidt
R. Kall
Roetgen
Schwammenauel Dam
89
Kesternich
Simmerath
Urft Dam
R. Roer
Mützenich
Monschau
Höfen

to notice a striking contrast. Surgeons observed that 'the German soldier shows an aptitude for recovery from the most drastic wounds far above that of the American soldier'. This difference was apparently due to 'the simple surgical fact that American soldiers, being so much better fed than the Germans, generally have a thick layer of fat on them which makes surgery not only more difficult and extensive, but also delays healing. The German soldier on the other hand, being sparsely fed and leaner, is therefore more operable.'

To the dismay of divisional commanders, First Army headquarters was unmoved by the casualties of the 9th Division's offensive and still took no account of the terrain. Once again Hodges insisted on attacking through the most difficult parts and the thickest forest, where American advantages in tank, air and artillery support could never play a part. He never considered advancing on the key town of Schmidt from the Monschau corridor to the south, a shorter and generally easier approach. The trouble was that neither his corps commanders nor his headquarters staff dared to argue with him. Hodges had a reputation for sacking senior officers.

The First Army plan for the Hürtgen Forest had never mentioned the Schwammenauel and Urft dams south of Schmidt. The idea had simply been to secure the right flank and advance to the Rhine. Hodges did not listen to any explanation of the problems the troops faced. In his view, such accounts were simply excuses for a lack of guts. Radios worked badly in the deep valleys, heavy moisture and dense pinewoods. A back-up signaller was always needed since the Germans targeted anyone with a radio pack on his back. The Germans were also swift to punish any lapses in wireless security. The slip of a battalion commander who said in clear over the radio 'I am returning in half an hour' led to two of his party being killed in a sudden mortar bombardment on their customary route back to the regimental command post.

The trails and firebreaks in the forest were misleading and did not correspond to the maps, which inexperienced officers found hard to read anyway. 'In dense woods,' a report observed, 'it is not too infrequent for a group to be completely lost as to directions and front line.' They needed the sound of their own artillery to find their way back. Sometimes they had to radio the artillery to fire a single shell on a particular point to reorientate themselves. And at night men leaving their foxhole could get completely lost just a hundred metres from their position, and would have to wait until dawn to discover where they were.

Most unnerving of all were the screams of those who had stepped on an anti-personnel mine and lost a foot. 'One man kicked a bloody shoe from his path,' a company commander later wrote, 'then shuddered to see that the shoe still had a foot in it.' American soldiers soon found that the Germans prided themselves on their skills in this field. Roadblocks were booby-trapped, so the trunks dropped across trails as a barrier had to be towed away from a distance with long ropes. New arrivals had to learn about 'Schu, Riegel, Teller and anti-tank mines'. The Riegel mine was very hard to remove as it was 'wired up to explode upon handling'. Germans laid mines in shellholes where green troops instinctively threw themselves when they came under fire. And well aware that American tactical doctrine urged troops to approach a hill whenever possible via 'draws', or gullies, the Germans made sure that they were mined and covered by machine-gun fire.

Both sides mined and counter-mined in a deadly game. 'When mines are discovered,' a report stated, 'this same unit places its own mines around the enemy mines to trap inspecting parties. The Germans, in turn, are liable to booby-trap ours, and so on.' A member of the 297th Engineer Combat Battalion noticed a mine poking through the surface of the ground. Fortunately for him, he was suspicious and did not go straight to it. A mine detector showed that the Germans had buried a circle of other mines all around it and he would have had a leg blown off. 'The Germans are burying mines as many as three deep in the soft muddy roads in this sector,' Colonel Buck Lanham's regiment reported soon after reaching the Hürtgen Forest. The engineers would locate and remove the top one, not realizing that there were more. Once spotted, they resorted to blowing them with dynamite and then repairing the hole in the road with a bulldozer.

Another danger was from trip-wires among the pine trees. Officers complained that soldiers spent so much time staring at the ground just in front of them in an attempt to spot wires and mines that they never looked up and around when on patrol. The Americans also improvised trip flares in front of their forward positions, with wires stretched out in several directions between the trees. These consisted of a half-pound block of TNT taped to a 6omm mortar illuminating shell, with a firing device. They soon discovered that they had to be sited at least fifty yards in front of the machine-gun pits covering the approach, otherwise the gunner would be blinded by the light. But in the Hürtgen Forest nothing was simple. As another officer observed: 'The effective range of rifle fire in woods and forests seldom exceeds fifty yards.'

Both sides suffered badly from the chilling autumn rains. Even when it was not pouring down, the trees dripped ceaselessly. Rusty ammunition caused stoppages. Uniforms and boots rotted. Trench foot could lead rapidly to debilitation, and even the need to amputate. American officers were slow at first to recognize the gravity of the problem. Regiments, weakened by the loss of so many men, made efforts to issue a fresh pair of socks to each man with his rations. Men were told to keep their spare socks dry by putting them inside their helmet, and to use the buddy system, rubbing each other's feet briskly, and sleeping with their feet up to help the circulation.

The constant chill felt by men soaked to the skin for days on end in water-filled foxholes made battalion officers aware of the need to allow men to get warm at least once a day. Bell tents with heaters inside were set up behind the lines, with hot coffee and hot food on offer. Another heated tent was used for drying uniforms. But all too often the constant attacks and the Germans' aggressive patrolling prevented those in the forward foxholes from getting away. Trench-foot rates soared as the men were simply doomed to shiver under pelting rain and chew on cold rations. As a heater and cooker, some resorted to using a C-Ration can filled with earth and soaked in gasoline, which they dug into a hole a foot deep. They would then warm up their food or liquid in a larger No. 10 can which had been perforated round the top.

Resilient constitutions, both mental and physical, were needed in such conditions, especially when the snow began to fall in November at higher altitudes. 'Men over thirty are too old to stand up under combat conditions,' a VII Corps officer observed, 'while men under twenty are not sufficiently matured, mentally and physically.' Unfortunately, the vast majority of replacements were either under twenty or over thirty.

Even providing overhead cover for the two-men foxholes was a dangerous matter. The German artillery fired tree bursts, deliberately exploding their shells in the tops of the tall pines to rain splinters and metal shrapnel down on anyone sheltering below. So part of the foxhole had to be covered with logs under a thick layer of earth, camouflaged in turn with moss or branches. But cutting logs to size with an axe was dangerous. The sound carried a long way and the Germans, knowing that men were above ground, would fire a rapid mortar barrage. Hand-saws had to be used instead.

The Germans, as had been their practice in Normandy and on the eastern front, manned their foremost line very lightly, relying on auto-matic weapons. They then used better-quality troops to launch their counter-attacks, backing them with tanks. And when the Americans attacked, they did not shrink from calling down artillery fire on their own positions. The Americans soon discovered that they could do the same, because with the shells coming in from behind, the spray of deadly splinters and shell fragments went forward against the attackers rather than down on their own men, sheltering in their foxholes. 'It took guts, but it worked,' a colonel commented.

On 1 November, Hodges accompanied by Gerow, the V Corps com-mander, visited the headquarters of the 28th Division at Rott. He told 'Dutch' Cota, who had so proudly watched his men march through Paris, that they would be attacking the next morning as the first stage before VII Corps began to advance on their left. The plan, Hodges assured him, was 'excellent'. In fact the plan was just about as inept as it could be. Not only was the 28th to advance across the steepest ridges and valleys, but Hodges ordered Cota to split his division in different directions, effectively making his attacking force far weaker than the defenders. Not even a whole regiment was to advance on the town of Schmidt. Cota tried tactfully to point out the flaws but his objections were ignored.

Obstinacy and a failure to listen were even greater at the top of the Third Reich. The very next morning, General der Flieger Kreipe, hav-ing been forced to resign as chief of staff of the Luftwaffe, made his farewell to Reichsmarschall Göring on his special train at the Wolfss-chanze. The conversation came round to the outcome of the war. 'Certainly there will be a Nibelungen battle,' Göring said, 'but we will stand at the Vistula, at the Oder or at the Weser River.' Kreipe doubted that a civilian population could be expected to engage in such suicidal warfare. He begged the Reichsmarschall 'to prevail upon the Führer to see to it that politics will take a hand in the matter. Göring was silent for a while,' he wrote in his diary, 'and finally told me that he was unable to do this since this would rob the Führer of his self-confidence.'

At 09.00 on 2 November, just as Kreipe met Göring, the 28th Infantry Division advanced eastwards out of a small salient into the mist-covered forest. The 110th Infantry Regiment on the right suffered badly from machine guns in pillboxes of the Siegfried Line which had not been dealt with earlier. The 109th Infantry on the left were equally unfortunate, running straight into an unmarked minefield covered by heavy fire. The German 275th Infanterie-Division defending the sector was by then experienced in forest fighting, but had been ground down so badly that its commander, Generalleutnant Schmidt, clamoured for its relief. Some of his soldiers, on surrendering to the Americans, claimed that mines had been laid behind as well as in front to prevent desertion. Several of their comrades had been executed for making the attempt.

In the centre, the American 112th Infantry Regiment attacked down towards the village of Vossenack, running along to the end of a saddle-back ridge above the 200-metre-deep ravine of the Kall river. Artillery concentrations of white phosphorus shells set most of the houses on fire. Sherman tanks fired at the church steeple, on the assumption that it contained at least a German artillery observer or snipers. Expecting a counter-attack after they had occupied the smoking village, the company commander told his men to dig in and have their rifles ready. To his surprise 'one big, old country boy remarked, "The last time I fired this thing, it cost me 18 bucks in a summary court. I was liquored up on Calvados."'

On 3 November at dawn, the 112th Infantry began to advance down the very steep slope to the River Kall below and then climb up the equally steep escarpment on the south-east side which led to the village of Kommerscheidt. One battalion, displaying considerable endurance, leap-frogged on ahead towards the town of Schmidt, which it seized to the astonishment of the utterly unprepared German troops there. Sergeant John M. Kozlosky stopped a horse-drawn ammunition wagon. 'When the driver found that Kozlosky could speak Polish, he jumped from the wagon and kissed Kozlosky on both cheeks.' He was one of the many Poles forced into the Wehrmacht. Below Schmidt lay the great, meandering Schwammenauel reservoir and its dam, just two and a half kilometres from where the soldiers of the 112th stood. Cota could not resist basking in the congratulations he received on this triumph, even if it seemed too good to be true.

Only a few days before, officers at First Army headquarters had suddenly realized that if the Germans opened the dams when American forces downstream were trying to cross the River Roer, a wall of water could sweep away pontoon bridges and cut off any troops in bridgeheads on the east bank. Hodges started to take this in only when news of the capture of Schmidt arrived, but it was too late to do anything. And to make a bad situation worse, Hodges had just encouraged Collins to delay the VII Corps attack until a fourth division arrived to reinforce his advance. As a result the 28th Division was left totally exposed.

Cota's division could hardly have been a worse choice for such a hopeless task. Earlier losses meant that most of its troops were replacements and it had a very high rate of self-inflicted wounds and desertion. As a warning, Private Eddie Slovik, a repeat deserter from the division, was selected as the only soldier in the United States Army in Europe to be executed for the offence.

The Germans had been taken by surprise because they could not understand the reason for the strong American attacks in the Hürtgen Forest, 'after the effectiveness of the German resistance' against the 9th Division the previous month. But, in one of those coincidences of war, Generalfeldmarschall Model, the commander-in-chief of Army Group B, was holding a map conference at that very moment in Schloss Schlenderhan, near Quadrath, west of Cologne. He and his staff were looking at the possibility of an American attack along the boundary between the Fifth Panzer Army and the Seventh Army. So as soon as Model received word of the American occupation of Schmidt, he wasted no time. He sent Generalleutnant Straube, the commander of the LXXIV Corps in charge of the sector, straight back to his headquarters. Then, with General Erich Brandenberger of the Seventh Army and General der Panzertruppe Hasso von Manteuffel of the Fifth Panzer Army, he worked out their best response with the other officers present.

The 116th Panzer-Division was ordered to move with all speed to attack the northern flank of the American advance along with the 89th Infanterie-Division. The 116th Panzer was now commanded by Generalmajor Siegfried von Waldenburg, following the storm created by his predecessor, Generalleutnant Graf von Schwerin, who had cancelled the evacuation of Aachen. Waldenburg also left the map exercise rapidly with his operations officer, Major Prinz zu Holstein, to rejoin their division. Model, who had been ordered by Führer headquarters not to commit the 116th Panzer, felt obliged to ignore this instruction purely 'to prevent American troops from spilling out of the woods on to the open ground'.

That night, men of the 3rd Battalion of the 112th Infantry Regiment holding Schmidt were exhausted after their efforts. Rather than dig foxholes, they went to sleep in houses. Their officers never imagined that the Germans would react immediately, so they did not send out patrols or position outposts. As a result the battalion was totally surprised when German infantry and tanks appeared at dawn, following a sudden artillery bombardment. Short of bazooka rounds and shocked by the unexpected attack from three directions, most of the battalion panicked. In the confusion, some 200 men ran straight into more Germans coming from the south-east, and only sixty-seven of them were left alive afterwards. Officers lost control of their men. The rest of the battalion, abandoning their wounded, rushed back towards Kommerscheidt to join up with the 1st Battalion.

In his command post at Rott, some thirteen kilometres to the west of Schmidt, Cota at first had little idea of the disaster overtaking his division. On 8 November, he was inundated by a chain of commanders. General Hodges arrived to find 'General Eisenhower, General Bradley and General Gerow talking the situation over with General Cota. Pleasantries were passed until the official party left,' Hodges's aide recorded, 'then General Hodges drew General Cota aside for a short sharp conference on the lack of progress made by 28th Division . . . General Hodges, needless to say, is extremely disappointed over the 28th Division's showing.' Hodges also blamed Gerow, the corps commander, even though the supposedly 'excellent' plan, sending a single division alone into the Hürtgen and then splitting it up, had been the work of his own First Army headquarters. He forced Cota to send an order to the 112th

Infantry to retake Schmidt, which revealed his total ignorance of what was happening on the ground.

Sherman tanks sent forward to take on the Panther and Mark IV panzers could not negotiate the steep winding tracks, the mines and the mud. Low cloud and rain meant that the fighter-bombers could not take off. And all the time, the two American battalions cut off in Kommerscheidt were subjected to concentrated shelling from tanks and all the artillery battalions which Model had ordered in from neighbouring corps. On 7 November, the 2nd Battalion in Vossenack broke and ran. Cota sent in the 146th Engineers, fighting as infantry, and they managed to hold on to the western part of Vossenack against panzergrenadiers and tanks. The situation was so grave that part of the 4th Infantry Division had to reinforce the 28th Division.

On the night of 8 November, American artillery laid a heavy bombardment around Kommerscheidt to allow the survivors of the two battalions to sneak out through the Kall ravine. The 28th Infantry Division had been forced back almost to where it had started, having suffered 5,684 battle and non-battle casualties. For Cota, who had watched his division so proudly in Paris, it must have been the most bitter day of his life. The 112th Infantry alone had lost more than 2,000 men and was now no more than 300 strong. As one of Bradley's staff officers observed: 'When the strength of an outfit in the line drops below a certain point, something very bad happens to it and its effectiveness falls away sharply. What happens to it is that there are not enough experienced men left in it to make the replacements – "the reinforcements" – savvy.'

German propaganda wasted no time in boasting of the successful counter-attack, as well as the recapture of Goldap in East Prussia and the failure of the Red Army to take Budapest. 'The surrounded American task force was destroyed. The villages of Vossenack and Kommerscheidt have been cleared of the small groups, which defended themselves desperately, but then gave up their senseless resistance.'

General Hodges refused to consider another plan. Even now, knowing the importance of the dams, he did not plan to swing round to the south. He ordered the 1st, the 8th and the 104th Infantry Divisions as well as the 5th Armored Division and the rest of the 4th Division into the

Hürtgen Forest. This would constitute the right flank of the joint Ninth and First Army offensive. On 12 November, the British Second Army began its offensive east from its Nijmegen salient. Despite the rain, mud and mines, over the next ten days it cleared the west bank of the Maas up to Venlo and Roermond, both close to the Dutch–German border. Also that day, the 1st Division left its rest area west of Aachen in trucks for the northern sector of the forest.

The third offensive into the Hürtgen Forest began, after several delays, on 16 November. By then sleet had started to turn to snow on the higher ground. The 1st Division in the north was to advance from the Stolberg corridor on the town of Düren, which along with Esch-weiler and Jülich was almost totally flattened under the weight of 9,700 tons of bombs dropped by the Allied air forces. Düren was also shelled nightly by American artillery.

Soon after the leading elements of the 1st Division had entered the pinewoods, they and their supporting tanks came under heavy artillery and small-arms fire from the 12th Volksgrenadier-Division. 'There was a stream of wounded soldiers coming out of the woods,' wrote the nov-ice machine-gunner Arthur Couch. 'One man I noticed was holding onto his stomach in an effort to hold in a large wound that was allowing his intestines to spill out. Quickly a front line medic came up and helped the man lie down and he put on a large bandage around his stomach and then injected him with morphine. An old sergeant told me to lie low behind large rocks and then move towards the last German artillery shell blast. He said that was the safest thing to do since the German gunners always turned the crank on their gun a few notches to hit another position. I did run into the last shell burst and the next shell landed 30 yards away. This was life-saving advice.'

Once again, as a 1st Infantry Division officer observed, the Germans tried to pin the American attackers down with small-arms fire 'then blast hell out of us with artillery and mortars'. Newcomers had been told to stand close behind a large tree, as it offered some protection from tree bursts. The one thing to avoid was lying flat on the ground as that increased your chances of being hit by shards of steel or wood splinters. The Americans tried to use heavy 4.2-inch mortars in support, but their crews soon found a wide dispersion in the fall of their rounds because of the effect of the cold, wet weather on the propellant. And when the ground was saturated, the base plate would be hammered further into the mud with each round.

'The German artillery', wrote Couch, 'was pre-aimed on the forest roads and also had been set to explode when hitting a tree top so the shell fragments sprayed down on us. This caused many dangerous wounds or deaths. I was seeing many wounded or dying men . . . at first I used to kneel down and talk to them but I soon found that too much to bear. I think seeing such wounds was starting to break through my defensive shield.' His greatest admiration was for the medics who ran to help the wounded 'even under heavy artillery or machine guns while we would stay in more protected places'.

In the forest, most German soldiers lost their fear of tanks. They could stalk them with the Panzerfaust. Or at a slightly longer range, they used the Panzerschreck, known as an 'Ofenrohre' or 'stovepipe', which was a larger version of the American bazooka. The German soldier or *Landser* also used the Panzerfaust as close-range artillery in the forest. Not surprisingly, as the chief of staff of the Seventh Army pointed out, the Germans found it 'easier to defend in the woods than in the open', because American tanks had such difficulties operating there. Engineers would remove most of the mines along the narrow, muddy tracks, but almost always one would be missed and the first tank through would be immobilized and block the route.

The 1st Infantry faced bitter resistance, and heavy artillery fire. 'Just before dawn,' continued Couch, 'a large bombardment began mainly hitting the trees above us. Being night and really dangerous, the new troops became very anxious and started moving around in panic. I tried to hold onto one or two of them, saying stay in your foxholes or you may get killed . . . This was the first time I had seen battlefield panic and could understand how some men get very traumatized and shell-shocked . . . Other later cases were sent to the rear for treatment. It is too dangerous for the rest of us to have such disturbances in our midst while we need to move forwards.'

The 4th Division, with Colonel Buck Lanham's 22nd Infantry Regiment in the centre, set out eastwards up the great ridge which ran down to Schmidt. The plan was to begin with Grosshau almost at the top, while the 8th Division on its right attacked the village of Hürtgen, and then Kleinhau. But the casualty rate for every metre of ground gained was appalling. American commanders had no idea that the reason for the desperate German defence was to prevent a breakthrough just north of the start-line for the forthcoming Ardennes offensive.

Even the tiny villages, often no more than a hamlet in size, had their own church solidly built in the same grey and brown stone. Schmidt's 275th Infanterie-Division had sent a number of men off for intensive sniper-training courses. American officers had to wear their field glasses inside their shirt to avoid being targeted, and yet, as Colonel Luckett of the 4th Division pointed out, visibility seldom stretched beyond seventy-five yards, making it very difficult for snipers on the ground. The Germans also made use of a flak battery of 88mm guns south-west of Mariaweiler, which fired at Allied bombers on their way to German cities. At the same time, a forward observation post could warn them if their guns needed to be switched to an anti-tank role.

Schmidt's officers could rely on local foresters for much of their intelligence in the area, which gave them a great advantage. The Americans, they noticed, bothered to carry out reconnaissance only when about to attack a particular sector, which thus revealed their objective for the next day. German officers and NCOs were adept at exploiting American mistakes. Junior American commanders were often tempted to pull back at night after taking ground, but the Germans would move in and it would become impossible to dislodge them next day. And an attack was not the only time GIs bunched together. Whenever a prisoner was captured, 'twelve to twenty men will pile around, and that is going to cause a lot of casualties'.

The Germans kept their tanks well dug in and camouflaged, and used them mostly as a psychological weapon. 'In the daytime,' an American officer reported, 'they are comparatively quiet, but at dawn, dusk and at intervals during the night they become active. They continually move around and shoot, just enough to keep our troops in an almost frantic state of mind.' American officers resolved to keep their tank destroyers well forward to reassure their men. Infantry tended to panic and retreat once their supporting tanks moved back to replenish with fuel and ammunition, so whenever possible a reserve platoon of tanks needed to be ready to take their place. It was not easy because armoured vehicles were so vulnerable in the dark woods. Each platoon of light tanks needed a squad of infantry, and a mine-removal squad from the engineers. Tank crews seem to have been even more frightened than the infantry in the forest. 'One time we didn't get out of the tanks for four days,' recorded one soldier. 'Heavy artillery, 88s, mortars, screaming meemies [from the German Nebelwerfer rocket launcher] pounding in all around us. You got out of your tank to take a leak and you were a dead duck. We used our damn helmets and dumped them out of the turret.'

As Colonel Lanham's 22nd Infantry Regiment slogged its way up the thickly wooded hill towards the hamlet of Kleinhau, it found that the Germans had cut the lower branches from the trees to the front to provide better fields of fire for their MG-42 machine guns. A sudden charge forced the first outposts to flee, but further on the Americans were stopped by a 'booby-trapped stretch of tangle-foot barbed wire twenty-five yards deep'. As they surveyed the obstacle, a sudden salvo of mortar fire hit them. This was just the start of their Calvary. All three of Lanham's battalion commanders were killed. In one of the most horrific incidents, three German soldiers stripped a badly wounded American of his possessions, then placed an explosive charge under him which would explode if he was moved. He was not found for seventy hours, but had just enough strength left to warn his rescuers.

The 4th Infantry Division gradually adapted to forest fighting. Each company was divided into two assault groups and two support groups. The assault groups carried only personal weapons and grenades. The support groups behind, keeping just within sight, had the mortars and machine guns. The scouts and the assault group in front needed to maintain 'direction by compass' because it was so easy to lose all sense of direction in the woods. As they advanced, the support group would reel out signal wire for communications, but also, rather like Hansel and Gretel, to guide runners, ammunition carriers and litter bearers.

American divisions in the forest soon found that tracks, firebreaks and logging trails should be used not as boundaries but as centre lines. Units should advance astride them, although never up them because they were so heavily booby-trapped and targeted by the Germans in their artillery fire-plans. The Germans had zeroed in their mortars on every track, as part of the 1st Infantry Division had found to its cost; so to save lives the division attacked through the forest itself. It also sited command posts well away from trails, even though this too cost time.

In mid-November the weather turned very cold. Many exhausted men had thrown away their heavy wool overcoats when they became impregnated with rain and mud. 'A heavy snow two feet or more fell on the whole forest,' wrote Couch with the 1st Infantry Division. 'One day we were walking through a forward area where another company had made an earlier attack. I saw a line of about six soldiers standing leaning forward with pointed rifles in the deep snow – seemingly in an attack. But I then noticed they didn't move at all. I said to a comrade: they must be dead and are frozen stiff as they were hit. I had taken the precaution of stuffing my left breast pocket with German coins to block a bullet or shrapnel to my heart – but I knew it was silly.'

Further south, General Patton continued to pressure his commanders to attack. On Saturday 11 November, the 12th Army Group diarist joked that it was both 'Armistice Day and Georgie Patton's birthday: the two are incompatible'. Exactly a week later, Patton's Third Army finally encircled Metz, and four days later resistance within the fortress city ceased. Patton's obsession with capturing Metz had led to heavy losses among his own troops. His arrogance and impatience, after the lightning victories of the summer, had contributed greatly to the heavy casualties. The constant rain, which had swollen the Moselle over its flood plain, made the crossing south of Metz a sodden nightmare. Patton told Bradley how one of his engineer companies had taken two days of frustration and hard work to connect a pontoon bridge across the fast-flowing river. One of the first vehicles across, a tank destroyer, snagged on a cable which then snapped. The bridge broke loose and swung downstream. 'The whole damn company sat down in the mud', Patton related, 'and bawled like babies.'

In the south, a US Seventh Army attack on the Saverne Gap in mid-November enabled the French 2nd Armoured Division to break through and into Strasbourg itself, thundering right up to the Kehl bridge over the Rhine. And on the 6th Army Group's right flank, General de Lattre's First Army liberated Belfort, Altkirch and Mulhouse to advance south of Colmar, where it would be halted by German resistance within what became known as the 'Colmar pocket'.

The defence of Strasbourg was an inglorious episode in the history of the German army. The SS had looted Strasbourg before withdrawing. According to one general defending Strasbourg, soldiers ordered to 'fight to the last round' tended to throw most of their ammunition away before the battle, so that they could claim they had run out and then surrender. Generalmajor Vaterrodt, the Wehrmacht commander, was scornful about the behaviour of senior officers and Nazi Party officials. 'I am surprised that Himmler did not have anyone hanged in Strasbourg,' he told fellow officers after he had been captured. 'Everyone ran away, Kreisleiter, Ortsgruppenleiter, the municipal authorities, the mayor and the deputy mayor, they all took to their heels, government officials – all fled . . . When things began getting a bit lively in the early morning they crossed the Rhine.' The Landgerichtspräsident or chief judge of Strasbourg was seen fleeing with a rucksack towards the Rhine. Vaterrodt had more sympathy in his case. 'He was right. He had had to sign so many death warrants, summary sentences, that it was really terrible.' The judge was an Alsatian born in Strasbourg, so he would have been the first to be tried or lynched.

Many German officers turned up with their French girlfriends, claiming 'I've lost my unit.' 'They were all deserters!' Vaterrodt exploded. The most spectacular was Generalleutnant Schreiber, who arrived in Vaterrodt's office and said: 'My staff is down there.' Vaterrodt looked out of the window. 'There were about ten wonderful brand-new cars down there, with girls in them, staff auxiliaries, and over-fed officials, with a terrific amount of luggage which of course consisted mainly of food and other fine things.' Schreiber announced that he intended to cross the Rhine. 'Then at least I shall be safe for the moment.'

The liberation of Strasbourg by General Leclerc's 2nd Armoured Division produced great joy in France, and for Leclerc it was the culmination of his promise at Koufra, in North Africa, that the *tricolore* would fly again from the cathedral. For them the liberation of Strasbourg and Alsace, taken by the Germans in 1871 and 1940, represented the final objective in France. Leclerc was admired and liked by senior American officers. The same could not be said of the mercurial and flamboyant General de Lattre de Tassigny, who believed it was his duty to keep complaining about the failure to supply enough uniforms and weaponry to his forces in the First French Army on the extreme southern flank. To be fair to him, he faced immense problems, integrating some 137,000 untrained and unruly members of the French Resistance into his army. De Gaulle wanted to start withdrawing colonial forces to make the First Army appear more ethnically French, and the North African and Senegalese colonial troops had suffered terribly in the cold of the Vosges mountains. In heavy snow, Lattre's First Army had finally broken through the Belfort Gap to the Rhine just above the Swiss frontier.

On 24 November, Eisenhower and Bradley arrived to visit Lieutenant General Jacob L. Devers, who commanded the 6th Army Group with Lieutenant General Alexander M. Patch's Seventh Army and Lattre's First French Army. Devers was an ambitious young general who put many backs up, including Eisenhower's. He had not had a chance to discuss his plans with SHAEF, largely because Eisenhower took little interest in his southern flank. Devers was convinced he could cross the Rhine easily at Rastatt, south-west of Karlsruhe, despite some counterattacks on his left flank. He had clearly expected that Eisenhower would be thrilled at the possibility of seizing a bridgehead across the Rhine. But as Devers outlined the operation he handled his arguments badly, and became deeply upset when the Supreme Commander rejected his plan out of hand. The fault lay mainly with Eisenhower, who had his eyes on the Ruhr and Berlin and had never really considered what his strategy should be in the south. He simply wanted to follow his overall idea of clearing the west bank of the Rhine all the way from the North Sea to Switzerland. Eisenhower's decision showed an unfortunate lack of imagination. A bridgehead across the Rhine at Rastatt would have offered a useful opportunity, and if carried out quickly, it might well have disrupted Hitler's planning for the Ardennes offensive.

As the fighting in the Hürtgen Forest ground on, both sides relied more and more on artillery. Schmidt's division alone had a total of 131 guns in direct support, although its artillery regiments were equipped with a mixture of German, Russian, Italian and French guns, which made ammunition resupply difficult. The American concentration of firepower was even greater.

The result was a chaotic nightmare of trees smashed, shredded, gashed and sliced by shellfire and mortars, bodies mangled by mines, abandoned helmets and rusty weapons, the burned-out carcasses of vehicles, ammunition containers, ration packs, gasmasks and sodden

mud-encrusted overcoats abandoned because of their weight. 'Especially distressing was the personal clothing of the soldiers,' General
Straube, the German corps commander, admitted. In the wet and
intense cold his men suffered from hypothermia, trench foot, frostbite
and illness. Yet mortar rounds caused the largest proportion of battle
casualties on both sides.

Many German officers believed that the fighting in the Hürtgen
Forest was worse than fighting in the First World War, or even on the
eastern front. One described it as 'an open wound'. Generalmajor
Rudolf Freiherr von Gersdorff called it a 'death-mill'. Hemingway,
having attached himself again to Lanham's 22nd Infantry, witnessed the
scenes of snow, mud and smashed pines. He said that the Hürtgen was
'Passchendaele with tree bursts'.

Hemingway, again armed with a Thompson sub-machine gun despite
the recent inquiry into his martial activities, was also carrying two canteens, one filled with schnapps and the other with cognac. He certainly
demonstrated his own fearlessness under fire on several occasions, and
even took part in one battle. Journalism was not high on his priorities.
He referred to himself mockingly as 'Old Ernie Hemorrhoid, the poor
Poor Man's Pyle', in a mild jibe against Ernie Pyle, the most famous
American war correspondent. But he studied the men around him
and their conduct under fire because he had plans for writing the
great American novel about the war. As his biographer observed,
'Ernest gloried in the role of senior counsellor and friend to both
officers and men.' He was fascinated by the nature of courage and
derided psychiatrists' views about a man's breaking point.

J. D. Salinger, little more than a mile away with the 12th Infantry
Regiment, continued to write short stories furiously throughout this
hellish battle, whenever, as he told his readers, he could find 'an unoccupied foxhole'. This activity seems at least to have postponed
Salinger's own psychological collapse until the end of the war.

Combat exhaustion, that military euphemism for neuro-psychiatric
breakdown, spread rapidly. 'After five days up there you talk to the
trees,' ran one of the few jokes. 'On the sixth you start getting answers
back.' With perhaps cynical exaggeration one of Bradley's staff officers, who visited the sector, wrote: 'The young battalion commanders
who came out of the Hürtgen Forest were as near gibbering idiots as

men can get without being locked up for it.' One of them apparently said to him: 'Well, it's not too bad until the doughs get so tired that when they are coming out of the line and there is a dead dough from their own outfit lying on his back, in their way, they are just too god-dam tired to move their feet and they step on the stiff's face, because what the hell . . .'

Stress made the men yearn for nicotine and alcohol. Most officers were generous in sharing their own privileged supplies of whisky and gin, but rumours of cigarette rations being stolen by quartermasters in the rear to sell on the black market could almost provoke a riot. 'The men accept poor or short rations without grumbling,' remarked an officer with the 4th Division; 'in fact, [they] would rather go short on rations to get more cigarettes.'

Physical casualties also soared. 'You drive by the surgical tents in the morning, going up, and there are two or three stiffs there on the ground; you come back in the afternoon and there are thirty or forty . . . They are short-handed in the Graves Registration squad.' In the first three days of the offensive, the 22nd Infantry in the 4th Division suffered 391 battle casualties, including 28 officers and 110 NCOs. Sometimes new company and platoon leaders survived for such a short time that their men never even knew their names.

German losses were also severe. Model, determined to 'keep control of the dominant terrain', threw one hastily organized battalion or regiment after another into the battle. More elderly policemen and under-trained Luftwaffe ground crew were marched forward to die. Many were killed by American artillery before they even reached the front line. Whenever the sky cleared, American fighter-bombers attacked German artillery batteries using white phosphorus bombs. Although freezing in his threadbare uniform and badly under-nourished due to meagre and infrequent rations, the German *Landser* fought on because there appeared to be no alternative.

Constant German counter-attacks against the 1st, 4th and 8th Infantry Divisions delayed the American advance through the smashed woodland, but painfully and slowly it continued: whatever the cost, and despite the freezing rain, and the mud and the mines which prevented tanks from coming up to support them. American troops became embittered. 'Our men appear to have developed fully a requisite psychological attitude towards battle,' a sergeant wrote in his diary. 'They are killers. They hate Germans and think nothing of killing them.'

For 23 November, Thanksgiving Day, Eisenhower had ordered that every soldier under his command should receive a full turkey dinner. Battalion cooks tried to comply in the Hürtgen Forest, if only with turkey sandwiches, but as men climbed out of their foxholes to line up, they were hit by German artillery fire. A major who witnessed that day of heavy casualties confessed that he had never been able to eat another Thanksgiving dinner again. He 'would get up and go to the backyard and cry like a baby'.

Nobody felt there was much to celebrate. It needed another six days of very heavy casualties to take Kleinhau and Grosshau. The 8th Division finally captured the village of Hürtgen in a mad charge followed by close-quarter fighting in the houses, with grenades, rifles and Tommy guns.

The 83rd Division began to replace the 4th Infantry Division. These troops too were shaken by the damage caused by 'tree bursts that sent shell fragments screaming from the treetops in every direction'. To prepare for their assault on the village of Gey, the massed artillery organized a 'time on target', with every gun synchronized to fire at the same moment at the same target. They nevertheless faced 'gruelling house-to-house combat' when they entered the village. It was not until the end of the first week in December that the Americans were out of the forest, and looking down on the open countryside of the Roer valley. But they had still failed to capture the town of Schmidt and the dams. RAF Bomber Command, after repeated requests, finally made three attempts to destroy the dams, with five cancellations due to bad weather. Little damage was done and Bomber Command refused to try again. Finally, Hodges decided to try attacking towards them from the south-west with the 2nd Infantry Division, but the great German offensive soon halted that attempt. The dams would not be secured until February 1945.

The cost to both sides in battle casualties, nervous breakdown, frostbite, trench foot and pneumonia had been horrendous. In October, some 37 per cent of US troops had to be treated for common respiratory diseases, the worst level in the whole war. Fighting in the Hürtgen Forest produced 8,000 cases of psychological collapse on the American side. The Wehrmacht did not acknowledge this to be a legitimate reason to be spared front-line duty, so it had no figures. 'There were few cases of combat exhaustion,' the chief German medical officer said later. 'However since these men were not relieved, I could not say what per-cent this would be of total casualties.' 'In some cases,' wrote Brandenberger's chief of staff at Seventh Army, 'soldiers were found dead in their foxholes from sheer exhaustion.'

In the Hürtgen Forest campaign, the United States Army suffered 33,000 casualties out of the 120,000 men deployed. The 4th Infantry Division alone sustained 'more than 5,000 battle casualties and over 2,500 non-battle losses'. To help the division to recover, General Hodges ordered it to move to the 'quiet' VIII Corps sector across the Ardennes. Over the next twelve days, the 4th Division's three regiments took over the positions of the 83rd Infantry Division and came under the com-mand of Troy Middleton's VIII Corps, with its headquarters in Bastogne. The 4th Division had to man a fifty-six-kilometre front, yet it was only at half strength when the German Ardennes offensive struck a few days later.

6

The Germans Prepare

On 20 November, Hitler boarded his special train in the camouflaged siding in the Wolfsschanze. The Führer's *Sonderzug* included a flak wagon at both ends with four quadruple guns, two armoured coaches and six passenger coaches in between. All were painted dark grey.

Hitler must have known in his heart that he would never return to East Prussia, but in a characteristic act of denial he ordered the building work on defences to continue. His staff and his secretary Traudl Junge also climbed aboard the train 'with the rather melancholy feeling of saying a final farewell'. Hitler, who spoke only in a loud whisper, was nervous because next day in Berlin a specialist was going to remove a polyp from his vocal chords. Hitler admitted to Traudl Junge that he might lose his voice. 'He knew very well', she wrote, 'that his voice was an important instrument of his power; his words intoxicated the people and carried them away. How was he to hold crowds spellbound if he couldn't address them any more?' His entourage had been begging him for weeks to speak to the nation. 'My Führer, you must address the German people again. They've lost heart. They have doubts about you. There are rumours that you're not alive any more.'

Hitler wanted to reach Berlin after dark. He said that this was to keep his presence there a secret, but his entourage knew that he did not want to see the effects of Allied bombing. When they disembarked at the Grunewald station and drove off to the Reichschancellery, 'the column of cars tried to drive down streets that were still intact', wrote Junge. 'Once again, Hitler had no chance to see Berlin's wounds as they really were. The dipped headlights of the cars merely touched on mounds of rubble to right and left of the road.'

Hitler's most important reason for coming to Berlin was to supervise the planning for the Ardennes offensive, the vision which had come to him when bedridden in the second week of September at the Wolfs-schanze. Hitler had been sick with an attack of jaundice, and was therefore unable to attend the situation conferences. 'Hitler had all day in which to think,' Generaloberst Jodl later recalled. 'I saw him alone as he lay in bed – he usually disliked anyone seeing him in bed except his aides – and he spoke of the idea. I made a rough sketch on a map, show-ing the direction of attack, its dimensions, and the forces required for it.'

Hitler was determined never to negotiate, a fact of which Göring was well aware when he rejected General der Flieger Kreipe's entreaty to persuade the Führer to seek a political solution. Hitler continued to convince himself that the 'unnatural' alliance between the capitalist countries of the west and the Soviet Union was bound to collapse. And he calculated that, instead of being ground down in defensive battles on both eastern and western fronts, a final great offensive stood a far better chance of success. 'By remaining on the defensive, we could not hope to escape the evil fate hanging over us,' Jodl explained later. 'It was an act of desperation, but we had to risk everything.'

On the eastern front, a concentrated attack with thirty-two divisions would be absorbed and smothered by the immense forces of the Red Army. A sudden victory on the Italian front would change nothing. But Hitler believed that in the west, by driving north to Antwerp, two panzer armies could split the western Allies, forcing the Canadians out of the war and perhaps even the British in 'another Dunkirk'. It would also put paid to their threat to the war industries of the Ruhr.

Hitler had selected the Ardennes as the sector for the breakthrough because it was so thinly held by American troops. He was certainly conscious of the success of the 1940 attack on that sector, and wanted to repeat it. The great advantage was the thickly forested Eifel region on the German side of the frontier, which offered concealment for troops and tanks from Allied airpower. Everything would depend on surprise and on the Allied leadership failing to react quickly enough. Eisenhower, he assumed, would have to consult with his political mas-ters and other Allied commanders, and that could take several days.

Until Hitler's unexpected announcement at the Wolfsschanze on 16 September, only Jodl knew of the Führer's plan. From then on, everyone informed had to sign a piece of paper accepting that they would be executed if they mentioned it to anyone not specifically authorized. Jodl used his small staff for working out details of the plan according to Hitler's wishes. Keitel, although theoretically in charge of the OKW, was not involved in the planning, only in the allocation of fuel and ammunition for the operation. And Rundstedt, despite his position as commander-in-chief west, received no information at all. This was why he was so irritated later when the Americans kept referring to the 'Rundstedt offensive' as if it had been his plan.

On 22 October, Rundstedt's chief of staff General der Kavallerie Siegfried Westphal and Model's chief of staff General der Infanterie Hans Krebs answered a summons to the Wolfsschanze. Fearing a tirade from Hitler over the fall of Aachen and suspecting that their request for more divisions would be angrily rejected, they were surprised when made to sign a pledge of secrecy on pain of death before entering the conference room. Jodl's deputy presented a secret study entitled 'Wacht am Rhein' – 'Watch on the Rhine', a codeword designed to give an entirely defensive impression. There was at that stage no hint of the Ardennes offensive, just the transfer of troops to the western front in the general area of Aachen, supposedly to counter-attack an imminent American onslaught.

After lunch, the two chiefs of staff were included in Hitler's daily situation conference. A number of officers were asked to leave after the general briefing, and about fifteen men remained in the room. Hitler began to speak. The western front, he said, had been asking for reinforcements, and considering the fact that during the First World War there had been 130 German divisions, this was understandable. He had not been able to reinforce it because he could not afford more troops just for defence. But now things were different because he had evolved a plan for a surprise attack towards Antwerp. It would take place south of Liège, and would be supported by 2,000 aircraft, an exaggerated figure which no officer present believed for a moment.

He wanted to launch the attack in November, the period of fogs, although he realized that it would take most of the month to prepare. The main breakthrough would be made by the Sixth Panzer Army just south of the Hürtgen Forest. Manteuffel's Fifth Panzer Army would support its left flank, while the Seventh Army would in turn guard against counter-attacks from Patton's Third Army to the south. Westphal had many questions to put to Jodl afterwards, but found himself 'whisked away'. He had been tempted to say that the forces allocated were clearly insufficient even to reach the River Meuse, but he knew that if he had raised these objections, the 'Wehrmachtführungsstab [operations staff] probably would have accused me of defeatism'.

Westphal briefed Rundstedt on returning to Schloss Ziegenberg, the headquarters of the commander-in-chief west near Frankfurt-am-Main. It was next to the carefully camouflaged Adlerhorst, Hitler's western field headquarters, which Albert Speer had built for him before the campaign of 1940. Westphal also reported his impression that even Jodl probably did not believe that they would ever get to Antwerp.

Although Rundstedt cannot have been pleased at the lack of prior consultation, he was determined not to allow such an over-ambitious operation to proceed without modification. Model, the commander-in-chief of Army Group B, had similar feelings when briefed by his own chief of staff. One can only speculate as to his reaction on hearing that he was strictly forbidden from using any of the divisions earmarked for the great offensive. They had to be withdrawn from the front to be re-equipped, reinforced and retrained. The American attack into the Hürtgen Forest forced him to break that order less than two weeks later when he had to send forward the 116th Panzer-Division to help retake Schmidt. A number of other divisions nominated for the offensive also had to be brought in to prevent a collapse in the Hürtgen Forest. And further south the 17th SS Panzergrenadier-Division *Götz von Berlichingen*, which was needed to hold the advance of Patton's Third Army, never could be extracted to join the Ardennes offensive as planned. These 'German divisions were gradually worn down and could no longer be reconditioned prior to the Ardennes offensive', acknowledged the chief of staff of the Seventh Army.

'The old Prussian' and the short, aggressive Model could hardly have been more different in appearance, tastes and political outlook, but they at least agreed that Hitler's 'grand slam', or 'large solution', was one of his map fantasies. Rundstedt maintained that the only realistic option on the Ardennes–Aachen front was a double envelopment, with the two panzer armies wheeling inside the great bend of the Meuse to cut off

Hodges's First Army and part of Lieutenant General William H. Simpson's Ninth Army, while the Fifteenth Army further north near Roermond swung out to meet them near Liège. This alternative became known as the 'small solution' or 'little slam'. Model was sceptical about the Fifteenth Army's role. He wanted to use any spare forces as a follow-up to the main attack, broadening the breakthrough as they advanced, creating 'a snowplow effect'.

On 27 October, at a conference at Model's headquarters near Krefeld, the plans were discussed with the army commanders: SS-Oberstgruppenführer Sepp Dietrich of Sixth Panzer Army, Manteuffel of the Fifth Panzer Army and Brandenberger of the Seventh Army. Model, accepting that he would not be able to get his version of the 'small solution' approved by the OKW without his chief's support, acceded to Rundstedt's plan. But even Jodl's gradual attempts to win the Führer round to a 'small solution' made no headway. Hitler stubbornly ignored warnings that much greater forces would be needed, not just to reach Antwerp, but to secure the corridor against Allied counter-attacks.

Jodl warned Rundstedt that the Führer was immovable, so the commander-in-chief west put his views in writing. He clearly could not face another frenzied meeting with Hitler, outraged at the idea that any of his generals could disagree with him. Even Model's later tactic of suggesting the 'small solution', to be followed upon success by a drive north to Antwerp, was firmly rejected. Hitler thought that the American forces in front of Aachen were too powerful, so the only way to weaken them was by outflanking them across the Meuse and then cutting off their supply base.

Generaloberst Heinz Guderian again protested at the concentration of all available German forces in the west. He knew that the Red Army was preparing to strike its next blow on the eastern front as soon as the ground froze hard enough for its tank armies to charge forward from the Vistula. 'In our current situation,' Jodl explained to him on 1 November, 'we cannot shrink from staking everything on one card.' Guderian's son was to take part in the Ardennes offensive as Ia, or chief operations officer, of the 116th Panzer-Division.

The field commanders knew that fuel was going to be the chief problem, despite all assurances that they would receive what was needed. On 23 November, at a major conference in Berlin, they raised the question.

Dietrich complained that there was no sign of the supplies he had been promised. General Walter Buhle of the OKW tried to prove that they had been delivered by showing pieces of paper, but most of the fuel supplies were still stuck east of the Rhine as a result of Allied bombing. Manteuffel, knowing the effects of the difficult terrain and the mud on fuel consumption, had requested fuel for 500 kilometres, but his army received enough only for 150 kilometres. Keitel had accumulated 17.4 million litres of fuel, but Jodl later admitted that Keitel wanted to hold some back 'on principle, otherwise the commanders would have been too extravagant with it.'

Any hope of keeping to Hitler's original plan of attacking in November disappeared. Even the beginning of December looked increasingly uncertain. The transport of fuel, ammunition and the divisions themselves was delayed, partly due to Allied bombing of the transport network and partly due to the earlier difficulties of withdrawing formations to prepare. Hardly a single panzer division found the time and fuel to train many of the novice tank drivers. German forces on the western front had been receiving priority for the replacement of panzers, assault guns and artillery. Waffen-SS divisions received the bulk of the new equipment and had the pick of reinforcements, but even then they tended to be mainly youngsters transferred from the Luftwaffe and Kriegsmarine. The shameless preference for SS formations, which had Hitler's backing, was justified on the grounds that the Sixth Panzer Army had the major breakthrough role, but Jodl conceded later that the panzer divisions in Manteuffel's Fifth Panzer Army were more effective. 'There was a certain political interference in the conduct of the war,' he said.

On 2 December, Model came to Berlin with Manteuffel and Sepp Dietrich, who had been Hitler's loyal escort commander from the Nazis' street-fighting days. Both men also supported the 'small solution'. Hitler insisted that the Antwerp plan remain as he had stated. All preparations were to be made on that basis. Rundstedt did not attend the conference. He sent instead his chief of staff Westphal, who said virtually nothing. Hitler later 'expressed his astonishment at this conduct' to Jodl. But Rundstedt was clearly signalling what he thought of the whole project over which he had no control. The final orders were annotated by the Führer 'Not to be altered'. Rundstedt and Model were told expressly that their task was simply to pass on orders from the OKW 'to their subordinate commands'.

Model appears to have been fatalistic. He took the view that this was a 'last gamble' and he had no choice but to carry it out. Manteuffel later said that it was at this conference on 2 December that he privately decided that his 'final objective would be the Meuse' and not Brussels, as Hitler insisted for his army. He knew that 'the Allied ability to react would be the cardinal factor'.

Manteuffel was a tough little cavalryman who had served in the Zieten Hussars in the First World War. During the revolutionary upheavals which followed the Armistice he became adjutant to the Freikorps von Oven, which took part in suppressing the Spartacists in Berlin and the Räterepublik in Munich. In the Second World War he rapidly proved himself to be an outstanding leader on the eastern front, first with the 7th Panzer-Division and then with the Panzergrenadier-Division *Grossdeutschland*. 'Surprise, when it succeeds,' he explained, 'is a decisive part of the success of the panzer formation. Slackness, softness, etcetera amongst all ranks must be sternly put down.'

Hitler's obsession with secrecy never slackened. No troops were to be briefed until the evening before the attack. Even regimental commanders would know nothing until the day before. No registering of artillery could take place in advance. Despite pleas from the army commanders, the OKW, on Hitler's instruction, refused permission to brief anyone other than corps commanders, their chief artillery officers and one staff officer. Commanders of corps artillery had to reconnoitre all the gun positions themselves. Not surprisingly, many officers were soon able to work out that a major offensive was in preparation, since the artillery dispositions alone indicated that the deployments were not for defensive purposes.

Troops, as they moved on night marches into their concentration areas in the Eifel, were to be billeted in villages by day, with all vehicles concealed in barns. There were to be no fires and no movement in daylight in case of American reconnaissance flights. Charcoal was provided for cooking as it made little smoke. German officers were amazed that Allied air reconnaissance failed to spot villages and woods 'full to bursting point'. They half expected a massive air attack at any moment.

Maps were to be distributed only at the very last moment, for security reasons. Total radio silence was to be observed, but that also meant signals nets could not be established until the opening bombardment.

For the move to their attack positions, all roads were restricted to one-way traffic. No routes were to be marked in case this was spotted by enemy agents. Recovery vehicles were to be ready to cope with breakdowns. Storch aircraft would fly constantly overhead at night to check on progress and to spot any lights showing, but also to disguise the noise of engines. The civilian population was to be tightly controlled and all telephone lines in the Eifel must be cut. Gestapo officers were sent forward to check on all security measures. Volksgrenadier divisions received the order to take away their men's paybooks and identity documents so that they would be shot as spies if they deserted.

A fake headquarters north of Aachen transmitting instructions gave the impression that the Sixth Panzer Army was in position there, ready to counter-attack an expected American offensive across the River Roer. And a fake Twenty-Fifth Army was created in the same way as the Allies had invented a 1st US Army Group in eastern England before D-Day. Manteuffel himself 'started a rumour in a restaurant early in December, to the effect that we were preparing to attack in the Saar area in January. I mentioned this in a loud voice to some of my commanders while we were having dinner one night.'

Goebbels, meanwhile, kept repeating the mantra of the Nazi leadership that 'the political crisis in the enemy camp grows daily'. But many of their most loyal followers were not convinced by this message of hope; they simply felt that there was no choice but to fight on to the bitter end. A secret recording of a captured Waffen-SS Standartenführer revealed the diehard view of the moment. 'We have all been brought up from the cradle to consider Leonidas's fight at Thermopylae as the highest form of sacrifice for one's people,' he told a fellow officer. 'Everything else follows on from that and if the whole German nation has become a nation of soldiers, then it is compelled to perish; because by thinking as a human being and saying – "It is all up with our people now, there's no point in it, it's nonsense" – do you really believe that you will avoid the sacrifice of an appreciable number of lives? Do you think you will alter the peace terms? Surely not. On the other hand it is well known that a nation which has not fought out such a fateful struggle right to the last has never risen again as a nation.'

The vision of Germany as a phoenix arising from the ashes had a wide currency among true believers. 'The only thing is to continue the fight until the last,' said Generalleutnant Heim, 'even if everything is destroyed. Fighting until the last moment gives a people the moral strength to rise again. A people that throws in the sponge is finished for all time. That is proved by history.'

Tensions between the Waffen-SS and the German army were growing because of Hitler's insistence on saving SS formations in a retreat while ordinary divisions were left to fight on as a rearguard. And the SS never forgot a perceived injury. An officer in the 17th SS Panzergrenadier-Division claimed that, in the escape from the Falaise pocket at the end of the battle for Normandy, General der Panzertruppe Freiherr von Lüttwitz of the 2nd Panzer-Division had refused to lend a vehicle to evacuate the wounded commander of the SS Division *Leibstandarte*, who had been shot in the thigh. 'What a filthy trick!' he said. He then asserted that Lüttwitz himself had been saved by the commander of an SS panzergrenadier battalion.

'There were many comments', acknowledged General Warlimont, 'to the effect that the SS no longer considered itself a member of the Wehrmacht but had its own organisation.' Sepp Dietrich wanted his Sixth Panzer Army to be designated an SS panzer army, but this was denied because he had non-SS formations in his command. Dietrich even refused to have General der Artillerie Kruse as his chief artillery officer because he was not a member of the Waffen-SS. Manteuffel, like many others, had little respect for Dietrich's generalship. He thought that the Sixth Panzer Army 'was not commanded as one formation, and its component parts did not fight with the same sense of duty as the Army divisions'. Dietrich was regarded as a bad joke by senior army officers. When asked the objectives of his Sixth Panzer Army in the first and second days of the offensive, he is said to have replied: 'Objectives, objectives! If I had to give everybody objectives, wherever should I be? You general staff officers!'

Oberstleutnant von der Heydte was even more scathing, after meeting him to discuss his parachute drop in front of the Sixth Panzer Army. He said that Dietrich liked to pose as 'a people's general', but he was 'a conceited, reckless military leader with the knowledge and ability of a good sergeant. He has no moral scruples.' Heydte, although a German nationalist, detested the Nazis. As a cousin of Oberst Claus

Graf von Stauffenberg, he had been exasperated by a questionnaire following 20 July which asked whether he was related to aristocracy of non-German blood or to the former ruling house of Germany, or whether he had been educated abroad or in a Jesuit institute. When Heydte asked about his overall plan, Dietrich could say only that it was to push through to Antwerp 'and then give the English a good beating'.

Heydte, the head of the Fallschirmjäger Army Combat School, had first been warned of his mission by Generaloberst Kurt Student on the evening of 8 December at Student's headquarters in Holland. 'The Führer has ordered a parachute attack in the framework of a powerful offensive,' Student told him. 'You, my dear Heydte, are ordered to carry out this task.' He was to assemble a force of some 1,200 men to drop behind enemy lines to seize key road junctions. He rejected Heydte's suggestion of using his 6th Fallschirmjäger-Regiment, since that might be spotted by the enemy and secrecy was vital.

Kampfgruppe Heydte was to drop on the first night south of Eupen. Its mission was to block American reinforcements coming south from the Aachen sector. Over the next two days, Heydte received his men and sent them off to Sennelager for a short and intensive training course. Hitler's refusal to attempt airborne operations after the heavy losses on Crete in 1941 meant that many had never received proper training, and even some of the veterans had not been up in an aircraft since that invasion.

Heydte then went to Limburg to see General Pelz to discuss aircraft requirements. He was not impressed. 'There was nothing but French girls in the mess of the XII Flieger Korps commanded by Pelz at Limburg,' he noted.* Pelz complained of their disastrous situation and said: 'Germany's last reserves of fuel are being thrown into this Ardennes enterprise.' Heydte discovered that 112 Junkers 52 transports had been allocated for the mission; but half of the pilots had never dropped para-

---

* It is striking how many accounts at this time refer to young French women who had accompanied their lovers on the retreat to Germany because they knew that the Resistance would seek revenge for their *collaboration horizontale*. It is, however, very hard to get an idea of their subsequent fate. Many of them must have lost their 'protector' in the savage fighting over the last six months of the war. And German women, convinced that French women had done nothing since 1940 except try to seduce their menfolk, would not have taken them in.

troopers, nor flown over enemy territory, nor been trained to fly in formation. 'Only two pilots were old Stalingrad flyers,' he noted, referring to those veterans who had flown in and out of the Stalingrad encirclement during the doomed attempt to resupply Paulus's Sixth Army in December 1942.

On 11 December, taking the most experienced pilot with him, Heydte went on to see General der Flieger Beppo Schmidt, the most disastrous intelligence officer the Wehrmacht ever produced. Schmidt had constantly predicted all through the Battle of Britain that RAF Fighter Command was at its last gasp, yet Göring had protected and promoted his toady ever since. Schmidt, 'who was heavily under the influence of alcohol', declared that 'Success or failure in the German attack on Antwerp will decide the outcome of the war.' Schmidt told Heydte that he was to split his force in two, with one group to drop west of Malmédy and the other near Eupen. Heydte said this was ridiculous. They would be too small to be effective since many men would not make the dropping zone. And when Heydte warned that the lack of training of both pilots and paratroopers was so serious that the operation would fail, Schmidt cursed his two visitors and dismissed them for questioning the abilities of Luftwaffe personnel.

After a long drive through the night, Heydte went on to see Generalfeldmarschall Model in a hunting lodge south of Münstereifel. Model was blunt. He said the operation was not his idea and asked whether it stood a one in ten chance of success. Heydte had to agree that it was possible. Model apparently replied that 'the entire offensive had not more than a ten percent chance of success', but 'it was the last remaining chance of concluding the war favourably'. Model then sent him to see Sepp Dietrich, whose headquarters were half an hour's drive further to the south.

While Heydte waited most of the morning to see Dietrich, an orderly-room clerk told him the secret plan for sabotage operations by a Kampfgruppe led by Otto Skorzeny, an astounding breach of security for which he could have been shot. Finally, Heydte was shown into Dietrich's office. Heydte thought he looked like 'an old non-commissioned officer permanently addicted to alcohol'. Dietrich opened the conversation by demanding: 'What can you paratroopers do, anyhow?' Heydte replied that, if told the mission, he could judge whether or not it was possible.

Failing to obtain a clear reply, Heydte then asked what was known of enemy strength in the area. 'All that was known', Heydte recorded, 'was that the front line was held by American units; and that behind them there were only "a couple of bank managers and Jewboys"', in Dietrich's words. 'As for tactical and operational reserves, nobody could tell me anything.'

Heydte later entertained fellow officers in captivity with his version of how the conversation went, imitating Dietrich's thick Swabian accent. When he tried to explain some of the problems the operation faced, Dietrich clearly considered this defeatism. The offensive would crush the Americans.

'We'll annihilate them,' he shouted.

'But what about the enemy, Herr Oberstgruppenführer?'

'Good Lord, I don't know. You'll find out soon enough.'

'Who will you send in first?'

'I can't tell you yet – whoever is the first to turn up.'

Heydte's account continued: 'When I added that you can only jump when the wind is favourable, he said: "Well, I'm not responsible for the Luftwaffe's shortcomings! It's just another example of their uselessness."'

The only useful aspect to this bizarre encounter was that Dietrich agreed he should not split his force in two. Heydte discovered more from Dietrich's chief of staff, SS-Brigadeführer Krämer – 'a highly overstrung and overworked man', which was hardly surprising since he had to do everything for Dietrich. Krämer told him that the panzer spearhead of the 12th SS Division *Hitler Jugend* would be with them 'within twenty-four hours'. Heydte demanded an artillery forward observation officer to drop with them and he was provided with SS-Obersturmführer Etterich. Heydte then heard that the drop was to take place on the morning of 16 December between 04.30 and 05.00 hours, just before the opening bombardment. Motor transport would be laid on to take his force to the airfields at Paderborn and Lippspringe.

The other special operation which the OKW planned was a commando venture, using picked troops in captured American vehicles and uniforms to penetrate Allied lines and cause mayhem in the rear. Hitler had summoned SS-Obersturmbannführer Otto Skorzeny to East Prussia on 21 October for a personal briefing long before Rundstedt or

Model knew anything of the offensive. 'Skorzeny,' Hitler said, 'this next assignment will be the most important of your life.' Skorzeny, two metres tall and with a large scar on his left cheek, towered over the bent and sickly Führer. Heydte described the huge Austrian as a 'typical evil Nazi' who used 'typical SS methods. So he formed a special body of people of the same type as himself.' General der Panzertruppe von Thoma also regarded Skorzeny as an Austrian criminal, and described him as 'a real dirty dog . . . shooting is much too good for him'.

Skorzeny was given unlimited powers to prepare his mission. His officers obtained whatever they wanted simply by saying 'order from the Reichsführer'. Officers and NCOs from the army, Waffen-SS, Kriegsmarine and Luftwaffe who spoke English were ordered to report to the camp at Schloss Friedenthal outside Oranienburg for 'interpreter duties'. Around half of them came from the navy. There they were interrogated in English by SS officers. They were told that they would be part of a special unit designated the 150th Panzer-Brigade and were sworn to secrecy. They had to sign a paper which stated: 'Everything I know about the commitment of 150th Panzer-Brigade is secret. Secrecy will be maintained even after the war. Breach of the order is punishable by death.' Their commander, the wonderfully named Oberstleutnant Musculus, had blond hair and facial scars from student duels. He promised them that the activities of the 150th Panzer-Brigade would have a 'decisive effect on the course of the war'.

A young naval officer, Leutnant zur See Müntz, was sent along with all the others to the heavily guarded camp of Grafenwöhr. He was then given the task of collecting 2,400 American uniforms, including those of ten generals and seventy officers, from prisoner-of-war camps by 21 November. Müntz first went to Berlin to the department of prisoners of war. The officer in charge, Oberst Meurer, was taken aback by the Führer order they presented signed by Hitler himself. He mentioned that such activities were illegal under international law, but provided them with written instructions to all camp commanders. Müntz set off with a truck and various helpers to collect the uniforms as well as identity papers, paybooks and so forth, but they had great difficulty obtaining what they needed from the prisoner-of-war camps. At Fürstenberg-an-der-Oder, the camp commandant refused the order to strip field jackets from eighty American soldiers. Müntz was recalled to Grafenwöhr in case the Red Cross heard of the row and word of it then reach the Allies. His mission partly failed because of the grave shortage of US Army winter clothing, as GIs had already found to their cost in the Hürtgen Forest, Lorraine and Alsace.

At Grafenwöhr, all ranks had to salute in the American style, they were fed on K-Rations and were kitted out in the few uniforms which Müntz and his group had managed to obtain. Every order was given in English. They were made to watch American movies and newsreels to learn the idiom, such as 'chow-line', and to improve their accent. They also spent two hours a day on language and American customs, including how to eat 'with the fork after laying down the knife'. They were even shown how to tap their cigarette against the pack in an American way. All the usual commando skills were also taught, such as close-quarter combat training, demolition and the use of enemy weapons.

When given more details of the forthcoming Operation *Greif*, as it was called, those who expressed doubts about going into action in American uniforms were threatened by SS-Obersturmbannführer Hadick. He 'emphasized that the Führer's orders would be obeyed without question, and that anyone who chose to disagree would be sentenced to death'. Morale was also rather shaken when they were issued with ampoules of cyanide 'concealed in a cheap cigarette-lighter'.

Men from SS units almost worshipped Skorzeny as a super-hero after his exploits in Italy and Budapest, while he treated them with 'conspicuous friendship'. One of them wrote later: 'he was our pirate captain'. Many rumours ran around the camp about what their true mission was likely to be. Some thought that they were to be part of an airborne operation to reoccupy France. Skorzeny himself later claimed that he had encouraged the story that certain groups would be tasked with heading to Paris, to kidnap General Eisenhower.

Kampfgruppe Skorzeny was split into a commando unit, Einheit Steilau, and the 150th Panzer-Brigade. For the commandos, Skorzeny picked 150 men out of 600 English-speakers. Mounted mostly in Jeeps and wearing American uniforms, they included demolition groups to blow up ammunition and fuel dumps and even bridges; reconnaissance groups to scout routes to the Meuse and observe enemy strength; and other teams to disrupt American communications by cutting wires and issuing false orders. Four men were mounted in each Jeep, which was a mistake since the Americans themselves seldom packed as many on board, and each team had a 'speaker', the one with the best grasp of American idiom. The German soldiers in American uniforms waiting to advance in their Jeeps were clearly nervous. In an attempt to reassure them, an officer from brigade headquarters told them that 'according to the German radio, US soldiers in German uniforms had been captured behind the German lines, and that . . . a lenient view would be taken, and the US soldiers treated as prisoners of war'.

The 150th Panzer-Brigade was much stronger with nearly 2,000 men, including support units. There was a paratroop battalion, two tank companies with a mixture of M-4 Shermans and badly disguised Panthers, panzergrenadier companies, heavy mortars and anti-tank guns in the event of their securing one of the Meuse bridges at Andenne, Huy or Amay. The plan was to get ahead of the panzer spearheads once they reached the Hohes Venn plateau on a line with Spa, by taking side roads and tracks. They would hide up by day, then race forward in the dark to seize the three bridges.

Skorzeny also had plans to blow up the five bridges over the upper Rhine at Basle, in case the Allies entered Switzerland to outflank German defences in the south. In fact on 5 December SHAEF studied the possibility of outflanking German forces in the south by going through Switzerland, but Eisenhower turned this idea down. (Stalin, who clearly hated the Swiss, had urged the Allies at the Teheran conference a year before to attack southern Germany through Switzerland.)

As X-Day for the Ardennes offensive approached, the defensive cover-name was changed from *Wacht am Rhein* to *Herbstnebel*, or 'Autumn Mist'. The delays in the delivery of fuel and ammunition became worse and the attack had to be pushed back to dawn on 16 December. Altogether some 1,050 trains were needed to bring the divisions to their concentration areas. Each panzer division needed seventy trains alone.

So far, nobody below the level of corps command had been informed. But SS-Obersturmbannführer Joachim Peiper of the 1st SS Panzer-Division *Leibstandarte Adolf Hitler* guessed what was afoot on 11 December when Krämer, the Sixth Panzer Army's chief of staff, wanted to discuss a hypothetical offensive in the Eifel region. He asked Peiper how long it would take a panzer regiment to move eighty kilometres at night. To be sure of his answer, Peiper himself took out a Panther for a test run over that distance in darkness. He realized that moving a whole division was a much more complicated matter, but what he and his superiors had underestimated was the state of the roads and the saturated ground in the Ardennes.

Hitler reached his western headquarters at the Adlerhorst that day in a long motorcade of huge black Mercedes. His main concern was maintaining secrecy. He had become nervous when Allied bombers flattened the town of Düren, the main communications centre just behind the start-line for the operation. His mood swings were highly erratic, from total dejection to groundless optimism. According to his Luftwaffe adjutant Oberst von Below, he 'was already seeing in his mind's eye the German spearhead rolling into Antwerp'. The next morning, Sepp Dietrich was summoned to his bunker concealed under fake farm buildings.

'Is your army ready?' Hitler asked straight out.

'Not for an offensive,' Dietrich claimed to have replied.

'You are never satisfied,' the Führer answered.

Late that afternoon, buses brought divisional commanders to the Adlerhorst to be addressed by Hitler. Each officer was searched by SS guards and had to surrender his pistol and briefcase. At 18.00 hours, Hitler limped on to the stage. Generals who had not seen him for some time were shocked by his physical deterioration, with pallid face, drooping shoulders and one arm which shook. Flanked by Keitel and Jodl, he sat behind a table.

He began with a long self-justification of why Germany was in the state it was at that stage of the war. A 'preventative war' had been necessary to unify the German peoples and because 'life without *Lebensraum* is unthinkable'. Never for a moment did he consider how other nations might react. Any objection was part of a conspiracy against Germany. 'Wars are finally decided by the recognition on one side or the other that the war can't be won any more. Thus, the most important task is to bring the enemy to this realization. The fastest way to do this is to destroy his strength by occupying territory. If we ourselves are forced on to the defensive, our task is to teach the enemy by ruthless strikes that he hasn't yet won, and that the war will continue without interruption.'

Hitler reminded the assembled generals that some of them had feared taking the offensive against France in 1940. He claimed that the Americans had 'lost about 240,000 men in just three weeks' and 'the enemy might have more tanks, but with our newest types, ours are better'. Germany was facing a fight that had been inevitable, which had to come sooner or later. The attack had to be carried through with the greatest brutality. No 'human inhibitions' must be allowed. 'A wave of fright and terror must precede the troops.' The purpose was to convince the enemy that Germany would never surrender. 'Never! Never!'

Afterwards the generals went to a party to toast Rundstedt's sixty-ninth birthday at his headquarters in the nearby Schloss Ziegenberg, a gloomy building rebuilt in neo-Gothic style. Nobody felt much like celebrating. According to Dietrich, they did not dare discuss the offensive because of the death penalty threatened against anyone who mentioned it.

On 13 December, Dietrich visited the headquarters of Army Group B. Model said to him that this was 'the worst prepared German offensive of this war'. Rundstedt noted that out of the thirty-two divisions promised, four divisions were withdrawn just before the attack, including the 11th Panzer-Division and the 17th SS Panzergrenadier-Division. Only twenty-two were assigned to take part in the opening of the offensive. The rest were held back as an OKW reserve. While most generals were deeply sceptical of the operation's chances of success, younger officers and NCOs, especially those in the Waffen-SS, were desperate for it to succeed.

Peiper's regiment received its march order from east of Düren to its assembly area behind the front. It set off after dark following the plain yellow arrows which marked the route. No divisional insignia or numbers were shown. The night and the following morning were foggy, which allowed the men to slip into their assembly areas without being spotted by air reconnaissance. Other divisions also removed their divisional insignia from vehicles just before the advance.

Joachim, or 'Jochen', Peiper was twenty-nine years old and good looking with his brown hair slicked back. In the Waffen-SS he was seen as the beau idéal of a panzer leader, a convinced Nazi and utterly ruthless. In the Soviet Union he was well known for torching villages and killing all the inhabitants. On 14 December, shortly before noon, he reported to the headquarters of the 1st SS Panzer-Division *Leib-standarte Adolf Hitler* where Brigadeführer Wilhelm Mohnke issued its orders for X-Day on 16 December. The division had been reinforced with an anti-aircraft regiment with 88mm guns, a battalion of heavy howitzers and an extra engineer battalion for repairing bridges. Each Kampfgruppe was to be accompanied by one of the Skorzeny units, with captured Shermans, trucks and Jeeps, but the division had no control over them. On his return Peiper briefed his battalion commanders in a forester's hut.

Only on the evening of 15 December were officers allowed to brief their troops. Hauptmann Bär, a company commander in the 26th Volksgrenadier-Division, told his men: 'In twelve or fourteen days we will be in Antwerp – or we have lost the war.' He then went on to say: 'Whatever equipment you may be lacking, we will take from American prisoners.' Yet, in SS formations especially, the mood was one of fierce exultation at the prospect of revenge. NCOs appear to have been among the most embittered. Paris was about to be recaptured, they told each other. Many regretted that the French capital should have been spared from destruction while Berlin was bombed to ruins. In the 10th SS Panzer-Division *Frundsberg*, the briefing on the offensive produced 'an extraordinary optimism' because the Führer had 'ordered the great blow in the West'. They believed that the shock of an unexpected attack would represent a massive blow to Allied morale. And according to an officer in the highly experienced 2nd Panzer-Division, 'the fighting spirit was better than in the early days of the war'. Dietrich's Sixth Panzer Army alone had more than 120,000 men, with nearly 500 tanks and assault guns and a thousand artillery pieces. Manteuffel's Fifth Panzer Army had another 400 tanks and assault guns. The Allied command had no idea of what was about to hit them on their weakest sector.

7

Intelligence Failure

Hitler's prediction of tensions in the Allied camp did come about, but certainly not to the degree he had hoped. Both Field Marshal Sir Alan Brooke, the chief of the imperial general staff, and Montgomery had again become concerned with the slowness of the Allied advance, which they ascribed to Eisenhower's incapacity as a military leader. Both wanted a single ground force commander, ideally in the shape of Bernard Law Montgomery. Yet Brooke thought Montgomery harped on about it too much. He was awake to the political reality that everything had changed. The war in north-west Europe had become an American show, as Britain struggled to maintain its armies around the world. So if there were to be a single ground commander, in Brooke's view, it would have to be Bradley and not Montgomery. But the diminutive field marshal had clearly learned nothing and forgotten nothing, except his promise to Eisenhower that he would hear no more on the subject of command from him.

On 28 November, Eisenhower came to 21st Army Group headquarters at Zonhoven in Belgium. Montgomery always pretended to be far too busy to visit his Supreme Commander even when little was happening on his front. Eisenhower should not have put up with his behaviour. He sat in Monty's map trailer while Montgomery strode up and down, lecturing him for three hours on what had gone wrong, and why a single ground commander was needed. Montgomery felt that the natural dividing line was the Ardennes, and that he should command all the Allied forces north of that sector, which would have given him most of the First US Army and all of Lieutenant General William H. Simpson's Ninth Army. Unfortunately, Eisenhower's silence – he was speechless from exhaustion and boredom – gave Montgomery the idea that it indicated tacit consent with his argument that the Allies had suffered a strategic reverse by failing to reach the Rhine and by the fruitless bloodbath in the Hürtgen Forest. Afterwards, to the astonishment of his own military aide, the field marshal sent a signal to Brooke in London indicating that Eisenhower had agreed with everything he said. And in a cable to Eisenhower on 30 November, Montgomery outlined what he thought had been agreed.

The next day Eisenhower visited Bradley at his headquarters in the Hôtel Alfa in the city of Luxembourg. Bradley was a pitiful sight in bed, suffering from flu and hives. Although Eisenhower was furious with Montgomery over his allegation of a strategic reverse, the letter which he dictated in reply was not pointed enough to penetrate Montgomery's armoured complacency. A meeting on 7 December was agreed in Maastricht.

On Wednesday 6 December, Eisenhower returned to Bradley's headquarters, bringing his deputy Air Chief Marshal Tedder to discuss tactics before meeting Montgomery. Major Chester B. Hansen, Bradley's aide, feared that his general was 'pathetically alone'. 'It is his knowledge of the critical times facing him that has caused the nervousness now evident in him for the first time. He is not irritable but he is more brusque than usual, he looks tired and the slight physical irritations have combined to wear him down physically as well as mentally.' Eisenhower listened to him, 'with his face heavily wrinkled as he frowned, his neck stuck deeply into the fur collar of the flying jacket he wears'.

Bradley was also exasperated with the Allies' lack of progress. 'If we were fighting a reasonable people they would have surrendered a long time ago,' he said. 'But these people are not reasonable.' Hansen then added in his diary: 'The German has proved unexpectedly resistant, however, and he dies only with great difficulty ... He has been told by Goebbels that this is a fight to the finish, that the weak shall be exterminated in the labor camps of Siberia. It is little wonder, therefore, that we find them fighting our advance savagely, causing us to kill them in great numbers.' Goebbels, in an attempt to stop German soldiers surrendering in the west, had indeed put out a story that the Americans had agreed to hand over all their prisoners of war to the Soviets for reconstruction work. He came up with the slogan 'Sieg oder Sibirien!' – 'Victory or Siberia!'

The next day at Maastricht, with Montgomery, Hodges and Simpson, Eisenhower discussed the next stage. He spoke of 'sledgehammer blows that will carry them across the Roer and up to the banks of the Rhine'. Eisenhower then expressed his concerns about crossing the Rhine. He was afraid of mines or ice floes destroying pontoon bridges, thus cutting off any troops in the bridgehead. Field Marshal Brooke had been horrified when Eisenhower told him in mid-November that the Allies probably would not be across the Rhine until May 1945. This remark, coming at the end of Brooke's tour of the front, strongly influenced his view that Eisenhower was not up to the task of Supreme Commander.

Montgomery once again put forward his arguments for a heavy attack across the Rhine north of the Ruhr industrial region while all the other American armies were virtually halted. Eisenhower, no doubt gritting his teeth, once again repeated his position that a thrust towards Frankfurt was also important and he had no intention of stopping Patton. 'Field Marshal Montgomery', the notes of the meeting recorded, 'could not agree that a thrust from Frankfurt offered any prospect of success. In his view, if it were undertaken, neither it nor the thrust north of the Ruhr would be strong enough . . . Field Marshal Montgomery said that the difference of view about the Frankfurt–Cassel thrust was fundamental.' To avoid a clash, Eisenhower tried to convince him that the difference was not very great. Montgomery's 21st Army Group would have the major role with Simpson's Ninth Army under his command.

Bradley had to hide his anger when Montgomery went on to argue that 'all operations north of the Ardennes should be under one command; all south of the Ardennes under another'. This would mean leaving Bradley with just the Third Army. Eisenhower retorted that future operations dictated that the Ruhr in front of them should be the dividing line. Bradley made his feelings clear to Eisenhower soon afterwards. If his 12th Army Group were to be placed under Montgomery, then he would regard himself as relieved of his duties for having failed in his task as a commander.

Most of the action at that time was taking place on the Third Army front. Patton's forces were crossing the River Saar in several places, and a few days later the last fortress in the Metz area was taken. 'I think only Attila [the Hun] and the Third Army have ever taken Metz by assault,' Patton wrote with satisfaction in his diary. He was also preparing a major offensive to begin on 19 December. Yet it is wrong to suggest that Montgomery was acting through jealousy of Patton, as some have suggested. He was far too self-absorbed to be envious. He also appeared quite incapable of judging the reactions of others to what he said. In fact, one might almost wonder whether Montgomery suffered from what today would be called high-functioning Asperger syndrome.

Patton was becoming infuriated with the one element he could not control, the relentless rain. On 8 December, he rang the Third Army chaplain, James O'Neill. 'This is General Patton. Do you have a good prayer for weather?' The chaplain asked if he could call back. He could not find anything in the prayer books, so he wrote out his own. 'Almighty and most merciful Father, we humbly beseech Thee, of Thy great goodness, to restrain these immoderate rains with which we have had to contend. Grant us fair weather for Battle. Graciously hearken to us as soldiers who call upon Thee that, armed with Thy power, we may advance from victory to victory, and crush the oppression and wickedness of our enemies, and establish Thy justice among men and nations. Amen.' Patton read and firmly approved. 'Have 250,000 copies printed and see to it that every man in the Third Army gets one.' He then told O'Neill that they must get everyone praying. 'We must ask God to stop these rains. These rains are the margin that holds defeat or victory.' When O'Neill encountered Patton again, the general was in bullish form. 'Well, Padre,' said Patton, 'our prayers worked. I knew they would.' And he cracked him across the helmet with his riding crop to emphasize the point.

In the south, the neglected US Seventh Army in Alsace redeployed towards the northern flank of its salient to support Patton's offensive in Lorraine with its own attack up towards the area of Bitche. This meant that the neighbouring French First Army under General de Lattre de Tassigny felt exposed. Lattre considered his forces undermanned, partly because so many French units were still besieging German garrisons on the Atlantic coast. This, he maintained, was the reason for his army's inability to crush the Colmar pocket despite the addition of a US infantry division, a failure which prompted many disobliging remarks from American officers. To make matters worse, the bitter cold of the Vosges mountains had badly affected the morale of his troops.

*

One of the great debates about the Ardennes offensive has focused on the Allied inability to foresee the attack. There were indeed many fragmented pieces of information which taken together should have indicated German intentions, but as in almost all intelligence failures, senior officers discarded anything which did not match their own assumptions.

Right from the start, Hitler's orders for total secrecy cannot have been followed. Word of the forthcoming offensive even circulated among senior German officers in British prisoner-of-war camps. In the second week of November, General der Panzertruppe Eberbach was secretly recorded saying that a Generalmajor Eberding, captured just a few days before, had spoken of a forthcoming offensive in the west with forty-six divisions.* Eberbach believed this was true, and that it was a last try. Even a Leutnant von der Goltz, captured on South Beveland during the clearing of the Scheldt, had heard that 'the big offensive, for which they were preparing 46 divisions, was to start in November'. These secretly recorded conversations were reported by MI 19a on 28 November to the War Office in London and sent on to SHAEF, but this rather vital information does not appear to have been taken seriously. No doubt it was simply dismissed as a desperately optimistic rumour circulating among captured officers, especially since the figure of forty-six divisions seemed so impossibly high.

During the first week of November, a German deserter recounted in a debriefing that panzer divisions redeployed to Westphalia were part of the Sixth Panzer Army. This also highlighted the fact that SHAEF intelligence had not heard of the Fifth Panzer Army for several weeks. Both SHAEF and Bradley's 12th Army Group assumed that the Germans were preparing a strong counter-attack against an American crossing of the Roer. A German spoiling attack before Christmas was also considered to be quite likely, but hardly anybody expected it to come from the Eifel and through the Ardennes, even though the Germans had used this route in 1870, 1914 and 1940.

---

* The secret recording of conversations among selected German prisoners of war was carried out by the Combined Services Detailed Interrogation Centre (CSDIC). Interpreters, most of whom were German Jewish refugees, listened to conversations picked up by concealed microphones and recorded on wax discs. Transcripts of relevant material were distributed afterwards to the War Office, Admiralty, the Secret Intelligence Service, ministries and also SHAEF from 1944.

The Allies could not believe that the Germans in their weakened state would dare to undertake an ambitious strategic offensive, when they needed to husband their strength before the Red Army launched its own winter onslaught. Such a gamble was definitely not the style of the commander-in-chief west, Generalfeldmarschall Gerd von Rundstedt. This was true, but the Allied command had gravely underestimated Hitler's manic grasp on the levers of military power. Senior officers have always been encouraged to put themselves in their opponents' boots, but it can often be a mistake to judge your enemy by yourself. In any case, SHAEF believed that the Germans lacked the fuel, the ammunition and the strength to mount a dangerous thrust. And the Allies' air superiority was such that a German offensive into the open would surely play into their hands. In London, the Joint Intelligence Committee had also concluded that 'Germany's crippling shortage of oil continues to be the greatest single weakness in her capacity to resist.'

Wehrmacht troop movements into the Eifel around Bitburg were observed, but other divisions seemed to move on so it was assumed the area was just a staging post, or a sector for preparing new formations. Unfortunately, the Ardennes sector was deemed a low priority for air reconnaissance, and as a result of bad weather very few missions were flown in the region. Just six days before the great attack in the Ardennes, Troy H. Middleton's VIII Corps headquarters in Bastogne concluded: 'the enemy's present practice of bringing new divisions to this sector to receive front line experience and then relieving them out for commitment elsewhere indicates his desire to have this sector of the front remain quiet and inactive'. In fact the Germans were playing a clever form of 'Find the Lady', shuffling their formations to confuse Allied intelligence.

Patton's Third Army headquarters noted the withdrawal of panzer formations, and his chief intelligence officer, Brigadier General Oscar W. Koch, feared that VIII Corps in the Ardennes was very vulnerable. The conclusion of many, including General Bradley, was that the Germans might well be planning a spoiling attack to disrupt Patton's major offensive due to begin on 19 December. A number of other intelligence officers became wise after the event and tried to claim that they had predicted the great offensive, but nobody had listened. Several within SHAEF and Bradley's 12th Army Group did indeed predict an attack, and a couple were very close to getting the date right, but none of them specifically identified the Ardennes as the threatened sector in time.

Eisenhower's senior intelligence officer Major General Kenneth Strong included an offensive in the Ardennes as one of several options. This had made a marked impression on Eisenhower's chief of staff Bedell Smith in the first week of December. Bedell Smith told Strong to go to Luxembourg and warn Bradley, which he did. In their conversation, Bradley said that he was 'aware of the danger', but that he had earmarked certain divisions to move into the Ardennes area should the enemy attack there.

The most controversial Cassandra was Colonel B. A. Dickson, the G-2 (or senior intelligence officer) at US First Army. A colourful character, Dickson was not always trusted by his peers because he had an unfortunate knack of identifying German divisions in the west when their position had been confirmed on the eastern front. In his report of 10 December, he commented on the high morale of German prisoners, which indicated a renewed confidence. Yet even though he noted a panzer concentration in the Eifel, he predicted that the attack would come further north in the Aachen area on 17 December. Several prisoners of war had spoken of an attack to recapture Aachen 'as a Christmas present for the Führer'. Then, on 14 December, Dickson received the debriefing of a German-speaking woman who had reported troop concentrations and bridging equipment behind enemy lines in the Eifel. Dickson was now convinced that the attack was definitely coming in the Ardennes between Monschau and Echternach. Brigadier General Sibert at Bradley's 12th Army Group, irritated by Dickson who loathed him in return, rejected his report as no more than a hunch. Dickson was told on 15 December to take some leave in Paris.

Hitler's order for total radio silence among the attack formations had been followed, thus depriving Bletchley Park analysts of a clear picture through Ultra material. Regrettably, SHAEF relied far too much on Ultra intelligence, and tended to think that it was the fount of all knowledge. On 26 October, however, it had alighted upon 'Hitler's orders for setting up a special force for special undertaking in west. Knowledge of English and American idiom essential for volunteers.' And on 10 December, it worked out that radio silence had been imposed on all SS formations, which should have rung an alarm bell at SHAEF.

Unlike the German army the Luftwaffe had once again been incredibly lax, but SHAEF does not appear to have reacted to Bletchley transcripts. Already on 4 September, the Japanese ambassador in Berlin had reported after interviews with Ribbentrop and Hitler that the Germans were planning an offensive in the west in November 'as soon as replenishing of air force was concluded'. The subsequent inquiry into the intelligence failure stated, 'The GAF [Luftwaffe] evidence shows that ever since the last week in October, preparations have been in train to bring the bulk of the Luftwaffe on to airfields in the West.'

On 31 October, 'J[agd]G[eschwader] 26 quoted Goering order that re-equipment of all fighter aircraft as fighter bombers must be possible within 24 hours.' This was significant because it could certainly indicate preparations for an attack in support of ground troops. And on 14 November, Bletchley noted: 'Fighter units in West not to use Geschwader badges or unit markings'. On 1 December, they read that courses for National Socialist Leadership Officers had been cancelled owing to 'impending special operation'. The Nazi over-use of the word 'special' was probably the reason why this was not seized on. And on 3 December, a report was called for by Luftflotte Reich 'on measures taken for technical supply of units that had arrived for operations in the west'. The next day fighter commanders were summoned to a conference at the headquarters of Jagdkorps II. Soon after, the whole of SG 4, a specialized ground-attack Geschwader, was transferred to the west from the eastern front. That should have raised some eyebrows.

The head of the Secret Intelligence Service considered it 'a little startling to find that the Germans had a better knowledge of the US order of battle from their signals intelligence than we had of the German order of battle from Source [Ultra]'. The reason was clear in his view. 'Ever since D-Day, US signals have been of great assistance to the enemy. It has been emphasized that, out of thirty odd US divisions in the west, the Germans have constantly known the locations, and often the intentions, of all but two or three. They knew that the southern wing of US First Army, on a front of about eighty miles, was mostly held either by new or by tired divisions.'

The understandably tired 4th and 28th Infantry Divisions were licking their wounds after the horrors of the Hürtgen Forest. They had been sent to rest in the southern Ardennes, a steeply sloped area known as the 'Luxembourg Switzerland', and described as a 'quiet paradise for weary troops'. It seemed to be the least likely sector for an attack. The men were billeted in houses, to make a change from the extreme discomforts of foxholes in the Hürtgen Forest.

In the rear areas, soldiers and mechanics settled down with local families, and the shops were stocked with US Army produce. 'The steady traffic and the slush soon gave nearly every village the same drab, mud-splashed touch. In most of the drinking and eating places the atmosphere was that of some far western town of the movies where the men gathered at night to spice their lives with liquor. These soldiers, for the most part, had made their deal with the army. They didn't care for the life, but they proposed to make the best of it.'

The Germans, despite all orders forbidding reconnaissance, had a very clear picture of certain sectors of the front, especially those which were lightly held, such as the 4th Infantry Division frontage in the south. German civilians could move back and forth, slipping between outposts along the River Sauer. The Germans were thus able to identify observation posts and gun positions. Counter-battery fire was an essential part of their plan to protect their pontoon bridges over the Sauer in the first vital hours of the attack. Some of the more experienced agents even mingled with off-duty American soldiers in villages behind the lines. After a few beers, many soldiers were happy to chat with Luxembourgers and Belgians who spoke a little English.

Locals ready to converse were rather fewer than before. The joy of liberation in September and initial American generosity had turned sour later in the autumn as collaborators were denounced and suspicions increased between Walloon and German-speaking communities. Resistance groups made increasingly unjustifiable demands for food and supplies from farmers. But, for the eastern cantons closest to the fighting along the Siegfried Line, the greatest dismay was caused by the decision of the American civil affairs administration to evacuate the majority of civilians between 5 and 9 October. Only a small picked number would be allowed to remain in each village to look after livestock. In one way, this would prove to be a mercy because even more farming families would have been killed otherwise.

Over the previous 150 years, the border areas of Eupen and St Vith had moved back and forth between France, Prussia, Belgium and Germany, depending on the fortunes of war. In the Belgian elections of April 1939, more than 45 per cent of those in the mainly German-speaking 'eastern cantons' voted for the Heimattreue Front which wanted the area reincorporated into the Reich. But by 1944 the privilege of belonging to the Reich had turned bitter. The German-speakers of the eastern cantons had found themselves treated as second-class citizens, jokingly known as *Rucksackdeutsche* who had been gathered up and carried along after the Ardennes invasion of 1940. And so many of their young men had been killed or crippled on the eastern front that now most German-speakers longed for liberation by the Reich's enemies. Yet there were enough left still loyal to the Third Reich to constitute a considerable pool of potential informers and spies for German intelligence, known as *Frontläufer*.

Parties from the divisions in the Ardennes were allowed back to the VIII Corps rest camp at Arlon or to Bastogne, where Marlene Dietrich went to perform for the GIs, crooning huskily in her long sequinned gown which was so close-fitting that she wore no underwear. She nearly always sang 'Lili Marlene'. Its lilting refrain had gripped the hearts of Allied troops, despite its German provenance. 'The bloody Heinies!' wrote one American soldier. 'When they weren't killing you they were making you cry.'

Dietrich loved the response of the soldiers, but she was much less enamoured of the staff officers she had to deal with. 'La Dietrich was bitching,' Hansen wrote in his diary. 'Her trip among the corps of the First Army had been a rigorous one. She didn't like the First Army. She didn't like the competition between corps, armies and divisions. Most of all she disliked the colonels and generals of Eagle Main [12th Army Group rear headquarters] at Verdun where she lived on salmon because her meal times did not correspond to the chow periods and no one took an interest in her.' She also claimed that she caught lice, but that did not stop her from accepting General Bradley's invitation to cocktails, dinner 'and a bad movie' at the Hôtel Alfa in Luxembourg. General Patton, whom she claimed to have slept with, was clearly much more her sort of general. 'Patton believes earnestly in a warrior's Valhalla,' Hansen also observed that day.

On the evening of Sunday 10 December, there was a heavy fall of snow. The next morning, Bradley, now partially recovered, went to Spa to see Hodges and Simpson. It would be their last meeting for some time. He returned in the afternoon after a long drive past Bastogne.

Snow covered the whole area and the roads were thick with slush as a result of the blizzard the previous night. A pair of shotguns which he had ordered were waiting for him. General Hodges seemed to have had the same idea. Three days later, he spent 'a good part of the afternoon' with Monsieur Francotte, a renowned gunmaker in Liège, ordering a shotgun to be made to his specifications.

Bradley's headquarters remained quietly optimistic about the immediate future. That week staff officers concluded: 'It is now certain that attrition is steadily sapping the strength of German forces on the western front and that the crust of defence is thinner, more brittle and more vulnerable than it appears on our G-2 maps or to the troops in the line.' Bradley's chief worry was the replacement situation. His 12th Army Group was short of 17,581 men, and he planned to see Eisenhower about it in Versailles.

At a press conference on 15 December to praise the IX Tactical Air Command, Bradley estimated that the Germans had no more than six to seven hundred tanks along the whole front. 'We think he is spread pretty thin all along,' he said. Hansen noted that as far as air support was concerned, 'Little doing today . . . Weather prevents their being operational even a quarter of the time.' The bad visibility to prevent flying, which Hitler had so earnestly desired, was repeated day after day. It does not, however, appear to have hampered artillery-spotting aircraft on unofficial business in the Ardennes. Bradley received complaints that 'GI's in their zest for barbecued pork were hunting [wild] boar in low-flying cubs with Thompson submachine guns.'

Also on 15 December, the G-3 operations officer at the daily SHAEF briefing said that there was nothing to report from the Ardennes sector. Field Marshal Montgomery asked General Eisenhower if he minded his going back to the United Kingdom the next week for Christmas. His chief of staff, General Freddie de Guingand, had just left that morning. With regrettable timing on the very eve of the German onslaught, Montgomery stated that the shortages of 'German manpower, equipment and resources precluded any offensive action on their part'. On the other hand, VIII Corps in the Ardennes reported troop movements to its front, with the arrival of fresh formations.

In the north of the VIII Corps sector, the newly arrived 106th Infantry Division had just taken over the positions of the 2nd Infantry

1. US Infantry advancing through a hole blasted in the Siegfried Line, or Westwall, in October 1944.

2. Fallschirmjäger mortar crew in the Hürtgen Forest. Mortars accounted for the highest number of casualties on both sides.

3. 1st Infantry Division in the Hürtgen Forest.

4. Medics with wounded soldier.

5. French troops in the Vosges. The North African soldiers in the First French Army attacking the Colmar Gap south-west of Strasbourg suffered terribly from the cold.

6. 7 December 1944, Maastricht meeting with (*l* to *r*) Bradley, Tedder, Eisenhower, Montgomery and Simpson.

7. German prisoners captured in early December in the Hürtgen Forest near Düren.

8. Generalfeldmarschall Walter Model, commander-in-chief Army Group B.

9. Field Marshal Montgomery appears to be lecturing an increasingly exasperated Eisenhower once again.

10. General der Panzertruppe Hasso-Eccard Freiherr von Manteuffel of the Fifth Panzer Army.

11. Oberstgruppenführer-SS Sepp Dietrich of the Sixth Panzer Army wearing his Knight's Cross with oak leaves.

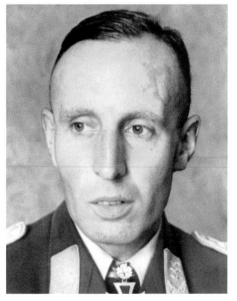

12. Oberst then Generalmajor Heinz Kokott, the rather more enlightened commander of the 26th Volksgrenadier-Division at Bastogne.

13. Oberstleutnant Friedrich Freiherr von der Heydte, the law professor turned paratroop commander.

14. The briefing of panzer commanders in a snow flurry just before the Ardennes offensive on 16 December 1944.

15. Two SS panzergrenadiers enjoying captured American cigarettes.

16. 16 December. A Königstiger tank of the Sixth Panzer Army carrying soldiers of the 3rd Fallschirmjäger-Division on the first day of the advance.

17. German infantry in a Volksgrenadier division advance loaded down with machine-gun belts and panzerfaust anti-tank grenade launchers.

18. The first killing of American prisoners by SS panzergrenadiers from the Kampfgruppe Peiper in Honsfeld who then proceeded to loot the bodies. The boots have been removed from the victim on the left.

19. SS panzergrenadiers from the Kampfgruppe Hansen pass a burning convoy of American vehicles near Poteau.

Division on a hogsback ridge of the Schnee Eifel. 'My men were amazed at the appearance of the men from the incoming unit,' wrote a company commander in the 2nd Division. 'They were equipped with the maze of equipment that only replacements fresh from the States would have dared to call their own. And horror of horrors, they were wearing neckties! Shades of General Patton!'* During the handover a regimental commander from the 2nd Division told Colonel Cavender of the 423rd Infantry: 'It has been very quiet up here and your men will learn the easy way.' The experienced troops pulling out took all their stoves with them. The green newcomers had none to dry out socks, so many cases of trench foot soon developed in the damp snow.

Over the following days the 106th Division heard tanks and other vehicles moving to their front, but their lack of experience made them unsure of what it meant. Even the experienced 4th Division to their south assumed that the engine noises came from one Volksgrenadier division being replaced by another. In fact there were seven panzer and thirteen infantry divisions in the first wave alone, coiled ready for the attack in the dark pinewoods ahead.

In Waffen-SS units especially, the excitement and impatience were clearly intense. A member of the 12th SS Panzer-Division *Hitler Jugend* wrote to his sister on the eve of battle. 'Dear Ruth, My daily letter will be very short today – short and sweet. I write during one of the great hours before an attack – full of unrest, full of expectation for what the next days will bring. Everyone who has been here the last two days and nights (especially nights), who has witnessed hour after hour the assembly of our crack divisions, who has heard the constant rattling of Panzers, knows that something is up and we are looking forward to a clear order to reduce the tension. We are still in the dark as to "where" and "how" but that cannot be helped! It is enough to know that we attack, and will throw the enemy from our homeland. That is a holy task!' On the back of the sealed envelope he added a hurried postscript: 'Ruth! Ruth! Ruth! WE MARCH!!!' That must have been scribbled as they moved out, for the letter fell into American hands during the battle.

---

* General Patton was renowned for making his military police charge any soldier without a necktie for being improperly dressed.

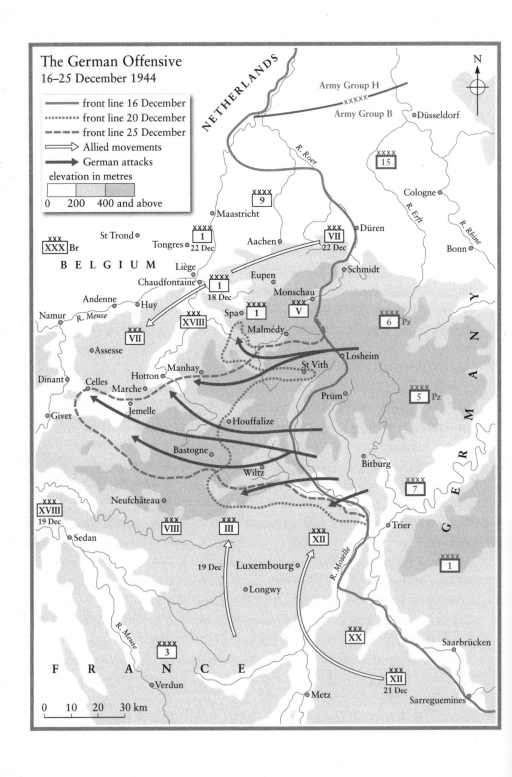

The German Offensive
16–25 December 1944

front line 16 December
front line 20 December
front line 25 December
Allied movements
German attacks
elevation in metres

0   200   400 and above

N

NETHERLANDS

Army Group H
Army Group B

Düsseldorf

R. Roer

XXXX
15

R. Erft

R. Rhine

XXXX
9

Cologne

Maastricht

St Trond

XXXX
1
22 Dec

Tongres

Aachen

XXX
VII
22 Dec

Düren

Bonn

Schmidt

BELGIUM

Liège

Eupen

XXX
Br

XXX
XXX

Chaudfontaine

XXXX
1
18 Dec

Spa

XXXX
1

Monschau

XXX
V

XXXX
6   Pz

Andenne

Huy

Malmédy

Namur

R. Meuse

XXX
XVIII

XXX
VII

Assesse

Losheim

Manhay

St Vith

Dinant

Celles

Hotton

XXXX
5   Pz

Marche

Prüm

Jemelle

Givet

Houffalize

Bastogne

Bitburg

Wiltz

XXXX
7

Neufchâteau

XXX
VIII

XXX
III

XXX
XVIII
19 Dec

XXX
XII

Trier

Sedan

19 Dec

Luxembourg

R. Moselle

GERMANY

XXXX
1

Longwy

XXX
XX

Saarbrücken

R. Meuse

XXXX
3

F R A N C E

XXX
XII
21 Dec

Verdun

Metz

Sarreguemines

0   10   20   30 km

8

Saturday 16 December

At 05.20 hours on 16 December, ten minutes before 'zero hour', the artillery of Sepp Dietrich's Sixth Panzer Army opened fire. Most American soldiers, avoiding the chill of damp snow in the sixteen hours of darkness, were asleep in farmhouses, foresters' huts, barns and cowbyres. Dawn was not due until 08.30. Along most of the front, south from the Monschau Forest, the terrain was reminiscent of the Hürtgen, with thick woods, rocky gorges, small streams, few roads and saturated firebreak trails so deep in mud that they were almost impassable to vehicles.

German artillery commanders, knowing that American soldiers preferred shelter, always targeted houses. Sentries were told they should never be in the house by the door. They should be in a foxhole a short distance away to cover it in the event of German surprise attacks. Sentries, having seen flashes like summer lightning on the horizon, rushed in to wake those inside. But it was only when the shells began to explode all around that there was a panic-stricken scramble by the men to extricate themselves from their sleeping bags, and grab equipment, helmets and weapons.

There had been odd bombardments before, but this was much more intense. Some of the civilians allowed to stay in the forward area to look after their livestock were terrified to see shells setting hay-barns alight, with the fire quickly spreading to the farmhouse. Unable to control the blaze, they fled with their families towards the rear. Some were killed in the bombardment. In the tiny village of Manderfeld, five died, including three small children.

To the south, on the Fifth Panzer Army frontage, artillery batteries remained silent. Manteuffel had disregarded Hitler's insistence on a long opening bombardment. He considered such a barrage to be 'a World War I concept and completely out of place in the Ardennes, in view of the thinly held lines . . . Such a plan would merely be an alarm clock to the American forces and would alert them to the daylight attack to follow.' A few days earlier, Manteuffel had sneaked forward in disguise to reconnoitre the deep valley of the River Our, and the River Sauer at the southernmost end. The Sauer was 'a significant obstacle due to its steep banks and limited crossing sites'.

He then questioned his soldiers and officers on the habits of the Americans opposite them. Since the 'Amis' retired after dark to their houses and barns, and only returned to their positions an hour before dawn, he decided to cross the river and infiltrate their lines without waking them up. Only when the attack had really started did his army use searchlights, bouncing their beams off low cloud to create artificial moonlight. This helped his infantry spearheads find their way forward in the dark woods. His engineer battalions meanwhile had started bridging the River Our, so that his three panzer divisions, the 116th, the 2nd and the Panzer Lehr, could surge forward.

Hitler had laid down in his prescriptive way that infantry divisions would make the breakthrough so that the precious panzer divisions would start fully intact for the Meuse bridges. The first reports to reach the Adlerhorst were most encouraging. Jodl reported to Hitler 'that surprise had been achieved completely'. Surprise had indeed been achieved, but what the Germans really needed was momentum to turn surprise into a paralysing shock. Some American troops lost their heads and began to save themselves. In many cases, frightened civilians begged to be allowed to accompany them. A few of the German-speakers still loyal to the Reich, on the other hand, watched the chaotic scenes with undisguised satisfaction. 'If in places there was panic,' an officer in the 99th Division reported, 'in other places there was supreme valor.' These feats of extraordinary courage would slow down the German onslaught with critical results.

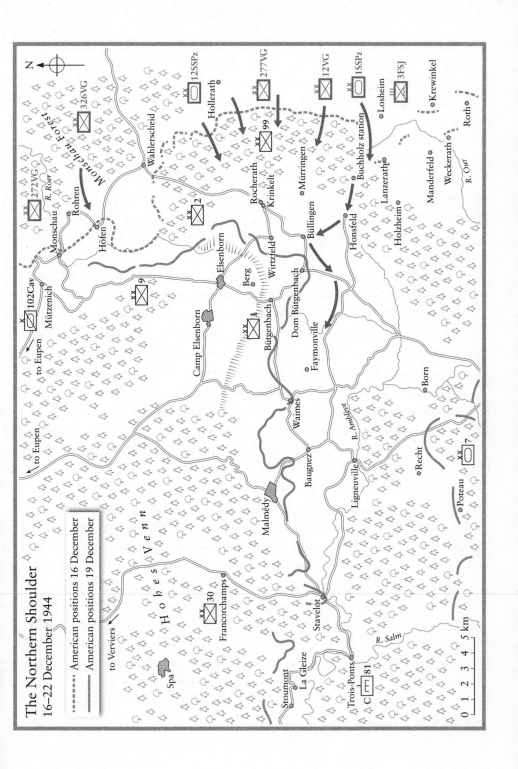

The Northern Shoulder
16–22 December 1944

American positions 16 December
American positions 19 December

Four kilometres north of Manderfeld, the hamlet of Lanzerath stood opposite the Losheim Gap, the line of advance of the 1st SS Panzer-Division led by the Kampfgruppe Peiper. Almost on the top of a ridge, it had a magnificent view out towards Germany. On a knoll, overlooking the houses and the road, an outpost of eighteen soldiers from the intelligence and reconnaissance platoon of the 394th Regiment of the 99th Division manned foxholes on hillside pasture. To their right rear a thick pinewood offered a means of escape, but also a route for an attacking force to outflank them. The importance of this position lay in the fact that a couple of hundred metres to the left was the road junction leading north-west to Honsfeld, and then to the valley of the River Amblève.

Even though the inexperienced 99th Division was part of V Corps, this platoon commanded by Lieutenant Lyle J. Bouck Jr was just over the boundary into the VIII Corps sector, which at its northern end was weakly held by the 14th Cavalry Group. Some tank destroyers attached to the 14th Cavalry were down below them among the houses. When the eastern horizon came alive with the flashes from the muzzles of hundreds of guns, the reconnaissance platoon had ducked down into its foxholes. Lanzerath was an obvious target for German artillery. The soldiers were grateful for the overhead cover on their well-constructed trenches, which had been prepared by the 2nd Division. After the bombardment lifted, they saw the tank destroyers down in the village pull out past them and then turn left down the Honsfeld road. 'They might at least wave goodbye,' one soldier remarked.

Bouck radioed his regimental headquarters to report on the bombardment, and he was told to send a small patrol into Lanzerath to check and observe. Now in the grey, dawn light, he took three men down to have a look. They entered a house to hear a man talking German. Lanzerath, only just within the Belgian border, was very much part of the Germanophone eastern cantons. Bouck's men were convinced the man was talking to the enemy and he had to stop them from killing him. As the light improved a little on that heavily overcast morning, they saw large numbers of figures in the distance approaching in a column. They would be coming up the road past the platoon's position. Bouck ran back to radio a request for artillery fire on the road below Lanzerath, but he was met by disbelief at regimental headquarters.

Through his field glasses, Bouck watched what turned out to be a twin column of German paratroopers in their distinctive helmets and smocks marching, with a file on either side of the road. Their weapons were slung, not at the ready, and they had no scouts out ahead or on the flanks. They could have been on a route march. This was the 9th Regiment of the 3rd Fallschirmjäger-Division, whose task was to break open the front for the Kampfgruppe Peiper. The platoon waited tensely, their machine guns and other automatic weapons cocked ready for the perfect ambush. Bouck wanted the main body to be within their field of fire before his men opened up. He then sighted a small group who were clearly officers. He signalled to his men to prepare to open fire. But at the very last moment a little fair-haired girl of about thirteen rushed out of a house and pointed up the hill at the recon platoon's position. Bouck hesitated, not wanting to kill the girl, but the German officer screamed an order, and his men threw themselves into the ditches on either side of the road.

The ambush may have aborted, but the opportunities for killing the under-trained teenagers had not disappeared, due to the obduracy of their commander. He sent them into one frontal attack after another. The recon platoon machine-gunners simply scythed them down as they struggled to climb a snow-fence across the field just below the American positions. The range was so short that they could see their faces clearly. Bouck radioed a second time, urgently requesting artillery support. He was told that the guns were on other fire missions. He asked what he should do. 'Hold at all costs!' came the reply. Several of his men had been hit, but they were able to fight on.

Sickened by piles of dead and the wounded building up in the fields below, Bouck could scarcely believe that the German regimental commander could continue this futile sacrifice instead of trying to outflank them. A white flag appeared, and Bouck ordered a ceasefire while German medical orderlies collected their wounded. The battle began again and continued until after dark, by which time Bouck and his men were almost out of ammunition. Only after nightfall did the German commander attempt to outflank the defenders. They rushed and overran the position. Bouck and almost all his men were taken prisoner. His platoon had held off a whole regiment for a day, killing and wounding over 400 paratroopers, at a cost of just one man dead and several wounded. But it was the delay inflicted which counted most.

Peiper knew that it had been a mistake to let the infantry go first, and he was furious. Already his Kampfgruppe had been held up because the bridge over the railway line north-west of Losheim, which had been blown by the Germans during their withdrawal three months earlier, had not been repaired. It was not ready until 19.30 hours that evening. The 12th Volksgrenadier-Division's horse-drawn artillery also went ahead of Peiper's column, adding to the delay. The roads were clogged but Peiper ordered his vehicles 'to push through rapidly and to run down anything in the road ruthlessly'. In his impatience to get ahead, he told his tank commanders to drive on through an American minefield: five panzers were disabled as a result.

His divisional headquarters ordered him to divert to Lanzerath to meet up with that part of the 3rd Fallschirmjäger-Division which had been repulsed. Peiper was to take over the regiment and attack. According to one inhabitant of Lanzerath, Peiper's men were highly agitated as they entered the village, 'shouting that they were going to drive the Americans all the way back to the Channel', and they kept saying that their troops were already on the Meuse at Liège.

Peiper showed his contempt for the parachute regiment officers, who insisted the American positions were very strong although they had not been near them. He was also exasperated with the Kampfgruppe Skorzeny combat team attached to his force, with four Shermans, trucks and Jeeps. 'They might just as well have stayed at home,' he said later, 'because they were never near the head of the column where they had planned to be.' Peiper ordered his men and the paratroopers forward towards Buchholz and Honsfeld.

The small force from the 99th Division, surrounded at Buchholz station, fought off attacks from the 3rd Fallschirmjäger. A young forward observation officer was sent to direct artillery support. 'We pulled our jeep off the road and backed it into a barn,' he recorded later. 'It was a quiet, cold night . . . We could clearly hear the SS panzer troops shouting back and forth, the racing of tank engines, the squeal of bogie wheels.' On their SCR-536 radio, they also heard German signallers taunting them in English. 'Come in, come in, come in. Danger, danger, danger. We are launching a strong attack. Come in, come in, anyone on this channel?' The defenders of Buchholz station were doomed when Peiper's flak panzers arrived. They mounted quadruple 20mm guns that could obliterate any defenders unprotected by concrete, or by several inches of armour-plate.

On Peiper's right flank, the 12th SS Panzer-Division *Hitler Jugend* was struggling as it advanced slowly on the twin villages of Rocherath and Krinkelt. This division, which had been ground down by the British and Canadians in Normandy, had never fully recovered. 'There were fellows among them whose discipline was not quite up to standard,' an officer in another SS formation commented. 'These were boy-scout types and the sort of swine who think nothing of cutting a man's throat.' The division also seemed to lack technical skills. The *Hitler Jugend* suffered a high rate of mechanical breakdowns with its Panther Mark V panzers.

At the northernmost end of the 99th Infantry lines, the 3rd Battalion of the 395th Infantry held the village of Höfen just south of Monschau. The small Höfen salient in the Monschau Forest was an obvious target for attack. Generalfeldmarschall Model wanted to break through either side of Monschau to block the roads to Eupen and Aachen, and stop any American reinforcements coming from the north. He forbade any bombardment on Monschau itself. At Höfen, however, the American battalion found artificial moonlight playing in its favour. As the 326th Volksgrenadier-Division advanced through the mist, the glow silhouetted the approaching German infantry. 'At 06.00 the Germans came,' an officer reported. 'Out of the haze, they appeared before the battalion position. They seemed to be in swarms moving forward in their characteristic slow walk. The artificial moonlight outlined the approaching Germans perfectly against the backdrop of snow, and every weapon the battalion possessed opened fire . . . The German losses were terrific and at 06.55, they began to withdraw.' The battalion's ten 81mm mortars were also used, and when communications were restored with the 196th Field Artillery, they added their fire.

Less than two hours later, another, stronger attack began, reinforced by tanks and armoured cars. 'On the K Company front, the German infantry moved forward of the tanks and shouting like wild men, they charged the company position.' The assault was fought off only after the mortars and artillery – the 155mm 'Long Toms' – targeted the sector. At 09.30 came yet another attack. A large number of Germans managed to seize four houses. The battalion commander ordered his two 57mm anti-tank guns to start smashing the walls with armour-piercing rounds. Rifle and automatic fire was concentrated on all the windows to prevent the Germans shooting at the anti-tank gun crews. 'From the screams within the house one could readily ascertain that the anti-tank guns were creating havoc.' A reserve platoon crept up and began throwing white phosphorus grenades through the windows. The survivors soon surrendered. Some seventy-five dead were apparently found inside.

The 2nd Battalion of the 393rd Infantry had been attached to the 2nd Division, which had just started a new V Corps advance north towards the Roer dams near Schmidt. When they heard heavy firing to the south they thought that the rest of the division was now joining in the same attack. They still had no idea of the German offensive.

An aid man called Jordan, helped by a couple of riflemen, began bandaging the wounded in the comparative shelter of a sunken road. 'We administered plasma to a boy whose right arm was attached by shreds,' a soldier recounted, 'tried to soothe him and held cigarettes for him to smoke. He was already in shock, his body shaking badly. Shells exploding hundreds of feet away made him flinch. "Get me out of here! For God's sake get me out of here. That one was close – that one was too damn close. Get me out of here," he kept saying.' Jordan, the aid man, received a bullet through the head. 'We heard later that day that our boys shot a German medic in retaliation, somewhat mitigated by the fact that he was carrying a Luger.' Not knowing what was going on, and angry at having to give up ground they had just taken in the advance towards the dams, they were ordered to halt and turn round. Orders were to withdraw south-west towards Krinkelt to face the 12th SS Panzer-Division.

While most of the 99th Division fought valiantly in the desperate battles, 'a few men broke under the strain', an officer acknowledged, 'wetting themselves repeatedly, or vomiting, or showing other severe physical symptoms'. And 'the number of allegedly accidental rifle shots through hands or feet, usually while cleaning the weapon, rose sharply'. Some men were so desperate that they were prepared to maim themselves even more seriously. A harrowing example in the 99th Infantry Division was a soldier who was said to have 'lain down beside a large tree, reached around it, and exploded a grenade in his hand'.

*

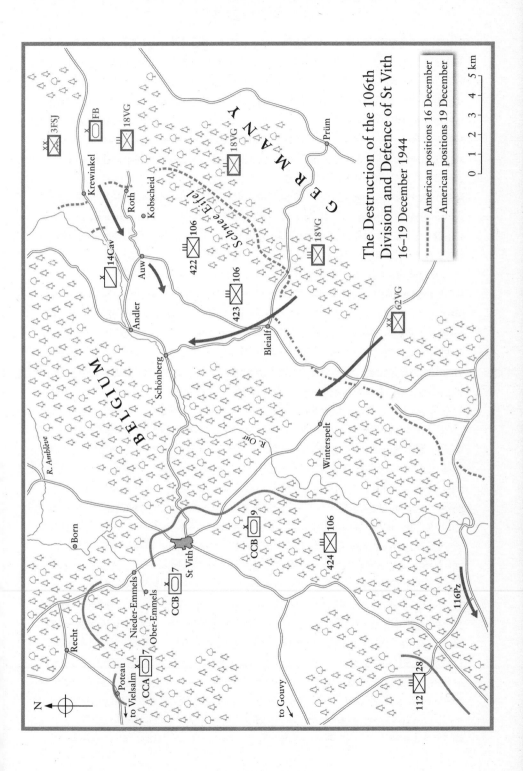

The Destruction of the 106th
Division and Defence of St Vith
16–19 December 1944

American positions 16 December
American positions 19 December

0 1 2 3 4 5 km

GERMANY

BELGIUM

Schnee Eifel

R. Amblève

R. Our

3FSJ
FB
18VG
Krewinkel
Roth
Kobscheid
14Cav
Auw
Andler
Schönberg
422 106
423 106
18VG
18VG
62VG
Bleialf
Winterspelt
Prüm
Born
St Vith
CCB 9
CCB 7
424 106
116Pz
Recht
Nieder-Emmels
Ober-Emmels
Poteau
to Vielsalm
CCA 7
112 28
to Gouvy

N

The newly arrived and even less experienced 106th Infantry Division to the south, in the Schnee Eifel, would be shattered by the German offensive over the next three days. It was rapidly outflanked when the 14th Cavalry Group in the Losheim Gap, covering the area between the 99th Division and the 106th, retreated without warning. This also left the right flank of the 99th vulnerable. As its 395th Infantry Regiment pulled back in desperate haste, soldiers bitterly remembered the slogan 'The American Army never retreats!' Having received no rations, they forced open some drums of dried oatmeal. So desperate were they that they tried to stuff handfuls of it into their mouths and fill their pockets. An officer recorded that one soldier even offered another $75 for a thirteen-cent can of Campbell's soup.

The cavalry group had faced an almost impossible task. Strung out in isolated positions across a front of nearly nine kilometres, its platoons could only attempt to defend fixed positions in villages and hamlets. There was no continuous line and the cavalry was not manned, trained nor equipped for a stationary defence. All it had were machine guns dismounted from reconnaissance vehicles, a few anti-tank guns and a battalion of 105mm howitzers in support. The very recent arrival of the 106th meant that no co-ordinated plan of defence had been established.

In the days before the offensive, German patrols had discovered that there was a gap nearly two kilometres wide between the villages of Roth and Weckerath in the 14th Cavalry sector. So, before dawn, the bulk of the 18th Volksgrenadier-Division, supported by a brigade of assault guns, advanced straight for this hole in the American line, which lay just within the northern boundary of the Fifth Panzer Army. Manteuffel's initial objective was the town of St Vith, fifteen kilometres to the rear of the American front line on the road from Roth.

In the murky grey daylight, the men of the 14th Cavalry at Roth and Weckerath found that the Germans were already behind them, having slipped through partly concealed by the low cloud and drizzle. Communications collapsed as shell bursts cut field telephone cables and German intercept groups played records at full volume on the wavelengths which the Americans used. The surrounded cavalry troopers in Roth fought on for much of the day, but surrendered in the afternoon.

The 106th Division did not collapse immediately. With more than thirty kilometres of front to defend, including a broad salient just forward of the Siegfried Westwall, it faced major disadvantages, especially when its left flank was burst open on the 14th Cavalry sector around Roth. With eight battalions of corps artillery in support, it inflicted heavy casualties on the volksgrenadiers, used as cannon fodder to break open the front for the panzer divisions. But the 106th Division did little to counter-attack the flank of the German breakthrough on its left, and this would lead to disaster the next day.

As Model's artillery chief observed, the difficult terrain of wooded country slowed the advance of the German infantry and made it very hard for his artillery to identify its targets. Also Volksgrenadier divisions did not know how to make proper use of artillery support. They were not helped by the strict orders on radio silence, which had prevented signals nets from being established until the opening bombardment.

Communications were even worse on the American side. Middleton's VIII Corps headquarters in Bastogne had no clear idea of the scope of the offensive. And at First Army in Spa, General Hodges assumed that the Germans were mounting 'just a local diversion' to take the pressure off the V Corps advance towards the Roer river dams. And yet although V-1 'buzz-bombs', as the Americans called them, were now passing overhead every few minutes to bombard Liège, Hodges still did not recognize the signs.* Despite General Gerow's urging, he refused to halt the 2nd Division's advance north. In Luxembourg at 12th Army Group headquarters during the 09.15 briefing, the G-3 officer reported no change on the Ardennes sector. By then General Bradley was on his way to Versailles to discuss manpower shortages with General Eisenhower.

A diary kept by Lieutenant Matt Konop with the 2nd Division's headquarters gives an idea of how Americans, even those close to the front, could take so long to comprehend the scale and scope of the German offensive. Konop's entry for 16 December began: '05.15: Asleep in Little Red House with six other officers – hear loud explosions – must be a dream – still think it's a dream – must be our own artillery – can't be, that stuff seems to be coming in louder.' Konop got up in the dark

* The worst disaster resulting from the V-1 bombardment took place in Antwerp that evening when one struck a cinema, killing nearly 300 British and Canadian soldiers and wounding another 200 as well as many civilians.

and padded to the door in his long johns. He opened it. An explosion outside sent him scurrying back to wake everyone else. They all rushed down into the cellar in their underclothes, finding their way with flashlights. Eventually, when the shelling eased, they returned upstairs. Konop called the operations section to ask if there was anything unusual to report. 'No, nothing unusual,' came the answer, 'but [we] had quite a shelling over here. Nothing unusual reported from the lines.' Konop crawled back to his mattress, but could not get back to sleep.

It was still dark at 07.15 when he reached the command post at Wirtzfeld. The progress of the 2nd Division's advance appeared satisfactory on the situation map. Its 9th Infantry Regiment had just captured the village of Wahlerscheid. An hour later Konop looked round Wirtzfeld. There were no casualties from the shelling, except that a direct hit on a heap of manure resulted 'in the pile being suddenly transported over the entire kitchen, mess-hall and officers' mess of the Engineer Battalion'. Later in the morning, he agreed with the division's Catholic chaplain that after the morning's bombardment they should be careful about holding mass in the church next day because it was an obvious target.

At 17.30 hours, Konop saw a report that German tanks had broken through the 106th Division. This was described as a 'local enemy action'. Having nothing else to do, he returned to his room to read. He then spent the evening chatting with a couple of war correspondents who had arrived to doss down. Before going to 'hit the hay', he showed the two journalists the door to the cellar in case there was another bombardment the next morning.

Cota's 28th Division, adjoining the 106th to the south-west, was initially taken by surprise because of the bad visibility, but the Germans' use of artificial moonlight proved a 'blunder'. 'They turned searchlights into the woods and then on clouds above our positions, silhouetting their [own] assault troops. They made easy targets for our machinegunners.'

Fortunately, before the offensive began the division had trained infantry officers and NCOs to act as forward observers for the artillery. One company of the division's 109th Infantry Regiment, which was dug in, brought down 155mm howitzer fire just fifty metres in front of its own position during a mass attack. It claimed a body count of 150 Germans afterwards for no American casualties.

The compulsion to exaggerate achievements and the size of enemy forces was widespread. 'Ten Germans will be reported as a company,' a battalion commander in the division complained, 'two Mark IV tanks as a mass attack by Mark VIs. It is almost impossible for commanders to make correct decisions quickly unless reports received are what the reporter saw or heard and not what he imagined.'

The 112th Infantry Regiment of Cota's 28th Division found that 'on the morning of the initial assault, there were strong indications that the German infantry had imbibed rather freely of alcoholic beverage . . . They were laughing and shouting and telling our troops not to open fire, as it disclosed our positions. We obliged until the head of the column was 25 yards to our front. Heavy casualties were inflicted. Examination of the canteens on several of the bodies gave every indication that the canteen had only a short time before contained cognac.'

Waldenburg's 116th Panzer-Division attacked on the boundary between the 106th and 28th Divisions. But, instead of finding a gap, the Germans were taken in the flank by the extreme right-hand battalion of the 106th and a platoon of tank destroyers. In the forest west of Berg, Waldenburg reported, the assault company of his 60th Panzergrenadier-Regiment was not merely stopped but 'nearly destroyed' when the Americans 'fought very bravely and fiercely'. The Germans rushed forward artillery to cover the river crossings, but the woods and hills made observation very difficult and the steep slopes offered few places to site their batteries.

Waldenburg's 156th Panzergrenadier-Regiment to the south, on the other hand, advanced rapidly to Oberhausen. Then he found that the dragons' teeth of the Siegfried Line defences made it impossible for the panzer regiment to follow its prescribed route. He had to obtain permission from his corps headquarters to allow it to follow the success of the 156th Panzergrenadiers who had seized crossing points over the River Our. The heavy rains and snow in the Ardennes had made the ground so soft that panzer units were restricted to surfaced roads. Tank tracks churned the mud of lesser routes to a depth of one metre, making them impassable for wheeled vehicles, and even other panzers. The bad weather which Hitler had wanted to shield his forces from Allied airpower

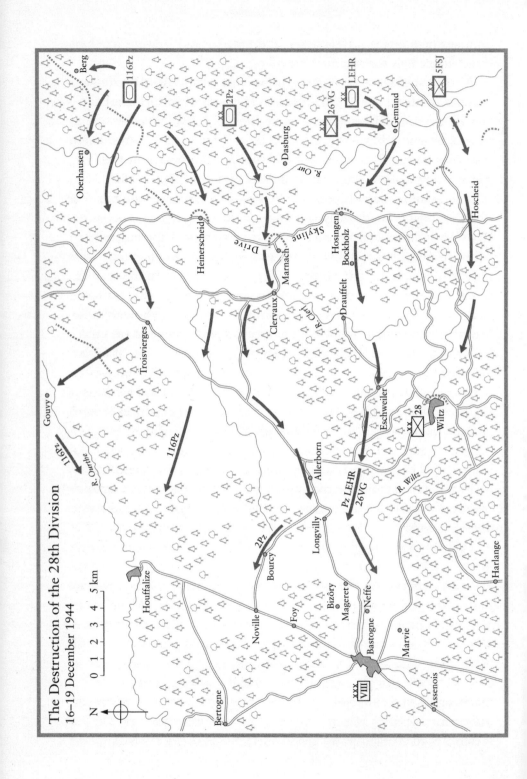

The Destruction of the 28th Division
16–19 December 1944

N

0 1 2 3 4 5 km

Berg
116Pz
Oberhausen
2Pz
Dasburg
R. Our
LEHR
26VG
Gemünd
5FSJ
Hoscheid
Heinerscheid
Skyline Drive
Marnach
Hosingen
Bockholz
Clervaux
R. Clerf
Drauffelt
116Pz
Troisvierges
Gouvy
Eschweiler
Wiltz
28
111Pz
R. Ourthe
Allerborn
Pz LEHR
26VG
R. Wiltz
Harlange
Longvilly
2Pz
Bourcy
Houffalize
Noville
Foy
Bizôry
Mageret
Neffe
Bastogne
Marvie
Assenois
VIII

came at a high price, and so did the wild, forested terrain, with which he had concealed his purpose.

Further south, the 26th Volksgrenadier-Division had the task of opening the front for Manteuffel's most experienced formations, the 2nd Panzer-Division and the Panzer Lehr Division. They hoped to reach Bastogne, which lay less than thirty kilometres to the west as the crow flies, during that night or early the next morning. But General-major Heinz Kokott, the commander of the 26th Volksgrenadiers, had an unpleasant surprise. The 28th Division fought on even after its line along the high ground and road known as 'Skyline Drive' had been broken. What had not been expected, he wrote later, 'was the fact that the remnants of the beaten units did not give up the battle. They stayed put and continued to block the road.' This forced the German command to accept that 'the infantry would actually have to fight its way forward', and not just open a way for the panzer divisions to rush through to the Meuse. 'At the end of the first day of the offensive, none of the objectives set by the [Fifth Panzer] Army were reached.' The 'stubborn defense of Hosingen' lasted until late in the morning of the second day.

Even though the 26th Volksgrenadiers eventually forced a crossing, repairs to the bridge over the Our near Gemünd were not ready until dusk at 16.00 hours. Traffic jams with the vehicles of both the 26th Volksgrenadier and the Panzer Lehr built up, because the Americans had blocked the road to Hosingen with enormous craters and 'abatis' barriers of felled trees. German pioneer battalions had to work through the night to make the road passable. The 26th Volksgrenadier lost 230 men and eight officers, including two battalion commanders, on the first day.

On the American 28th Division's right flank, the German Seventh Army pushed forward the 5th Fallschirmjäger-Division to shield Manteuffel's flank as his Fifth Panzer Army headed west for the Meuse. But the 5th Fallschirmjäger was a last-minute replacement to the German order of battle and struggled badly. Although 16,000 strong, its officers and soldiers had received little infantry training. One battalion, commanded by the flying instructor Major Frank in the 13th Fallschirmjäger-Regiment, had twelve officers with no field experience. Frank, in a conversation secretly taped after his capture, told another officer that his NCOs were 'willing but inept', while his 700 soldiers were mostly just sixteen or seventeen years old, but 'the lads were wonderful'.

'Right on the very first day of the offensive we stormed Führen [held by Company E of the 109th Infantry]. It was a fortified village. We got to within 25 metres of the bunker, were stopped there and my best Kompaniechefs were killed. I stuck fast there for two and a half hours, five of my runners had been killed. One couldn't direct things from there, the runners who returned were all shot up. Then, for two and a half hours, always on my stomach, I worked my way back by inches. What a show for young boys, making their way over flat ground and without any support from heavy weapons! I decided to wait for a forward observation officer. The Regimental commander said: "Get going. Take that village – there are only a few soldiers holding it."

'"That's madness," I said to the Regimentskommandeur.

'"No, no, it's an order. Get going, we must capture the village before nightfall."

'I said: "We will too. The hour we lose waiting for the forward observation officer I will make up two or three times over afterwards . . . At least give me the assault guns to come in from the north and destroy their bunker."

'"No, no, no."

'We took the village without any support and scarcely were we in it when our heavy guns began firing into it. I brought out 181 prisoners altogether. I rounded up the last sixty and a salvo of mortar shells fell on them from one of our mortar brigades right into the midst of the prisoners and their guards. Twenty two hours later our own artillery was still firing into the village. Our communications were a complete failure.'

The divisional commander Generalmajor Ludwig Heilmann clearly had no feeling for his troops. Heydte described him as 'a very ambitious, reckless soldier with no moral scruples', and said that he should not be commanding a division. His soldiers called him 'der Schlächter von Cassino', the butcher of Cassino, because of the terrible losses suffered by his men during that battle. And on the first day of the Ardennes offensive, his units were battered by American mortar fire as they floundered across the River Our, which was fast flowing and had a muddy bottom.

Just to the south the American 9th Armored Division held a narrow three-kilometre sector, but was pushed back by the 212th Volksgrenadier-Division. To its right, outposts of the 4th Infantry Division west and south of Echternach failed to see German troops crossing the Sauer before dawn. Their outposts on bluffs or ridges high above the river valley may have had a fine view in clear weather, but at night and on misty days they were blind. As a result most of the men in these forward positions were surrounded and captured very rapidly because German advance patrols had slipped through behind them. A company commander, while finally reporting details of the attack by field telephone to his battalion commander, was startled to hear another person on the line. A voice with a heavy German accent announced: 'We are here!' One squad in Lauterborn was caught entirely by surprise and taken prisoner. But the over-confident Germans marched them down the road past a mill, which happened to be occupied by Americans from another company who opened fire. The prisoners threw themselves in the ditch where they hid for several hours, and then rejoined their unit later.

Once again, field telephone lines back from observation posts were cut by shellfire and radios often failed to work due to the hilly terrain and damp atmospheric conditions. Signals traffic was in any case chaotic, with careless or panic-stricken operators jamming everyone else. Major General Raymond O. Barton, the commander of the 4th Infantry Division, only heard at 11.00 hours that his 12th Infantry Regiment either side of Echternach was under strong attack. Barton wasted no time in committing his reserve battalion and sending in a company from the 70th Tank Battalion. As darkness fell later that afternoon, the 12th Infantry still held five key towns and villages along the ridge route of 'Skyline Drive'. These were the all-important crossroads which blocked the German advance. 'It was the towns and road junctions that proved decisive in the battle,' concluded one analysis.

The 4th Infantry had also dropped tall pines across the roads to make abatis barriers, which were mined and booby-trapped. The division's achievement was all the more remarkable when considering its shortages in manpower and weaponry after its recent battles in the Hürtgen Forest. Ever since the fighting in Normandy, the 4th Infantry Division had seized as many Panzerfausts as it could to use them back against the

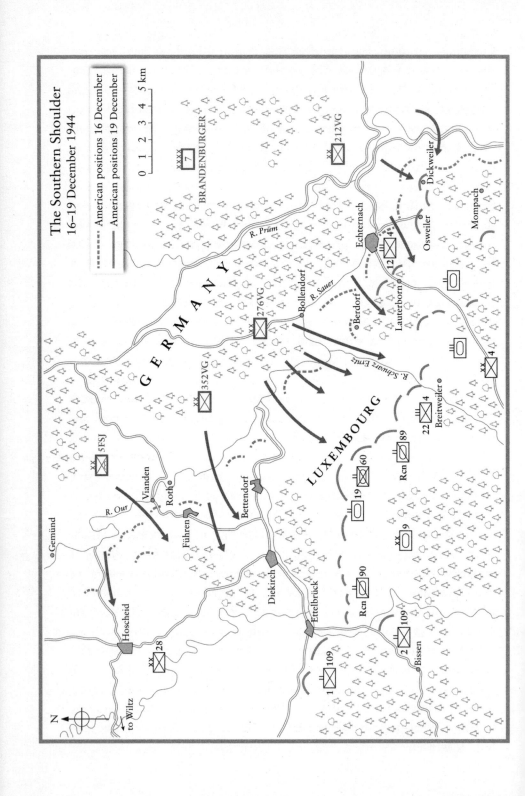

The Southern Shoulder
16–19 December 1944

- - - - - American positions 16 December
————— American positions 19 December

0 1 2 3 4 5 km

BRANDENBURGER

7 (XXXX)

212VG (XX)

Dickweiler

Mompach

Echternach

Osweiler

12 4 (XX)

R. Prüm

Bollendorf

R. Sauer

Berdorf

Lauterborn

276VG (XX)

R. Schwarz Ernz

4 (XX)

Breitweiler

352VG (XX)

22 4 (XX)

LUXEMBOURG

89 Rcn

60 19 (XX)

G E R M A N Y

5FSJ (XX)

Vianden

Roth

R. Our

Gemünd

Führen

Bettendorf

9 (XX)

Diekirch

90 Rcn

Ettelbrück

2 109 (XX)

Bissen

Hoscheid

28 (XX)

1 109 (XX)

N

to Wiltz

Germans. Although their effective range was only about forty metres, the infantrymen found them much more powerful in penetrating the Panther tank than their own bazooka. Forty-three of their fifty-four tanks were still undergoing repair in workshops to the rear. This did not prove as disastrous as it might have done. Manteuffel had wanted to provide Brandenberger's Seventh Army with a panzer division to break open the southern shoulder, but none could be spared.

General Bradley's journey that day on the icy roads from Luxembourg to Versailles took longer than expected. Eisenhower was in an expansive mood when he arrived, for he had just heard that he was to receive his fifth star. Bradley congratulated him. 'God,' Eisenhower answered, 'I just want to see the first time I sign my name as General of the Army.'

Major Hansen, who had accompanied Bradley, returned to the Ritz where Hemingway was drinking with a large number of visitors. 'The room, with two brass beds,' wrote Hansen, 'was littered in books which overflowed to the floor, liquor bottles and the walls were fairly covered with prints of Paris stuck up carelessly with nails and thumbtacks.' After talking with them for a time, Hansen 'ducked out and walked wearily to the Lido where we saw bare breasted girls do the hootchy kootchie until it was late'.

At the end of the afternoon, while Eisenhower and Bradley were discussing the problem of replacements with other senior officers from SHAEF, they were interrupted by a staff officer. He handed a message to Major General Strong who, on reading it, called for a map of the VIII Corps sector. The Germans had broken through at five points, of which the most threatening was the penetration via the Losheim Gap. Although details were sparse, Eisenhower immediately sensed that this was serious, even though there were no obvious objectives in the Ardennes. Bradley, on the other hand, believed that this was simply the spoiling attack he had half expected to disrupt Patton's offensive in Lorraine. Eisenhower wasted no time after consulting the operations map. He gave orders that the Ninth Army should send the 7th Armored Division to help Troy Middleton in the Ardennes, and that Patton should transfer his 10th Armored Division. Bradley remarked that Patton would not be happy giving it up with his offensive about to start in three days. 'Tell him', Eisenhower snarled, 'that Ike is running this war.'

Bradley had to ring Patton straight away. As he had predicted, Patton complained bitterly, and said that the German attack was just an attempt to disrupt his own operation. With Eisenhower's eyes upon him, Bradley had to give him a direct order. The men of the 10th Armored Division were horrified to hear that they were to be transferred from Patton's Third Army to First Army reserve. 'That broke our hearts because, you know, First Army – hell we were in Third Army.' Patton, however, had an instinct just after the telephone call that it 'looks like the real thing'. 'It reminds me very much of March 25, 1918 [Ludendorff's offensive]', he wrote to a friend, 'and I think will have the same results.'

Bradley then rang his headquarters in Luxembourg and told them to contact Ninth Army. He did not expect any trouble there. Lieutenant General William H. Simpson was a tall but quietly spoken Texan known as 'the doughboy general', whom everybody liked. He had an engaging long face on a bald head with prominent ears and a square chin. Simpson was examining the air-support plan for crossing the Roer when at 16.20 hours, according to his headquarters diary, he received a call from Major General Allen, the chief of staff at 12th Army Group. 'Hodges [is] having a bit of trouble on his south flank,' Allen said. 'There is a little flare-up south of you.' Simpson immediately agreed to release the 7th Armored Division to First Army. Exactly two hours later, Simpson rang to check that the advance party of the 7th Armored Division was on its way.

Eisenhower and Bradley, having despatched the two divisions, drank a bottle of champagne to celebrate the fifth star. The Supreme Commander had just received a supply of oysters which he loved, but Bradley was allergic to them and ate scrambled eggs instead. Afterwards they played five rubbers of bridge, since Bradley was not returning to Luxembourg until the following morning.

While the two American generals were in Versailles, Oberstleutnant von der Heydte in Paderborn was woken from a deep sleep by a telephone call. He was exhausted because everything had gone wrong the night before and he had not been to bed. His Kampfgruppe had been due to take off in the early hours of that morning, but most of the trucks to bring his men to the airfield had not received fuel in time, so the operation had been postponed; then it looked as if it would be cancelled. General Peltz, the Luftwaffe general on the telephone, now told him that the jump was back on because the initial attack had not progressed as rapidly as hoped.

When Heydte reached the airfield, he heard that the meteorological report from Luftflotte West estimated a wind speed of twenty kilometres per hour over the drop zone. This was the highest speed permissible for a night drop on a wooded area, and Heydte was being deliberately misinformed so that he would not cancel the operation. Just after all the paratroopers had climbed aboard the elderly Junkers 52 transport planes, a 'very conscientious meteorologist' rushed up to Heydte's plane as it was about to taxi, and said: 'I feel I must do my duty; the reports from our sources are that the wind is 58 kph.'

The whole operation turned into a fiasco. Because most of the pilots were 'new and nervous' and unused to navigating at night, some 200 of Heydte's men were dropped around Bonn. Few of the jumpmasters had ever performed their task before, and only ten aircraft managed to drop their sticks of paratroopers on the drop zone south of Eupen, which had been marked by two magnesium flares. The wind was so strong that some paratroopers were blown on to the propellers of the following aircraft. Survivors of the landing joined up in the dark by whistling to each other. By dawn Heydte knew that his mission was 'an utter failure'. He had assembled only 150 men, a 'pitifully small muster', he called it, and very few weapon containers were found. Only eight Panzerfausts out of 500 were recovered and just one 81mm mortar.

'German People, be confident!' stated Adolf Hitler's message to the nation. 'Whatever may face us, we will overcome it. There is victory at the end of the road. Under any situation, in battle where the fanaticism of a nation is a factor, there can only be victory!' Generalfeldmarschall Model declared in an order of the day to the troops of Army Group B: 'We will win, because we believe in Adolf Hitler and the Greater German Reich!' But that night some 4,000 German civilians died in an Allied bombing raid on Magdeburg, which had been planned before the offensive.

Belgian civilians at least had the choice of fleeing the onslaught, but some stayed with their farms and animals, resigned to another German occupation. They did not know, however, that the SS Sicherheitsdienst security service was following hard on the heels of Waffen-SS formations. As far as these SD units were concerned, the inhabitants of the eastern cantons were German citizens and they wanted to know who had disobeyed the orders in September to move east of the Siegfried Line with their families and livestock. Locals avoiding service in the Wehrmacht and those who had collaborated with the Americans during the autumn were liable to arrest, and even execution in a few cases. But their main targets were those young Belgians in Resistance groups which had harried the retreating German forces in September.

General Hodges, finally aware of the danger, ordered the 1st Division then resting behind the lines to prepare to move. 'We heard a siren-like sound', wrote Arthur Couch, 'and an announcement that all American troops were to return to their units and prepare to move out – there had been a large German attack in the Ardennes area. We gathered our combat gear and climbed onto trucks taking us to the new front line. We were told that a German tank attack had broken through an inexperienced new division straight from America. They were in a chaotic retreat.' At 22.00 hours, another order from First Army headquarters instructed the 2nd Division to halt its attack north and prepare to move back towards the eastern flank of the Elsenborn ridge to block the advance of the 12th SS Panzer-Division.

After all the delays on the first day, that night Peiper forced his men forward to Honsfeld. His Kampfgruppe had been allotted 'the decisive role in the offensive', and he had no intention of failing. 'I was not to bother about my flanks, but was to drive rapidly to the Meuse river, making full use of the element of surprise.' His column of tanks, half-tracks and other vehicles stretched almost twenty-five kilometres in length, and because the roads were so narrow he could not change the order of march. He therefore decided to have a strong fighting element right at the front, with panzergrenadiers mounted in half-tracks, followed by a company of Panthers and Mark IV tanks. The heavy battalion of Tiger tanks would follow on behind.

Before the offensive began, Peiper really had believed that if the

German infantry managed to break through at dawn on 16 December as planned, then he could reach the Meuse in just over twenty-four hours. Now he knew that his test-drive of a Panther over eighty kilometres before the offensive had been utterly misleading. The farm roads allotted to him were muddy tracks. The fact that the Führer himself had chosen Peiper's route for him was hardly a consolation in the circumstances. As Manteuffel had predicted, the panzers' fuel consumption in this terrain was more than twice what Keitel and the OKW had estimated. Having been warned at the divisional briefing that two trainloads of fuel had failed to arrive and that the spearheads were to make use of captured supplies, Peiper consulted his map. The divisional Ic intelligence officer had marked the position of American fuel dumps at Büllingen and Stavelot. However, the main US Army gasoline dump at Francorchamps between Malmédy and Spa, which held more than 2 million gallons, was not shown.

9

Sunday 17 December

For Lieutenant Matt Konop with the 2nd Infantry Division headquarters, the first sign of anything 'unusual' came on the second morning when the telephone by his mattress rang shortly before seven. The operations officer told him that a report had come in of paratroopers landing south of Eupen, and that some thirty German tanks had broken through to their east. Konop turned on the light and reached for a map to try to work out if anything important was going on. A few minutes later the telephone rang again.

'Say, Konop, I want you to alert everybody.' Konop could not identify the voice. 'Get every gun, man and whatever you can get to prepare a last ditch defense of the C[ommand] P[ost]! Enemy tanks have broken through and are on the road to Büllingen now.'

'Yes, sir,' Konop replied. 'By the way, who is this?'

'This is General Robertson,' replied his divisional commander, a man known for his calm, good sense. Konop felt obliged to remind him that the only soldiers available were 'those men who drive the trucks and former battle exhaustion cases'. Robertson told him to get together every individual he could find. So Konop formed cooks, clerks, drivers and any man who could still hold a weapon into an improvised defence platoon and rushed them down the road from Wirtzfeld. He could already hear machine-gun fire in the distance while he placed bazooka teams and their two 57mm anti-tank guns to cover any side tracks which a panzer commander might select. He put a cook sergeant and his own Jeep driver to man a .50 machine gun and set up observation posts with radios. A

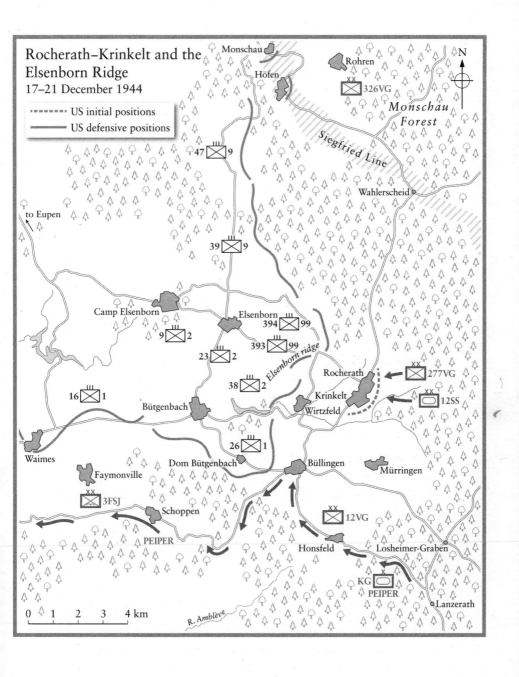

Rocherath–Krinkelt and the
Elsenborn Ridge
17–21 December 1944

▪▪▪▪▪▪▪ US initial positions
━━━━━ US defensive positions

N

Monschau
Höfen
Rohren
326VG
Monschau
Forest
Siegfried Line
Wahlerscheid
47 9
39 9
to Eupen
Camp Elsenborn
Elsenborn
394 99
9 2
393 99
23 2
Elsenborn ridge
Rocherath
277VG
38 2
Krinkelt
12SS
Bütgenbach
Wirtzfeld
16 1
26 1
Waimes
Dom Bütgenbach
Büllingen
Mürringen
Faymonville
3FSJ
Schoppen
12VG
PEIPER
Honsfeld
Losheimer-Graben
KG
PEIPER
Lanzerath

0 1 2 3 4 km

R. Amblève

military police officer arrived with twenty men, and even though his 'snowdrops' were armed only with pistols, they too went into the line.

General Hodges had at last been forced to face reality. At 07.30 hours on 17 December, twenty-four hours after the German offensive began, he finally allowed General Gerow, the commander of V Corps, to halt the 2nd Division in its attack north from Wahlerscheid. Gerow wanted to pull it back towards the twin villages of Rocherath–Krinkelt, which were now threatened. The 99th Division had been forced to retreat by the 277th Volksgrenadier-Division and the 12th SS Panzer-Division *Hitler Jugend*. He and General Robertson agreed that they must protect the road north from Rocherath–Krinkelt to Wahlerscheid so that he could extricate his two regiments.

Gerow did not subscribe to the pointless slogan that the American army never retreats. He had immediately sensed that holding the northern shoulder of the breakthrough was what mattered, and the key to that would be the Elsenborn ridge, which began just west of Rocherath–Krinkelt. They had to hold the twin villages long enough to establish firm positions along the ridge, where he was already bringing in artillery regiments.

Robertson ordered forward his only reserve, a battalion of the 23rd Infantry Regiment, from Elsenborn in trucks. These troops dismounted east of Rocherath, and looked with foreboding at the thick pinewoods. All they knew was that a unit of the 99th Division, which 'had had the hell knocked out of them', was withdrawing in front of the 12th SS *Hitler Jugend*. Behind them, bursts of firing could be heard as anti-aircraft half-tracks blazed away at the V-1 buzz-bombs flying overhead. 'The snow around the road junction had been churned into a yellowish mixture of snow and dirt from recent heavy shelling,' wrote Charles MacDonald, a company commander.

He took his men forward to the edge of the woods. Even in the open, visibility extended no more than a hundred metres in the damp mist. They could hear small-arms fire ahead of them, mainly the ripping noise of rapid-fire German automatic weapons, rather than the slower, more deliberate cadence of their American counterparts. Then, a salvo of 'screaming meemies' came over. As soon as MacDonald's men heard artillery shells they picked a thick pine tree to stand behind, hoping to avoid any splinters from an overhead burst. With little enthusiasm except the instinct of self-preservation, MacDonald's company returned to digging foxholes. It was hard work with the small shovels because of the tree roots under the wet snow.

The threat that morning to the 2nd Division's headquarters in Wirtzfeld, which Lieutenant Konop prepared to defend, did not come from the *Hitler Jugend* Division to the east: it came from Peiper's Kampfgruppe to the south. Peiper, horrified by the state of the tracks he was expected to follow, had decided to ignore his orders and the route prescribed by Hitler. His corps commander later agreed. 'Owing to the wretched condition of the roads,' he wrote, 'the wheeled vehicles had be towed in places for considerable distances.'

Before dawn on 17 December, the Peiper Kampfgruppe launched an attack on Honsfeld. Its leading vehicles simply followed in the wake of a retreating American column. Even though the small American force was taken by surprise, the Kampfgruppe lost two Mark V Panthers, but captured a large number of trucks and half-tracks. Peiper's SS panzer-grenadiers executed nineteen American prisoners in a field, and two villagers who were made to face a wall were shot in the back of the head. For the panzergrenadiers, it could have been the eastern front again where they had slaughtered prisoners and civilians without a second thought. They proceeded to loot the houses and the chapel. Peiper detailed a small group to stay behind to guard his line of communications. Two days later, five of these panzergrenadiers forced Erna Collas, a beautiful sixteen-year-old girl, to show them the way to a farm. She was never seen again until her body was found in a foxhole five months later. She had been riddled with bullets, almost certainly after she had been raped.

Peiper decided to leave most of the trucks in Honsfeld because of the mud, and ordered the commander of the 9th Fallschirmjäger-Regiment to stay there to mop up and secure the area. Then, instead of driving due west to the valley of the Amblève as he had been instructed, Peiper pushed north to Büllingen where the American 2nd Division's fuel dump was marked on his map. The Kampfgruppe took the village un-opposed soon after 08.30 hours that Sunday morning, and destroyed twelve American light aircraft parked on a landing strip. A civilian emerged wearing a swastika armband to greet them. He gave the Nazi salute as each vehicle passed, then showed the SS soldiers where the Americans stored their fuel. The panzergrenadiers put their prisoners to work refuelling vehicles and loading jerrycans on to the half-tracks. One wounded soldier was finished off with a *Kopfschuss*, a pistol shot through the head at close range, but according to civilian witnesses the other prisoners were more fortunate than their comrades in Honsfeld. The American official history, on the other hand, states that fifty were shot at Büllingen.

Just west of Büllingen, Company B of the 254th Engineer Battalion was overrun by German tanks. The panzers did not just 'iron' the fox-holes by charging over them, they halted to twist back and forth on their axis to collapse the trench walls and bury the occupants in mud and snow. Fortunately, help was on the way. The 26th Infantry Regiment of the 1st Division, after travelling in trucks through the early hours, reached Camp Elsenborn on the ridge at 09.00 hours. One of its battalions was immediately sent south to Bütgenbach.

On the way down, it skirmished with an advance patrol of paratroopers from the 3rd Fallschirmjäger's reconnaissance battalion. After urging the civilians in Bütgenbach to shelter in their cellars, the Americans pushed on towards the next hamlet of Dom Bütgenbach, two kilometres west of Büllingen, where they heard that SS troops had taken the village. On some high ground by the road, they found a scratch force made up of around fifty clerks and supply personnel from the 99th Infantry Division who had been taken in hand by a captain from a tank-destroyer battalion. The battalion of the 26th Infantry wrongly assumed that the enemy force in Büllingen was from the 12th *Hitler Jugend* Division. These infantrymen could not understand why it did not continue to attack north. But the reason for the lull was that Peiper's spearhead had already set off south-west, to regain the route to the Amblève valley.

Despite the delays in the initial breakthrough, German morale was high. 'I think the war in the west is again turning,' wrote a Gefreiter in the 3rd Panzergrenadier-Division, waiting that day to advance. 'The main thing is that the war will soon be decided and I will be coming home again to my dear wife and we can again build a new home. The radio is now playing bells from the homeland.'

*

General Bradley, returning that morning from Paris to Luxembourg in his own olive-drab Cadillac, found an escort of machine-gun-mounted Jeeps waiting for him in Verdun because of reports of German paratroopers. Hansen asked about the possibility of moving 12th Army Group headquarters, because German divisions were now less than thirty kilometres to their north. 'I will never move backwards with a headquarters,' Bradley replied. 'There is too much prestige at stake.' This defiance would serve him ill over the next few days.

Both men sensed that a German reoccupation of the Grand Duchy might be brutal after the warm welcome its people had accorded to the Americans less than three months before. When entering the city of Luxembourg, Bradley saw the Stars and Stripes hanging from a house. 'I hope he doesn't have to take it down,' he murmured. The city of Luxembourg had so far been spared the full horrors of war. It was dubbed 'the last air-raid shelter in Europe', because it had not been bombed by either the RAF or the USAAF.

The Cadillac drew up outside the 12th Army Group's forward headquarters known as 'Eagle Tac', four blocks from the general's residence in the Hôtel Alfa. Bradley hurried up the stairs. He came to a halt in front of the situation map and stared at it in fascinated horror. 'Pardon my French,' he said, 'I think the situation justifies it – but where in hell has this son of a bitch gotten all his strength?'

Bradley and his staff were shaken by the way German intelligence had identified the weakest part of their whole front. And since the Americans' policy was one of attack, their lines had not been built in depth with reserve formations. Yet Bradley still wanted to believe that a major redeployment could be avoided. First Army at Spa that day wondered 'whether 12th Army Group fully appreciates the seriousness of the situation'. Third Army also appears to have been surprised at the slow reaction. 'The Army Group commander called General Patton on the phone,' the chief of staff recorded, 'and told him that he might have to call on him for two more divisions. The decision was not to be made for forty-eight hours.'

At Ninth Army headquarters, nobody seemed to have any idea of the size of the attack. Staff officers could indulge only in confused speculation. A Luftwaffe attack on their front prompted suggestions that this was 'a diversion for a larger counter-offensive in First Army zone'.

Ninth Army staff officers told war correspondents desperate for information that 'everything depends on what troops are at von Rundstedt's disposal'.

Back at SHAEF, the danger became clearer thanks to some captured German instructions. Eisenhower ordered that all reserve formations should be brought in. He told Bedell Smith, Strong and Major General John Whiteley, the British head of the operational planning staff, to organize the details. In the chief of staff's office, the three men stood around a large map spread out on the floor. Strong pointed with a German ceremonial sword to Bastogne. The town was the hub of the central Ardennes, and most of the main roads leading to the Meuse passed through it. It was the obvious place to block the German advance to the Meuse, and everyone present agreed.

SHAEF's immediate reserve consisted of the 82nd and 101st Airborne Divisions, resting in Reims after their operations in Holland. The question was whether they could reach Bastogne before Manteuffel's panzer spearheads arrived from the east. Strong considered it possible, and the orders for them to move were issued immediately.

It was ironic that Bradley's headquarters in Luxembourg should have feared an ambush by Heydte's paratroopers, for they had dropped more than a hundred kilometres to the north as the crow flies. And Heydte, accepting that there was little he could do with such a weak force, decided to hide most of his men in the forest. He sent out standing patrols to watch the main roads from Eupen to Malmédy and from Verviers. They were to ambush single Jeeps and messengers. Once the sounds of battle came closer, then perhaps his men could assist by seizing a key point just before Dietrich's tanks arrived. His standing patrols soon collected a range of prisoners and a haul of intelligence on the American order of battle, but since their radios had been lost in the parachute drop Heydte had no way of passing the information back. He had asked Sepp Dietrich for carrier pigeons, but the Oberstgruppenführer had simply laughed at the idea.

On the evening of 17 December, Heydte's force doubled in size to around 300 men when more stragglers and a large group which had dropped too far to the north joined them. That night he released all his prisoners and sent them off with some of their own wounded. Then he moved camp. Heydte and his men had no idea of the course of events, except for the rumble of artillery from the Elsenborn ridge more than a dozen kilometres to their south.

While the 99th Division was being battered east of Rocherath–Krinkelt, the 106th Division to its south was in an even worse state, attacked by the 18th and 62nd Volksgrenadier-Divisions. Major General Alan W. Jones, the 106th's hapless commander, felt powerless as he sat in a school in St Vith, which he had taken over as his command post. Two of his regiments, the 422nd and the 423rd, were almost surrounded in the Schnee Eifel, while his third regiment, the 424th, was holding the line down to the south with a combat command of the 9th Armored Division. His son was with the headquarters of one of the beleaguered regiments, which increased his anxiety.*

The day before, Jones had failed to comprehend the gravity of the German thrust through the 14th Cavalry's position on his north flank, and he had not reacted when its commander Colonel Mark Devine warned that he was having to pull back. Devine added that he would try to counter-attack with the 32nd Cavalry Squadron, but their attack was repulsed in the afternoon, and most of his force withdrew to the north-west unable to close the widening breach. Only a single cavalry troop remained in the valley of the River Our, attempting to block the road to St Vith. Jones sent his last reserve battalion to Schönberg in the valley, but it became lost in the dark and turned in the wrong direction. And on the right of the 106th Division's sector, the 62nd Volksgrenadier-Division had forced Jones's right-hand regiment, the 424th, back towards the village of Winterspelt and the River Our.

General Jones, overtaken by events, had tended to rely on the promise of help from outside rather than on his own actions. He expected Combat Command B of the 7th Armored Division to be with him in St Vith by 07.00 hours on Sunday 17 December. He was counting on it to launch a counter-attack to free his two regiments. When Brigadier General Bruce C. Clarke, a 'great bear of a man', arrived at his command post at 10.30 hours, Jones asked him to mount an attack immediately. Clarke had

* See map, The Destruction of the 106th Division, p. 119 above.

to tell him that he was on his own. His tanks had been held up by chaotic traffic, caused by units falling back in panic. Jones now bitterly regretted having committed the 9th Armored Division combat command to his right flank the evening before. The two men could only sit and wait.

To Clarke's astonishment, he heard Jones tell his corps commander in Bastogne on the telephone that the situation was under control. Jones's mood veered between irrational optimism and despair. Clarke was even more concerned because there was little radio contact with the two regiments out on the Schnee Eifel, apart from their demands for resupply by airdrop.* Colonel Devine of the 14th Cavalry Group then appeared in the command post, claiming that German tanks were just behind him. Jones and Clarke saw that Devine had lost his nerve, so Jones told him to report to General Middleton in Bastogne. Yet Devine had not imagined the German tanks. Another SS Kampfgruppe was breaking through ten kilometres to the north.†

At 14.30 hours, they heard small-arms fire. Jones and Clarke went up to the third floor of the school and sighted German troops emerging from the woods in the distance. Jones told Clarke that he should now take over the defence of St Vith. Clarke accepted, but wondered what troops he had, apart from the two engineer service companies and headquarters personnel already out on the road east to Schönberg. Half an hour later this force, miraculously joined by a platoon of tank destroyers, was attacked. The tank destroyers managed to scare the panzers back into the woods beyond the road. But the main reason for the slowness of the German advance on 17 December came from the state of the roads and the traffic jams, which blocked artillery and other panzer units coming forward.

Volksartillerie units had not moved forward because their draught horses could not cope with hauling heavy guns through the deep mud

---

* 'One futile effort' was made the next day, but due to bad co-ordination with Transport Carrier Command no drop took place.

† Staff officers described Devine as 'excited, nervous, over-talkative, agitated, could barely control his actions, and gave undue attention to trivial personal injuries. At no time did he present the appearance of a competent commander.' He was treated with sedatives in hospital and released on 19 December, but was then found directing traffic in La Roche-en-Ardenne while trying to order a battalion of tanks to turn round. He was again sedated and evacuated.

churned up by panzer tracks. Even some of the self-propelled artillery of the 1st SS Panzer-Division had to be left behind because of the shortage of fuel. Both Model and Manteuffel were seething with impatience. Model, on finding several artillery battalions still in their original positions, ordered General der Panzertruppe Horst Stumpff to court-martial their commanders. 'When I told him it was because of the fuel shortages and road conditions that they hadn't moved, he rescinded the order.' At one stage, out of sheer frustration, Manteuffel began to direct traffic at a crossroads. 'I expected the right-hand corps to capture St Vith on the first day,' he acknowledged later. Like Bastogne, St Vith's network of paved roads was vital for a rapid advance to the Meuse.

While the Germans held back east of St Vith and made little more than skirmishing thrusts, Clarke sent his operations officer out on the road west to Vielsalm to await his combat command. The scenes along the road shocked officers in the 7th Armored Division. 'It was a case of "every dog for himself"; it was a retreat, a rout,' one officer wrote. 'It wasn't orderly; it wasn't military; it wasn't a pretty sight – we were seeing American soldiers running away.' At one stage the combat command took two and a half hours to move five kilometres, and then they had to bulldoze vehicles off the road.

In Malmédy, their artillery encountered civilians fleeing in a variety of vehicles, with 'panic stricken soldiers running through the square towards the west . . . A field hospital north of Malmédy was being evacuated and ambulances were darting up and down. A truck loaded with nurses went through the square at top speed. The nurses' hair was flying.' Just over a kilometre from St Vith, part of Clarke's combat command came around a bend and spotted three panzers and an infantry company coming towards them. They quickly set an ambush, 'head-on at the bend of the road at point-blank range'. The three panzers were knocked out, and the infantry scattered, losing some fifty men.

Clarke himself went to the Vielsalm road and was horrified to see a field artillery battalion retreating, having abandoned its guns. He asked his operations officer why he had let them block the road. He replied that the lieutenant colonel in command had threatened to shoot him if he interfered. Clarke found him and said that he would shoot him if he did not get his trucks off the road. The lieutenant colonel, intimidated by Clarke's superior rank and build, finally did as he was told.

Another artillery officer proved very different. Lieutenant Colonel Maximilian Clay appeared with a battalion of self-propelled 105mm guns, saying he wanted to help. His 275th Armored Field Artillery Battalion had been supporting the 14th Cavalry Group, which was now far away to the north. Clarke welcomed him warmly and told him where to go. Finally, at 16.00 hours, Clarke's own reconnaissance squadron arrived, followed by the rest of his combat command. Clarke sent them straight through the town to strengthen the thin defence line on the eastern side. Not long afterwards, Clarke's divisional commander Brigadier General Robert W. Hasbrouck joined Jones and Clarke to discuss the situation. He too had been disturbed by 'the continuous stream of frenzied soldiers hurrying to the "safety" of the rear'. To Jones's despair, Hasbrouck ruled out a counter-attack to rescue the two stranded regiments. Holding on to St Vith was far more important. Jones observed bitterly that no general in the American army had lost a division so quickly. Late that afternoon, the two prongs of the 18th Volksgrenadier-Division closed on Schönberg and cut off the two regiments completely.

The defence of St Vith would take the form of a large horseshoe. The town stood on a small hill, which was surrounded a couple of kilometres further out by a circular ring of higher hills covered in woods, which the infantry, the reconnaissance squadron and the scratch units would defend with support from the tanks. 'The build-up of a defensive cordon around the town', wrote Hasbrouck, 'was a piecemeal procedure with units being placed in the line as they arrived in Saint Vith.' At that stage they did not know that the Kampfgruppe Hansen, based on the 1st SS Panzergrenadier-Regiment, had slipped through to their north and attacked Combat Command A of the 7th Armored near Recht. This was the panzer unit which had so unsettled Colonel Devine. The battle between the Americans and the SS lasted all night. The luckier villagers managed to escape to a nearby slate quarry, while their houses were blasted from both sides. These unfortunate 'border Belgians' were regarded with suspicion by American soldiers because they spoke German and had framed photographs of sons in Wehrmacht uniform. And Germans distrusted them because they had defied the September order to move into Germany beyond the Siegfried Line. Around a hundred men from St Vith had been killed serving in the German forces during the war. Others had deserted and were now determined not to be caught by the Feld-gendarmerie or the SD, following closely behind the lead formations.

Peiper's long column had turned west, picking up speed. By midday it was close to the crossroads at Baugnez, five kilometres south-east of Malmédy. Peiper despatched a small force of panzergrenadiers and tanks to Baugnez to reconnoitre. His troops had just missed bumping into Combat Command R of the 7th Armored Division, on its way south to support the defence of St Vith.

Oblivious to the threat ahead the next unit of the 7th Armored Division, part of the 285th Field Artillery Observation Battalion, followed on through Malmédy. As the men were driven in open trucks through the town, locals who knew of the sudden German advance from refugees tried to warn them by pointing ahead shouting, 'Boches! Boches!', but the soldiers did not understand and just waved back. Their vehicles motored on towards the crossroads at Baugnez, and there the convoy ran straight into the SS half-tracks and panzers.

The German tanks opened fire. Trucks were set ablaze as men tumbled off to seek shelter or run for the forest. Panzergrenadiers rounded up some 130 prisoners and herded them into a field by the road. The SS took rings, cigarettes, watches and gloves from their prisoners. When one of their officers opened fire, they began to shoot their prisoners with automatic weapons and the tanks joined in with their machine guns. Some American soldiers made it to the trees, others feigned death, although many were still shot through the head with pistols. Although the mass killing took place at Baugnez, it was to become infamous as the Malmédy massacre. Altogether, eighty-four Americans died, as well as several civilians who tried to shelter some escapees.

Peiper, who had continued on the road to Ligneuville, was not present when the killings took place. But if one takes into account the murder of prisoners in Honsfeld, to say nothing of his record of extreme brutality on the eastern front, one cannot imagine that he would have objected. He claimed later that the firing started only when the prisoners ran for the trees. The few soldiers who escaped the massacre made it back to American lines by the late afternoon.

A patrol from an engineer combat battalion in Malmédy reached Baugnez that same afternoon after the departure of the SS, and saw the

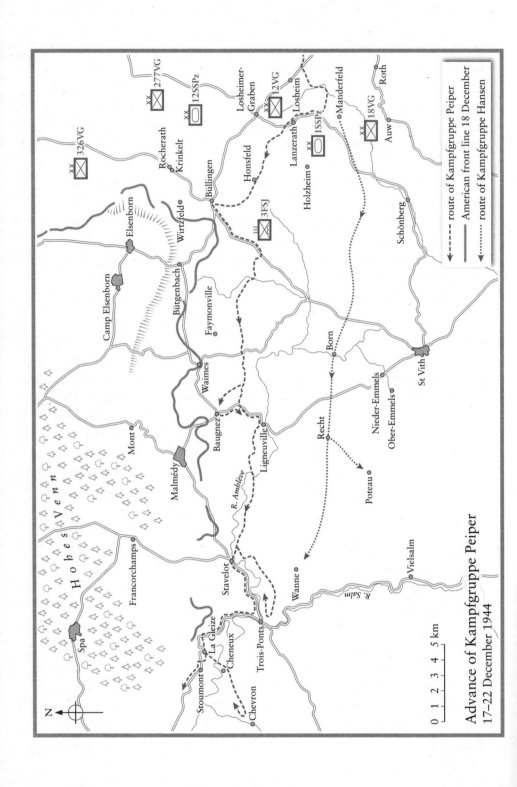

277VG

125SPz

326VG

12VG

Losheimer-
Graben

Losheim

1SSPz

Manderfeld

18VG

Roth

Auw

Rocherath

Krinkelt

Honsfeld

Lanzerath

Losheim

Holzheim

Schönberg

Büllingen

Elsenborn

Wirtzfeld

3FSJ

Bütgenbach

Faymonville

Born

St Vith

Camp Elsenborn

Waimes

Nieder-Emmels

Ober-Emmels

Mont

Baugnez

Ligneuville

Recht

Malmédy

R. Amblève

Poteau

H o h e s   V e n n

Francorchamps

Wanne

Vielsalm

R. Salm

Stavelot

La Gleize

Cheneux

Trois-Ponts

Spa

Stoumont

Chevron

N

---- route of Kampfgruppe Peiper
—— American front line 18 December
...... route of Kampfgruppe Hansen

Advance of Kampfgruppe Peiper
17–22 December 1944

0 1 2 3 4 5 km

bodies. A military policeman on traffic duty at the crossroads, who had witnessed the whole incident, was brought to First Army headquarters at Spa. He described to Hodges and his assembled officers how the prisoners had been 'herded together into a side field and an SS officer fired two shots from his pistol and immediately there came the crackle of machinegun fire and whole groups were mown down in cold blood'. Staff officers at Spa were shaken and furious. 'Immediate publicity is being given to the story,' General Hodges's chief of staff noted. Word spread like wildfire to all command posts, to SHAEF and to the 12th Army Group in Luxembourg, where Hansen recorded that the news 'took the breath away from the room for an instant – as though the room had suddenly become a vacuum'. Major General Elwood R. Quesada of IX Tactical Air Command made sure that his pilots were fully briefed the next morning. Revenge was clearly going to be the order of the day.*

Peiper's spearhead pushed on to Ligneuville where it met heavy resistance for the first time in the form of American tanks. A short, fierce battle left a Panther and two half-tracks burning, while the Americans lost two Shermans and an M-10 tank destroyer. Peiper's men shot another eight American prisoners. Ahead in the town of Stavelot on the River Amblève, civilians were appalled to see their American liberators fleeing in vehicles. Many began to pack bags with their valuables and some food. They feared more German vengeance after the Resistance actions in September. Twenty-two men and women had been killed then in nearby Werbomont by German troops and Russian auxiliaries. The rush to escape beyond the River Meuse and the chaos which that would cause on the roads prompted the American authorities to forbid any civilian movement. Fortunately for the Americans and the fleeing Belgians, Peiper halted his column at dusk just short of Stavelot.

Since the main road was on the side of a very steep hill there was no room for Peiper's tanks to manoeuvre, and the sharp curve in the road just before entering the town meant that the defenders could focus all their anti-tank fire on one point. Peiper pulled back his Kampfgruppe

---

* When news of the massacre reached England, German army generals held prisoner there were shaken. 'What utter madness to shoot down defenceless men!' said one. 'All it means is that the Americans will take reprisals on our boys.' Another added: 'Of course the SS and the paratroopers are simply crazy, they just won't listen to reason.'

and bombarded the village with mortar and artillery fire instead. Meanwhile he sent off some of his tanks to find a way to bypass Stavelot to the south, by crossing the River Salm at Trois-Ponts. But as other vehicles followed they were hit in the flank by a circuitous American counterattack from Stavelot. This was beaten off, but Peiper ordered another assault on the town, this time using his panzergrenadiers on foot. But after suffering nearly thirty casualties, he decided to wait for the rest of his panzergrenadier battalion to catch up. As night fell, the Kampfgruppe could see in the distance the lights of American military vehicles escaping to the west, so they opened fire with their tanks at maximum range on the road.

While the Peiper Kampfgruppe forged west down the valley of the Amblève, more battalions from the US 1st Division arrived to strengthen the southern approach to the Elsenborn ridge. The 2nd Battalion of the 26th Infantry prepared positions facing Büllingen during the afternoon. It was ready with four M-10 tank destroyers in support, to take on the advancing Germans who had been held back by American artillery fire from the ridge behind them.

The vital battle to defend the ridge was already taking place on its eastern flank around Rocherath–Krinkelt. General Robertson of the 2nd Division, having thrown his 23rd Infantry Regiment into a line east of the twin villages as the 99th Division was beaten back, began bringing the 38th Infantry back down the road from Wahlerscheid. A barrage by American artillery at midday kept the Germans' heads down as they pulled back from their forward positions. In such a confused situation, friendly fire was a real danger. That morning, a P-47 Thunderbolt pilot jettisoned his bombs to engage a Messerschmitt over the 3rd Battalion and caused twelve casualties.

With reinforced platoons flanking the eastern side of the Wahlerscheid–Rocherath road, General Robertson himself went out to meet the battalions with trucks to take them to the new positions near Rocherath.

At least the far left of the line, some fourteen kilometres north of Elsenborn, appeared solid. The 326th Volksgrenadier-Division had attempted one attack after another on either side of Monschau, but American artillery had broken each one. The new top-secret proximity, or Pozit, fuse was used on shells for the first time in action, without authority from higher command, but with great success as they exploded over the attackers in accurate air bursts.

An armoured infantry battalion from the 5th Armored Division would reach Mützenich to strengthen the line not long after dark. And to their rear the 18th Regiment from the 1st Infantry Division was starting its sweep of the forests south of Eupen, to deal with Heydte's isolated paratroopers. General Gerow was puzzled as to why the Sixth Panzer Army had not attacked in much greater strength on the northern flank, rather than concentrate its forces just south of the Elsenborn ridge. This was of course at Hitler's insistence, but Manteuffel still felt that Dietrich had made a great mistake in restricting himself to such a narrow frontage, with so little room for manoeuvre.

East of Rocherath–Krinkelt, as the light began to fade and the sound of firing came closer, the soldiers of Robertson's 2nd Division dug harder and harder to make their foxholes deep enough under the snow before the tanks of the SS *Hitler Jugend* Division hit them. Their sweat would turn very cold as soon as they stopped. There were chaotic scenes as the 1st Battalion of the 9th Infantry Regiment moved into its positions under fire from the wooded high ground to its east. Many of the men from the shattered 99th Division were so determined to escape that they would not listen to orders to halt and join the defensive line. 'Against this demoralizing picture, the Battalion moved in with orders to hold,' its commander, Lieutenant Colonel McKinley, reported. 'Streams of men and vehicles were pouring down the forest roads through the junction in wild confusion and disorder. Control in the 99th Division had been irretrievably lost and the stragglers echoed each other with remarks that their units had been surrounded and annihilated. One of our own battalions from the 23rd Infantry had also been engulfed in what actually was a flight to the rear.'

McKinley's men laid 'daisy-chains' or 'necklaces' of six anti-tank mines each across any track or approach likely to be used by German tanks. The first attack came as darkness fell. Artillery fire along the length of the approach road proved effective, to judge by the 'screaming among the enemy'. During a lull, men slipped forward to lay anti-tank mines borrowed from the tank-destroyer battalion, and two-man bazooka teams improved their positions covering the road, knowing full well that they were in the target zone of their own artillery.

The American infantry's 57mm anti-tank gun stood little chance of knocking out a German Panther tank except from the side or rear, at close range. And tank-destroyer units with towed guns were at a severe disadvantage in the mud and snow, when limbering up to pull back. 'In heavy and close combat,' one analysis stated, 'the towing vehicle was often destroyed while the gun, dug in, remained intact.'

Lieutenant Colonel Barsanti of the 38th Infantry warned his platoon commanders that because of all the men from the 99th Division pulling back through their positions, they were not to open fire until they had positively identified the enemy. In the darkness it was impossible to be sure until they came close. As a result, two German tanks got through his K Company using their spotlights to blind the men looking out from their foxholes. But the two tanks were knocked out, one by artillery, the other by a bazooka team. Panzergrenadiers came close behind. 'One enemy soldier came so close to the position that he grabbed the barrel of a light machinegun and the gunner was forced to finish him off with a .45 pistol.'

Members of one company, forced to pull back from its forward position in a wood, 'plunged through the thickly interlaced branches of little firs. Bullets followed us,' their commander wrote, 'lashing the firs on all sides, and I wondered if maybe I had been hit. I felt no pain, but I could not see how any human being could endure those hails of bullets and not be wounded.' He wrote later of their escape back to Rocherath: 'I felt like we were helpless little bugs scurrying blindly about now that some man monster had lifted the log under which we had been hiding.'

The SS panzergrenadiers attacked using automatic weapons and throwing potato-masher grenades. One SS man seized a prisoner, and forced him to walk and answer challenges. Both he and his luckless human shield were shot down. Yet some stragglers who arrived from the 99th Division in the middle of this night battle were identified in time and not killed by their own side. A medic from the 99th also arrived, but he was a prisoner sent by the Germans. Apparently, some 150 Americans were surrounded by 200 Germans in the area shelled by the field artillery battalions on the Elsenborn ridge. 'The Germans had sent him to the US positions to try to get them to surrender on threat of annihilation of the prisoner GIs.'

During a lull in the battle, to the astonishment of the defenders, a large convoy of trucks full of troops from the 99th Division appeared. Their officers asked for directions to Camp Elsenborn. It was a miracle that they had come through the German units without being identified as American.

In the holding battle forward of Rocherath–Krinkelt, bazooka teams were sent to deal with the panzers. Whenever they achieved a hit, forcing the Germans inside to bale out, 'the crews were picked off by American riflemen', as Lieutenant Colonel McKinley observed. At 22.00 hours, two sergeants from his battalion grabbed a can of gasoline and crept up in the dark on a panzer, which although immobilized was causing heavy casualties with its machine gun and main armament. They poured the fuel over the tank and set it alight. Fifteen minutes later, a lieutenant stalked a Mark VI Tiger with a bazooka and knocked it out. But the attacks continued throughout the night in waves, and the main assault would not come until shortly before dawn the next morning.

In the south, Manteuffel's Fifth Panzer Army was having greater success against Cota's 28th Infantry Division due east of Bastogne. The 28th, which had been badly weakened in the Hürtgen Forest, was still short of men and weapons. But even though battered by the 116th Panzer-Division, the 2nd Panzer-Division and the Panzer Lehr, Cota's men managed to inflict considerable casualties and slow them down by holding crossroads and villages for as long as possible. The German corps commander considered the 28th to be 'a mediocre division with no reputation as a great fighting unit'. But although the 28th had certainly lost most of its experienced men in the Hürtgen Forest, some of its companies performed a heroic and vital role.

When fighting to defend a small town east of Wiltz, soldiers from Cota's 109th Infantry Regiment sighted tanks. They thought they were Mark VI Tigers, but they might have been Mark IVs which looked similar although much smaller. They had no anti-tank gun. 'A group of men nearby had a couple of bazookas and ammunition,' an officer recorded later, 'but said that they did not know how to use them. I took one and bumped right into a Tiger as I came round a corner. The tank was head on but I let it have one anyway, hitting it right in front. The tank stopped but was not damaged and fired its 88 at the house I had ducked behind. I then got up in the second story of an adjoining house where I was to the flank and above the tank. I fired two more shots at it; the first striking the rear deck at an angle. It exploded but the tank did not appear to notice it. My third shot hit the turret just above where it joins the hull of the tank. It didn't penetrate but a lot of sparks flew and it must have jarred the crew as the tank immediately backed up and withdrew to a position about 800 yards away from which they shelled us.' The bazooka was not as powerful as its shoulder-launched counterpart, the German Panzerfaust. From the front, all that could be achieved was a broken track. But if hunting groups managed to get round the back of a Tiger or a Panther with a bazooka, then they stood a chance. It was generally agreed that the anti-tank rifle grenade was a dangerous waste of time.

On the 28th Division's northern flank, the ancient town of Clervaux above the River Clerf came under threat. The attack of the 116th Panzer-Division to the north was pushing back the 112th Infantry of the 28th Division up into the 106th Division's sector, where it became the far-right flank in the defence of St Vith. Clervaux, where Colonel Fuller commanding the 110th Infantry had set up his command post in a hotel, was partly shielded by the resolute defence of Marnach by one of his companies. But the 2nd Panzer-Division forced on past this obstacle. At 05.00 on 17 December, a field artillery battery five kilometres north-east of Clervaux was overrun by panzergrenadiers.

Before dawn German patrols reached Clervaux, which had already been infiltrated by an artillery observation team equipped with a radio. Then infantry slipped in unobserved and concealed themselves in the pharmacy just below the mainly fifteenth-century castle, with round towers surmounted by spires like witches' hats. The castle still stands on a rocky spur projecting into the middle of the town, which curves round it in a horseshoe. By 09.30, Panther tanks and self-propelled assault guns were in action from the high ground overlooking Clervaux. General Cota sent a platoon of Shermans and some infantry to help Fuller, who had no more than his regimental headquarters personnel and sixty men retrieved from the divisional rest centre. As darkness fell that afternoon, Fuller reported to Cota in Wiltz that the town was surrounded and a panzer was 'sitting in his front door firing in'. At an aid station someone called out, 'If you're a Jewish GI, throw your dog tags away because there are SS troops here.' At least one soldier tossed his, marked with an 'H' for 'Hebrew', into a pot-bellied stove.

The headquarters personnel with soldiers from the rest centre pulled back to the castle, where they continued to hold out on the following day. Among the civilians sheltering in the castle was the sixteen-year-old Jean Servé, who described how in one room a GI was playing the piano while an American sniper, with a cigarette hanging from his lips, was calmly shooting Germans, one after another. Servé watched as one of his victims rolled down the hill behind the Hôtel du Parc. As the battle continued, the wounded were placed in the cellars along with the civilians. But soon the defenders ran out of ammunition, and with the castle on fire they had no choice but to surrender.

Next to the 28th Division on the southern flank was General Barton's 4th Infantry Division. It too had been badly weakened in the Hürtgen Forest, but at least its attackers were less formidable than Manteuffel's panzer divisions. Barton's 12th Infantry Regiment held the towns of Dickweiler, Echternach, Osweiler, Lauterborn and Berdorf against the 212th Volksgrenadier-Division. His plan had been to deny the Germans use of the road network west of the Sauer by occupying villages and hamlets at key intersections with a company apiece. The main thrust hit the 2nd Battalion of the 22nd Infantry Regiment, but it held its ground. Almost all these defended points were surrounded. But by the evening of 17 December the situation had been stabilized with the arrival of task forces from the 10th Armored Division, and they were soon relieved.

The 'Tigers of the Tenth' moved north through Luxembourg on 17 December. The news that they were to lead the fight back against the offensive was greeted with elation, for they had feared they were destined to be a rearguard. Late that afternoon, Combat Command A under Brigadier General Edwin W. Piburn 'rolled headlong into a very surprised German force' near the Schwarz Erntz gorge. The battle continued for three days, but the German advance was halted. The southern shoulder was secure.

At First Army headquarters in Spa, however, the mood on the evening of 17 December was sombre, with the Peiper Kampfgruppe forging west and the 28th Division unable to hold back Manteuffel's panzer divisions. 'The G-2 estimate tonight', the war diary recorded, 'says that the enemy is capable of attempting to exploit his initial gains by driving through our rear areas and seizing bridgeheads over the Meuse river.'

The greatest threat was to Bastogne. The Panzer Lehr Division was heading due west straight for its southern side, while the 2nd Panzer-Division was aiming to circumvent it to the north. The 26th Volksgrenadier-Division was to take the town. They all received orders from General der Panzertruppe Heinrich Freiherr von Lüttwitz, who commanded the XLVII Panzer Corps. The 5th Fallschirmjäger-Division to the south was held up at Wiltz by Cota's 28th Division. There was no mention of Bastogne in its orders from the Seventh Army. It was just told 'to advance as rapidly as possible, to secure a large enough area for General von Manteuffel's Fifth Panzer Army to maneuver in'. But that afternoon Lüttwitz suddenly became aware of Bastogne's importance to the Americans. His headquarters intercepted a radio message saying that an airborne division would be coming to Bastogne in convoys of trucks. This presumably came from the US military police radio net, which broadcast in clear and gave the Germans some of their best intelligence. Lüttwitz was confident that his panzer divisions would get there first.

After their extended combat role in Holland in waterlogged foxholes, both the 82nd and the 101st Airborne Divisions were recuperating at the French camp of Mourmelon-le-Grand near Reims. Their rest period had consisted of playing football, compulsive gambling, drinking cheap champagne and indulging in bar-room brawls between the two divisions. The decision taken that morning in Versailles to pass XVIII Airborne Corps from SHAEF reserve to the First Army at first led to a good deal of confusion. A number of senior officers were absent. Major General Matthew B. Ridgway, the corps commander, happened to be in England. Major General Maxwell D. Taylor, the commander of the 101st, was back in the United States. His deputy, Brigadier General Gerald J. Higgins, was also in England, lecturing on Operation Market Garden. So Brigadier General Anthony C. McAuliffe, the 101st Division's artillery commander, had to take their men into battle.

McAuliffe, on receiving the order at 20.30 hours to prepare to move, immediately summoned unit commanders and staff for a meeting. 'All I know of the situation', he told them, 'is that there has been a break-through and we have got to get up there.' Many of their men were on leave in Paris, determined to enjoy themselves in an unrestrained air-borne way, especially those who, following their wartime tradition, had pinned their 'Dear John' letters from unfaithful sweethearts on the unit noticeboard. Orders went out to the military police in Paris to round up all the airborne personnel, while an officer commandeered a train to bring them back. Many of those snatched back from leave were the worse for wear from their excesses. And 'most of them, to hear them tell it,' remarked Louis Simpson, 'were suffering from *coitus interruptus*'. There had been a good deal of jealousy from those who had lost all their back pay gambling and could not afford to go.

The 101st was well below strength and had not yet been re-equipped. Some 3,500 men had been lost during the fighting in Holland, and the division received comparatively few replacements during its time at Mourmelon. So after receipt of the movement order, prisoners on disciplinary sentences, mostly for fighting or striking an NCO, were released from the stockade and ordered to report immediately to their companies. Officers went to the military hospital and called for those almost cured to discharge themselves. On the other hand, some com-manders advised their officers to leave behind any men whose nerves were still badly shaken. There had been several suicides from combat fatigue in the previous ten days, including the divisional chief of staff who had put his .45 automatic in his mouth and pulled the trigger.

The 82nd had had more time to integrate replacements and re-equip after the losses in Holland, while the 101st was short of everything, especially winter clothing. During that night, everyone tried to beg, borrow or steal whatever they were missing. Quartermasters simply opened their stores. Com Z, meanwhile, rose to the challenge of assem-bling enough ten-ton trucks to move two divisions. Their exhausted drivers, who had been with the Red Ball Express, were not exactly enthusiastic at the prospect of delivering airborne troops to the front line in the Ardennes, but they more than did their duty.

Even though SHAEF tried to suppress news of the German advance, word spread rapidly. The rumour was that the Germans were heading for Paris. French collaborators in prison began to celebrate and taunt their guards. This was unwise. Many of their jailers came from the

Resistance and they swore that they would shoot every one of them before the Germans arrived.

Partly due to the lack of clear information, anxiety in Paris had reached a feverish level. General Alphonse Juin accompanied by other senior French officers came to SHAEF at Versailles to discuss the break-through. They were met by General Bedell Smith. 'As we walked through the halls,' Bedell Smith wrote later, 'I saw the officers casting puzzled glances into offices where normal routine seemed to be going on. Then a French general behind me said to our Intelligence Chief, General Strong: "What! You are not packing?"'

Ernest Hemingway heard of the German attack at the Ritz in the Place Vendôme, where he was installed with his paramour, Mary Welsh. She had returned from a dinner with the air force commander Lieutenant General 'Tooey' Spaatz, during which aides had rushed in and out bearing urgent messages. The Ritz lobby was in chaos, with officers running backwards and forwards. Although still not recovered from the bronchitis he had picked up in the Hürtgen Forest, Hemingway was determined to rejoin the 4th Infantry Division. He started to pack and assemble his illegal armoury. 'There's been a complete breakthrough,' he told his brother Leicester, who was passing through Paris. 'This thing could cost us the works. Their armor is pouring in. They're taking no prisoners . . . Load those clips. Wipe every cartridge clean.'

10

Monday 18 December

The main attack against the last battalion of the 2nd Infantry Division in front of Rocherath–Krinkelt came at 06.45 hours, more than an hour before dawn. The Germans followed their usual practice of making the maximum amount of noise in night attacks, with 'yells, catcalls and many other forms of noises including banging on mess gear'. The battle continued for four hours, with the American field artillery taking on fire mission after fire mission in support of the forward infantry foxholes. In a number of cases, companies were calling for fire on their own positions as they were overrun. Lieutenant Colonel McKinley's 1st Battalion of the 9th Infantry Regiment had covered other units as they pulled back to the twin villages.

Again at first light twelve panzers, each escorted by a platoon of panzergrenadiers, advanced out of the mist until halted by artillery fire. The 2nd Division found that it would have been far more useful to have a dozen bazooka teams than three 'cumbersome' 57mm anti-tank guns in the anti-tank platoon. 'The 57mm anti-tank guns proved very unsatisfactory, only one effective hit being scored on the turret of one enemy tank,' an after-action report stated. Another officer described it as 'practically a useless weapon'. Lieutenant Colonel McKinley thought the 57mm had 'no place in an infantry battalion', because it was so hard to manoeuvre in mud, and it was impossible to put into position if the enemy was already in contact. He wanted tank destroyers as an integral part of the unit so that they did not disappear whenever they felt like it. But that day at Rocherath–Krinkelt, tank destroyers, as well as Shermans, bazookas and the artillery accounted for a number of Panther and Mark IV tanks.

The Americans always tried to prevent the Germans from recovering and repairing disabled panzers, or from using them as temporary firing positions just in front of their lines. So whenever the SS panzergrenadiers were forced back 'tanks knocked out of action, but not destroyed, were set afire with gasoline-oil mixes poured on them, and with thermite grenades set in gunbarrels which burned through the barrels'.

But then another attack overran the front line. Panzers fired down into the foxholes, and twisted back and forth on top to bury the men in them. Only twelve soldiers from one platoon of around thirty men emerged alive. The left-hand platoon of one company had no anti-tank ammunition left, so some six or seven men started to run towards the rear in despair. McKinley stopped them and sent them back to their platoon. Aid men, struggling heroically to evacuate the wounded through the snow, improvised sleds by nailing raised crosspieces to a pair of skis to carry a litter.

In due course the battalion received orders to pull back, but the fighting was so close that McKinley felt that he would not be able to extricate any of his men. At the critical moment, however, four Shermans from the 741st Tank Battalion appeared. They were able to cover the withdrawal, even scoring hits on three German tanks. 'When the Battalion assembled in Rocherath,' McKinley recorded, 'it was found that of the total strength of 600 men that had started the fight, 197 were left, including attachments.' Yet only nine men from the whole of the 2nd Division abandoned the battle and headed for the rear. They were picked up by military police as 'stragglers'. Most men found that they did not get the 'shakes' at the height of a battle: it hit them afterwards when the firing had died away.

The sacrificial stand of the 1st Battalion of the 9th Infantry Regiment helped save the rest of the 2nd Division, and thwart the breakthrough of the 12th SS Panzer-Division. But even McKinley acknowledged afterwards that 'it was artillery that did the job', saving his unit from complete destruction. All the time remnants of the 99th Division, which had faced the initial onslaught, continued to slip through to American lines. They were directed back to Camp Elsenborn where they were fed and ammunitioned, then placed in a new line behind Rocherath–Krinkelt. One battalion commander, accused by his own officers of 'cowardice and incompetence', was relieved.

Around 10.00, a group of seven American trucks approached. A tank destroyer fired a round over the leading truck at a range of 500 metres, compelling it to halt. A patrol went forward to make sure that the trucks were genuine, and not captured vehicles. But as they came close, men in the trucks opened fire. It had been a 'Trojan Horse trick' to penetrate American lines in the confusion. Around 140 German soldiers leaped from the trucks and tried to escape back towards the woods. The battalion's mortars and heavy machine guns opened up, and the battalion commander estimated that three-quarters of them were killed, but a number may have feigned death and crept away later. Several of the wounded were taken prisoner, and proved to be members of the 12th SS Division *Hitler Jugend*. One of the more badly hit refused a transfusion of American blood at the aid station.

The battle for the twin villages continued, with civilians trapped and deafened from explosions in their cellars. As the fog lifted at about 08.30 hours and daylight strengthened a little, the woods beyond the snow-fields became visible. More Panther and Mark IV tanks advanced accompanied by groups of panzergrenadiers and some broke into Rocherath–Krinkelt. The mortar officer in the 38th Infantry Regiment formed four bazooka teams, for stalking tanks around the village. Some men wore goggles because of the flash when firing, but only noticed the burns on their face later. The worst fate was to find a dud round stuck in the bazooka and see the enemy tank traverse its gun towards you. Guile was needed. 'A tank was observed approaching on a road,' V Corps reported. 'A sergeant stationed a bazooka in concealment on each side of the road, and then drove a herd of cows out in front of the tank. The tank slowed to a halt, was knocked out by bazooka fire, and the crew killed by small arms fire as they baled out.'

German tanks began blasting houses at point-blank range, even sticking their gun through a window. 'The bayonet was little used,' another American officer observed later, 'even in close-in fighting in Rocherath where rifle butts or bare fists seemingly took preference.' Two Shermans parked by the battalion command post in Rocherath and crewed by a mixture of 'gunners, drivers, assistant drivers, cooks and mechanics' fought back. Lieutenant Colonel Robert N. Skaggs suddenly saw a

Mark VI Tiger tank approaching some American soldiers guarding German prisoners of war. Skaggs alerted the two tanks and they both opened fire. They missed. The Tiger halted and traversed its turret to fire back at both of them, but both of its shots also missed. Allowed a second chance, the scratch crews of the two Shermans made sure that they did not miss again, and the Tiger burst into flames. As soon as a German tank was hit, American infantry brought their rifles up to their shoulders ready to shoot down any of the crew trying to escape from the turret or hull. If they were on fire and screaming, then they were simply putting the poor bastard out of his misery. Captain MacDonald of the 2nd Division 'saw a soldier silhouetted against the tracers, throw a can of gasoline at a tank. The tank burst into flames.'

In another incident in the twin villages, the crew of a Sherman of the 741st Tank Battalion 'observed a Mark VI [Tiger] approaching frontally. The tank commander knew the difficulty of penetrating the frontal armor, and desired to utilize the faster turret action of the Sherman. The tank was quickly turned round and routed round a small group of buildings to enable the Sherman to bring fire to bear on the side or rear of the Mark VI. The German simultaneously sensing the maneuver followed, and the two tanks were chasing each other round in a circle endeavoring to get into position to fire. The team mate of the Sherman observed the action, [and] as the Mark VI in its course around the buildings exposed its rear, brought fire to bear on it and knocked it out.' The two commanders jumped out to shake hands jubilantly, climbed back into their tanks and then went back to work.

Rifle grenades again proved useless, and only one tank was disabled in this way. A sergeant saw a 'man from another outfit' fire six or seven rounds of anti-tank grenades at a panzer, and although they were hitting the target they had no effect. In other cases too, the grenades 'just glanced off'.

One Mark VI Tiger in Krinkelt in front of the church began firing at the battalion command post. Lieutenant Colonel Barsanti sent out five bazooka teams to stalk the tank. They achieved two hits, but the Tiger was barely damaged. Even so, its commander decided that it was too exposed in the village and made a run for it towards Wirtzfeld. But as the tank charged off, it rounded a corner at full speed and flattened a Jeep. The two occupants had managed to throw themselves into a ditch just in time. This slowed the Tiger just enough for the crew of a 57mm anti-tank gun to get off a round which wrecked the turret traverse mechanism. As it continued on its way, a Sherman fired and missed, but a tank destroyer further down the road brought it to a halt with two rounds. Riflemen then picked off the black-uniformed crew as they tried to escape. 'None of them got away.'

The 2nd Division later claimed that in the extended battle around Rocherath–Krinkelt seventy-three panzers had been knocked out by Shermans, bazookas, tank destroyers and artillery, while two Mark VI Tigers had been knocked out by bazookas. These, of course, were rare victories during that onslaught. American losses in men and tanks were very heavy. On the other hand, the determination to fight back and make the enemy pay dearly for every step of his advance proved probably the most important contribution to the eventual outcome of the Ardennes offensive. The Sixth Panzer Army had underestimated both the power of American artillery and the commanding position of the Elsenborn ridge. The SS divisions were sharply disabused of their arrogant assumptions about the low quality of American infantry units.

The fighting went on all day and into the night, with more and more buildings ablaze. The artillery observer from the 99th Division who had been sent forward to Buchholz on the first evening gazed at the conflagration in Rocherath–Krinkelt and kept thinking of a line from an Alan Seeger poem: 'But I've a rendezvous with death at midnight in some flaming town.'

While the fighting in Rocherath–Krinkelt reached its climax, part of the 1st Infantry Division five kilometres to the south-west was consolidating its positions and patrolling to establish the direction and strength of the German advance. Sepp Dietrich, frustrated by the fierce American defence of the twin villages, ordered the 277th Volksgrenadier-Division to continue the attack there. The 12th SS Panzer meanwhile was to move to the south-west, and advance from Büllingen and push further west towards Waimes. The small town of Waimes contained the 47th Evacuation Hospital and part of the 99th Division's medical battalion. General Gerow ordered a mixed force from the 1st Division with tank destroyers, light tanks and engineers to extricate the medics and the wounded in time.

The *Hitler Jugend* was to find that the southern flank of the Elsenborn ridge was as strongly held as the eastern flank. The 1st Division alone was backed by six battalions of artillery and a battery of 8-inch guns. The Americans were also fortunate that the ground was so soft in many places that it made off-road movement for the German tanks almost impossible. When American anti-tank guns and tank destroyers knocked out the leading panzer on a road, the others were blocked. Anti-aircraft half-tracks with quadruple .50 machine guns known as 'meatchoppers' then proved very effective in forcing back the SS panzergrenadiers.

Neither General Gerow nor General Hodges had any idea that Hitler had forbidden the Sixth Panzer Army to head north towards Liège. The Führer, wanting to avoid the concentration of American forces around Aachen, had dictated that the SS panzer divisions strike due west towards the Meuse and not vary their route. But Peiper's direction of advance had already convinced the American command that they had to extend the northern shoulder westward. General Ridgway's XVIII Airborne Corps was to establish a defensive line from Stavelot, deploying both the experienced 30th Infantry Division and the 82nd Airborne, which was already heading for Werbomont.

Following the Malmédy massacre of the day before, the American command issued an urgent warning to all troops: 'It is dangerous at any time to surrender to German tank crews, and especially so to tanks unaccompanied by infantry; or to surrender to any units making a rapid advance. These units have few means for handling prisoners, and a solution used is merely to kill the prisoners.' The lesson was: 'Those that fought it out received fewer losses. Those that surrendered did not have a chance.'

Peiper launched his attack on Stavelot at dawn, having let his exhausted men catch up on sleep during the night. Major Paul J. Solis had arrived in the early hours with a company of the 526th Armored Infantry Battalion, a platoon of anti-tank guns and a platoon of towed tank destroyers. He was still positioning his men and guns when they were surprised by two Panther tanks and a company of panzergrenadiers, charging around the hillside on the road to the bridge over the Amblève. The first Panther was hit and caught fire, but it had built up such momentum that it smashed into the anti-tank barrier erected across the road. The second

Panther pushed on and occupied the bridge in Stavelot, to be followed rapidly by the panzergrenadiers.

The Americans did not have time to blow up the bridge. Solis's force was driven back into the town. Peiper's men alleged, without any justification, that Belgian civilians fired on them and they proceeded to shoot twenty-three of them, including women. After heavy fighting throughout the morning, Solis's small force had to withdraw a little way up the road to Francorchamps and Spa. The main American fuel dump at Francorchamps had not been marked on Peiper's map, and he decided to carry on west along the valley of the Amblève. In any case, General Lee's Communications Zone troops had succeeded in evacuating the bulk of the fuel supplies potentially within Peiper's grasp. Between 17 and 19 December, American supply troops removed more than 3 million gallons of fuel from the Spa–Stavelot area. The biggest Allied loss was 400,000 gallons, destroyed on 17 December by a V-1 strike on Liège.

That afternoon a misleading report reached Hodges's headquarters that Spa itself was threatened. General Joe Collins, who was sitting next to the First Army commander, heard its chief intelligence officer whisper to Hodges: 'General, if you don't get out of town pretty quickly, you are going to be captured.'

'The situation is rapidly deteriorating,' the headquarters diary noted. 'About three o'clock this afternoon there were reports that tanks were coming up from Stavelot headed towards Spa. Only a small roadblock and half-tracks stood between them and our headquarters.' Hodges rang Simpson, the Ninth Army commander, at 16.05. 'He says that the situation is pretty bad,' Simpson recorded. 'He is ready to pull out his establishment. He is threatened, he says.' Spa was evacuated, and the whole of First Army staff moved to its rear headquarters at Chaudfontaine near Liège, which they reached at midnight. They learned later that, as soon as they left Spa, 'American flags, pictures of the President and all other Allied insignia were taken down and that the mayor released 20 suspected collaborationists out of jail.'

Earlier that evening two officers from the 7th Armored Division, who had just returned from leave, found that their formation had left Maastricht. Setting out to find them, they first went to Spa and in Hodges's abandoned headquarters they gazed in astonishment at the situation maps which had not been removed in the rush to evacuate. They took them down and carried on to St Vith, where they handed them over to Brigadier General Bruce Clarke. Clarke studied the maps in dismay. They revealed, as nothing else could, the First Army's failure to understand what was going on. 'Hell, when this fight's over,' Clarke said, 'there's going to be enough grief court-martialling generals. I'm not in the mood for making any more trouble.' He promptly destroyed them.

Peiper, in an attempt to find an alternative route, had sent off a reconnaissance force of two companies south of the Amblève to Trois-Ponts, a village on the confluence of the Amblève and the Salm. It appears that they became hopelessly lost in the dark. From Trois-Ponts the road lay straight to Werbomont. Peiper, having forced the Americans out of Stavelot, left behind a small detachment on the assumption that troops from the 3rd Fallschirmjäger-Division would arrive, and then set off for Trois-Ponts himself.

The 51st Engineer Battalion, which had been based at Marche-en-Famenne operating sawmills, had received orders the evening before to make for Trois-Ponts to blow the three bridges there. Company C arrived while Peiper's force was attacking Stavelot and set to work placing demolition charges on the bridge over the Amblève and the two bridges over the Salm. They also erected roadblocks across the road along which the Peiper Kampfgruppe would come. A 57mm anti-tank gun and its crew were pressed into service, as was a company of the 526th Armored Infantry Battalion on its way to St Vith to join up with the rest of the 7th Armored Division.

At 11.15 hours, the defenders of Trois-Ponts heard the grinding rumble of tanks approaching. Peiper's vanguard included nineteen Panthers. The crew of the 57mm anti-tank gun were ready and its first round hit the track of the leading Panther, bringing it to a halt. The other tanks opened fire and destroyed the gun, killing most of its crew. At the sound of firing the engineers blew up the bridges. Peiper's route to Werbomont was blocked. The defenders in houses on the west bank opened fire on panzergrenadiers trying to cross the river. Using various ruses, including a truck towing chains to make the noise of tanks and infantrymen firing bazookas to imitate artillery, the defenders convinced Peiper that their force was much stronger than it was.

Furious at this setback, Peiper decided to return to Stavelot and take the road along the north bank of the Amblève instead. His column thundered along the road towards La Gleize. The steep, forested slopes on the north side of the valley allowed no room for manoeuvre. Peiper still felt that, if only he had enough fuel, 'it would have been a simple matter to drive through to the River Meuse early that day'.

Finding no resistance in La Gleize, Peiper sent off a reconnaissance group who discovered a bridge intact over the Amblève at Cheneux. They were seen by an American spotter aircraft flying under the cloud. Fighter-bombers from IX Tactical Air Command were alerted and soon dived into the attack, despite the bad visibility. The Kampfgruppe lost three tanks and five half-tracks. Peiper's column was saved from further punishment by the early fall of darkness at 16.30 hours, but the Americans now knew exactly where they were. The 1st SS Panzer Corps, which had been out of radio contact with Peiper, also found out by intercepting the Americans' insecure transmissions.

Peiper pushed on under the cover of darkness but when the lead vehicle reached a bridge over the Lienne, a small tributary of the Amblève, it was blown up in their faces by a detachment from the 291st Engineer Combat Battalion. Peiper, who suffered from heart problems, must have nearly had a stroke at this further setback. He sent a tank company to find another bridge to the north, but just as they thought they had found one unguarded, they were attacked in a well-executed ambush. It was in any case a fruitless diversion because the bridge was not strong enough for their seventy-two-ton Königstiger tanks. Thwarted and with no more bridges left to try, the column turned round with great difficulty on the narrow road and returned to La Gleize to rejoin the Amblève valley to Stoumont three kilometres further on. Peiper halted the column to rest for the night before attacking Stoumont at dawn. This at least gave civilians in the village the chance to get away.

Peiper had no idea that American forces were closing in. A regiment of the 30th Infantry Division already lay ahead, blocking the valley road another two and a half kilometres further on, and the 82nd Airborne was starting to deploy from Werbomont. The trap was also closing behind him. A battalion from another regiment in the 30th Infantry Division, strengthened with tanks and tank destroyers, relieved Major Solis's men north of Stavelot, and that evening fought its way into the northern part of the town.

*

While the 82nd Airborne had rushed on ahead to Werbomont, the 101st started to mount up back at Mourmelon-le-Grand. A long line of 380 ten-ton open trucks were waiting to take up to fifty men apiece. Roll calls by company took place. Men bundled up 'in their winter clothing looked like an assembly of bears'. Many, however, lacked greatcoats and even their paratrooper jumpboots. One lieutenant colonel, who had just arrived back from a wedding in London, would march into Bastogne still in his ceremonial Class A uniform. The division band, which had been ordered to stay behind, formed up in angry mood. Its members asked the chaplain whether he could speak to the commander of the 501st Parachute Infantry Regiment, to persuade him to allow them to go. He said that the colonel was too busy, but tacitly agreed that they could always climb aboard with the others. He knew that every man would be needed.

The first trucks left at 12.15 with airborne engineers, the reconnaissance platoon and part of divisional headquarters. The orders were to head for Werbomont. Brigadier General McAuliffe left almost immediately, and two hours later the first part of the main column set off. Altogether 805 officers and 11,035 enlisted men were going into battle. Nobody knew exactly where they were headed, and many thought it strange that they were not going to parachute into battle, but were being transported in like ordinary 'straight-leg' infantry. Packed into the open trucks, they shivered in the cold. The column did not stop, and as there was no room to move to the back to relieve themselves over the tailgate, they passed around an empty jerrycan instead. When darkness fell later in the afternoon, the drivers switched on their headlights. The need for speed was deemed to be greater than the risk of encountering a German night-fighter.

When McAuliffe reached Neufchâteau, thirty kilometres south-west of Bastogne, an MP flagged down his command car. He was given a message from Middleton's VIII Corps headquarters to say that the 101st Airborne had been attached to his command, and that the whole division should head straight for Bastogne. The advance party, unaware of the change of plan, had already gone on to Werbomont, forty kilometres further north as the crow flies. McAuliffe and his staff officers drove on to Bastogne and, just before dark, found General Troy Middleton's corps headquarters in a former German barracks on the north-west edge of the town. The scenes of panic-stricken drivers and soldiers flee-ing on foot heading west were not an encouraging sight.

McAuliffe found Middleton briefing Colonel William L. Roberts of Combat Command B of the 10th Armored Division, one of the two formations which Eisenhower had ordered to the Ardennes that first evening. Roberts had a better idea of how desperate the situation was than McAuliffe. That morning General Norman Cota had sent him an urgent request to come to the aid of his battered 28th Division near Wiltz, where the 5th Fallschirmjäger-Division was attacking. But Rob-erts had received firm orders to go straight to Bastogne, so was forced to refuse. The Panzer Lehr Division and the 26th Volksgrenadier had already broken through just to the north, heading for the town.

'How many teams can you make up?' Middleton asked Roberts.

'Three,' he replied.

Middleton ordered him to send one team to the south-east of War-din, and another to Longvilly to block the advance of the Panzer Lehr. The third was to go north to Noville to stop the 2nd Panzer-Division. Although Roberts did not like the idea of splitting his force into such small groups, he did not contest Middleton's decision. 'Move with the utmost speed,' Middleton told him. 'Hold these positions at all costs.'

In the race for Bastogne, hold-ups on the roads caused tempers to flare in the XLVII Panzer Corps. But the main setback to the timetable had been caused by the courage of individual companies from the 28th Infantry Division. Their defence of road junctions along the north–south ridge road known as 'Skyline Drive', at villages such as Heinerscheid, Marnach and Hosingen, had made a critical difference. 'The long resistance of Hosingen', Generalmajor Heinz Kokott acknowledged, 'resulted in the delay of the whole advance of 26th Volksgrenadier-Division and thereby of Panzer Lehr by one and a half days.' Company K's defence of Hosin-gen until the morning of 18 December, as the commander of Panzer Lehr also recognized, had slowed his division so much that it 'arrived too late in the Bastogne area'. This proved decisive for the battle of Bastogne, when every hour counted.

General Cota in Wiltz knew that his division was doomed. He ordered unsorted Christmas mail to be destroyed to keep it from the Germans, so letters, cards and packages were piled up in a courtyard, doused with

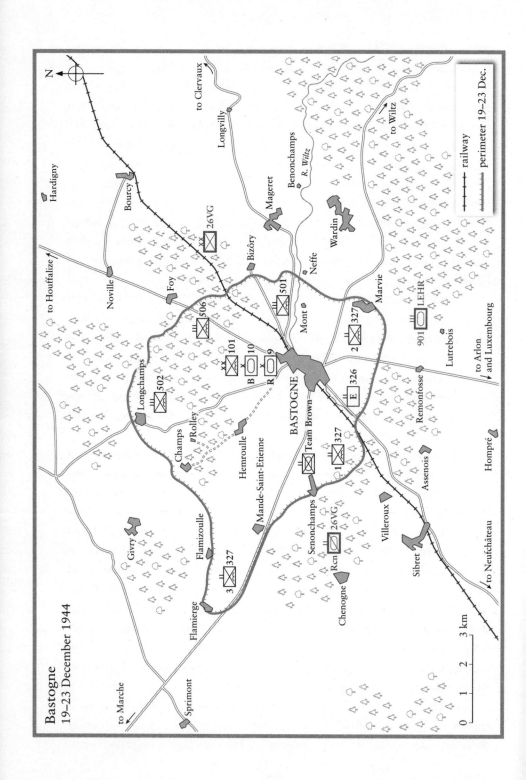

Bastogne
19–23 December 1944

N

to Marche

to Houffalize

to Clervaux

to Wiltz

to Arlon
and Luxembourg

to Neufchâteau

Sprimont

Givry

Flamierge

Flamizoulle

3 327

Longchamps

502

Champs

Rolley

Hemroulle

Mande-Saint-Etienne

Senonchamps

26VG Rcn

Chenogne

Villeroux

Sibret

Assenois

Hompré

Hardigny

Bourcy

Noville

Foy

506

101

502

B 10

R 9

26VG

Bizóry

501

Mont

Neffe

Mageret

Benonchamps

R. Wiltz

Wardin

Marvie

2 327

901 LEHR

Lutrebois

Remonfosse

E 326

Team Brown

1 327

BASTOGNE

Longvilly

| railway |
| perimeter 19–23 Dec. |

0   1   2   3 km

gasoline and set on fire. During the afternoon, the remnants of the 3rd Battalion of the 110th Infantry fell back towards Wiltz. The hungry and exhausted men formed up to defend the howitzers of a field artillery battalion south-east of Wiltz, while Cota prepared to pull his divisional command post back to Sibret, south-west of Bastogne.

That morning, in mist and drizzle, the spearhead of the Panzer Lehr had finally crossed the bridge over the River Clerf near Drauffelt while the 2nd Panzer-Division crossed at Clervaux, having been delayed by the defence of the town and its castle. Congestion was then caused by tanks breaking down – the Panthers were still the most susceptible to mechanical failure – while the horse-drawn artillery of an infantry division struggling on the same muddy track as armoured formations produced furious scenes.

The commander of Panzer Lehr, Generalleutnant Fritz Bayerlein, a short and aggressive veteran of North Africa and Normandy, blamed his corps commander for having allowed this chaos. Congestion was so bad that the marching infantry of the 26th Volksgrenadier reached Nieder Wampach at about the same time as the panzer troops in their tanks and half-tracks. When vehicles bogged down in the mud, infantrymen took their heavy machine guns and mortars off the vehicles and carried them on their shoulders.

As darkness was falling on 18 December, and the Panzer Lehr advanced on Bastogne, Bayerlein witnessed a tank battle going on near Longvilly. 'Panzer Lehr, with their barrels turned northward,' he wrote, 'passed by this impressive spectacle in the twilight which, cut by the tracer bullets, took on a fantastic aspect.' In fact one of his own units was involved. Middleton had ordered Combat Command R of the 9th Armored Division to defend the main routes to Bastogne from the east. After some initial skirmishes against roadblocks and outposts in the late afternoon, the Shermans and half-tracks of Task Force Rose and Task Force Harper were caught between the spearhead of the 2nd Panzer-Division, a 26th Volksgrenadier-Division artillery regiment, and a company of tanks from the Panzer Lehr. Once the first tanks to be targeted had burst into flames, the panzer gunners kept firing at the other vehicles silhouetted by the blaze. Bayerlein attributed their success to the accuracy and longer range of the Mark V Panther's gun. American crews abandoned their vehicles whether hit or not, and escaped towards Longvilly.

The Germans boasted later that as a result of this action they captured twenty-three Sherman tanks, fourteen armoured cars, fifteen self-propelled guns, thirty Jeeps and twenty-five trucks, all undamaged. Although the German account of their success was exaggerated, the one-sided battle near Longvilly was a very nasty blow for the Americans.

The only welcome development that evening in Bastogne was the arrival of the 705th Tank Destroyer Battalion, which had managed to fight its way through from the north. Colonel Roberts of the 10th Armored Division had already briefed his three team leaders and sent them on their way. Each had a mixture of Sherman tanks, armoured cars and half-tracks carrying the infantry. Team O'Hara set off to Wardin where it took up position on some high ground just to the south of the village. There was no sign of the Germans, but small groups of exhausted men from the 28th Division, bearded and filthy from three days of fighting, came through heading for Bastogne.

Major William R. Desobry of the 20th Armored Infantry Battalion was ordered north to Noville. An MP led the way in a Jeep to put him on the right road as they had no maps. On reaching the edge of Bastogne, the MP said: 'Noville is two towns up, straight down the road.' Desobry sent the reconnaissance platoon on ahead, through Foy and on to Noville. Both villages were deserted.

Desobry set up a defence on the north and eastern side of Noville with outposts of infantry squads and pairs of Sherman tanks guarding the roads coming in, then got some sleep soon after midnight. He knew that there was a big battle to come. 'We could hear gunfire out to the east and to the north and we could see flashes. We could see searchlights and so on. During the night a number of small units came back into our lines and a lot of stragglers. They essentially told us horror stories about how their units had been overrun by large German units with lots of tanks, Germans in American uniforms, Germans in civilian clothes and all sorts of weird tales.'

Roberts had given Desobry the authority to grab any stragglers and take them under command, but he found that their 'physical condition and mental condition was such' that it was easier to send them on to the rear. The only groups that seemed to be worth taking on were an infantry platoon from the 9th Armored Division and a platoon of engineers, but even the engineers were sent on their way the next morning. Reinforcements were coming in the shape of paratroopers, but Desobry sensed that the Germans would attack before they arrived.

Lieutenant Colonel Henry T. Cherry's team, with the 3rd Tank Battalion, a company of infantry, some engineers and a platoon of the 90th Cavalry Squadron, advanced from Bastogne towards Longvilly and the sound of firing. They halted short of the village, whose narrow street was jammed with rear-echelon vehicles from Combat Command R. Colonel Cherry went forward on foot to find out what was happening, but none of the officers in their temporary command post seemed to have any idea of the situation. As at Wardin, stragglers from the 28th were retreating to Bastogne.

Cherry positioned his tanks and infantry a kilometre west of Longvilly and returned to report to Colonel Roberts in Bastogne. He set off back to his men shortly before midnight, and heard over the radio that the remnants of Combat Command R of the 9th Armored Division had pulled out completely. On reaching Neffe, Cherry was warned by a wounded soldier that the road ahead had been cut at Mageret by a reconnaissance group from the Panzer Lehr. Cherry called one of his officers on the radio to tell him to send a small force back to clear them out. But when the half-track with two squads of infantry reached Mageret, they found the German force consisted of three tanks and a company of infantry.

When Colonel Cherry heard what they had discovered, he knew that Longvilly could not be defended, despite Colonel Roberts's admonition to hold it 'at all costs'. He ordered his team to pull back to Neffe, fighting their way through if necessary. Cherry, having spotted an ancient chateau with thick walls, decided to set up his command post there. Like Desobry, he sensed that the real battle would start in the morning.

Even though his panzer divisions had at last broken through in the south, General der Panzertruppe von Manteuffel was furious at the delays in capturing St Vith. Part of the trouble came from the fact that the only roads west led through the town, and the boundary with the Sixth Panzer Army lay just six kilometres to the north. And since, in Manteuffel's view, Dietrich's army was already attacking on far too narrow a front, some of his forces had moved on to Fifth Panzer Army routes, increasing the traffic chaos.

Shortly after dawn, the Germans attacked Hasbrouck's defence line in front of St Vith. Panzers fired tree bursts, bringing down pine branches which made the Americans duck deep in their foxholes. Volksgrenadiers attacked, firing automatic weapons. The 18th Volksgrenadier-Division was considerably more experienced than the 62nd advancing towards the south of St Vith. A second attack late in the morning was supported by a massive Ferdinand self-propelled gun, but a Sherman knocked it out twenty-five metres from the American positions with an armour-piercing round which bounced and penetrated its belly.

A Greyhound armoured car concealed in some trees slipped in behind a Tiger tank on the Schönberg road so as to fire its puny 37mm gun at point-blank range. The Tiger commander, on spotting it, tried to traverse his turret round to engage, but the crew of the Greyhound managed to get within twenty-five metres and fire off three rounds into the thinly protected rear of the Tiger. 'There was a muffled explosion, followed by flames which billowed out of the turret and engine ports.'

The third attack came in the afternoon, with a battalion of infantry supported by four tanks and eight self-propelled assault guns. The assault was only broken up by the enfilade fire of Shermans. The temperature dropped sharply that day, with some snow flurries.

Manteuffel, seeing little progress, decided to commit his reserve in the form of the *Führer Begleit* Brigade commanded by Oberst Otto Remer. That afternoon, Remer received the order to advance to St Vith, but his column of vehicles was soon brought to a halt by the appalling conditions of the roads. One of Remer's officers recorded that the '*Führer Begleit* Brigade was involved in a vast traffic jam with two other infantry formations, all claiming the same road'. Remer ordered his men to keep 'pushing forward and not to worry about minor considerations'. When told to advance further round to the north, Remer at first 'declined to move in that direction', but eventually took up position in a wood south of Born. As the Führer's favourite, he could clearly get away with behaviour which would have landed any other officer in front of a court martial. Remer's high-handed attitude during the offensive became something of a black joke among fellow commanders.

All major American headquarters lacked information on the true state of affairs. Hodges's First Army staff now at Chaudfontaine appeared to be paralysed in the face of disaster, while at Simpson's Ninth Army headquarters in Maastricht officers appeared very optimistic. 'There's not the slightest feeling of nervousness in American quarters with regard to an attack,' the Australian war correspondent Godfrey Blunden wrote. 'On the contrary there is satisfaction that the enemy has chosen to join battle [in the open] instead of lying down behind a barrier of mud and water.' Reports of air battles above the clouds at altitudes of up to 20,000 feet, between P-47 Thunderbolts and Focke-Wulf 190s and Me 109s caused great excitement.

General Bradley still had no idea that General Hodges had abandoned his headquarters at Spa. At 22.30 hours, Bradley rang Patton to summon him to Luxembourg for a conference as soon as possible. Patton and three key staff officers left within ten minutes. As soon as Patton arrived, Bradley again said to him: 'I feel you won't like what we are going to do, but I fear that it's necessary.' Bradley was surprised at how nonchalant Patton was about postponing his offensive in the Saar. 'What the hell,' he said. 'We'll still be killing Krauts.'

On the map Bradley showed the depth of German penetration, which was also much greater than Patton had imagined. Bradley asked him what he could do. Patton answered that he would halt the 4th Armored Division and concentrate it near Longwy, prior to moving north. He could have the 80th Infantry Division on the road to Luxembourg by the next morning, with the 26th Infantry Division following within twenty-four hours. Patton rang his chief of staff and told him to issue the necessary orders and assemble transport for the 80th Division. He confessed that driving back in the dark with no knowledge of how far the Germans had advanced rattled him. 'A very dangerous operation, which I hate,' he wrote in his diary.

When Patton called Luxembourg on his return, Bradley said: 'the situation up there is much worse than it was when I talked to you'. He asked Patton to get the 4th Armored moving immediately. 'You and a staff officer meet me for a conference with General Eisenhower at Verdun at approximately 1100.'

11

Skorzeny and Heydte

Eight of Obersturmbannführer Skorzeny's nine Jeep teams had slipped through American lines on the night of 16 December. They consisted of the best English-speakers, but even they were not good enough. Some carried vials of sulphuric acid to throw in the faces of guards if stopped. Some groups cut wires and carried out minor sabotage, such as changing road signs. One even managed to misdirect an entire infantry regiment. But the greatest success of the operation, combined with Heydte's disastrous parachute drop near Eupen, was to provoke an American over-reaction bordering on paranoia.

A Jeep with four men was stopped at a bridge on the edge of Liège by military police. The four soldiers wore US Army uniforms, and spoke English with an American accent, but when asked for a work ticket they produced several blanks. The MPs ordered them out, found German weapons and explosives, and swastika brassards under their uniform. The Jeep, it turned out, had been captured from the British at Arnhem.

Their officer, Leutnant Günther Schultz, was handed over to Mobile Field Interrogation Unit No. 1. Schultz appeared to co-operate fully. He admitted that he had been part of Skorzeny's Einheit Steilau and told the team from the Counter Intelligence Corps that, according to his commander Major Schrötter, 'the secret orders of the *Fernaufklärer* [long-range reconnaissance teams] were to penetrate to Paris and capture General Eisenhower and other high ranking officers'. All of this came from the rumour at the Grafenwöhr camp which Skorzeny had encouraged, but it is still not clear whether Schultz himself believed it, or whether he hoped to cause chaos, or perhaps in a wild attempt to impress his interrogators to save his skin.

Schultz told them of an 'Eisenhower Aktion' carried out by a 'special group' commanded by an 'Oberleutnant Schmidhuber', directly under Skorzeny's orders. Approximately eighty people were involved in the plot to kidnap or assassinate General Eisenhower. They would rendez-vous at the Café de l'Epée or the Café de la Paix in Paris, he was not sure which. He also claimed that Brandenburger commandos, who had crossed the Soviet frontier just before the invasion in June 1941, were involved. Another report claimed that they 'may have a captured Ger-man officer as a ruse, pretending to take him to higher headquarters for questioning'. Despite the improbable image of eighty German soldiers meeting in a Parisian café, the Counter Intelligence Corps believed Schultz's account. The next morning, Eisenhower's security was stepped up to such a degree that he almost found himself a prisoner.

General Bradley made sure that when he went out he was sandwiched between another machine-gun-mounted Jeep in front and a Hellcat tank destroyer behind. He had been told by the Counter Intelligence Corps, alarmed by the assassination rumours, that he should not use a car, especially getting in and out on the street outside the main entrance of the Hôtel Alfa in Luxembourg. In future, he was to use the kitchen entrance round the back, and his room was changed to one further back in the hotel. All plates with a general's stars had been removed from vehicles and even those on his helmet had to be covered over.

The idea of German commando troops charging around in their rear areas turned the Americans into victims of their own nightmare fan-tasies. Roadblocks were set up on every route, greatly slowing traffic because the guards had to interrogate the occupants to check that they were not German. Instructions were rushed out: 'Question the driver because, if German, he will be the one who speaks and understands the least English . . . Some of these G.I. clad Germans are posing as high-ranking officers. One is supposed to be dressed as a Brigadier General . . . Above all don't let them take off their American uniform. Instead get them to the nearest PW cage, where they will be questioned and eventually put before a firing squad.'

American roadblock guards and MPs came up with their own ques-tions to make sure that a vehicle's occupants were genuine. They included a baseball quiz, the name of the President's dog, the name of the current husband of Betty Grable and 'What is Sinatra's first name?' Brigadier General Bruce Clarke gave a wrong answer about the Chicago Cubs. 'Only a kraut would make a mistake like that,' the MP declared. Having been told that he should look out 'for a kraut posing as a one-star general', he was convinced he had discovered his man, and Clarke found himself under arrest for half an hour. Even General Bradley was stopped and held for a short time, despite having given the right answer to the capital of Illinois. The MP thought differently.

British personnel in the American Ninth Army rear area aroused considerable suspicion during the panic. The actor David Niven, a Phantom reconnaissance officer in Rifle Brigade uniform, was challenged by one American sentry with the question: 'Who won the World Series in 1940?'

'I haven't the faintest idea,' Niven claimed to have replied with characteristic insouciance. 'But I do know that I made a picture with Ginger Rogers in 1938.'

'O.K. beat it, Dave,' came the reply, 'but watch your step for Crissake.'

At a more senior level Major General Allan Adair, the commander of the Guards Armoured Division, accompanied by his ADC, was stopped at a checkpoint manned by African-American soldiers. Adair's much loved but famously incompetent ADC Captain Aylmer Tryon could not find their identity documents. After much fruitless searching for them, the large NCO finally said, to Adair's delight, 'General, if I were you, I'd get myself a new aide.'

Another way of checking was to make the soldier or officer in question lower their trousers to check that they were wearing regulation underwear. A German Jew, who had escaped to England soon after Hitler came to power, asked his commanding officer in the Royal Army Service Corps for permission to visit Brussels. Born Gerhardt Unger, he had, like many other soldiers of German Jewish origin, anglicized his name in case of capture by the Nazis. On the evening of 16 December, Gerald Unwin, or Gee, as he was known, began drinking with some American soldiers from the First Army in a bar. They told him of their German Jewish intelligence officer, a Lieutenant Gunther Wertheim. Gunther was his cousin and had escaped from Germany to America. So, on the spur of the moment, he decided to accompany his new friends back to their unit when they left early the next morning.

As they came closer to the Ardennes front, they became aware of heavy firing in the distance and scenes of panic. At a roadblock near Eupen, Gee was arrested. He had no movement order or authorization to be in the area, and although he wore British uniform, he spoke with an unmistakable German accent. Hauled off to an improvised cell-block in a local school, Gee was fortunate not to have been shot out of hand in the atmosphere of rumour and fear then caused by Heydte's paratroopers. He was saved for the moment by the fact that his underwear was standard British army issue, but he was locked up nevertheless in the school until summoned for interrogation the next day. As he was marched into the room, the intelligence officer gasped in astonishment: 'Gerd?' he said. 'Gunther!' Gee exclaimed in relief, on seeing his cousin.

One of Skorzeny's teams was captured on the evening of 18 December at Aywaille, less than twenty kilometres from the Meuse. The three men were found with German papers, and large sums in American dollars and British pounds. They were tried and sentenced to death five days later. Altogether sixteen members of Einheit Steilau were captured and sentenced to 'be shot to death with musketry'. One group asked for a reprieve on the grounds that they were following orders, and faced certain death if they had refused to do so. 'We were sentenced to death,' their appeal stated, 'and are now dying for some criminals who have not only us, but also – and that is worse – our families on their conscience. Therefore we beg mercy of the commanding general; we have not been unjustly sentenced, but we are de facto innocent.' Their appeal was refused and the sentences confirmed by General Bradley.

One of the group taken at Aywaille repeated the story about the plan to seize or kill General Eisenhower, thus confirming the worst fears of the Counter Intelligence Corps. There were also reports of a group of Frenchmen, former members of the Vichy Milice and the SS *Charlemagne* Division, who had been given the task of penetrating Allied lines to sabotage fuel dumps and railway cars. They were said to be wearing American coats, and pretending to be forced labourers who had escaped from a factory.

Another three members of Einheit Steilau, due to be executed at Eupen on 23 December, made a last request just before their execution.

They wanted to hear some Christmas carols sung by German nurses interned near by. While the firing squad stood ready, 'the women sang in clear strong voices'. The guards looked at the condemned men, and apparently 'hung their heads struck by the peculiar sentimentality of it all'. The officer in command of the squad was 'half afraid that they'd shoot at the wall instead of the man when the command was given'.

On 23 December, when British troops from the 29th Armoured Brigade guarded the bridge over the Meuse at Dinant, 'visibility was almost nil' due to fog, the commanding officer of the 3rd Royal Tank Regiment wrote. 'An apparently American Jeep drove through one of the road blocks approaching the bridge on the east side of the river. This road block, as were all the others, was mined by the 8th Rifle Brigade who had established a movable barrier and arranged for mines to be pulled across the road should any vehicle break through the barrier without stopping. As we were by now in contact with the Americans, this Jeep was not fired on, but as it refused to stop the mines were drawn across the road and it was blown up.' It was found to contain three Germans. Two were killed and one taken prisoner.

This was probably the same incident (recorded with a certain artistic licence by Bradley's aide Chester Hansen) in which four Germans in a Jeep lost their nerve on a guarded bridge and tried to smash their way through. The sentry pulled a string of mines across the road, and the Jeep blew up. Three of the Germans were killed instantly, the fourth wounded. The guards walked up, shot the fourth one dead, then tipped the Jeep and all the bodies into the river, 'swept up the bridge' and resumed their post.

Skorzeny's 150th Panzer-Brigade proved a complete anticlimax. Their tanks, most of which were German Mark IVs and Panthers unconvincingly camouflaged to look like Shermans, were painted in olive-drab paint with the white Allied star, in some cases with the surrounding circle omitted. Skorzeny himself knew that they would not have fooled the Americans except perhaps at night. He soon gave up all idea of thrusting through to the Meuse bridges after being bogged down in mud and thwarted by the immense traffic jams which built up behind the 1st SS Panzer-Division. On the evening of 17 December he asked Sepp Dietrich to commit his force instead as an ordinary panzer brigade. Dietrich gave his consent and told Skorzeny to take his force to Ligneuville. Dietrich had another reason for agreeing so readily. The commanding general of I SS Panzer Corps asked for Skorzeny's forces to be withdrawn, as they were 'hindering the operation of the corps by driving between vehicles and doing exactly as they pleased'.

On 21 December, the 150th Panzer-Brigade attacked north to Malmédy in a freezing fog. They forced back a regiment of the 30th Infantry Division until the American artillery ranged in, using the new and highly secret Pozit fused shells, which exploded on proximity to their target. More than a hundred men were killed and 350 wounded in the day's fighting, including Skorzeny, who was badly wounded in the face by shrapnel and nearly lost an eye. The 150th Panzer-Brigade was withdrawn entirely from the offensive and Operation *Greif* was over. But in its only action it managed, purely by chance, to sow confusion, just as Einheit Steilau had done. First Army became convinced by the attack on Malmédy that the Sixth Panzer Army was preparing a drive north.

The original contributor to Allied confusion, Oberstleutnant von der Heydte, was increasingly depressed in his Kampfgruppe's forest hide-out south of Eupen. He was bitter about the 'amateurish, almost frivolous manner displayed at the higher levels of command, where the order for such operations originated'. Dietrich had assured him that he and his men would be relieved within a day. But there was no indication of a breakthrough round Monschau, and the American artillery on the Elsenborn ridge to the south still thundered away. Without radios, there was no hope of discovering the progress of the battle.

Heydte's 300 paratroopers had little food left, having jumped with emergency rations: two rolls of pressed bacon, two portions of sausage, two packets of 'Soya Fleischbrot', dextro-energen tablets, some of the German army hard bread called *Dauerbrot*, marzipan and Pervitin, a benzedrine substitute which had by then been banned. Under the cover of darkness, a group of his men had crept up to an American artillery battery during the night of 17 December and managed to steal some boxes of rations. But these did not last long when divided between 300 men.

Heydte's outposts near the road never attempted to attack a convoy, but picked off single vehicles. The Americans found a single strand of wire stretched across at neck height for anyone sitting in a Jeep. This was attributed to Heydte's men, and it prompted the decision to fit an angled iron attachment on the front of Jeeps to cut any wires strung across roads or trails. There were very few incidents of this sort, but it was considered necessary to reassure drivers, especially when they advanced further into Germany because of the rumours of Werwolf resistance groups made up of Hitler Youth fanatics.

On 17 December Sergeant Inber of the 387th Anti-Aircraft Artillery, driving south from Eupen, overtook a slow column of trucks with ease. But 400 metres ahead of it he was 'ambushed, captured and whisked off the road before the leading vehicle of the convoy reached the point'. Inber was led off to Heydte's main lair, about a kilometre into the woods, where the paratroopers treated him well. Heydte told Inber that he would release him if he could guide two of his injured men to an American aid station. The other American wounded whom they had captured were placed by the road where an ambulance could pick them up.

Isolated paratroopers and air crew from the scattered drop soon fell into American hands. A survivor from a Junkers 52, brought down behind the Ninth Army, told his interrogators that they had 'taken off believing they were on a practice flight, but learned while in the air that they were on a special mission'.

After moving their hiding place, Heydte's force clashed on 19 December with some of the troops from the 18th Infantry Regiment of the 1st Division who were combing the forest. There were a dozen casualties on both sides. Some of the soldiers searching for the German paratroopers did not report the parachutes they found; they simply cut them up to make silk scarves.

Heydte, who was sickening and suffered from trench foot, gave up any idea of an advance on Eupen and decided to move east instead toward Monschau. His men were visibly weakened by malnutrition. They struggled through forest and marshes, and were soaked in the freezing waters of the Helle river which they had to wade. On 20 December, after another, heavier skirmish, Heydte told his men to make their way back to German lines in small groups. Altogether thirty-six were captured, but the rest reached safety. The thirty-seven fatal casualties in the Kampfgruppe were entirely from anti-aircraft fire on the first night.

On 22 December Heydte, by then feeling very ill and utterly exhausted, went into Monschau on his own and broke into a house. When discovered by a civilian, he was relieved when the man told him that he would have to report him to the American military authorities. After a spell in hospital, Heydte was transferred to a prison camp in England. It was comfortable, but he and other officers held there never realized that their conversations were being recorded.

12

Tuesday 19 December

On 19 December at dawn, Peiper's Kampfgruppe attacked Stoumont with a battalion of panzergrenadiers, a company of paratroopers, and tanks in support on the road. The first assault failed. Stoumont seemed solidly held, and the 119th Infantry of the 30th Division launched a counter-attack on their right flank. But a little later in the thick morning mist the trick of Panther tanks charging at maximum speed worked once more. The anti-tank gunners did not stand a chance in the bad visibility. Only ghostly bazooka teams stalking panzers in the fog managed to achieve a couple of kills from the rear. A 90mm anti-aircraft gun sent to Stoumont in desperation managed to knock out a Tiger from the 501st Heavy Panzer Battalion.

Peiper's Kampfgruppe cleared Stoumont nevertheless, crushing the infantry company defending it. Two platoons of Shermans arrived too late, and had to pull back. Peiper's force pushed on four kilometres to the west to Stoumont station. American officers assembled a scratch force just in time. It included the reserve battalion from the 119th, fifteen incomplete Shermans extracted from a nearby ordnance depot by the newly arrived 740th Tank Battalion, a battery of howitzers and another 90mm anti-aircraft gun. With short cliffs on the north side of the road, rising to steep, wooded hillsides above, and a sharp drop on the south side down to the railway track along the river, this position could not be outflanked. Even though First Army headquarters feared that Peiper's force would turn north towards Liège, Stoumont station would be the furthest point of his advance. The rest of the 30th Infantry

Division and General Jim Gavin's 82nd Airborne were concentrating in the area just in time: the 30th to counter-attack the German spearhead and the 82nd to advance from Werbomont to support the defenders of St Vith.

Around 260 Belgian civilians, in an attempt to escape the fighting in Stoumont itself, went down into the cellars of the Saint-Edouard sanatorium, which from the steep hillside overlooked the Amblève valley. But the Germans took over the building as a strongpoint. Priests held masses to calm the frightened women and children when the Americans counter-attacked next day and fought their way in.

The civilians thought they were saved, and greeted the GIs with joy, but the Germans came back in the night. 'Sister Superior led the crowd in reciting twelve rosaries for those fallen in battle.' The Americans again launched an attack, with Sherman tanks firing at point-blank range into the sanatorium. The roof collapsed, walls were blasted down, and parts of the basement ceiling came down in a cloud of dust and smoke. The priest gave general absolution, but by a miracle none of the women and children was hurt.

On the morning of 19 December, Peiper heard that the Americans had retaken Stavelot to his rear, thus cutting his Kampfgruppe off from any hope of resupply when it was almost out of fuel. He sent his reconnaissance battalion back to retake the small town. Peiper sensed failure. He still bitterly regretted that his Kampfgruppe had been forced to wait for the infantry to open the way on the first day of the offensive. It should have been a surprise attack without artillery preparation, he believed, but with armoured combat teams as well as infantry. In the subsequent advance west, the long snaking column had proved a big mistake. They should have had many smaller groups, each one probing for intact bridges and a way through.

His Waffen-SS troopers continued to kill prisoners at almost every opportunity. In La Gleize on the route back, a member of the 741st Tank Battalion, cut off by the German attack the day before, remained hidden in the church. 'From his place of concealment,' a report stated, 'this soldier observed the [German] tanks and infantry halt an American armored car. The occupants surrendered and were told to get out. They were promptly fired upon by machine weapons as they stood there with hands up. The Germans then took the vehicle and moved away.' And

Rottenführer Straub of the reconnaissance battalion later recounted another incident to fellow prisoners from the 26th Volksgrenadier-Division. 'Our battalion advanced to Stavelot and on to La Gleize. From there we went back to Stavelot. Our Sturmführer just shot [prisoners] outright . . . There were twelve of them the first time. He just shot them because they were in the way.'

SS panzergrenadiers convinced themselves of the most extraordinary stories to justify their actions. An eighteen-year-old soldier from the 1st SS Panzer-Division told a fellow prisoner of war that the reputation of one of their senior NCOs for shooting unarmed men was so well known that they had to deal with Americans who pretended to surrender but were secretly bent on revenge. 'Some of them came along', he said, 'waving a white flag and we knew very well that they were out for our Oberscharführer, because he'd killed so many of them, so we took our machine pistols and shot them before they could do a thing. That's the way we work.'

After dark on the evening of 19 December, American soldiers from the 105th Engineer Battalion managed to infiltrate Stavelot and destroyed the main bridge across the Amblève, despite enemy tank and machine-gun fire. Peiper was furious: part of his force was now cut off north of the river and there was little sign of bridging equipment coming up from his division.

The 3rd Fallschirmjäger-Division, which Peiper's Kampfgruppe had expected to catch up with them, was just one of Sepp Dietrich's formations battering away without success at the southern edge of the Elsenborn ridge. The I SS Panzer Corps headquarters had sent the paratroopers to take Faymonville and then Waimes, from where the American field hospital had been evacuated. But the bulk of the 3rd Fallschirmjäger never advanced further than Faymonville.

The lack of progress by the Sixth Panzer Army had started a cascade of criticism from Hitler and the OKW, via Rundstedt and Model down to a frustrated and angry Dietrich. In a fresh attempt, Dietrich ordered the 12th SS Panzer-Division to move round from Rocherath–Krinkelt to attack the American 1st Infantry Division positions from Büllingen. The Germans urgently needed to open the road west to Malmédy. Panzergrenadiers of the SS *Hitler Jugend*, battalions of the 12th Volksgrenadier and tanks assembled in the early hours in Büllingen ready to crush the American 26th Infantry Regiment. The battle for Dom Bütgenbach was to be as intense as that for Rocherath–Krinkelt to the north-east.

To continue the attacks around Rocherath–Krinkelt and Wirtzfeld, Dietrich sent in his reserve, the 3rd Panzergrenadier-Division, to support the 12th and 277th Volksgrenadiers. The hard pounding intensified, as the massed American artillery regiments on the Elsenborn ridge smashed every village in range now held by the Germans. Their first priority on the morning of 19 December was to break up the renewed attacks against Rocherath–Krinkelt, a task at which the 155mm Long Toms excelled. But the casualty rate among young artillery officers acting as forward observers was very high.

In the shattered twin villages, the remaining units of the 2nd Division and the Sherman and tank-destroyer platoons continued to fight off the volksgrenadiers and panzergrenadiers. They also prepared their withdrawal to new positions on the side of the Elsenborn ridge. During the afternoon, they started to destroy vehicles, guns and equipment which would have to be left behind. Radiators and oil reservoirs were emptied and the engines revved until they seized. Artillerymen rolled thermite grenades into their gun barrels. And at 17.30 hours, just over an hour after dark had fallen, the first units began their withdrawal. Along the rutted road, engineers had taped TNT blocks to the trees on either side, ready to blow them down to block the way.

Exhausted after the three-day battle of Rocherath–Krinkelt which had blunted the Sixth Panzer Army, the men slipped and slid in the muddy slush, cursing and sweating. They were so tired that on firmer patches they fell asleep as they continued to trudge forward. Late that night, a small patrol sneaked back to the edge of the twin villages. They returned to report that there were around a thousand Germans there with about a hundred American prisoners.

A dozen kilometres to the south, the two unfortunate regiments of the 106th Division, trapped in the Schnee Eifel east of St Vith, tried to fight their way back to American lines. The inexperienced officers and soldiers were utterly demoralized. They were short of ammunition, out of radio contact mainly due to German jamming, and the scale of the disaster appeared overwhelming. Many tried to raise each other's spirits with assurances that a relief force must be on its way.

Kurt Vonnegut, who was with the 423rd Infantry Regiment, described his comrades as a mixture of college kids and those who had enlisted to avoid jail. Many were 'poor physical specimens' who 'should never have been in the army'. Few had received infantry training. Vonnegut was a battalion scout who knew about weapons only because his 'father was a gun-nut, so [he] knew how all this crap worked'.

Some tried to get away in vehicles, but when the Germans opened fire with anti-tank guns, they abandoned them and immobilized the rest. Their commanders, who were 'flying blind', sent off scouts to find out what was happening, but they could not even find the artillery battalion which was supposed to be supporting them. The Germans had brought up loudspeakers to play music by Benny Goodman, Artie Shaw and other American bandleaders, interrupted with promises of 'showers, warm beds, and hotcakes for breakfast if you surrender'. This provoked an obscene chorus in response. One soldier in a ditch, weeping violently, shouted: 'Go blow it out your ass, you German son of a bitch!'

The two regimental commanders decided to give up when their units were bombarded by German artillery from all sides. At 16.00 hours an officer went forward waving a snow cape. Officers and men were marched off with their hands on their heads, stumbling and tripping. Their guards later told them to put the contents of their pockets into their helmet liners so that they could pick out what they wanted. A large number found themselves herded into a farmyard surrounded by a stone wall. At dusk a voice called out: 'Do not flee. If you flee, you will be machine weaponed.' They could only cling together for warmth in the long, cold night.

Vonnegut called it 'the largest surrender of Americans under arms in American military history'. (In fact the surrender at Bataan in 1942 was much greater, but the capitulation of some 8,000 men in the 106th was certainly the biggest in Europe.) Vonnegut and a dozen others tried to find their way back to American lines through the snow-bound forest, but the Germans of the 18th Volksgrenadier-Division who were mopping up trapped them in the bed of a creek. Loudspeakers broadcast an order to surrender. To hurry them, the Germans fired tree bursts over their heads. Deciding that they had no alternative, the cornered Americans stripped their weapons and threw the working parts away. They emerged with their hands up, and thus began their imprisonment which, in Vonnegut's case, led to Dresden and the firestorm of February 1945, described in *Slaughterhouse Five*.

Officers at VIII Corps headquarters in Bastogne were horrified when they heard of the surrender. The deputy chief of staff 'inferred that the two surrounded regiments might have put up a stronger fight. He characterized a force of that size as "two wildcats in a bush" which might have done some clawing of the enemy instead of surrendering as they eventually did.'

The Germans could not believe how many men they had surrounded. One of their officers wrote in his diary: 'Endless columns of prisoners pass; at first, about a hundred, later, another thousand. Our vehicle gets stuck on the road. I get out and walk. Model himself directs traffic. (He's a little undistinguished looking man with a monocle.) The roads are littered with destroyed American vehicles, cars and tanks. Another column of prisoners pass. I count over a thousand men. In Andler there is a column of 1,500 men with about 50 officers and a lieutenant colonel who had asked to surrender.'

To Model's frustration, German traffic east of St Vith was hardly advancing. The 7th Armored Division's artillery kept up a steady bombardment on the approach roads. After the previous day's failure to take St Vith, the Germans tried probing and outflanking movements mainly against the 31st Tank Battalion. The 38th Armored Infantry Battalion was 'licking its wounds' after the mauling it had received, and platoons needed to be amalgamated because of their losses. But even so the Germans seemed to have come off worst.*

In the trees in front of them, the 38th Armored Infantry reported, 'the only Jerries we found were dead ones – most of them killed apparently as they tried to dig themselves in behind some tree or fallen log. Those who were not equipped with shovels had attempted to scoop shallow holes with their helmets, bayonets and even with their fingernails.' A firebreak, which had been covered by a heavy-machine-gun section on the right flank, was found to have 'nineteen paratroopers

---

* See map, The Destruction of the 106th Division, p. 119 above.

stretched out at almost parade-ground intervals, five yards apart, each one with at least five to eight slugs in his chest or throat'. According to Major Boyer, the 'paratroopers' were later found to have been wearing *Grossdeutschland* uniform and insignia 'under their jump jackets'. During another attack that afternoon, the 90mm guns of a tank-destroyer platoon managed to knock out a Mark V Panther tank and one of the two assault guns supporting the infantry.

The main threat to Brigadier General Hasbrouck's defence line lay in the north where the 18th Volksgrenadiers and the *Führer Begleit* Brigade were pushing round. But although the *Führer Begleit* saw itself as an elite formation, it also had its psychological casualties. Apparently one member of its staff, Rittmeister von Möllendorf, was 'hysterical and a nervous wreck. He cries whenever Hitler's name is mentioned.'

An even greater threat to Hasbrouck's rear came when the 9th SS Panzer-Division *Hohenstaufen* followed the same route a little further north, via Recht and Poteau, which the Kampfgruppe Hansen had taken earlier. In the fighting near Poteau, an SS runner received a stomach wound when an American shell exploded. As his comrades put him on a stretcher, with some of his intestines protruding, one of them made a move to take his steel helmet off, but he begged him to leave it on. At company headquarters an Unterscharführer tried to remove the helmet, but the man screamed his protest. By the time they reached the dressing station, he was barely conscious. A medic 'lifted the man's head up, undid the chin strap and took the helmet off. The top of the skull with the brain came off with it. The man must have realised that he had taken another piece of shrapnel right under the rim of his helmet. It had sheared through his skull. He lived until his helmet was removed.'

Hasbrouck knew that if the Germans diverted south and took Vielsalm and Salmchâteau some ten kilometres to the west of St Vith, then his forces would be cut off. But both the 9th SS Panzer and the 116th Panzer-Division twenty kilometres to the south-west were heading towards the Meuse either side of the St Vith breakwater. He knew he simply had to hold on there to block the 18th and 62nd Volksgrenadier-Divisions which, having now dealt with the two beleaguered American regiments in the Schnee Eifel, could concentrate all their strength against St Vith.

*

Verdun, in the words of one of Bradley's staff officers, was 'an ugly professional garrison town', with a population considered hostile by the Americans. 12th Army Group's rear headquarters was based 'within great loops of barbed wire, up and down which sentries walked'.

Eisenhower arrived with Air Chief Marshal Tedder in the Supreme Commander's armour-plated Cadillac. Patton appeared in his 'fabulous Jeep with plexiglass doors and thirty caliber machinegun mounted on a post'. Together with the two American army group commanders, Bradley and Devers, they trooped upstairs in the grey stone barracks followed by a bevy of staff officers. A single pot-bellied stove was the only source of heat in the long room, so few outer clothes were removed.

Resolved to set the right tone, Eisenhower opened proceedings. 'The present situation is to be regarded as one of opportunity for us and not of disaster,' he said. 'There will be only cheerful faces at this conference table.'

'Hell, let's have the guts to let the sons of bitches go all the way to Paris,' Patton called down the table. 'Then we'll really cut 'em off and chew 'em up.' This prompted nervous laughs. Patton's instinct to attack the enemy salient at the base found few supporters. Eisenhower was unamused. 'George, that's fine,' he said. 'But the enemy must never be allowed to cross the Meuse.'

Thanks to fresh Ultra intercepts, SHAEF by now had a much clearer picture of German ambitions in Operation *Herbstnebel*. Eisenhower was determined to rise to the challenge as a field commander, and not preside over the battle as a distant figurehead. This feeling may well have been strengthened by the suspicion that he had not imposed himself strongly enough over the past months.

Standing by the large map of the Ardennes hanging on the wall, staff officers briefed the assembled array of generals on the situation. Eisenhower then listed the divisions being brought over to France. Commanders could give ground if necessary, but there was to be no withdrawal behind the Meuse. General Devers's 6th Army Group in Alsace was to extend north to take over part of Patton's Third Army front. This was to free up Patton's divisions for a counter-attack from the south.

'When can you start?' Eisenhower asked, turning to Patton.

'As soon as you're through with me.'

Eisenhower wanted him to be more specific. Patton could not resist a display of bravado. 'On the morning of December 21st, with three divisions', he replied.* 'The 4th Armored, the 26th and the 80th.' Patton did not say that a combat command of the 4th Armored and a corps headquarters were already on the move, and the rest were starting to leave that morning. The idea that the bulk of an army could be turned around through ninety degrees to attack in a different direction within three days produced stunned disbelief around the table.

'Don't be fatuous, George,' Eisenhower said. 'If you try to go that early, you won't have all three divisions ready and you'll go piecemeal. You will start on the twenty-second and I want your initial blow to be a strong one!' Eisenhower was right to be concerned that an over-hasty attack would reduce the desired effect. But there can be little doubt that Third Army's energy and staff work produced one of the most rapid redeployments known in the history of warfare.

All through the meeting, Patton's superior General Bradley said very little. Already suffering from stress and hives, he was also a martyr to his sinuses. Bradley felt very much on the defensive since it had been his decision to leave the Ardennes weakly defended. He felt completely sidelined, for Eisenhower was taking all the decisions and giving orders to Patton over his head. Bradley had also isolated himself by refusing to move his headquarters from the city of Luxembourg on the grounds that this would frighten its inhabitants, but pride certainly played a large part in that decision. In any event, the result was that he remained cut off from Hodges's First Army headquarters near Liège by the German advance. Neither he nor any of his staff officers had visited an American headquarters since the offensive began. To make his mood even worse, Bradley clearly felt snubbed after the meeting when he invited Eisenhower to lunch. The Supreme Commander declined the offer, saying he would have a sandwich in the car on his way back to Versailles.

As Eisenhower was about to get into the staff car, he turned again to Patton. 'Every time I get a new star I get attacked,' he joked, referring

* In most accounts of the meeting, Patton apparently said the morning of 21 December, but in his own diary Patton puts 22 December. It is impossible to tell whether this was what he believed he said at the time, or whether he changed it because he recognized that Eisenhower was right.

also to his previous promotion just before Rommel's surprise offensive at Kasserine in Tunisia.

'And every time you get attacked, I pull you out,' Patton retorted, clearly feeling on top of the world. He then went to a telephone and called his own headquarters in Nancy to confirm the movement order for his divisions using a prearranged codeword. Patton returned, smoking a cigar, to talk to Bradley, who, according to his aide Chester Hansen, was 'fighting mad'.

'I don't want to commit any of your stuff [i.e. formations] unless I have to,' Bradley said to Patton. 'I want to save it for a damn good blow when we hit back and we're going to hit this bastard hard.' This suggests that Bradley still resented Eisenhower's decision that Patton should launch a rapid counter-attack. But when Bradley and his retinue drove back towards Luxembourg, they passed a convoy of Patton's III Corps already on the road. Third Army staff had not wasted a moment.

Eisenhower had been right to dismiss Patton's instinct to cut off the German offensive at its base. Although American forces in the Ardennes had doubled to nearly 190,000 men, they were still far too few for such an ambitious operation. The Third Army was to secure the southern shoulder and the city of Luxembourg, but its main priority was to advance north to Bastogne where the 101st Airborne and part of the 10th Armored Division were soon to be surrounded.

The situation in the whole area was chaotic. Colonel Herman of the 7th Tank Destroyer Group took over the defence of Libramont, southwest of Bastogne. Nobody there knew what was happening, so he stopped all stragglers and even an artillery column passing through the town. 'Where are you going?' he demanded.

'We're retreating, sir,' came the reply.

'The hell you are,' said Herman. 'This is where you turn around and fight.' By midnight on 19 December, Herman had collected a force of some 2,000 men, to which he added another leaderless artillery battalion the next morning.

Resistance still continued in Wiltz even though the road west to Bastogne had been cut by German patrols, thus blocking efforts to resupply the remnants of the 28th Division in the town with rations and ammunition. At 14.30 the 5th Fallschirmjäger-Division, blowing whistles and supported by forty tanks and self-propelled assault guns, attacked the town from several sides. By nightfall, the defenders had been pushed back to the centre of the town, amid burning buildings. General Cota sent a message to their commander: 'Give them hell!' That night survivors were ordered to break into small groups and head for Bastogne. A convoy of thirty vehicles tried to leave but ran into heavy fire and was abandoned. Having blown the bridges, the last engineer unit did not leave Wiltz until 11.00 the next day.

The trucks and trailers heading for Bastogne packed with paratroopers were directed to Mande-Saint-Etienne, half a dozen kilometres to the west, so as not to clog the town. Roads leading out of Bastogne were blocked by panic-stricken army drivers trying to escape. Even their officers had to be threatened with pistols to force them to move their vehicles aside to allow the 101st Airborne through. Paratroopers frozen from the long journey jumped down stiffly. Everybody realized the need for speed, with two panzer and one infantry division closing on Bastogne. Those who had to shoulder mortar tubes and their base-plates staggered along under the load like 'a hod-carrying Egyptian slave', in the words of Louis Simpson with the 327th Glider Infantry.

Unaware of the vital part played by the shattered 28th Division, the paratroopers of the 101st Airborne were disgusted by the bearded and filthy stragglers fleeing west through the town. They grabbed ammunition, grenades, entrenching tools and even weapons from them or from abandoned vehicles to make up for their own shortages. Belgian civilians, on the other hand, emerged from their houses with hot soup and coffee for the soldiers, and walked along beside them as they gulped it down.

The first regiment to arrive, Colonel Julian Ewell's 501st Parachute Infantry Regiment, marched east towards Longvilly in the pre-dawn darkness to support Team Cherry of the 10th Armored. The men could hear firing ahead through the damp, chill fog. Soon they encountered traumatized survivors from the destruction of Combat Command R the evening before, who told them: 'We have been wiped out.'

Colonel Cherry had reached the chateau just south of Neffe during the night of 18–19 December, but any hope of making it his command post was dashed at dawn. The reconnaissance platoon of the 3rd Tank Battalion and part of the 158th Engineer Combat Battalion holding the crossroads in Neffe were attacked by an advance detachment of the

Panzer Lehr. A bazooka team knocked out one Mark IV tank, but the weight of machine-gun fire and shellfire coming at the reconnaissance platoon was so great that they had to pull back along the road which ran up a valley to Bastogne.

Two men managed to warn Cherry in the chateau of what had happened. Another four tanks including a Mark VI Tiger, as well as an armoured car and another hundred panzergrenadiers, were sighted coming from the east. Cherry and his handful of headquarters personnel prepared to defend the chateau, a square solid building with a single tower. They dismounted the machine guns from their vehicles and set them up in the windows. For Cherry, it was terrible moment. His main force between Mageret and Longvilly had been cut off, and was blocked in a traffic jam with the remnants of the 9th Armored Division's Combat Command R. Cherry could only watch as the Germans prepared their trap.

At around 13.00 hours the noise of battle became audible. The 77th Grenadier-Regiment of the 26th Volksgrenadier-Division launched an immediate attack on the jammed column. Artillery and assault guns joined in as well as a company of tanks from the Panzer Lehr. 'The surprise was complete,' the rather professorial Generalmajor Kokott noted. The Americans were surrounded, and chaos ensued as vehicles collided with each other as they tried in vain to escape. The battle was over in an hour and a half. Only a few vehicles managed to escape towards the north. Several officers and a hundred men were captured.

As they approached Neffe, Colonel Ewell's 1st Battalion of the 501st Parachute Infantry could hear shooting clearly through the fog and drizzle. Ewell spread his men out on both sides of the road with the order to dig in. As they were preparing foxholes, tanks could be heard. Desperate cries for bazooka teams followed.

The 2nd Battalion, meanwhile, was moving to defend Bizôry, two kilometres to the north of Neffe. It too would be caught in a bitter battle, and was soon renamed 'Misery'. Morale among the German forces had been greatly boosted by the two highly successful engagements against American armoured columns, but they were about to receive a sharp disappointment. Later that afternoon the 26th Volksgrenadier reconnaissance battalion and the 78th Grenadier-Regiment found themselves involved in heavy fighting around both Mageret and Bizôry.

The attack on Bizôry produced 'painful losses'. Part of the Panzer Lehr Division was also heavily engaged at Neffe. The Americans had won the race to Bastogne, with their reinforcements.

Colonel Ewell established a defensive line along high ground less than three kilometres west of Bastogne's market square. 'The enemy had made good use of the time!' the commander of the 26th Volksgrenadiers acknowledged ruefully. And the Panzer Lehr was so desperate for fuel that it was reduced to draining the tanks of captured or knocked-out vehicles.

This 'day of surprises' made it clear to Bayerlein that the higher command idea of taking Bastogne off the march was now impossible. But the commander of the XLVII Panzer Corps, General der Panzertruppe Freiherr von Lüttwitz, blamed him for the failure to take Bastogne. Bayerlein retorted by blaming the 26th Volksgrenadier-Division, and Lüttwitz himself, who had slowed him down by committing the Panzer Lehr to battle east of the River Clerf contrary to the original plan. Bayerlein also said that Lüttwitz's leadership was 'not sufficiently coherent and energetic'. He had failed to concentrate the three divisions into a full-scale attack, and had allowed them to become 'scattered'.

That night the exhausted German troops dug in as the rain came on. 'Ammunition and rations were brought up,' recorded the commander of the 26th Volksgrenadiers. 'Now and then there was a nervous burst of machinegun fire or the thunder of mortar fire which lasted a couple of minutes and after a few salvos died down again.'

Eight kilometres north of Bastogne, the twenty-six-year-old Major William Desobry commanding the 20th Armored Infantry Battalion had spent an anxious night in Noville. The tall and athletic Desobry with his 400 men awaited the onslaught of what he would later discover to be the bulk of the 2nd Panzer-Division. At around 04.00 hours, Desobry's men noticed that no more stragglers were coming through. Soon afterwards, they heard the first shots. The outpost along the road to Bourcy, having opened fire, pulled back into the town as ordered. Its sergeant, who had been shot in the mouth, reported with difficulty that Germans had appeared in half-tracks.

Desobry could hear the distinctive noise of German armoured vehicles to the north. Although he knew that 'sounds at night are much louder and seem much nearer', this was clearly quite a force with tanks from the clanking noise of their tracks. 'Oh brother!' Desobry said to himself. 'There is really something out there.'

Heavy firing with automatic weapons and tank gunnery could be heard to the north-east. This came from the destruction of the third team from the 9th Armored Division's ill-fated Combat Command R. They had unfortunately withdrawn right into the path of the 2nd Panzer-Division. As at Longvilly the night before, German Panthers picked their targets with ease once the first vehicles were ablaze. Lieutenant Colonel Booth, the American commander, had a leg crushed under one of his own half-tracks as he tried to redeploy his trapped column. Survivors abandoned their armoured vehicles, and escaped across country towards Bastogne. Some 200 men were lost as well as all the Shermans and half-tracks.

The sergeant commanding Desobry's outpost on the northern route to Houffalize, however, felt that as he had seen some American tanks pulling back through their position earlier, they should check before opening fire. He gave his challenge in the darkness, and although he received an answer in English, he realized his mistake. A German tank opened fire, knocking out one of the Shermans. The remaining vehicles rapidly pulled back into Noville. Desobry immediately called in the third group to the north-west. Dawn brought little clarity to the situation because of a heavy ground fog, but soon the sound of German tanks could be heard coming down the northern road from Houffalize. The American defenders prepared their 57mm anti-tank gun and bazooka teams in a cemetery on the edge of Noville. As soon as the enemy vehicles emerged from the fog, they opened up with everything that they had against the Panther tanks and panzergrenadiers.

Two of the Panthers were disabled and provided a good roadblock. But just to make sure that German tank-recovery teams did not manage to sneak up, Desobry sent out a small group with explosives to blow their tracks and wreck their main armament. The ground everywhere was so waterlogged that the Germans would find it difficult to send their panzers round the knocked-out Panthers blocking the road. Desobry's small force was then strengthened by the arrival of five M-18 Hellcat tank destroyers from Bastogne. He kept them back as his reserve.

Later in the morning the fog began to lift, and to their horror the

Americans saw that the ridge to the north and north-east was covered in German panzers and half-tracks. The battle began in earnest. Many of the panzers got to within a hundred metres of the perimeter, and one even broke into the town before it was shot to a standstill. After an intense two-hour firefight, the Germans pulled back behind the ridge. Then the Germans tried probing attacks from different directions. They were not too difficult to fight off, but German mortar and artillery fire started to cause casualties.

Desobry ignored an order from Bastogne to send a patrol to Houffal-ize, because it would have had 'to go through the whole daggone German army to get there'. With Noville half surrounded by ridges, he suggested to his combat command headquarters back in Bastogne that it would be better if his force withdrew to defend the ridge between Noville and Foy. Colonel Roberts told him that it was his decision, but a battalion of the 101st Airborne was marching up the road from Bastogne to join him. Desobry sent a Jeep for the battalion's commander, Lieutenant Colonel James LaPrade, just before midday. LaPrade agreed entirely with Desobry's assessment that they had to take the ridgeline ahead if they were to hold Noville.

As with other battalions of the 101st Airborne, LaPrade's unit was short of weapons and ammunition. So the 10th Armored Division's service company loaded their trucks, drove up the road and threw the paratroopers what they needed: bandoliers of rifle ammunition, machine-gun belts, grenades, mortar and bazooka rounds and even spare weapons. As the parachute battalion reached Noville, Desobry called on the supporting artillery battalion to fire at the ridgeline. The paratroopers fanned out and went straight into the attack towards the ridge, with Desobry's Shermans firing in support. 'They spread out across the fields,' he wrote, 'and those guys when they attacked, did it on the dead run. They would run for 50 metres, hit the ground, get up and run.' But it turned out that the Germans had planned another attack at the same time, so the two sides 'were engaged in a head-on clash'. One company made it to the ridgeline, only to be counter-attacked by tanks and panzergrenadiers from beyond. All the companies were taking such heavy losses that LaPrade and Desobry agreed to pull everyone back into the village. The number of badly wounded men overwhelmed the tiny aid station set up in the village.

That night, Desobry and LaPrade conferred in their command post in Noville's school on what they could do to hold on to the village. General McAuliffe in Bastogne had asked General Middleton, who had been ordered to take his VIII Corps headquarters back to Neufchâteau, if he could pull back the force in Noville, but Middleton had refused. While Desobry and LaPrade were studying the map upstairs, the 10th Armored's maintenance officer, who was responsible for recovering damaged vehicles, drove up and parked right outside. This was contrary to all standard practice as it gave away the whereabouts of a command post. The Germans concentrated all their fire on the building. LaPrade and a dozen others were killed. Desobry, coated in dust, had a head wound, with one eye half out of the socket.

Desobry was evacuated in a Jeep. On the way back to Bastogne, they were stopped in Foy by a German patrol from the 26th Volksgrenadier-Division. The volksgrenadiers, seeing he was in a bad way, generously allowed the Jeep to continue. Desobry, despite his pain, was shaken to find that the Germans had cut the road behind his force at Noville. Just to the south of Foy, Easy Company of the 506th was digging in when they heard engines through the fog. A soldier said to Lieutenant Jack Foley, 'You know those sound like motorized vehicles.' 'Vehicles?' another soldier cried. 'Hell, they're tanks!' The fear was heightened because they could not see 'what was out there'. 'All you could do was hear.'

Desobry, in spite of his stroke of luck at being let through, was again to suffer the misfortunes of war. One of the most serious mistakes made in the defence of Bastogne was to leave the 326th Airborne Medical Company at a crossroads near Sprimont, a dozen kilometres north-west of the town. They had set up their tents and were already treating the first casualties to arrive as refugees continued to stream by. The company was so exposed that a surgeon went into Bastogne to ask General McAuliffe for permission to move into the town. 'Go on back, Captain,' McAuliffe said. 'You'll be all right.'

That night, as they were operating on badly burned men and other victims, a Kampfgruppe from the 2nd Panzer-Division attacked. Machine-gun fire ripped through the tents killing and wounding many of the men lying on stretchers. With no troops to defend them, the senior American officer had no option but to surrender immediately.

The Germans gave them forty-five minutes to load all the wounded, equipment and supplies on to their trucks.

Their German captors escorted them towards Houffalize. Desobry recovered consciousness on a halt in the journey and, on hearing German voices, thought that they must have taken many prisoners. He was cruelly disabused by his American driver. Desobry tried to persuade him to make a dash for it, but the driver was not prepared to take the risk. The bitter truth sank in. He was a prisoner of war.*

For the Germans of the 2nd Panzer-Division, it was a great coup to have captured so much equipment and medical supplies, especially morphine. For the 101st Airborne, it was a disaster. Their wounded were now condemned to suffer in fetid cellars and the garage of a barracks in Bastogne, where the short-staffed medics lacked morphine and other drugs. The conditions were primitive, with no latrine and a single electric light bulb in the main garage ward. The wounded were 'laid in rows on sawdust covered with blankets'. Those deemed unlikely to survive lay nearest the wall. 'As they died they were carried out to another building' used as a morgue.

Montgomery, at his tactical headquarters outside Zonhoven in Belgium, was deeply disturbed by the lack of information on the battles raging to his south. On the morning of 19 December he sent two of his young liaison officers, whom he used as old-fashioned 'gallopers', to report back on the state of the battle. They were accompanied by Lieutenant Colonel Tom Bigland, who was his link with Bradley. Driving through freezing fog in a Jeep, they headed for General Hodges's advance headquarters in Spa.

'We arrive at First Army HQ, located in an hotel,' Captain Carol Mather noted at the time, 'and find it abandoned. A hurried evacuation has evidently taken place. The tables in the dining room are laid for Christmas festivities. The offices are deserted.' The place felt like the *Marie Celeste*. 'The truth begins to dawn. The German attack is more

---

* Desobry encountered a number of paradoxes during his imprisonment, such as listening in a German hospital train near Münster to a recording of Bing Crosby singing 'White Christmas', while British bombers smashed the city. He was then held in a panzergrenadier training establishment in Hohne next to Belsen concentration camp, along with British paratroopers captured at Arnhem.

serious than we had thought, for the evacuation of the headquarters shows every sign of a panic move.' They collected some of the classified papers left lying around to prove that they had been there in case anyone disbelieved them later.

Montgomery did not wait for instructions from SHAEF. His staff officers began to issue detailed orders to the SAS and Phantom reconnaissance teams. Lieutenant General Brian Horrocks's XXX Corps received a warning order to move to defend the Meuse. Brigadier Roscoe Harvey, the commander of 29th Armoured Brigade, was summoned back from shooting woodcock. He expostulated that his brigade had not 'got any bloody tanks – they've all been handed in'. This was true. They were waiting to receive the new Comet, the first British tank produced in five years of war that would be a match for the Tiger and Panther. Harvey was told to take back his old Shermans, those that were still 'runners', and move with all speed to Dinant to block the very crossing points on the Meuse which Major General Erwin Rommel had seized in 1940.

Montgomery's gallopers meanwhile drove through 'oddly deserted countryside' to Hodges's rear headquarters at Chaudfontaine south-east of Liège, where they found him. 'He is considerably shaken,' Mather reported, 'and can give no coherent account of what has happened. Nor is he in touch with General Bradley's 12th Army Group. Communications seem to have completely broken down.' While Bigland set off on a circuitous route to Bradley's headquarters in Luxembourg, the two captains drove back to Zonhoven as quickly as the icy roads permitted.

Montgomery was 'clearly alarmed' when the two young officers recounted what they had seen. He told Mather to drive straight back to First Army headquarters. 'Tell Hodges he must block the Meuse bridges!' Mather asked how he was to transmit such orders when Hodges was not under 21st Army Group.

'Just tell him,' Montgomery said. 'The Liège crossings in particular must be defended at *all* costs. He *must* block the bridges by any means. Call up L[ine] of C[ommunications] troops. Use any obstacles he can find, including farm carts! He must hold the bridges all day tomorrow, and make sure that officers supervise each operation. You can tell him so from me!' Mather was also to inform Hodges that Phantom teams and SAS in Jeeps would be sent straight to the bridges. The British XXX

Corps would move with all speed to the north bank of the Meuse to block routes to Antwerp. Montgomery insisted that he must see Hodges the next morning. 'If possible bring him back here tonight!' Eisenhower, equally adamant about the Meuse crossings, had already given orders to General Lee's Com Z headquarters. It was to move any available engineer units to mine the bridges and send in scratch battalions of rear-area troops. The French also offered seven battalions, but they were poorly armed and trained.

Montgomery was already convinced, with a good deal of justification, that Bradley in Luxembourg could not direct First Army, which was cut off on the northern side of the German salient, or 'Bulge' as it was soon to be known. He told Major General Whiteley, the senior British operations officer at SHAEF, to tell Eisenhower that he should be put in command of all Allied forces north of the German salient. Whiteley, who was no admirer of the field marshal and his demands for increased powers, felt that this time he had a point. He discussed the situation with Major General Strong, Eisenhower's intelligence chief and a fellow Briton, and the two of them went that night to see Bedell Smith, the SHAEF chief of staff.

Bedell Smith, woken from his sleep, exploded at what he saw as a British plot. He called them 'Limey bastards' and told them that they should both consider themselves relieved of their duties. Then, after some reflection, he changed his mind. Bedell Smith was unimpressed by Hodges's First Army headquarters and its relationship with Bradley's 12th Army Group, but his real concern was that Bradley was out of touch. He rang Eisenhower to discuss giving Montgomery command of the northern front and suggested that this would also push the 21st Army Group into committing British forces to the battle.

Eisenhower agreed to the proposal, partly because Bradley had taken no steps to reinforce the line of the Meuse as he had ordered. He began to consult the map to decide where the boundary line should be drawn. He decided it would go from Givet on the Meuse, and run north of Bastogne to Prüm behind German lines. Montgomery would command all Allied forces to the north, thus leaving Bradley with just Patton's Third Army and Middleton's VIII Corps, which would be attached to it.

Bedell Smith rang Bradley in Luxembourg to warn him that Eisenhower thought of giving Montgomery command over the Ninth and

First Armies. According to Bedell Smith, Bradley admitted that he had been out of touch with Hodges and the First Army for two or three days. 'Certainly if Monty's were an American command,' Bradley acknowledged revealingly, 'I would agree with you entirely. It would be the logical thing to do.'

Next morning, Eisenhower rang Bradley to confirm his decision. Bradley had by now worked himself into a frenzy of outrage. 'By God, Ike, I cannot be responsible to the American people if you do this. I resign.'

'Brad, I – not you – am responsible to the American people,' Eisenhower replied. 'Your resignation therefore means absolutely nothing.' He then dealt with further complaints, and terminated the conversation by saying: 'Well Brad, those are my orders.'

A senior RAF officer present at 12th Army Group headquarters described how, after the call, an 'absolutely livid' Bradley 'walked up and down and cursed Monty'. Bedell Smith later found it ironic that 'Montgomery for a long time thought Bradley was very fond of him; he didn't know he couldn't stand him.' The dislike in fact went much deeper. Bradley saw Montgomery 'as the personal inspiration of all his troubles', an American staff officer remarked. 'He had long since acquired a distaste for the little man with the beret and the bark.' In his increasingly paranoid mood, a humiliated Bradley saw Eisenhower's decision 'as a slam to me'.

13

Wednesday 20 December

Captain Carol Mather left Montgomery's headquarters again at midnight, uneasy at his 'extremely delicate' mission to General Hodges. The journey, slowed by ice and roadblock guards checking for Skorzeny groups, took some two hours. From time to time V-1 missiles flew overhead through the night sky towards Liège. On arrival at First Army headquarters at Chaudfontaine, an MP took him straight to the bedroom of Hodges's authoritarian chief of staff, Major General Bill Kean. Many thought that Kean was the real army commander. Kean was in his pyjamas with a blanket round his shoulders telephoning.

Mather presented the handwritten letter from Montgomery. During a pause, Kean put his hand over the receiver and asked after Montgomery's chief of staff Major General Freddie de Guingand. They then went next door to wake Hodges. Mather described how the First Army commander sat up in bed also with a blanket round his shoulders to read Montgomery's letter. He felt that Hodges was 'completely out of touch' with events. He passed every question to Kean. 'On the important question of the Meuse crossings,' Mather recorded, 'General Hodges had nothing to say. He implied that it was of no great consequence and had been or would be looked after'.

Mather, suffering from loss of sleep, was back with Montgomery well before dawn. The field marshal sat up in bed sipping a cup of tea as he listened to Mather's report. He intended to meet Hodges later that day, but first he wanted an accurate picture of the German breakthrough. Five liaison officers, including two Americans attached to his headquarters, set off in Jeeps immediately. They wore the newly issued tank suits in pale-brown canvas to ward off the cold, but these increased the suspicions of nervous American soldiers manning roadblocks.

On that morning of 20 December, Montgomery took a call from Eisenhower. According to General Miles Dempsey, the commander of the Second British Army, who was with Montgomery when Eisenhower rang, the extraordinarily brief conversation went as follows:

'Monty, we are in a bit of a spot.'

'So I gathered,' the field marshal replied.

'How about taking over in the north?'

'Right.'

Montgomery drove to Chaudfontaine intending to sort out the situation. Mather's report had convinced him that Hodges was in a state of near collapse. In the memorable description of one of his own staff officers, the field marshal arrived at First Army headquarters 'like Christ come to clean the temple', even if Our Lord would not have appeared in a dark-green Rolls-Royce with pennants flying and motorcycle outriders.

Mather, although the most loyal of aides, felt that Montgomery put American backs up unnecessarily on his arrival by ignoring the American generals and summoning his liaison officers who had arrived with their reports of the fighting. 'What's the form?' he demanded, and they crowded round the bonnet of a Jeep with their maps. General Hodges and General Simpson, the commander of the Ninth Army, could only look on in embarrassment. 'It was a slight uncalled for on that day,' Mather wrote.

Montgomery had now taken command of all Allied armies north of that line from Givet on the Meuse to Prüm. He was also deeply concerned about Hodges. On his return, he telephoned Bedell Smith to say that as a British officer he was unwilling to relieve an American general, but that Eisenhower should consider it.* Bedell Smith asked for a twenty-four-hour delay. Montgomery sent a message the next day that things could stay as they were, even though Hodges was hardly the man

---

* There are several accounts of Hodges's collapse at this time. One comes in his aide's diary three days later. 'The General is now well located in a private home. With a chance for rest, and with good food again provided, he is obviously feeling fitter and better able to cope with the constant pressure of this work and strain.'

he would have picked. This was a view shared by Bedell Smith, who considered Hodges 'the weakest commander we had'.

Bradley later claimed that Montgomery and SHAEF had grossly exaggerated the danger for their own ends, to deprive him of the First Army. But the situation appeared desperate. Hodges was close to breaking down, and Kean had taken over. Even Kean said the following day that they would not know until Friday 'whether we can hold or will have to withdraw to a defense line such as the Meuse'.

Bradley clearly regretted having chosen the city of Luxembourg for his Eagle Tac headquarters and now felt trapped. It was not just a question of prestige, as he had said to Hansen. If he pulled out, the Luxembourgers would believe they were being abandoned to German vengeance. And even though Bradley tried to downplay the threat of the enemy offensive, his own staff officers took it very seriously. 'We sandwiched the thermite grenades in amongst the most secret of our papers,' one them wrote, 'to be ready to destroy them if we saw any grey uniforms across the hills.' But unbeknown to all of them, Generaloberst Jodl had persuaded Hitler not to include the city of Luxembourg as an objective in Operation *Herbstnebel*.

The capital of Luxembourg had in any case been ably defended by the 4th Infantry Division, holding the southern shoulder of the breakthrough. Its commander Major General Barton declared stoutly, if not very originally, during the battle: 'The best way to handle these Heinies is to fight 'em.' Barton had refused to allow his artillery battalions to move back. Their task was to maintain fire on the bridges over the Sauer, and he made sure that they were well defended by infantry. This prevented the Germans from bringing forward their heavy weapons, especially anti-tank guns. They were therefore unable to fight back effectively against the 10th Armored Division, which was arriving to support the 4th Division.

Like General Cota of the 28th Division, Barton used reinforced companies to hold key villages and thus block crossroads. Along with the 9th Armored Division on his immediate left, Colonel Luckett's task force was pushed back up the Schwarz Erntz gorge, but held fast at the village of Müllerthal to thwart the Germans as they attempted to break into the rear areas of the division.

20. American prisoners taken by the 1st SS Panzer-Division *Leibstandarte Adolf Hitler*.

21. 17 December. Part of the 26th Infantry Regiment (1st Infantry Division) arrives just in time to defend Bütgenbach at the base of the Elsenborn ridge.

22. Members of the same regiment manoeuvring an anti-tank gun in the mud as the Germans approach.

23. Belgian refugees leaving Langlir (south-west of Vielsalm) as the Fifth Panzer Army advances. Most wanted to cross the Meuse to escape the fighting and German reprisals for Resistance activities earlier in the year.

24. As the Germans advanced on the town of St Vith following the encirclement of the 106th Infantry Division, the people of Schönberg fled the fighting to shelter in caves.

25. American medics turned skis into improvised toboggans to drag the wounded on stretchers back to a point where they could be loaded on to Jeeps.

26. With a comrade already dead in the foreground, American troops dig in hastily on the forward edge of a wood to avoid the effect of tree bursts.

27. As the Germans advance on Bastogne and the first members of the 101st Airborne arrive to defend it, townsfolk start to flee in farm carts.

28. A platoon of M-36 tank destroyers emerge from the mist near Werbomont in support of the 82nd Airborne Division also rushed in by huge convoys of trucks.

29. German Volksgrenadiers taken prisoner in the fighting round the twin villages of Rocherath–Krinkelt.

30. Brigadier General Robert W. Hasbrouck, who commanded the 7th Armored Division and the defence of St Vith, receiving the silver star from Lieutenant General Courtney Hodges of the First Army.

31. In the wake of the scare caused by Otto Skorzeny's disguised commandos behind American lines, US military police check the identities of Belgian refugees near Marche-en-Famenne.

32. Dinant. Belgian refugees rush to cross the Meuse to safety to avoid German reprisals and the fighting.

In Berdorf, halfway down the east side of the gorge, a small mixed force of 250 men from the 10th Armored and two companies of the 4th Infantry had held on for three days. A heavy attack left them with little ammunition and many wounded in need of evacuation. Three assaults, supported by Nebelwerfer rockets and artillery, were beaten off. But just as the small force feared that they would not be able to hold back another attack, a group of two Shermans and three half-tracks broke through to the town with ammunition and supplies, and then left with the severely wounded. Later, the tank commander in Berdorf, Captain Steve Lang of the 11th Tank Battalion, received orders to withdraw. Each tank carried fifteen infantrymen, 'four inside and eleven clinging for life on the outside'. An artillery barrage was laid on to cover the noise of the tanks moving, and the small force managed to escape before the Germans discovered what was happening.

German attacks along that sector of the front began to weaken on 20 December, and the arrival of more units from General Patton's III Corps meant that the 212th and 276th Volksgrenadier-Divisions made no further advance to the south. Only thick fog prevented the Americans from counter-attacking. The stalwart defence of the southern shoulder meant that the Germans lacked room for manoeuvre, and that the Third Army could concentrate its forces against the encirclement of Bastogne.

Hemingway, eager not to miss the big battle even though he was suffering from influenza, managed to reach Colonel Buck Lanham's command post near Rodenbourg. The house had belonged to a priest suspected of being a German sympathizer. Hemingway took great delight in drinking a stock of communion wine and then refilling the bottles with his own urine. He claimed to have relabelled them 'Schloss Hemingstein 1944' and later drank from one by mistake.

The Germans had already found that their salient was too narrow and that Bastogne controlled the road network. Both Bayerlein of the Panzer Lehr and Kokott of the 26th Volksgrenadier-Division argued that since a swift attempt to take Bastogne had failed, then its defenders must be crushed by the whole corps. But General von Lüttwitz, the commander of XLVII Panzer Corps, was under strict instructions to send his two panzer divisions past Bastogne and straight on to the Meuse.

The German drive to the Meuse was also not helped when the 116th

Panzer-Division was ordered to change direction to the north-west. This 'caused a considerable waste of time', wrote its commander Generalmajor Siegfried von Waldenburg, and led to chaos on the overcrowded roads. This decision, he maintained, 'became fatal for the Division'.

The mixed force of paratroopers and 10th Armored in Noville, north of Bastogne, were attacked again and again in rushes by panzers and panzergrenadiers emerging out of the fog. They knew that the road behind them had been cut by another German unit, but not that the battalion of the 506th Parachute Infantry Regiment had been pushed back south of Foy. This would make their escape far more difficult. In the middle of the morning, the fog lifted, and the tanks of the 2nd Panzer-Division opened fire from the high ground. When radio contact was finally re-established with the beleaguered force in Noville, General McAuliffe told them to prepare to break out. He had decided that despite his orders from General Middleton not to pull them back, he must either rescue or lose them. He told Colonel Sink to launch a renewed assault on Foy to open the road, with his paratroopers of the 506th. German tanks were firing tree bursts in the woods just south of Foy to keep the paratroopers' heads down. Easy Company of the 506th had no anti-tank weapons, but fortunately the Germans never put in a proper armoured attack against them.

By a stroke of luck the fog rolled in again, just as the defenders of Noville were about to withdraw. The infantry left on foot, the wounded and the body of Lieutenant Colonel LaPrade were loaded on half-tracks, the Shermans carried as many men as possible, and the Hellcat tank destroyers acted as rearguard. Demolitions set in the church made the tower collapse across the road as planned. But, as they reached Foy, the armoured visor on the lead half-track came down, obscuring the driver's vision. He brought it to an abrupt halt, and all the following half-tracks rammed into one another: this gave three German panzers, out to the flank, stationary targets to fire at. The leading vehicles caught fire. A soldier further back in the column noted that 'the fog up front turned bright orange'. Crews baled out, and the same soldier watched from the ditch as German fire poured into the column. 'Dead were lying all around on the road and in the ditches. Some were hanging out of their vehicles; killed before they could get out and seek cover. Our trucks and half-tracks were either burning or had been torn to shreds.'

Chaos was finally averted when a Sherman, with paratroopers manning the gun, managed to knock out one of the tanks, and the other two pulled back rapidly. The force with which Desobry and LaPrade had held Noville had lost 212 men and eleven out of fifteen Shermans in less than two days.

General Troy Middleton's determination to maintain an extended perimeter had proved costly, but the sudden withdrawal from Noville seemed to encourage Lüttwitz in the belief that the capture of Bastogne would be straightforward. Generalmajor Kokott claimed that when Lüttwitz visited the headquarters of the 26th Volksgrenadier-Division at Wardin that morning, he said: 'The 2nd Panzer-Division has taken Noville. The enemy is in flight-like retreat to the south. 2nd Panzer-Division is in steady pursuit. The fall of Foy – if it has not already taken place – is to be expected at any moment. After taking Foy, the 2nd Panzer-Division will, according to its orders, turn west and drive into open country.' Lüttwitz, a large, smoothly shaved panzer general with a well-fed face and a monocle, also convinced himself that the Panzer Lehr Division had taken Marvie on the south-eastern edge of Bastogne. Lüttwitz strenuously asserted later that he had urged Fifth Panzer Army to capture Bastogne first, and Bayerlein believed his version.*

Kokott argued that the decision to send on the 2nd Panzer was the major mistake in the failure to take Bastogne. He blamed a lack of clear thinking at Fifth Panzer Army and XLVII Corps level. 'Is Bastogne to be captured? Or is Bastogne to be merely encircled and the Maas River reached?' Only with 2nd Panzer attacking from the north and west, and Panzer Lehr and the bulk of the 26th attacking from the south-west, could they sort out this 'Eiterbeule' or pus-filled boil. But in fact even Manteuffel himself had little say in the matter. Führer headquarters would brook no alteration to the plan.

Orders for the next day were categoric. The 2nd Panzer and Panzer Lehr were to push on westwards with the bulk of their force, leaving the

---

* Bayerlein claims that on 19 December, after the first attack failed, he had convinced Lüttwitz that the whole corps should be concentrated against Bastogne, because they could not afford to leave such a centre of road communications untaken in their rear. Lüttwitz is said to have referred the proposal upwards, but it was firmly rejected. Bayerlein heard from him that they 'considered Bastogne child's play'.

26th Volksgrenadier plus a panzergrenadier regiment from Panzer Lehr to encircle and capture Bastogne all on their own. 'The Division dutifully expressed its doubts,' wrote Kokott, but Lüttwitz dismissed them, apparently on the grounds that American forces in Bastogne could not be very strong, with 'parts of an Airborne division' and 'the remnants of those enemy divisions which had been badly battered at the Our River and which had taken refuge in Bastogne'. Corps headquarters apparently also believed that 'on the basis of prisoner of war interviews, the fighting quality of the forces inside Bastogne was not very high'.

The 26th Volksgrenadier, having expressed its need for artillery support in the attack ordered on Bastogne, was at least given time to deploy its 39th Regiment which had been guarding the southern flank, while most of the 5th Fallschirmjäger-Division was delayed in the Wiltz valley. Kokott was bemused by Lüttwitz's optimism. His two regiments confronting the Americans in the Foy–Bizôry sector had not detected any weakness. The rest of his division was then sent round to the south of Bastogne towards Lutrebois and Assenois, to attack the town from the south. But through gaps in the mist he spotted American vehicles rushing south from Neffe to Marvie. To the north, 'the deep rumble of artillery could be heard – in the wooded areas west of Wardin, in addition to the crashing impact of the mortars, the fire of rapid German and slower American machineguns was audible'. Roads and forest tracks had been blocked by craters, so the soldiers had to take their heavy weapons off the vehicles and manhandle them.

At about 13.00 hours, American artillery observers sighted the concentration of vehicles round the divisional headquarters of the 26th Volksgrenadiers in Wardin. Battalion salvoes crashed into the village 'with devastating effects on this assembly of men and machines', Kokott reported. That afternoon he heard that his reconnaissance battalion, when crossing the southern road to Arlon, had come into contact with the enemy. Matters were not helped by the chaos on roads and tracks south of Bastogne, with vehicles from the Panzer Lehr, the 26th Volksgrenadier and now an advance unit of the 5th Fallschirmjäger all trying to push on to the west but getting hopelessly entangled. Youngsters of the 5th Fallschirmjäger had to pull their own few vehicles when they broke down.

One of Kokott's Volksgrenadier battalions managed to break in from the north-east along a railway track, which was guarded by little more than a strong patrol because it was on the boundary between the 506th and the 501st Parachute Infantry Regiments. The patrol's resistance slowed the Volksgrenadier advance. Both Colonel Sink south of Foy and Colonel Ewell reacted quickly, sending a company each to block the penetration. Soon they found that the enemy force was larger than they had realized, and more units had to be hurried in, including, to their own disbelief, those who had escaped that day from Noville. The battle carried on well into the next day.

Another attack on the Neffe sector that evening by the Panzer Lehr was hit by a rapid response of concentrated artillery fire. McAuliffe could now count on eleven artillery battalions, several from the 101st, but also others from divisions which had withdrawn via Bastogne, including two battalions of African-American gunners. This gave him a total of around 130 pieces, but ammunition shortages would soon become a problem. Hellcats from the 705th Tank Destroyer Battalion firing tracer from their machine guns, as well as every automatic weapon in Ewell's 1st Battalion, caught the two battalions of panzergrenadiers in the open, exposed in the dark by the deathly glow of illuminating flares. They had been slowed down in this night attack by barbed-wire cattle fences. The carnage was sickening. Daylight next morning revealed a hideous sight of corpses caught on the wire like scarecrows battered by a freak storm.

General Middleton in his VIII Corps headquarters at Neufchâteau, some thirty kilometres south-west of Bastogne, was impatient for Patton's counter-attack from the south to begin. The 4th Armored Division Combat Command B had reached Vaux-les-Rosières halfway between the two towns. To the irritation of the commander of III Corps, Middleton's headquarters ordered it to send a combat team north immediately, rather than wait for the major attack which Patton had promised. Patton too was furious, and ordered the combat team to be recalled. Whether or not such a small force could have secured the road is open to question, but some historians believe that it would have made the advance from the south much less expensive in lives and tanks. In any case, the town of Bastogne was cut off from the south that evening, shortly after General McAuliffe had driven back from a meeting with

Middleton. The town was not entirely surrounded, but most people assumed it was.

For the paratroopers of the 101st, encirclement by the enemy was seen as part of the job. Louis Simpson, the poet and company runner, was sent back on an errand to battalion headquarters. On the way he came across a Sherman tank, with a sergeant from the 10th Armoured Division 'seated negligently in the turret, as if on the saddle of a horse'. Fifty metres down the road, a panzer burned. He asked the sergeant what had happened. 'They tried to get through,' the sergeant replied in a bored voice and turned away. Simpson pondered the fact that this was behind his own company's line. They would have been cut off if the 'appallingly casual' sergeant had not fired first. 'I saw Tolstoy's sergeant at Borodino, with his pipe stuck in his mouth, directing the fire of his battery. On men like this the hinge of battle swung. They did not see themselves in a dramatic role. They would do great tasks, and be abused for not doing them right, and accept this as normal.'

At battalion headquarters he heard that they were now surrounded within the Bastogne perimeter. When he returned to his foxhole in the snow, his neighbour called across: 'Welcome home! So what's new?'

'We're surrounded.'

'So what's new?'

First Army and Montgomery's headquarters lacked a clear idea of the situation round St Vith. Montgomery's instinct was to pull back Has-brouck's forces there before they were crushed, but the US Army had a proud dislike of abandoning ground. First Army wanted to send the 82nd Airborne forward to reinforce the defenders. At midday on 20 December, while they were discussing the problem, a letter reached Major General Bill Kean from Hasbrouck in St Vith outlining their embattled state. His horseshoe line extended from Poteau to the north-west of St Vith, down and round to Gouvy station to the south-west. His southern flank and rear were now totally exposed following the advance of the 116th Panzer-Division towards Houffalize.

Montgomery was convinced that the defence of St Vith had served its purpose well. The threat now lay further to the west, with three panzer divisions heading for the Meuse. He agreed, however, that the 82nd Airborne should continue its advance to the River Salm, but only to help extricate Hasbrouck's forces through the gap between Vielsalm and Salmchâteau.

In the afternoon the division's 504th Parachute Infantry Regiment advanced towards Cheneux, which was held by the light flak battalion of the SS *Leibstandarte* and a battalion of its panzergrenadiers. Colonel Reuben H. Tucker, the regimental commander, sent two companies into the attack through the mist. Coming under heavy machine-gun and 20mm-flak fire, they went to ground, suffering many casualties. When darkness fell, they pulled back to the woods behind. On hearing of this, Tucker ordered them to attack again. They managed to get closer in the dark, but barbed-wire fences across the fields held them up. Exposed to an even greater concentration of fire, men torn on the fences were shot down on all sides. The attack was about to stall when Staff Sergeant George Walsh yelled, 'Let's get those sons of bitches!' Only a handful of men made it to the roadblock on the edge of the village. One managed to throw a grenade into a flak half-track and a second cut the throat of a gunner on another. But the two companies suffered 232 casualties, including twenty-three killed. Their action was heroic, but Tucker's gung-ho decision was shockingly wasteful. The next day, Tucker sent another battalion around the flank, which is what he should have done the first time. With comparatively few losses, the 3rd Battalion took the village, along with fourteen flak wagons, another six half-tracks and a battery of self-propelled guns.

On 20 December the fighting round St Vith approached a climax as Model and Manteuffel became desperate to seize the town in an all-out assault. The Germans used their Nebelwerfer rocket launchers, targeting American mortar pits, whose crews were causing savage losses to the ranks of the Volksgrenadier battalions. Under heavy shellfire, many soldiers, bunched into a foetal position in the bottom of their foxholes, would keep repeating the 23rd Psalm, as a mantra to calm themselves 'in the valley of the shadow of death'.

Visibility was 'still very bad', Hasbrouck reported. 'Twenty-one enemy attacks were launched from north, east and south. Tanks were coming in from all directions accompanied by infantry.' The five American field artillery battalions fired almost 7,000 rounds on that day alone. 'The only way ammunition supply had been kept up was by hunting for and finding abandoned dumps toward the front . . . The 434th Field Artillery Battalion was reported to have fired even some old propaganda shells [used for leaflets] just to keep projectiles whistling around German ears.'

One attack was led by SS panzergrenadiers from the *Leibstandarte Adolf Hitler*, using a captured American half-track at the front of the column in the hope of confusing the defenders. But Shermans and bazooka teams managed to deal with them. 'We stressed to every man', wrote Major Boyer of the 38th Armored Infantry Battalion, 'that "no ammunition could be wasted – that for every round fired, a corpse must hit the ground," and that fire should be held until Germans were within 25 yards,' when fighting in the woods around the town. This order was also to discourage men from revealing their positions by firing too early.

Oberst Otto Remer's *Führer Begleit* Brigade finally did what it had been told, and began a probing attack on St Vith down the road from Büllingen. But Remer considered American resistance to be 'too heavy' and moved his brigade north and into thick woods below Born. He decided that he would take the main road west towards Vielsalm, but was then rather affronted when told to move back to the south. He claimed that he did not have enough fuel for his tanks, but the objective he had been given – the twin villages of Nieder-Emmels and Ober-Emmels – were little more than five kilometres away.

That evening after firing had died away, Hasbrouck's men could hear the sound of tanks. They knew that the Germans were almost certainly preparing an even greater onslaught for dawn the next morning.

With his Kampfgruppe under attack from all directions, Peiper brought back his outlying group from west of Stoumont. They then abandoned the town and pulled back to counter-attack the 117th Infantry from the 30th Division. Peiper had been bitter about the lack of support from his own division. He claimed later that he had been told that unless he reported on the state of his fuel supplies, he would not receive any more. Radio contact had been non-existent until the night before when an officer from the *Leibstandarte* had managed to get through, with a new and more powerful radio. Peiper learned that the division had sent forward the 2nd SS Panzergrenadier-Regiment to open a route. These troops had bridging equipment and before dawn they waded 'neck-deep' into the fast-flowing and freezing River Amblève supported by machine-gun and tank fire. But, by the light of illuminating flares fired overhead, American soldiers crouching at windows in houses which overlooked the river began to pick off the SS pioneers and panzergrenadiers. 'Them bastards was hopped up,' one of them said later. Three times the Americans were driven out of their positions in the houses by the river, 'forced out by direct fire from tanks, and three times the infantry came back and drove out the SS men'.

Peiper's panzergrenadiers had continued their casual killing of civilians. They had murdered two women and a man 'in a nearby street for no apparent reason', and later they put nine men against the walls of houses and killed them too. An SS trooper in an armoured vehicle 'emptied his machine gun into a house', killing a fourteen-year-old boy. The killing spree continued, but some bodies were not found until several days later. Belgian civilians were killed on the road towards Trois-Ponts: five were found shot in the head, while a woman was killed lying in bed. On the evening of 19 December, twenty townsfolk, mainly women and children, were forced out of a basement at gunpoint and shot by a hedge. Altogether more than 130 civilians, mostly women and children, were murdered in and around Stavelot. The young men had fled beyond the Meuse to avoid retribution for Resistance attacks in September, or to escape being marched off for forced labour in Germany. Waffen-SS claims that their killings were reprisals for partisans shooting at them had no basis in truth.

At 11.15 hours Peiper's troops again tried to establish a bridgehead over the river, with panzergrenadiers swimming and wading across. Rapid rifle and machine-gun fire killed many of them in the water and bodies were washed downstream. Only a few made it to the northern bank and they too were soon dealt with. A simultaneous attack was mounted from the west, forcing back the 1st Battalion of the 117th Infantry a hundred metres or so, where they held on until the firing petered out at dusk around 16.00 hours.

Peiper's difficulties had increased from another direction. Combat Command B of the 3rd Armored Division reached the Amblève valley that morning, coming from Spa via woodland tracks. One task force, commanded by Lieutenant Colonel William B. Lovelady, emerged from the trees on to the road between La Gleize and Trois-Ponts, and there surprised and destroyed a column of German trucks carrying fuel escorted by assault guns and infantry.

The desperate position of the Kampfgruppe Peiper was not due solely to the courageous resistance shown by the 30th Infantry Division, tank battalions and engineer units. The powerful defence of the Elsenborn ridge to the east had prevented the rest of the 1st SS Panzer-Division and the 12th SS *Hitler Jugend* from reinforcing Peiper's advance. II SS Panzer Corps, with the 9th SS Panzer-Division *Hohenstaufen*, had started to advance parallel with I SS Panzer Corps. The 2nd SS Panzer-Division *Das Reich* was supposedly following, but the single-track roads were so jammed with traffic that it had sought a route further south.

The Sixth Panzer Army blamed these failures on the fact that the only road was 'for the most part impassable because of the mire'. In many places, the mud was axle-deep, but in fact it was the American 1st Division's resolute defence of Bütgenbach which prevented the I SS Panzer Corps from using the much better road to the north. As a result, the 12th SS Panzer and the 12th Volksgrenadier-Division were kept battering away at the southern flank of the Elsenborn ridge, while the 3rd Panzergrenadier-Division and the 277th Volksgrenadiers attacked the eastern end above the twin villages of Rocherath–Krinkelt and Wirtzfeld. The 2nd Infantry Division continued to find that 'under almost continuous, heavy enemy artillery fire, wire lines went out nearly as soon as they were laid or repaired and communication was primarily by radio'.

Camp Elsenborn was a typical army post with officer apartments near the main gate, surrounded by single-storey barracks, garages and armouries. It stood in the middle of hilly, barren, windswept firing ranges. The barracks teemed with exhausted, dirty and bearded stragglers who were fed, rested briefly and then sent back into the line. Doctors and medics provided first aid to the wounded before evacuating them further back, now that the 47th Field Hospital in Waimes had been relocated just in time. Men discovered buddies they thought had been killed, and asked after others who were missing. Stories circulated of SS troopers killing wounded and executing prisoners and, coming on top of the news of the massacre at Baugnez, the determination to resist at all costs increased. Refugees packed the village of Elsenborn, and

American troops became deeply suspicious of them, seeing them as potential German sympathizers. But until they were evacuated on Christmas Day, their fate under German artillery fire was little better than if they had stayed in their farms and houses below.

On the eastern side of the Elsenborn ridge, the 2nd Infantry Division and the remnants of the 99th found digging in on the shale hillside very hard, so they filled wooden ammunition boxes with dirt, and covered their foxholes with doors ripped out of the barracks. Short of stretchers, they scrounged several from Camp Elsenborn, although they were still sticky with blood and smelled bad when warm. On the exposed hillside, they shivered in uniforms damp from the mud and wet snow, so they made makeshift heaters for their foxholes, either using some gasoline-soaked earth in a tin, or burning bits of wood in a jerrycan with a large hole cut out at the bottom as a fire-door. These inventions concealed the flames from observation, but the foxhole-dweller's unshaven face soon became impregnated with a black, oily grime. Many tried to create a warm fug in their foxhole by covering it and their stove with a water-proof cape, causing a few to asphyxiate themselves in the process. Almost everyone suffered from thudding headaches, brought on by the barrages fired over their heads by the field artillery just behind. The fact that the rounds were coming from their own guns did not stop men who had been under heavy enemy fire over the last few days from flinching at the noise.

They again faced the 3rd Panzergrenadiers, which consisted of little more than a large Kampfgruppe in its total strength, and the 277th Volksgrenadiers, worn down by the earlier battles. These two formations attacked north of Rocherath–Krinkelt past a crossroads the Germans named 'Sherman Ecke', or Sherman Corner, because of some knocked-out Sherman tanks with drooping barrels. But, as they mounted the little valley of the Schwalm, they were crushed by the weight of American artillery fire. 'The concentrated enemy artillery fire from the Elsenborn area was so strong', wrote the commander of the panzergrenadiers, 'that all roads leading to the front and all assembly areas were covered, and all our attacks brought to a standstill.'

The Elsenborn ridge provided the Americans with perfect fire positions for their sixteen field artillery battalions with 155mm Long Toms and 105mm howitzers, and seven battalions of corps artillery, including

4.5-inch and 8-inch guns. The longer-range artillery batteries were able to hammer villages and crossroads up to sixteen kilometres into the German rear. The unfortunate Belgian civilians trapped there could only sob and say their prayers in cellars, as their houses shook from the bombardment. 'Farmers learned to take care of cattle during the briefest of morning lulls that were soon known as the Americans' *Kaffeepause*.' It was impossible to bury the dead while the battle raged. Most were laid out in the local church wrapped in blankets. When the temperature dropped suddenly two days before Christmas, nobody could dig graves in the frozen ground.

During the night of 20–21 December, the Germans launched their largest attack on the southern flank against the 26th Infantry Regiment of the 1st Infantry Division around Dom Bütgenbach. Supported by more than thirty tanks and assault guns, two battalions of SS *Hitler Jugend* were sent into battle. A Belgian farmer had watched as twenty exhausted German youngsters, from fifteen to seventeen years old, were dragged weeping from his cellar in Büllingen by NCOs to force them into battle.

A total of twelve American artillery battalions and a battalion of 4.2-inch mortars placed 'a ring of steel' around the 1st Division's defensive positions. Yet a group of the *Hitler Jugend* panzers broke through on the 26th Infantry's right flank and began to 'iron' the foxholes of the forward defence line, running over them and firing into them. Arthur S. Couch was operating a 60mm mortar near battalion headquarters. 'Soon I noticed that tank shells were coming right over my head, along with tracer machine gun bullets. It was a foggy night so at first I couldn't see the German tanks, but as dawn started I could see a number of German tanks maneuvering around about 200 yards in front of my position. I soon ran out of mortar shells so I asked by radio for some more from battalion headquarters in a manor house about 400 yards to my left. To my welcome surprise, two men from battalion came running with large numbers of new shells in a cart. The German tanks seemed to know we had a mortar position but they couldn't see it in the foggy conditions. Another phone call said one of my mortar shells had landed in a German tank and blown it up. After a few more minutes I could see that a German tank was going along our front line and firing directly into the foxholes. I kept firing because I was very concerned that German infantry troops would soon be able to advance the 200 yards towards my position if I didn't stop them. I got word on my phone that German tanks were in the battalion headquarters.'

Several of these panzers were knocked out by anti-tank guns and Shermans, but only the arrival of a platoon of tank destroyers with the high-velocity 90mm gun managed to smash the attack. The losses inflicted on the *Hitler Jugend* were devastating. A Graves Registration unit counted 782 German dead. The 26th Infantry suffered 250 casualties.

More assaults on the ridge were mounted, but it became clear to both Rundstedt and Model that Hitler's beloved Sixth Panzer Army had utterly failed in its task, both around Monschau in the north, which was now reinforced with the 9th Infantry Division, and above all in front of Elsenborn. Its commander Sepp Dietrich was both angry and resentful, feeling that he was not to blame for the Führer's disappointment.

When the Ardennes offensive started, several British officers at 21st Army Group were teased by Belgian friends, who said that their Resistance groups were making preparations to hide them. When they replied that that would not be necessary as everything was well in hand, they received the answer: 'That is precisely what you said in 1940, and you left us next day.' Montgomery had no intention of allowing anything of the sort to happen again.

At 17.30 hours on 19 December, the day before Eisenhower gave him command in the north, Montgomery had ordered Lieutenant General Brian Horrocks's XXX Corps to secure the Meuse crossings. The 61st Reconnaissance Regiment in Bruges 'bombed-up, tanked up, loaded up and drove into the night'. Reinforced with an anti-tank troop, one squadron also headed to the bridge at Dinant. As well as watching for 'Germans masquerading as Yanks', they were to guard against enemy frogmen. Any flotsam in the river was blasted with Bren-gun fire. The 3rd Royal Tank Regiment, also at Dinant, worked with American MPs checking traffic and 'a small but steady trickle of American stragglers', as the bridges were prepared for demolition.

SAS and Phantom reconnaissance teams were already in position. On de Gaulle's orders, they were followed by the seven badly armed French battalions under Général de Division André Dody, and also by some scratch units from General Lee's Com Z supply troops. General

Bedell Smith was greatly relieved by the commitment of XXX Corps. He said later that 'I felt that we were all right if [the Germans] went north because if they angled towards Liège–Namur we had Horrocks's Corps of four veteran divisions. We knew Horrocks and knew he had good men.'

Because of their severe losses in tanks, the Americans also asked the British 21st Army Group for replacements. Altogether it would send about 350 Shermans, with the Guards Armoured Division bringing the first batch of eighty down itself with their radios removed, as the Americans used different sets.

While the line of the Meuse was secured, SHAEF's insistence on controlling news of the Ardennes offensive drew heavy criticism. This was partly an ineffectual attempt to conceal the fact that it had been caught out by the surprise attack. *Time* magazine soon declared that SHAEF and 12th Army Group 'clamped down a censorship thicker than the pea-soup fog that shrouded the great German counterattack'. And even when news was finally released, 'communiqués were as much as 48 hours behind the event', and deliberately vague. Some senior officers at SHAEF simply regarded journalists as an unnecessary evil. Bedell Smith told Third Army headquarters on the telephone: 'Personally I would like to shoot the lot of them.'

Not only correspondents complained. Senior British officers at SHAEF felt that this policy was having 'disastrous results on Belgian and French morale if not all western allies . . . It is undermining the credibility of our own news; it is encouraging people to listen to German broadcasts in order to find out the truth; and it is giving rise to a flood of rumours . . . The present SHAEF policy is merely leading the public to believe that serious disasters are being concealed.'

In Paris, many became convinced that the German attack was heading straight for the French capital. Wild rumours began to circulate. The Communists even tried to claim that the Americans had been so angry about the Franco-Soviet treaty signed in Moscow earlier that month by General de Gaulle that they were letting the Germans through simply to give the French a fright.

At the Adlerhorst Hitler was still elated, even though the advance was far behind schedule. News of the great counter-attack was released in

Germany. 'The wholly unexpected winter offensive in the Ardennes', wrote a staff officer with Army Group Upper Rhine, 'is the most wonderful Christmas present for our people. So we can still do it! . . . We had thought that this sixth Christmas of the war would hardly be festive and happy.' Unfortunately for the Nazis, the desperation to believe in something positive raised expectations far too high. Many persuaded themselves that France would be reconquered and the war brought to an end.

Some women were encouraged in this delusion by letters from their menfolk taking part in the battle. 'You cannot imagine what glorious hours and days we are experiencing now,' a Leutnant wrote to his wife. 'It looks as if the Americans cannot withstand our important push. Today we overtook a fleeing column and finished it . . . It was a glorious bloodbath, vengeance for our destroyed Homeland. Our soldiers still have the same old zip. Always advancing and smashing everything. The snow must turn red with American blood. Victory was never as close as it is now. The decision will soon be reached. We will throw them into the ocean, the arrogant big-mouthed apes from the New World. They will not get into our Germany. We will protect our wives and children from all enemy domination. If we are to preserve all tender and beautiful aspects of our lives, we cannot be too brutal in the deciding moments of this struggle.'

Goebbels noted that, following the announcement of the offensive, the entire Christmas ration of schnapps was consumed in Berlin. But sceptical Berliners, on the other hand, were less impressed. With characteristic gallows humour, they joked about the approach of a very unfestive Christmas: 'Be practical, give a coffin.' Their thoughts focused more on the threat from the east, and many privately prayed that the Americans would break through and reach the capital before the Red Army.

News of the offensive produced very different reactions among the German generals held prisoner in Britain. A secretly recorded conversation showed that Generalleutnant Ferdinand Heim, captured at Boulogne, Generaloberst Ramcke, the veteran paratrooper who had led the defence of Brest, and Standartenführer Kurt Meyer, the former commander of the 12th SS Panzer-Division *Hitler Jugend*, were all excited. Heim called it 'The Battle of the Long Nights'. 'Just rumble forward at night,' he cried out, 'just keep rumbling on!'

'Panzermeyer' agreed. 'The old principle of tank warfare: "forward, forward, forward!" . . . This is where the superiority of German leadership and especially of German junior commanders comes into play.' As a panzer leader, he was however concerned that the replacement tank gunners did not have enough experience. He was also in two minds whether the offensive might be over-ambitious and thus counter-productive, but Ramcke was having none of that. 'This offensive is terrific!' he insisted. 'The German people cannot be got down. You'll see that we shall chase the Allies right across France and hurl them into the Bay of Biscay!'

Others, on the other hand, were scathing. General der Panzertruppe Heinrich Eberbach said of Hitler: 'That man will never stop having illusions. When he is standing under the gallows he will still be under the illusion that he's not going to be hanged.' And Generalleutnant Otto Elfeldt, who had been captured in the Falaise Gap, reminded his listeners: 'It's Wednesday today, and if they have advanced only 40 kilometres in five days, I can only say that that is no offensive. A slow-moving offensive is no good at all because it allows the enemy to bring up reserves far too quickly.'

14

Thursday 21 December

By the morning of 21 December, the Kampfgruppe Peiper was in a desperate situation, 'pocketed without adequate supplies', as its leader put it. He received a message from 1st SS Panzer-Division that it intended to advance through Trois-Ponts to relieve him. But Peiper's reduced strength could not even hold Stoumont and Cheneux, and the relief force failed to get through. The enraged troops looted the Château de Detilleux south of the Amblève and destroyed whatever they did not take. Others in Wanne murdered five men and a woman, claiming that villagers must have been signalling to the American artillery. Another group of nine SS soldiers later seized food from a house in Refat and raped three women there after they had eaten.

In Stavelot on the morning of 21 December, another 100 German soldiers tried to swim the river to obtain a foothold on the north bank. Eighty of them were shot in the water by soldiers of the 117th Infantry who boasted of their 'duck shooting'; and the rest turned back. Peiper's position became even more critical when American combat engineers managed to block the road from Stoumont to La Gleize by blasting trees across it and mining the route. He had no alternative but to withdraw most of his remaining troops into La Gleize, where the 30th Division's artillery began to bombard the village.

The battle against the Kampfgruppe had become savage. 'After we saw those dead civilians in Stavelot, the men changed,' one of the soldiers recorded. 'They wanted to pulverize everything there was across the river. That wasn't impersonal anger; that was hatred.' Few SS soldiers were taken alive. Officers in the Waffen-SS apparently turned news of the Malmédy massacre to their own advantage, hoping to frighten their men into fighting to the bitter end. They told them that if captured, they would be tortured and then killed.

'The prisoner bag is thus far small,' an officer at First Army head-quarters noted. 'Our troops know of the atrocities committed by the enemy and know that now it is a matter of life or death, we or they.' A number of senior officers made it clear that they approved of revenge killing. When General Bradley heard soon afterwards that prisoners from the 12th SS Panzer-Division *Hitler Jugend* had spoken of their heavy casualties, he raised his eyebrows sceptically. 'Prisoners from the 12th SS?'

'Oh, yes sir,' the officer replied. 'We needed a few samples. That's all we've taken, sir.'

Bradley smiled. 'Well, that's good,' he said.

Bradley was encouraged by the sight of Patton's troops rolling north to attack Manteuffel's southern flank. He and members of his staff stood outside the Hôtel Alfa in Luxembourg on 21 December to watch the columns of 5th Infantry Division vehicles, 'caked in mud', passing through the city all day. 'The GIs looked cold,' Hansen wrote in his diary, 'bundled in brown against the winter wind that tore through their open vehicles, sitting stone-facedly on the piles of baggage in their trucks as they rode through town, staring back vacantly at the civilians who looked earnestly to them.'

Montgomery, all too conscious of the Germans' determination to cross the Meuse with their panzer divisions, recognized that First Army had to extend its line westward, well beyond the 30th Division's block on the Peiper Kampfgruppe. Major General Matthew B. Ridgway, a tall and formidable paratrooper who never appeared without grenades hooked on both shoulder straps of his webbing harness, had arrived to take command of the XVIII Airborne Corps west of the River Salm. Beyond, stretching towards the Meuse, Montgomery insisted on having the young Major General J. Lawton Collins in command of VII Corps. Montgomery regarded him as one of the very best American corps com-manders, and Hodges also rated him highly. The First Army chronicler noted that 'General Collins is full of his usual fighting Irish vigour.'

Collins was to have the 3rd Armored Division, the 84th Infantry Division and the 2nd Armored Division, Patton's old outfit known as 'Hell on Wheels'.

Ridgway, supported by Kean, the chief of staff First Army, and now Collins, argued that they should drive on St Vith while the defenders continued to hold out. 'Monty would come down about every other day to my command post,' Collins recorded. 'He would call Ridgway over to meet me at the same time, and would discuss the situation with us . . . I had gotten to know Monty well enough, and somehow or another we hit it off well. I could talk to him and disagree with him and he didn't get mad.' Montgomery opposed the idea of a corps attack towards St Vith partly on the grounds that a single road was insufficient to support a whole corps. 'Joe, you can't support a corps over a single road,' he said, no doubt remembering the route to Arnhem.

'Well, Monty, maybe you can't, but we can,' Collins retorted.

But both Hasbrouck, the commander of the 7th Armored Division, and Bruce Clarke of Combat Command B strongly disagreed with the plan to relieve St Vith. They felt afterwards that Montgomery had been right when he wanted to withdraw its defenders. They also thought that Ridgway was unnecessarily gung-ho and, as a paratrooper, did not understand the use of armoured formations.

Having heard the noise of tanks during the night of 20–21 December, the defenders of St Vith had expected an attack at dawn, but it did not come until towards the end of the morning. German volksgrenadiers began knocking out American machine-gun positions with grenades and the 'dread Panzerfaust'. They were so close that the American machine-gunners used 'swinging traverse', spraying fire in all directions. Hasbrouck's artillery battalions, although short of shells, responded to calls for fire missions within two to four minutes, 'bringing down fire within fifty yards of our own men'.

At 15.15 hours the battle died down, but Major Boyer suspected that it 'would prove to be only the lull before the storm'. They had no reserves left. Half an hour later, the German Nebelwerfer batteries suddenly opened fire again. Trees were lacerated. 'Huge gashes were cut in the logs over our holes, and all around us we could hear the crash and ripping of tree tops and even of trees as the merciless hail of steel swept and lashed through the forest. Again and again we heard the anguished scream of some man somewhere who had been hit, and yet all we could do was cower in our foxholes with our backs against the forward walls, hoping that we would not receive a direct hit. It seemed as if our very nerves were being torn out by the roots as the screaming steel crashed around us.'

The Germans attacked through the woods under the cover of the barrage. Boyer shouted out 'Heads up!' as the bombardment lifted. His infantrymen opened fire as the Germans tried to rush across the logging road. An American with a bazooka managed to knock out a self-propelled assault gun. And 'a Panther was destroyed when one soldier with a bazooka climbed out of his hole, ran forward and pressing his tube against the fender line, pulled the trigger. As he fired, he slumped to the ground dead.'

Two Panthers began methodically knocking out the foxholes one after another with direct fire. One of Boyer's officers called over the radio 'with tears in his voice' asking where the tank destroyers were to deal with the Panthers. 'Goddamn it, they've two heavy tanks here on the crest, and they're blasting my men out of their holes one at a time.' But no Shermans or tank destroyers were in their sector. Soon after nightfall, Boyer reported that he thought they could hold through the night, but just after seven the German onslaught began again, with Nebelwerfers and panzers eliminating foxholes one by one.

The German attacks came from three directions astride the main roads into the town from the north, east and south-east. The defenders were soon overwhelmed. Every machine gun in Boyer's battalion had been manned by several crews. 'As soon as one team was destroyed, it was replaced by other men.' By 22.00 'German tanks had blasted their way through the center of the line and were entering Saint-Vith.' This cut off the 38th Armored Infantry on the south-east side of the town after five days of battle with no sleep, little food and many suffering from frostbite. Boyer's battalion of 670 men was reduced to 185 men still on their feet. All the rest were dead or severely wounded. Snow began to fall heavily.

Brigadier General Clarke of Combat Command B issued the order: 'Reform. Save what vehicles you can; attack to the west through Saint-Vith. We are forming a new line west of the town.' Finding the order impossible to carry out, Boyer told his men to break out in groups of four or five, taking only personal weapons. He sent a runner to the mortar platoon with the instruction to destroy vehicles, but salvage their mortars and bipods. A medic volunteered to be left behind with the wounded. The exhausted men trudged through the falling snow into the forest. A point man led them by compass, and each soldier was told to hold on to the equipment of the one in front of him.

St Vith's streets were littered with rubble and broken glass, the slaughterhouse was on fire, and terrorized cattle rampaged in the streets. During the heavy shelling the day before, many civilians in the town had packed some belongings and sought refuge in the St Josef Kloster, which had solid vaulted cellars. As the bombardment intensified, Father Goffart decided to join the refugees below. 'He took a chalice and wafers with him and built a small altar in one of the subterranean storage rooms.' By the time of the all-out German attack that day, the place was so packed that nobody else could fit in. Many of them were wounded American soldiers who had dragged themselves there and forced the civilians to make room.

Soldiers retreating through the town included the intelligence and reconnaissance platoon of the 423rd Infantry, from the ill-fated 106th Division. 'Nothing much could be seen in the darkness but outlines in the snow,' one of them wrote, 'except when the blinding lights of the flares and muzzle blasts made it seem brighter than day.' The last three Shermans left in St Vith, with the intelligence and reconnaissance platoon alongside, 'proceeded cautiously down another street, the Rodterstrasse, that led to the northwest. At the edge of the town, some climbed aboard the tanks, lying as flat as they could, clinging to any-thing they could get hold of while the rest of the group flanked the tanks on foot. The tanks took off in the midst of a murderous crossfire coming from either side of the road – a crossfire marked by machineguns firing red tracers, scaring the living hell out us. Luckily, the Germans were firing too high and the tracers criss-crossed safely a few feet above our heads. At the top of a small hill about a mile to the west of town, we pulled off the road. The tanks took up position at the edge of a small patch of woods. The I&R moved down the forward slope of the hill a few yards, spread out and dug in as best we could.' The temperature had dropped significantly in the snowstorm.

The cold and famished Germans of the 18th and 62nd Volksgrenadier-Divisions charged into the town, desperate to seek shelter and loot what food they could find from houses and abandoned American stores. Hasbrouck's forces had pulled back to a new line west of St Vith, and now it was the turn of American field artillery battalions to bombard the doomed town.

To the north-west, Generalmajor Siegfried von Waldenburg's 116th Panzer-Division had orders to push on east of the River Ourthe to Hotton. The day before, Waldenburg's panzer group had attacked Samrée and Dochamps, while the 560th Volksgrenadier on their right had a harder fight. The Panthers managed to disable about a dozen American tanks in the battle, but they were so short of fuel that 156th Panzergrenadier-Regiment, the artillery and the reconnaissance battalion had to be halted. Relief came after capturing Samrée, where they discovered a fuel dump of 25,000 gallons, which Waldenburg described as 'a God-sent gift'. American prisoners told them that it had been sabotaged with sugar, but he claimed that it 'suited the German engines very well'.

'Nothing was to be seen of the long awaited II SS Panzer Corps,' he complained, but in fact the 2nd SS Panzer-Division *Das Reich* was not that far behind. Having been blocked near St Vith by the continuing traffic chaos on the roads, it had swung round to the south and was about to attack north against the line of the 82nd Airborne, but then had to wait for fuel supplies. The *Das Reich* burned with impatience at this hold-up. 'It was known that the army's 2nd Panzer-Division was pushing towards the west without meeting heavy enemy resistance and already was close to Dinant. No air activity – the route to the Meuse lies open – but the whole division is stuck for 24 hours unable to move because of a lack of fuel!' Montgomery was almost certainly right to extend the northern shoulder westward to face the threat, and reject the idea of an advance on St Vith as Ridgway and First Army wanted.

The 116th Panzer attacked Hotton later in the day with the 156th Panzergrenadier-Regiment supported by tanks, but they were repulsed by a battalion of the 325th Glider Infantry from the 82nd Airborne, a platoon of tank destroyers and some tanks from Major General Maurice Rose's 3rd Armored Division which had arrived in the early hours. The commander of the 116th Panzer-Division acknowledged that the Americans fought well. His Kampfgruppe lost several tanks and his men were exhausted. 'The troops began slowly to realize that the decisive plan must have failed, or that no victory could be won. Morale and efficiency suffered.'

The 2nd Panzer-Division, meanwhile, had only reached Champlon some eighteen kilometres to the south of Hotton as the crow flies. It had been held up at a crossroads south-east of Tenneville by just one company of the 327th Glider Infantry, and Lüttwitz later wanted to charge the divisional commander Oberst Meinrad von Lauchert with cowardice. As well as the battle at Noville, the division had also been delayed by the late arrival of fuel supplies. Some of its units had only just passed north of Bastogne.

Once the fighting was over, civilians in Bourcy and Noville emerged from their cellars to the sight of destruction all around, and the smell of damp smoke, carbonized masonry, burned iron and the seared flesh of farm animals killed in the bombardments. But even the comparative relief that the shelling had stopped was short lived. They found themselves rounded up by one of the SS security service groups from the Sicherheitsdienst. Brutal interrogations began, in an attempt to identify members of the Belgian Resistance and those who had welcomed the Americans in September. The SD officials had newspaper photographs with them of the event. One man in Bourcy, after a savage beating, was taken outside and killed with hammers. They had found a home-made American flag in his cellar. The group moved on to Noville where they murdered seven men, including the priest, Father Delvaux, and the village schoolmaster.

Patton had achieved miracles by regrouping his Third Army so rapidly, but he was hardly enthusiastic about having to concentrate on the relief of Bastogne. He would have much preferred to head for St Vith to cut off the Germans. He was also reluctant to wait until he had a larger force, as Eisenhower had ordered. 'Ike and [Major General] Bull [the G-3 at SHAEF] are getting jittery about my attacking too soon and too weak,' he wrote in his diary that day. 'I have all I can get. If I wait, I will lose surprise.' Never one to suffer from humility, Patton also wrote to his wife that day: 'We should get well into the guts of the enemy and cut his supply lines. Destiny sent for me in a hurry when things got tight. Perhaps God saved me for this effort.' But Patton's hubris was to embarrass him over the next few days when the breakthrough to Bastogne proved so much harder than he had imagined.

The reconnaissance battalion commanded by Major Rolf Kunkel and the 39th Fusilier Regiment from Kokott's 26th Volksgrenadier-Division were already seizing villages along the southern perimeter of Bastogne. They were followed by the lead Kampfgruppe of the Panzer Lehr. General Cota of the 28th Division, who had established his headquarters in Sibret, nearly seven kilometres south-west of Bastogne, attempted to organize its defence with a scratch force of stragglers. But they broke under the force of the attack, and Cota had to pull out rapidly. Kokott, visiting the sector, witnessed stragglers from the 28th Division and thought that they came from the Bastogne garrison. A Belgian he spoke to at Sibret assured him that the defenders of Bastogne were falling apart. He became much more hopeful, thinking that perhaps Lüttwitz's optimism was justified after all.

Kunkel's Kampfgruppe pushed north, causing considerable alarm in McAuliffe's headquarters because the VIII Corps artillery based round Senonchamps was vulnerable. Soldiers panicked in one field artillery battalion and fled; but a rapidly improvised force, backed by anti-aircraft half-tracks with quadruple .50 machine guns, arrived just in time. The 'meat-choppers' did their gruesome work, and Kunkel's attack collapsed.

The famished German troops took over farmhouses and villages, glad of shelter now that the temperature was dropping sharply. They slaughtered pigs and cows, seized food from families and exulted when they discovered abandoned stocks of American equipment and rations. They treated villagers with as much suspicion as many American soldiers treated the Belgians within the encirclement.

Further to the south the 5th Fallschirmjäger-Division had reached the road from Bastogne to Arlon, ready to block Patton's advance. The other German divisions had little confidence in their ability to halt a major counter-attack.

The fight to crush the German incursion along the railway track to Bastogne between Bizôry and Foy continued in the fog. Platoons of paratroopers advanced cautiously through pinewoods planted densely in neat rows with no underbrush. 'It was like a tremendous hall with a green roof supported by many brown columns,' wrote Major Robert Harwick, who commanded the 1st Battalion of the 506th which had escaped from Noville the day before. They paused at every firebreak and logging trail to observe, before crossing. Orders were given in whispers or by hand signals. From time to time shells from German guns exploded in the tree tops.

The German positions were well concealed, so the paratroopers had no idea where the shots were coming from when they were fired on. Once the enemy foxholes were spotted, the men in an extended skirmish line began to advance in short sprints, while others covered them in classic 'fire and maneuver'. Attacked from two directions, a number of the volksgrenadiers panicked. Some fled straight into the arms of Harwick's men and surrendered. 'Two prisoners came back,' Harwick wrote. 'They were terribly scared and kept ducking their heads as the bullets buzzed and whined. Finally, a close burst and they dove for a foxhole. The guard took no chances and threw a grenade in after them. He walked up to the hole and fired four shots from his carbine and returned to the fighting in front . . . The fight was not long, but it was hard – it was bitter, as all close fighting is. A wounded man lay near to where I had moved. I crawled over. He needed help badly. Beside him was an aid man, still holding a bandage in his hand but with a bullet through his head.'

His men brought in more prisoners once the battle was truly finished. 'One, terrified, kept falling on his knees, gibbering in German, his eyes continually here and there. He kept repeating in English, "Don't shoot me!" He finally fell sobbing on the ground and screamed as we lifted him. The rest had an attitude between this man and the coldly aloof lieutenant, who was so aloof, that somehow, somewhere, he got a good stiff punch in the nose.' The prisoners were forced to carry the American wounded back to the nearest aid station.

Bastogne itself was relatively well provided with food and large supplies of flour, but there was a distinct shortage of rations for the front line. The K-Rations brought for the first three days were soon used up, so soldiers survived mainly on hotcakes and pancakes.

McAuliffe's main concern was the shortage of artillery shells, especially the 105mm for the short-barrelled howitzers of the 101st Airborne field artillery. Fuel stocks were also a major worry. The tank destroyers and Shermans consumed a vast amount and they were essential in the defence. But, ever since the loss of the field hospital, the mounting number of wounded and the shortage of doctors haunted everyone. The low cloud cover meant that airdrops were out of the question. Like Patton and Bradley in Luxembourg, in fact like every commander and American soldier in the Ardennes, medical staff prayed for flying weather.

The German artillery began to concentrate that day on the town of Bastogne itself. The accuracy of their fire led to unjustified suspicions among the military police that there were fifth columnists among the refugees and civilians directing German fire. The town was an easy target, and those in the cellars of the Institut de Notre-Dame could feel the ground trembling. One shell hit a small ammunition dump, causing a huge explosion. McAuliffe had to move his headquarters down into cellars. He had been joined by Colonel Roberts, who, having conducted the operations of his 10th Armored Division combat command independently, was now under McAuliffe. The two men worked well together, and McAuliffe's expertise as an artilleryman was very useful in a defence which depended so much on that arm.

Since the 26th Volksgrenadier-Division was to be left with just a Kampfgruppe of the Panzer Lehr to take Bastogne, Lüttwitz the corps commander ordered General Bayerlein to send in a negotiator to demand the town's surrender to avoid total annihilation. Lüttwitz was under strict instructions from Führer headquarters not to divert any more troops for the capture of Bastogne, so this demand for surrender, which was to be delivered next day, was simply a bluff.

The defensive perimeter around Bastogne was porous to say the least, as the infiltration along the railway line had proved. Darkness in the long nights and bad visibility by day made it easy for German groups to slip through and cut a road behind forward positions, in an attempt to provoke a retreat. Whenever this happened, reserve platoons were sent off to deal with them, so there was a lot of 'rat-hunting' in damp woods as patrols searched for survivors. The low-lying fog also led to returning patrols being fired on by their own side, and to soldiers on both sides wandering into enemy-held territory by mistake. Captain Richard Winters, the executive officer with the 2nd Battalion of the 506th near Foy, even saw a German soldier with his trousers down, relieving himself behind their command post. 'After he was finished, I hollered to him in my best German, "Kommen sie hier!" (Come here), which he did. All the poor fellow had in his pockets were a few pictures, trinkets and the butt end of a loaf of black bread, which was very hard.'

The only reserve held back in Bastogne for emergencies was a scratch battalion of some 600 men known as 'Team SNAFU' (Situation Normal All Fucked Up). Stragglers from the 28th Infantry Division and survivors from the destruction of the 9th Armored Division combat command east of Bastogne, as well as soldiers suffering from borderline combat fatigue, were all drafted into it. One advantage of the encirclement meant that the defenders, using interior lines, could reinforce threatened sectors rapidly along the roads out of Bastogne. In the meantime, Team SNAFU was used to man roadblocks close to the town and to provide individual replacements for casualties in front-line units.

That night, it began to snow again, and a hard frost was about to set in. It brought mixed blessings, both for Hasbrouck's force holding on west of St Vith and for the 101st Airborne at Bastogne.

15

Friday 22 December

West of St Vith, the falling snow could have allowed Hasbrouck's depleted forces to disengage, but no permission to withdraw had arrived. General Ridgway still wanted them to hold out between St Vith and the River Salm.

In the early hours of the morning, Remer's *Führer Begleit* Brigade launched an attack on the small town of Rodt some four kilometres west of St Vith. Rodt was defended by American service troops – drivers, cooks and signallers – and by late in the morning Remer's well-armed force had cleared the place.

Some of Hasbrouck's men still remained out of contact north-east of St Vith, unaware of the general retreat. At 04.00 a company of armoured infantry received a radio message passed on by the 275th Field Artillery. 'Your orders are: Go west. Go west. Go west.' The company commander ordered his platoons to return from outposts one at a time in single file, with 'each man firmly gripping the belt or pack-straps of the man in front of him'. Visibility was almost non-existent in the heavy snow. They used a compass to aim west. On the way, trudging through the snow, the men became separated from each other, with most killed or captured. Those who escaped through the woods, small canyons and steep hills finally reached the line of light tanks and armoured cars which formed the rearguard of the 7th Armored Division.

The exhausted intelligence and reconnaissance platoon from the 106th Division, which had escaped St Vith with the three Shermans, was woken before dawn by their engines starting up. The tank crews had received an order to pull back, but they had not thought of warning the platoon which had been guarding them. 'We crawled wearily out of our makeshift foxholes and gathered together in the edge of the woods. Some of the guys had to be supported as they tried to stand, and to a man, walking was painful. Our legs had stiffened up over night and our near frozen feet had become more swollen as we crouched in our defensive positions.'

The tanks attracted German fire as they reached the road to Vielsalm, which revealed that the enemy had advanced beyond them. 'So, again in the cold wind and snow, we started cautiously southwest through the patch of woods.' They could hear the heavy fighting in Rodt as the *Führer Begleit* attacked. So 'taking advantage of scrub growth and the ever present fog, we made our way further southwest over country lanes until we came to the small village of Neundorf. Approaching the village over a small bridge, we came to a cluster of farmhouses at the edge of the village.'

'As we crossed this bridge,' another member of the platoon continued, 'we were met by a large number of Belgians – men, women and children. I explained who we were and what had happened in Saint-Vith. I shall never forget, as long as I live, the actions of these people. There they were, in front of the advancing German armies and in the midst of the fleeing American army. And what did they do? They very quickly divided us into small groups and took us into their homes. The group I was with, was taken to the home of a wonderful Belgian lady. I don't know how in the world she did it but it seemed, in minutes, she had a long table loaded with food. There was a huge pot of stewed meat, two large pitchers of milk, boiled potatoes, and loaves of hot bread. You can imagine what happened. We just gorged ourselves. There was a fire going in the fireplace, and it wasn't long before Irish [PFC John P. Sheehan] was asleep in an old rocking chair in front of the fire. We no sooner had finished eating than we heard the sound of German machine guns a short ways behind us. As we scrambled to leave, we took all the money we had been able to salvage, out of our pockets, and put it in the middle of the table. We could do no less for these wonderful people.'

The advance of the *Führer Begleit* had split Hasbrouck's force in two, so he had to pull back further to avoid encirclement. Hasbrouck was furious with Ridgway and his XVIII Airborne Corps headquarters, who wanted him to form a 'goose-egg'-shaped defence east of the River Salm. Hasbrouck was deeply concerned about his southern flank, because during the night he heard that his task force on the right had captured a German officer from the 2nd SS Panzer-Division *Das Reich*. If the *Das Reich* was heading for Gouvy, as the prisoner said, the very weak force there did not stand a chance. Later in the morning of 22 December a fresh German force around Recht, just north of Poteau, was identified as part of the 9th SS Panzer-Division *Hohenstaufen*. If it was heading for the River Salm, as appeared to be the case, then it threatened to cut off the line of retreat of Combat Command A of the 7th Armored Division. Its commander Colonel Rosebaum reacted quickly. He withdrew his tanks fighting the *Führer Begleit* and concentrated his force round Poteau to block the SS *Hohenstaufen*.

That morning one of Montgomery's British liaison officers appeared at Hasbrouck's command post in Commanster, twelve kilometres south-west of St Vith. He asked Hasbrouck what he thought should be done. Hasbrouck replied that if higher command believed it essential to maintain an all-round defence, then he would hold on as long as possible, but he considered that withdrawal was preferable because the woods and lack of roads made it an almost impossible terrain to hold. This was reported back to Montgomery.

Hasbrouck then sent a detailed assessment of his position to Ridgway. German artillery would soon be able to shell his men from all sides, and his supply route via Vielsalm was in danger with the advance of the SS *Das Reich*. He argued that his remaining forces would be of more use strengthening the 82nd Airborne to resist the *Das Reich*. Losses in infantry especially had been so great that he doubted whether they would be able to withstand another all-out attack. He added a postscript. 'I am throwing in my last chips to halt [the Germans] . . . In my opinion if we don't get out of here and up north of the 82nd before night, we will not have a 7th Armored Division left.'

Ridgway still rejected the recommendation to withdraw, but Montgomery overruled him in the middle of the afternoon during a visit to First Army headquarters. He sent a signal to Hasbrouck: 'You have accomplished your mission – a mission well done. It is time to withdraw.' It was indeed well done. Hasbrouck's very mixed force had managed to delay the Fifth Panzer Army's advance by nearly a whole week.

Fortunately for the Americans, the German stampede into St Vith had caused a massive jam. Many of the vehicles were American Jeeps and trucks captured in the Schnee Eifel, and their new owners refused to let them go. The Feldgendarmerie lost control, and a furious General-feldmarschall Model was forced to dismount and walk into the ruins of the town his troops had taken so long to seize. The chaos around the key road junction meant that the German commanders would take some time to redeploy their forces. This breathing space gave Brigadier General Clarke the chance to pull back his Combat Command B to a new line. Then an even greater miracle occurred. Hasbrouck's artillery had been down to their last rounds when a convoy of ninety trucks unexpectedly arrived that morning via circuitous back routes, with 5,000 shells for the 105mm howitzers.

The intelligence and reconnaissance platoon joined up with the 424th Infantry, the only regiment of the 106th Division to escape, having formed the right wing of Hasbrouck's force. For the first time they heard of the massacre near Malmédy. 'The line troops vowed that no prisoners would be taken in their sector,' wrote one of them. 'Two of the platoon, on liaison to one of the companies, were visiting the front line foxholes of one of the rifle platoons. Across a fifty yard gap in the woods, a white flag appeared, whereby a sergeant stood up and motioned the Germans to advance. About twenty men emerged out of the woods. After they had advanced closer to the line, the sergeant gave the command to open fire. No prisoners were taken.'

Only German troops who had circumvented St Vith were in a position to advance. That evening panzers and infantry attacked along the railway line to Crombach. The fight for Crombach was furious. One company fired 600 rounds in twenty minutes from its 81mm mortars and 'broke the base plates which were welded to the floor of the half-track'. German panzer crews used their trick of firing bright flares to blind American gunners and thus got off their rounds first with devastating effect.

As Hasbrouck had predicted, nearly the whole division was now coming under heavy shellfire. Orders for the withdrawal were issued, and the artillery began moving out at midnight. It began to freeze hard. To the joyful disbelief of Brigadier General Clarke, the ground finally became solid enough not only for cross-country movement, but also along the deeply mired woodland tracks. This was essential if they were to extricate all the different components towards the three-kilometre gap between Vielsalm and Salmchâteau, and the two bridges over the river. But German attacks during the night prevented the two combat commands from pulling out during darkness. The careful plan for the withdrawal was thrown out of synchronization, but despite many rear-guard skirmishes the bulk of the retreating forces managed to cross the River Salm on 23 December.

A survivor from one infantry company, who managed to escape with the 17th Tank Battalion, recounted how after several running firefights they finally reached the lines of the 82nd Airborne. A paratrooper digging a foxhole put down his shovel and said: 'What the hell are you guys running from? We been here two days and ain't seen a German yet.' The exhausted infantryman retorted: 'Stay right where you are, buddy. In a little while you won't even have to look for 'em.'

On the southern slope of the Elsenborn ridge, the 12th SS Panzer-Division *Hitler Jugend* again tried to break through with tanks at Büt-genbach. The American defenders herded civilians into the convent's cellars and provided them with food. In houses outside and on the edge of the town, women and children cowered in cellars as the house above them was fought over, captured and recaptured by both sides. Bazooka teams stalked panzers which had broken into the town. American fighter-bombers then attacked the village. One explosion threw a cow on to a farm roof. By the time the fighting had finished, the bodies of twenty-one civilians had been wrapped in blankets, ready for burial when the opportunity arose. Most were elderly and disabled residents from the nursing home.

This was the last major attempt to break the American defence of the Elsenborn ridge. The 12th SS *Hitler Jugend* Division was ordered to pull out and reorganize before being diverted to join the Fifth Panzer Army further south. Gerow's V Corps had defeated the attempt of the Sixth Panzer Army to break through.

In the early hours of 22 December, German Junkers 52 transport planes dropped fuel, rations and ammunition to Peiper's Kampfgruppe, but only about a tenth of the supplies could be recovered from the restricted drop zone. The Luftwaffe refused Sixth Panzer Army's requests for further missions. Attempts by the 1st SS Panzer-Division to break through to support and resupply Peiper were thwarted at Trois-Ponts by a regiment of the 82nd Airborne defending the line of the River Salm just below its confluence with the Amblève. General Ridgway knew that he needed to eliminate the Peiper Kampfgruppe in its pocket at La Gleize and Stoumont as soon as possible so that he could redeploy the 30th Division and the 3rd Armored Division. The threat was growing further west with the advance of the 116th Panzer-Division to Hotton, and the 2nd Panzer-Division on its left.

Ridgway had hoped for a clear sky that day, after the hard frost of the night before, but he soon heard that no aircraft would be flying in their support. At least Stoumont was finally cleared by the infantry from the 30th Division supported by Sherman tanks. The Germans pulled out, leaving wounded from all three battalions of the 2nd SS Panzergrenadier-Regiment. But west of Stavelot a panzergrenadier company slipped in to block the road and captured an American aid station. This was retaken by combat engineers and tanks next day.

Peiper acknowledged that his situation was 'very grave'. There was house-to-house fighting in La Gleize, where some buildings were burning from American artillery firing phosphorus shells. Peiper claimed that the church in La Gleize, 'conspicuously marked with a red cross', had been targeted by US tanks and artillery. His men, most of them still teenagers, were exhausted and half starved. Most of them wore articles of American uniform taken from the dead and prisoners because their own were falling to pieces. Since all attempts to break through by the relief force from his division had failed, Peiper decided that evening that his Kampfgruppe would have to fight its way out.

While Peiper's morale was sinking, Generalmajor Kokott on the south side of Bastogne began to feel much more optimistic. His 26th Volks-grenadier command post had just heard reports of the rapid advance of the panzer divisions towards the Meuse. He also began to think that perhaps Lüttwitz's corps headquarters must have good intelligence on the state of the American defenders of Bastogne, otherwise it would not have ordered just 'a single infantry division' to surround and capture the town. Lüttwitz, visited the night before by General der Panzertruppe

Brandenberger, was assured that the 5th Fallschirmjäger-Division could hold the southern flank against Patton's drive north from Arlon.

In bitterly cold weather, with more flurries of snow and the ground frozen hard, Kokott began a concentric attack. His 39th Regiment advanced on Mande-Saint-Etienne in the west, while his reconnaissance battalion, Kampfgruppe Kunkel, fought around Senonchamps and Villeroux, south-west of Bastogne. 'In the course of the [day],' Kokott recorded, 'news arrived from Korps [headquarters] to the effect that the commander in charge of the Bastogne forces had declined a surrender with remarkable brevity.'

When soldiers of the 327th Glider Infantry had seen four Germans coming towards them, waving a white flag, they assumed that they wanted to surrender. A German officer speaking English announced that according to the Geneva and Hague conventions they had the right to deliver an ultimatum. They produced their own blindfolds and were led to the company command post. Their letter was then sent to divisional headquarters. Brigadier General McAuliffe, who had been up all night, was catching up on sleep in the cellar. The acting chief of staff shook him awake, and told him that the Germans had sent emissaries asking the Bastogne defenders to capitulate or face annihilation by artillery fire. McAuliffe, still half asleep, muttered 'Nuts!' Not knowing what to recommend as a reply, one member of the 101st staff suggested that McAuliffe should use the same reply as he had given to the chief of staff. So back went the message to the unidentified 'German commander', who was in fact Lüttwitz, with the single word. Manteuffel was furious with Lüttwitz when he heard about the ultimatum. He regarded it as a stupid bluff, because the Germans simply did not have the artillery ammunition to carry out the threat. McAuliffe, on the other hand, could not be sure that it was a bluff.

The change in the weather meant that uniforms stood out conspicuously against the snow. In Bastogne and surrounding villages, American officers asked the local mayor if they could obtain sheets to be used as camouflage. In Hemroulle, the burgomaster went straight to the church and began to toll the bell. Villagers came running and he told them to bring their sheets as the American soldiers needed them. Some 200 were provided. The paratroopers began cutting them up to make helmet covers, or strips to wrap round rifle and machine-gun barrels. Those who made poncho-style capes for going out on patrol soon found, however, that they became damp and froze. This made them crackle and rustle as they moved. Other soldiers scoured Bastogne and its surrounding villages for cans of whitewash to camouflage their vehicles and tanks.

In their foxholes round the Bastogne perimeter, the ill-equipped paratroopers of the 101st suffered badly in the freezing temperatures, especially with their feet in sodden boots. Some soldiers discovered a store in Bastogne with a couple of thousand burlap sacks. These and others were distributed rapidly for the soldiers to wrap around their feet, yet non-battle casualties from trench foot and frostbite were soon to rise alarmingly.

Despite the wretched conditions, the paratroopers surprised the Germans by the vigour of their counter-attacks on that day. The Germans had begun by attacking the Mande-Saint-Etienne sector at dawn. During the fighting there, a family of refugees sought shelter along with others in the last house in the village. The two brothers who owned the farm milked the cows and brought in pails of it for their guests to drink in the attached stable. Suddenly, the door was kicked open and two German soldiers with 'Schmeisser' MP-40 sub-machine guns entered. The refugees cowered against the wall, because the two men appeared drunk. While one of them trained his weapon on the civilians, the other walked over to the pails of milk, undid his trousers and urinated in them one by one. They both thought that this was funny.

The 26th Volksgrenadier-Division lost just on 400 men in its attacks that day, and it had to bring in replacements from the divisional supply battalion and the artillery regiment as infantrymen to make up numbers. Because of the counter-attacks, Generalmajor Kokott even thought that the defenders were about to attempt a breakout from the encirclement. His men had heard from civilian refugees leaving Bastogne that there was great tension in the town and that vehicles were being loaded up. German shells during the night had hit the 101st Division's command post and killed several officers in their sleeping bags.

An airdrop planned for that day had to be cancelled because of the bad visibility. The 101st was running very short of artillery ammunition and the number of barely treated wounded was mounting fast. Yet morale was high, particularly when news of the rejected demand to surrender rapidly made the rounds. Some senior officers at SHAEF, particularly Major General Strong, the British chief of intelligence, feared that the 101st Airborne would not be able to defend Bastogne. 'I was never worried about the operation,' Bedell Smith said later. 'Strong was, however. He asked me three times in one day if I thought we would hold at Bastogne. I thought [we could]. He said, "How do you know?" I said: "Because the commanders there think they can hold." We had at Bastogne our best division. When the commander said [they were] OK, I believed he would [hold].'

Major General 'Lightning Joe' Collins wasted little time in organizing his VII Corps to resist the advance of the German panzer divisions heading for the Meuse. For the moment he had only the 84th Infantry Division, but the 2nd Armored Division was on its way, and so was the 75th Infantry Division. He travelled in an armoured car to reach the town of Marche-en-Famenne. 'The fog was sitting right on the tree tops,' he recorded later. There he found Brigadier General Alex Bolling, the commander of the 84th Infantry Division, who had pushed out reconnaissance forces to identify the enemy's line of approach. He was reassured to find Bolling 'very calm', but their conversation convinced him that Bradley was wrong to believe that his entire corps should be held back for a counter-attack. VII Corps was about to be 'engaged in a fight for its life'. Collins decided to set up his corps headquarters in a small chateau at Méan, fifteen kilometres due north of Marche.

The advance Kampfgruppe of the 2nd Panzer-Division had started early on 22 December heading for Marche. It met no resistance until it clashed with a detachment of Bolling's 335th Infantry Regiment at a crossroads two kilometres south of Marche, in rolling country of fields and woods. While a force of panzergrenadiers continued the battle, the lead elements of the 2nd Panzer turned west towards Dinant. Alarm was caused by an unconfirmed report from the British 23rd Hussars, forward of the Meuse crossing at Givet, that panzers had been sighted at Vonêche, a dozen kilometres to the south-east.

The lead elements of the 2nd Panzer were by then only twenty-five kilometres from the Meuse bridge at Dinant, but constant attacks by Bolling's division forced the 2nd Panzer to detach troops for flank protection. An attack from Marche by American infantry in the morning failed, but another, stronger attempt supported by tanks in the afternoon retook the high ground south-west of the town. A major reverse was prevented by the 2nd Panzer's anti-aircraft battalion taking on the Shermans in the open, but it suffered heavy losses in the process. That night the panzergrenadiers managed to retake part of the heights and open the road to the west.

American service troops and other detachments in the area soon woke up to the danger. One group, who had billeted themselves in the ancient Château d'Hargimont between Marche and Rochefort, slept in their uniforms and boots with grenades to hand in case they were surprised in the night by the German advance. On hearing gunfire, they pulled out rapidly and headed back towards Dinant. So too did most of the young Belgian men, either on bicycles or on foot. They had a well-justified fear of reprisals for the attacks by the Resistance in September, and they also knew that if they stayed, they risked being marched off to Germany for forced labour.

Taking refuge in cellars as artillery shells began to fall, Belgians had no idea of the state of the battle. They could, however, identify the different sounds made in the street by American boots with rubber soles and the hobnailed jackboots of the Germans. They backed away when Germans entered, not just from a fear of violence, but also because they knew the enemy soldiers were covered in lice. German troops during that advance were intent on searching for Americans in hiding or for members of the Resistance. Any young Belgian who had been unwise enough to pick up a couple of live rounds was liable to be shot as a 'terrorist' if searched. And when the Germans decided to make themselves at home, they stacked their rifles and Panzerfausts in a corner, which the civilians could not help eyeing nervously. The locals spoke Walloon among themselves, knowing that the soldiers could not understand, unless one of them happened to be a conscript from the eastern cantons.

In cellars, lit by storm-lamps or candles, the Ardennais sometimes sang folk-songs when there was a long lull. But when the shelling started again in earnest, people began reciting the rosary, their lips moving fast. Conditions during long periods of bombardment rapidly deteriorated, encouraging dysentery. Buckets could be taken up and emptied on the dung-heap only when there was a lull in the firing. Farmers and their sons would also rush out to milk cows in the byre and feed the pigs.

They brought back pails of milk for those sheltering downstairs to improve the diet of potatoes. If there was time, they would rapidly butcher livestock killed by shellfire. The fortunate would have brought an Ardennes ham, which they shared out. Many stuffed pails and bottles with snow and waited for it to melt as drinking water, because going to the pump was too dangerous. Those who fled to the woods when their homes were shelled could do no more than pack together for warmth. Their only water came from sucking icicles.

All over the Ardennes, the old and infirm were looked after in a community spirit; in fact examples of selfishness seem to have been rare. People whose houses had stone cellars would shelter neighbours who only had floorboards over theirs. And the owner of a local chateau with deep cellars would invite the villagers to take shelter there, but such a prominent building was always likely to attract the interest of artillery observers, whether Allied or German.

Generalmajor von Waldenburg, the commander of the 116th Panzer-Division, was in a bad mood that morning. At 04.00 hours, he had received an order from his corps commander to stop his attack on Hotton from east of the River Ourthe, which was valiantly defended by an American engineer battalion and service troops. Manteuffel wrongly believed that the defence was too strong and would hold up Waldenburg's division. He ordered the 560th Volksgrenadier-Division to take over at Hotton, while the 116th Panzer was to go back through Samrée and La Roche-en-Ardenne, then proceed north-west again on the other side of the Ourthe to break through between Hotton and Marche. Waldenburg was convinced that if they had been sent that way earlier, they could have advanced well beyond Marche by then. This diversion certainly allowed General Collins more time to organize his defence line further to the west.

In Luxembourg, General Bradley's staff noticed that he now seldom left his bedroom or office. But that morning Hansen entered Bradley's office to find him on his knees bent over a map on the floor, peering through his bifocals at the road net being used by the Germans, and marking routes with brown crayon. It was the day on which General Patton's attack from the south towards Bastogne began with III Corps, including the 4th Armored Division and the 26th and 80th Infantry Divisions on its right. XII Corps, starting behind the 4th Infantry Division on the southern shoulder, would also advance north with the 5th Division and part of the 10th Armored.

After the heavy snowfall of the night before, Hansen described the view from the hotel as 'a veritable postcard scene with tiny snow covered houses'. The fog had eased and the temperature had dropped, but low cloud cover still prevented the deployment of Allied airpower in all its strength. As the population of Luxembourg was still anxious, the 12th Army Group civil affairs officer decided to take Prince Jean, the son of the Grand Duchess Charlotte, round the city in a car, to reassure the people that he had remained with them. Bradley's staff were angry that Radio Luxembourg, with the most powerful transmitter in Europe, had gone off air when its staff pulled out in a panic, taking most of their technical equipment with them.

Fears over Skorzeny's commandos had still not been put to rest. Counter Intelligence Corps men were 'acutely worried over the safety of our generals', Hansen noted in his diary that day. 'German agents in American uniforms are supposedly identified by their pink or blue scarves, by two [finger] taps on their helmets and by the open top button on their coats and jackets. When Charlie Wertenbaker [of *Time* magazine] came this evening, we pointed to his maroon scarf, warned him of a shade of pink and he promptly removed it.'

Eisenhower, also suffocating under security precautions at Versailles, issued an order of the day to all formations. 'The enemy is making his supreme effort to break out of the desperate plight into which you forced him by your brilliant victories of the summer and fall. He is fighting savagely to take back all that you have won and is using every treacherous trick to deceive and kill you. He is gambling everything, but already in this battle, your unparalleled gallantry has done much to foil his plans. In the face of your proven bravery and fortitude, he will completely fail.'

The day before, in an attempt to defend Bradley from any suggestion that he had been caught off-guard in the Ardennes, Eisenhower recommended his promotion to full general. He wrote to General Marshall to say that the 12th Army Group commander had 'kept his head magnificently and . . . proceeded methodically and energetically to meet the situation. In no quarter is there any tendency to place any blame on Bradley.'

Bradley, egged on by his staff according to Bedell Smith, convinced himself that Montgomery had panicked. If nothing else, this completely distorted view demonstrated that his Eagle Tac headquarters in Luxembourg was totally out of touch with the reality on the ground. 'We learned that the entire British Army was in retreat,' wrote one of his staff officers. 'Leaving only a skeleton force in the line, and with remarkable agility for a man who was often so cautious, Montgomery moved the bulk of the British Second and the Canadian First Armies back from Holland to a defensive semicircle round Antwerp, prepared for the last ditch battle he apparently thought he would have to fight there.' Bradley's staff clearly had no idea that Horrocks's XXX Corps was on the Meuse, with the 29th Armoured Brigade already on the east bank, ready to link up with the right wing of Collins's VII Corps.

16

Saturday 23 December

All over the Ardennes, American commanders on the morning of 23 December gazed in wonder at the cloudless blue sky and blinding winter sun. The temperature had dropped even further, because a 'Russian High' of crystal-clear weather had arrived from the east. Air controllers joyfully reported 'visibility unlimited' and scrambled P-47 Thunderbolt fighter-bombers to go tank hunting. An ebullient General Patton exclaimed to his deputy chief of staff: 'God damn! That O'Neill sure did some potent praying. Get him up here, I want to pin a medal on him.' Chaplain O'Neill was rushed from Nancy to Luxembourg so that Patton could decorate him with the Bronze Star next day.

Bradley's staff, like many of the inhabitants of Luxembourg, went out into the street to squint up against the brightness at the condensation trails of Allied heavy bombers flying over to attack Trier and its marshalling yards. Morale soared in foxholes as men stared at the bombers and fighter-bombers once more streaming overhead, glinting like shoals of silver fish.

Allied air support produced another bonus. German artillery batteries did not want to reveal their gun positions by firing while there were fighter-bombers around. 'As soon as the enemy air force appeared the effect of the artillery was reduced to fifty or sixty percent,' Model's artillery commander reported.

Later in the morning, however, 12th Army Group headquarters was shaken to hear that part of the 2nd Panzer-Division was advancing on Jemelle, just east of Rochefort. This was the site of the army group's radio repeater station, and it was guarded by no more than a platoon of infantry and some tank destroyers. Bradley immediately called First Army headquarters to see if reinforcements could be sent, but 'as he was speaking the line went dead'. The soldiers guarding the repeater station had just removed all the tubes. They were withdrawing as the Germans approached, but they did not destroy the equipment in the hope that the place could be recaptured soon.

At least air-reconnaissance missions could now clarify the movements of the panzer divisions heading north-west for the Meuse. Yet First Army headquarters was still convinced that the Germans wanted to break through towards Liège. Staff officers did not know that Hitler had insisted on a drive westward.

General Rose, with his command post in the embattled town of Hotton, had been forced to split his 3rd Armored Division in all directions. One combat command was still tied down crushing the Kampfgruppe Peiper around La Gleize, while another was on its way to join him from Eupen. The rest of the division was split into three task forces. Two of them were ready to block the advance of the 2nd SS Panzer-Division *Das Reich* as it advanced up the road from Houffalize towards Manhay on the road to Liège, but Task Force Hogan was surrounded at Marcouray ten kilometres to the south-east of Hotton and out of fuel. An attempt to drop supplies was made that day, but the parachute bundles fell more than six kilometres away, and on the following day they fell nearly ten kilometres away.

On the Houffalize–Liège highway, Baraque-de-Fraiture consisted of three farmhouses by a crossroads close to a village called Fraiture. It lay on the boundary between the 82nd Airborne and the 3rd Armored Division and had been overlooked. But Major Arthur C. Parker III, a survivor of the 106th Division's débâcle in the Schnee Eifel, recognized the importance of its position. He had started to prepare a defence with his own gunners and a mixture of sub-units retreating that way. They included four anti-aircraft half-tracks with quadruple .50 machine guns – the notorious 'meat-choppers'.

The small force at 'Parker's crossroads', as Baraque-de-Fraiture was soon known, had been attacked before dawn on 21 December by a large fighting patrol from the 560th Volksgrenadier-Division. The

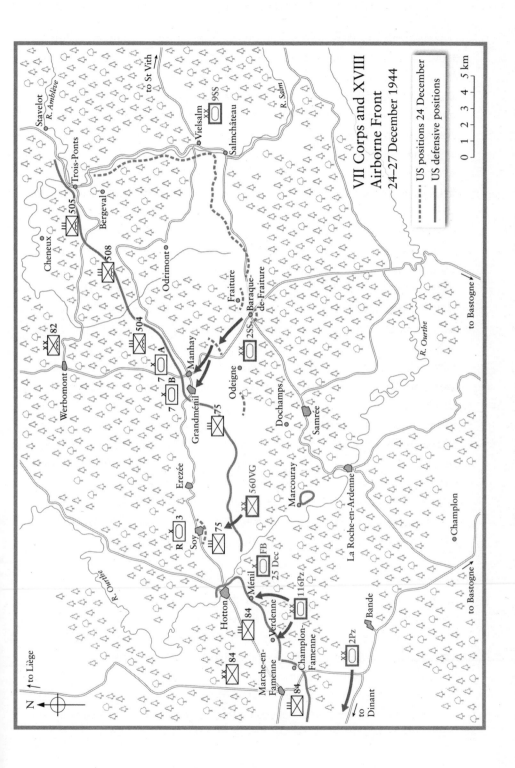

VII Corps and XVIII
Airborne Front
24–27 December 1944

- - - - US positions 24 December
———— US defensive positions

0 1 2 3 4 5 km

N
to Liège

to St Vith

Stavelot
R. Amblève
Trois-Ponts
Cheneux
Bergeval
Odrimont
Vielsalm
R. Salm
Salmchâteau
9SS

505
508
504
82
Werbomont
A 7
B 7
Grandménil
Manhay
Fraiture
Baraque-
de-Fraiture
2SS
Odeigne
75
Dochamps
Samrée
560VG
Erezée
R. Ourthe
Marcouray
La Roche-en-Ardenne
Champlon
to Bastogne
R. Ourthe
Soy
R 3
75
Ménil
FB
25 Dec
116Pz
Hotton
84
Verdenne
Champlon-
Famenne
Bande
2Pz
to Bastogne
Marche-en-
Famenne
84
84
to
Dinant

'meat-choppers' had cut them to pieces. Among the wounded, an officer from the SS *Das Reich* was identified. Task Force Kane defending Manhay to the north sent a reconnaissance platoon. And General Gavin, once aware of the danger, sent a battalion of the 82nd to Fraiture to protect Parker's left flank, and a company of the 325th Glider Infantry also arrived.

Little happened on 22 December because the *Das Reich* had been waiting for fuel supplies to arrive and for Remer's *Führer Begleit* to catch up. But at dawn on 23 December the 4th SS Panzergrenadier-Regiment attacked both the crossroads and the paratroopers at Fraiture, whom it surprised eating breakfast. The real attack on Parker's crossroads came late in the afternoon, with the whole of the 4th SS Panzergrenadiers and two companies of tanks. The fall of snow had revealed the defenders' positions, rather than camouflaging them, and their Shermans had no room for manoeuvre. Panzer gunners knocked out the armoured vehicles and shot up one foxhole after another. General Gavin had ordered the defenders to hold at all costs, but Parker's force was completely overwhelmed soon after nightfall. Three Shermans got away, and some men escaped into the woods when a herd of frenzied cows stampeded.

Gavin and Rose, afraid that the *Das Reich* would smash through Manhay and into their rear, scraped together whatever forces they could find. General Ridgway lost his temper at this unexpected threat, and ordered the exhausted survivors of the 7th Armored Division, who had just escaped across the River Salm, to hold Manhay. He was in an unforgiving mood after Hasbrouck and Clarke had opposed his plan to fight on west of St Vith, and then been supported by Montgomery.

In the early hours of 23 December, the headquarters of I SS Panzer Corps received a radio message from Kampfgruppe Peiper. 'Position considerably worsened. Meagre supplies of infantry ammunition left. Forced to yield Stoumont and Cheneux during the night. This is the last chance of breaking out.' American artillery and tanks continued to bombard La Gleize. The much feared Kampfgruppe, lacking both fuel and ammunition, was now powerless to respond.

Peiper held more than 150 American prisoners, including Major Hal McCown. He had already attempted to interrogate McCown and to proclaim his own belief in Nazism and its reasons for fighting the war. McCown had been moved to a small cellar that morning with four other American officers. During the afternoon, an American 105mm shell hit the wall, blasting a large hole in it and throwing the German guard halfway across the room. Another shell landed just outside, sending fragments and stones flying through the cellar. An American lieutenant was killed and three Germans were wounded.

Later, McCown was taken to see Peiper again, who told him that he was going to break out on foot but did not know what to do with his American prisoners. Peiper had just received permission to make his way back to German lines. He proposed a deal. He would leave all the prisoners and his own wounded behind, and take just McCown with him as a hostage. McCown would then be set free if the American commander released the German wounded. McCown replied that he obviously could not make any agreement about prisoners of war. All he could do was sign a paper saying that he had heard Peiper's suggestion. That night Peiper's men began to prepare their surviving vehicles for demolition. They would have to wade across the River Amblève in the dark to slip into the trees on the southern side.

The Ninth Army commander General Bill Simpson was proud of his 30th Division's ruthless fightback against the Peiper Kampfgruppe. 'American troops are now refusing to take any more SS prisoners,' his aide wrote, 'and it may well spread to include all German soldiers. While we cannot order such a thing, the C[ommanding] G[eneral] himself personally hopes that every GI will hear these stories and make that a battle rule, as the 30th Division did.' Simpson was pleased to hear that Germans now called the division 'Roosevelt's Butchers'. He had also received a report on prisoners taken in the Malmédy sector that their commanders had 'promised them that in this new fight they would not have to fight the 30th Div. They fear it that much.'

On the Elsenborn ridge, American artillery continued to pound the villages and towns below with white phosphorus and high explosive, even after the main attacks had petered out. The small town of Faymonville on the southern side, occupied by a detachment of the 3rd Fallschirm-jäger, had been targeted day after day. The local priest begged a German officer to arrange a ceasefire so that non-combatants could be evacuated.

On the morning of 23 December, the Germans instead simply ordered the 600 civilians trapped in Faymonville to leave for Schoppen, a village further behind the German lines. An officer told them that anyone who tried to walk towards American positions would be shot. The priest urged them to think again, but the Germans replied that they would start shooting his parishioners, five at a time, if they refused to leave.

At 11.00 hours, the terrified townspeople set off into the open. Unfortunately, the pilot of an American spotter plane saw the column trudging with difficulty through the deep snow, and identified it as an enemy concentration. American artillery on the Elsenborn ridge opened fire. As shells began exploding all around, the old men, women and children panicked, running in all directions. The priest ran back to Faymonville to ask the Germans to radio the Americans to cease their firing but they refused to do anything. Eight or so were killed or died later and many others were injured, before they reached the relative safety of Schoppen.

The German besiegers of Bastogne somehow still believed that the Americans were hoping to escape the encirclement. On 23 December, they tried to strengthen their presence on the west side of the town, continuing the attack round Senonchamps and Mande-Saint-Etienne to tighten the ring and to cut off any further 'attempts to break out'. Hitler, refusing to believe 'Manteuffel's report that he could not take Bastogne with the forces he had', sent an officer to check on 23 December. He, however, supported Manteuffel's assessment.

The defenders were certainly very short of food, but they still appear to have been better fed than Kokott's volksgrenadiers, whose supply situation was so bad that 'up to ten men had to share half a loaf'. And while American paratroopers suffered in the extreme cold from their lack of winter uniforms, they at least had villages round the perimeter in which they could warm up. Their volksgrenadier opponents were even worse off, which was why they stripped American bodies of boots and items of clothing for themselves. And in the continuing tension caused by the Skorzeny commandos, this led to the shooting of some of those who wore American kit when they surrendered. Apart from weapons, the only piece of German equipment which American soldiers hankered after was the German army's brilliantly simple knife–fork–spoon combination.

The Germans had also proved more foresighted by issuing snow camouflage suits, while the Americans had to improvise.

'The first enemy fighter-bombers', Generalmajor Kokott recorded,
'appeared towards 0900 hours, swooped down on communication roads
and villages and set vehicles and farmyards on fire.' Unfortunately for
the paratroopers on the south-western perimeter, little air support
appeared. The drastic drop in temperature during the night froze the
turret-traverse mechanism on many of their supporting tanks and tank
destroyers. Even anti-tank guns could not be moved as they had been
frozen into the ground. Cross-country movement for infantry was also
difficult, with a hard crust on the top of half a metre of snow.

The main German attacks that day to break the ring were mounted
against the Flamierge sector in the north-west at noon, and another
later against Marvie on the south-east side by the 901st Panzergrenadier-
Regiment from the Panzer Lehr Division. Towards the end of the
morning, however, an unexpected threat appeared from the south. The
Fifth Panzer Army had not imagined that General Patton would have
been able to move any of his forces north so quickly.

'Towards noon,' Kokott wrote, 'at first singly, but then in droves,
men of the 5th Fallschirmjäger appeared near the divisional command
post at Hompré. They were coming from the front lines and moving
east. Barely an officer was in sight. When questioned, the men yelled:
"The enemy has broken through! They've advanced north with tanks
and have captured Chaumont!"' Chaumont was no more than three
kilometres to the south of Kokott's headquarters.

The stragglers were soon followed by vehicles and the horse-drawn
carts of the Fallschirmjäger division. In no time at all, American fighter-
bombers had sighted the congestion in Hompré and wheeled in to
attack. Any German with a weapon began 'firing wildly' at the attacking
planes. 'Houses caught fire, vehicles were burning, wounded men were
lying in the streets, horses that had been hit were kicking about.'

This chaos coincided with a massive supply drop all around Bastogne. German soldiers, on seeing the quantity of white and coloured
parachutes to their north, assumed in alarm that this was the start of a
major airborne operation. They took up the cry: 'Enemy paratroopers
are landing to our rear!' Even Kokott was shaken by an eventuality that
he had never considered. But a sort of order was gradually established,

with volksgrenadiers halting the young soldiers of the 5th Fallschirm-jäger who were fleeing. An anti-aircraft battery near Hompré received the order 'about face'. The gunners were to switch from aerial targets to prepare their guns for ground operations.

Kokott then improvised combat groups, taking command of four tanks which happened to be near by, an artillery detachment and some engineers, and reorganized some of the fleeing paratroopers who had recovered from 'their initial shock'. He ordered them to move south to take up position blocking the roads. The situation soon appeared to be restored. The American armoured force in Chaumont had only been a reconnaissance probe by forward elements from Patton's Third Army and, lacking sufficient strength, it pulled back.

The first warning the Germans received of the American airdrop to resupply the 101st Airborne and its attached units came soon after mid-day. The 26th Volksgrenadier-Division received the signal: '*Achtung!* Strong enemy formation flying in from west!' The Germans sighted large aircraft flying at low level accompanied by fighters and fighter-bombers. They expected a massive carpet-bombing attack, and opened rapid fire with their 37mm anti-aircraft guns.

They do not seem to have noticed the first pair of C-47 transports which dropped two sticks of pathfinders at 09.55 that morning. On landing, the pathfinders had reported to McAuliffe's command post in Bastogne to establish the best sites for the drop zones. Their mission had been deemed essential by IX Troop Carrier Command, because of fears that Bastogne might have already been overrun. The pathfinders then set up their homing beacons just outside the town and waited until the drone of approaching aircraft engines gradually built to a roar.

'The first thing you saw coming towards Bastogne', recorded a radio operator in the first wave of C-47 transports, 'was a large flat plain completely covered with snow, the whiteness broken only by trees and some roads and, off in the distance, the town itself. Next, your eye caught the pattern of tank tracks across the snow. We came down lower and lower, finally to about 500 feet off the ground, our drop height.' As the parachutes blossomed open, soldiers emerged from their foxholes and armoured vehicles, 'cheering them wildly as if at a Super Bowl or World Series game', as one put it. Air crew suddenly saw the empty, snowbound landscape come alive as soldiers rushed out to drag the 'parapacks' to safety. 'Watching those bundles of supplies and ammunition drop was a sight to behold,' another soldier recounted. 'As we retrieved the bundles, first we cut up the bags to wrap around our feet, then took the supplies to their proper area.' The silk parachutes were grabbed as sleeping bags.

Altogether the 241 planes from IX Troop Carrier Command, coming in wave after wave, dropped 334 tons of ammunition, fuel, rations and medical supplies, including blood, 'but the bottles broke on landing or were destroyed when a German shell blew up the room where they were stored'. Nine aircraft missed the drop zone or had to turn back. Seven were brought down by anti-aircraft fire. Some air crew were captured, some escaped into the forest and were picked up over the following days, and a handful made it to American lines. 'Not a single German aircraft could be seen in the skies!' Kokott complained. Luftwaffe fighters did attempt to attack the supply drop, but they were vastly outnumbered by the escorts and were chased away, with several shot down.

As soon as the transport planes departed, the eighty-two Thunderbolts in their escort turned their attention to ground targets. They followed tank tracks to where the Germans had attempted to conceal their panzers, and attacked artillery gunlines. Despite the best efforts of the air controllers, the Thunderbolts made several attacks on American positions. In one case a P-47 began to strafe and bomb an American artillery battery. A machine-gunner fired back, and soon several aircraft joined in the attack. Only when an officer ran out waving an identification panel did the pilots understand their mistake and fly off.

The attack of the 901st Panzergrenadiers against Marvie went ahead after dusk following the departure of the fighter-bombers. Artillery fire intensified, then Nebelwerfer batteries fired their multi-barrelled rocket launchers, with their terrifying scream. The German infantry advanced behind groups of four or five panzers. The 327th Glider Infantry and the 326th Airborne Engineer Battalion fired illuminating flares into the sky. Their light revealed Panther tanks, already painted white, and the panzergrenadiers in their snowsuits. The defenders immediately opened fire with rifles and machine guns. Bazooka teams managed to disable a few of the tanks, usually by hitting the tracks or a sprocket, which brought them to a halt but did not stop them from using their main armament or machine guns.

A breakthrough along the road to Bastogne was only just halted after McAuliffe threw in his last reserves and ordered the artillery to keep firing, even though their stocks of shells were perilously low. In fact the defenders fought back so effectively that they inflicted grievous losses. Kokott eventually abandoned the action. He then received an order from Manteuffel's headquarters that he was to mount a major attack on Bastogne on Christmas Day. The 15th Panzergrenadier-Division would arrive in time, and come under his command. Kokott might have been sceptical of his chances, but the defenders were just as hard pushed, especially on the western side.

The Americans could not cover the perimeter frontage in any strength, and they sorely lacked reserves in the event of a breakthrough. With the front-line foxholes so spread out in places, paratroopers resorted to their own form of booby-traps. Fragmentation grenades or 6omm mortar shells were attached to trees with trip wires extending in different directions. Fixed charges of explosive taped to trunks could be detonated by pullwires running back to individual emplacements.

Just south of Foy, part of the 506th Parachute Infantry continued to hold the edge of the woods. Their observation post was in a house, outside which a dead German lay frozen stiff with one arm extended. 'From then on,' a sergeant remembered, 'it was a ritual to shake hands with him every time we came or left the house. We figured that if we could shake his hand, we were a helluva lot better off than he was.' Even with the sacks and bags from the airdrop, frostbite and trench foot affected nearly all soldiers. And Louis Simpson with the 327th Glider Infantry observed, 'in this cold the life in the wounded is likely to go out like a match'.

Facing the attack around Flamierge, Simpson wrote: 'I peer down the slope, trying to see and still keep my head down. Bullets are whining over. To my right, rifles are going off. They must see more than I do. The snow seems to have come alive and to be moving, detaching itself from the trees at the foot of the slope. The movement increases. And now it is a line of men, most of them covered in white – white cloaks and hoods. Here and there men stand out in the gray-green German over-coats. They walk, run and flop down on the snow. They rise and come towards us again.'

*

Bastogne had naturally been a priority for American air support, and so were the hard-pressed 82nd Airborne and the 30th Division on the northern flank. But the top priority that day, with half of all Allied fighter-bomber units allocated, had been to stop the German panzer divisions from reaching the Meuse.

From the moment the weather improved and the Allied air forces were out in strength, incidents of friendly fire, both from the air and from the ground, increased dramatically. Anti-aircraft gunners and almost anyone with a machine gun seemed almost physically incapable of stopping themselves from shooting at any aircraft. 'Rules for Firing' and instructions on 'Air-Ground Recognition' were forgotten. Soldiers had to be reminded that they were not to fire back at Allied aircraft who might be shooting them up by mistake. All they could do was to keep throwing out yellow or orange smoke grenades to make them stop, or firing an Amber Star parachute flare. The self-control of the 30th Infantry Division was the most sorely taxed. These soldiers had suffered attacks by their own aircraft in Normandy, and now in the Ardennes they were to suffer even more.

Bolling's 84th Infantry Division and parts of the 3rd Armored Division continued, with great difficulty, to hold a line south of the Hotton–Marche road against both the 116th Panzer-Division and the 2nd SS *Das Reich*. Combat Command A of the 3rd Armored was pushed further round to the west, as a screen for the assembly of Collins's VII Corps. The 2nd Armored Division, Patton's former command known as 'Hell on Wheels', was arriving by forced march in great secrecy for a counter-attack planned for 24 December. The advance of the 2nd Panzer-Division was faster than expected. But Collins had been greatly relieved to hear from Montgomery, 'chipper and confident as usual', that the bridges over the Meuse at Namur, Dinant and Givet were now securely defended by the British 29th Armoured Brigade. It was that night that the 8th Rifle Brigade killed two Skorzeny commandos in a Jeep. The main problem at the bridges was the flood of refugees fleeing across the Meuse to escape. 'The German push has unsettled the whole population,' wrote an officer with civil affairs, 'and they seem to fear the worst. Already the refugees are moving along the roads and we are out to stop them causing trouble to traffic.' Blocked at the bridges, Belgians resorted to boats to cross the Meuse.

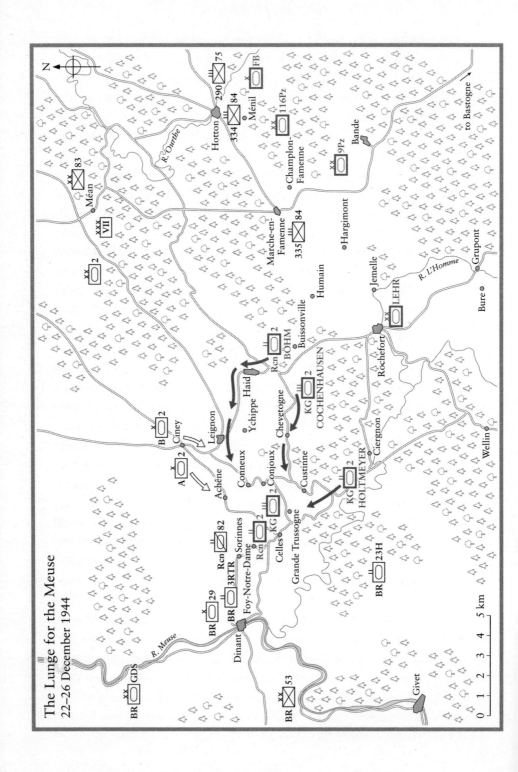

The Lunge for the Meuse
22–26 December 1944

N

to Bastogne

75
FB
290
84
Ménil
116Pz
Hotton
334
Champlon-
Famenne
83
Bande
Méan
9Pz
VII
Marche-en-
Famenne
84
Hargimont
335
2
Grupont
Humain
Jemelle
R. L'Homme
Buissonville
LEHR
Bure
2
Rochefort
Rcn
BÖHM
COCHENHAUSEN
2
Haid
KG
B
2
Ciney
Leignon
Ychippe
Chevetogne
Ciergnon
Wellin
A
2
Conneux
Conjoux
HOLTMEYER
Achêne
Custinne
2
KG
82
Custinne
Rcn
Sorinnes
2
KG
HOLTMEYER
3RTR
KG
Celles
2
R. Meuse
Foy-Notre-Dame
Rcn
Grande Trussogne
29
23H
BR
GDS
BR
BR
Dinant
BR
53
Givet
BR
0 1 2 3 4 5 km

Montgomery also assured Collins that the brigade would advance to link up with Collins's right flank on the next day, 23 December, but A Squadron of the 3rd Royal Tank Regiment commanded by Major Watts was already at Sorinnes, six kilometres east of Dinant. Watts had no idea where either the Americans or the Germans were, so he spread his eighteen tanks out to cover every route into Dinant, using them more like an armoured reconnaissance regiment. For the three armoured regiments in the brigade, the great frustration was to be going into battle with their 'battle-weary Shermans', rather than their new Comet tanks.

The British also started to receive valuable help from locals. The Baron Jacques de Villenfagne, who lived in the chateau at Sorinnes, just three kilometres north of Foy-Notre-Dame (not to be confused with the Foy near Bastogne), was a captain in the Chasseurs Ardennais and leader of the Resistance in the area. He acted as a scout for Watts's squadron on his motorcycle, and reported on the advance of the 2nd Panzer-Division in their direction.

The approaching battle made one thing very clear to farming folk. They needed to prepare food for what could be a long siege, sheltering in their cellars. At Sanzinnes, just south of Celles, Camille Daubois, hearing of the advance of German forces, decided it was time to slaughter his prize pig, a beast of 300 kilos. Because it was so large, he felt he could not do it himself, and called the butcher, who was about to take refuge beyond the Meuse. He only agreed to help with the slaughter, but when he arrived and saw the animal, he exclaimed: 'That's not a pig, that beast's a cow!' Not prepared to use the knife he insisted on an axe, with which he severed the head. They strung it up to drain the blood and the butcher dashed off. But when men from a Kampfgruppe of the 2nd Panzer arrived later, the pig's carcass disappeared, no doubt to their field kitchen known as a *Gulaschkanone*.

Oberst Meinrad von Lauchert, the commander of the 2nd Panzer-Division, split his force just north of Buissonville to search out the quickest route to the Meuse. The armoured reconnaissance battalion, under Major von Böhm, moved on ahead towards Haid and Leignon because it had been refuelled first. Two panzers in the lead sighted an American armoured car and opened fire. The armoured car was hit, but the crew escaped. Its commander Lieutenant Everett C. Jones got word to Major General Ernest Harmon, the commander of the 2nd Armored Division. The pugnacious Harmon, who was itching to go into the attack, ordered his Combat Command A under Brigadier General John H. Collier to advance immediately.

That evening the main panzer column, commanded by Major Ernst von Cochenhausen, reached the village of Chevetogne, a dozen kilometres north-west of Rochefort. The inhabitants of the village had so far had little more to fear than the V-1s flying overhead towards Antwerp, one of which had exploded in the woods near by. Apart from that, the war seemed to have passed them by. They had seen no American troops since the liberation of the area in September, and never imagined that the Germans would return.

Woken soon after midnight by the vibrations caused by tanks rumbling up the main street, the villagers crept to the windows of their houses to see if this force was American or German, but the vehicles were moving without lights and it was too dark to distinguish. The column came to a halt a little way up the hill, and then, to their alarm, they heard orders barked unmistakably in German. News of the massacres of civilians further east by the Kampfgruppe Peiper had spread rapidly. The black panzer uniforms with the death's-head badge prompted many to believe that these troops were also SS. But the 2nd Panzer-Division was different, and its behaviour towards civilians was on the whole correct. On entering a farm kitchen in Chapois, one of its officers warned the surprised housewife that she had better hide her hams. His soldiers were famished and they would not hesitate to take them.

In the early hours of 24 December, Kampfgruppe Cochenhausen reached Celles, a small and ancient town in a dip just a few kilometres south of Foy-Notre-Dame. Major von Cochenhausen attempted to push through the small town to head straight for Dinant, but the lead Panther tank hit a mine laid the day before by American engineers. According to local folklore, two German officers stormed into the little restaurant on the corner called Le Pavillon Ardennais. The *patronne*, Madame Marthe Monrique, who had just been woken by the blast, met them downstairs in her dressing gown. They demanded to know how many kilometres they still had to cover to reach Dinant. With great presence of mind, she apparently replied that there were only a dozen kilometres. 'But the road is mined, you know! The Americans have buried hundreds of mines.' Cursing, the Germans decided to pull back into nearby woods in case Allied aircraft caught them in the open at dawn.

Cochenhausen established his command post in the woods at a local grotto known as the Trou Mairia. His force included the 304th Panzergrenadier-Regiment, a battalion of the 3rd Panzer-Regiment, a panzer artillery regiment and most of the division's anti-aircraft battalion. Signs pointing to the divisional field hospital or *Feldlazarett* bore the trident symbol of the 2nd Panzer-Division. To prevent information getting back to the Allies, panzergrenadiers were put to work sawing down telephone poles and cutting wires. Another detachment of the 2nd Panzer-Division was just to the east at Conjoux. The villagers there were reminded how in September the local German commander had sworn, just before pulling out, that they would be back.

After Leignon, Böhm's Kampfgruppe had turned west in the night towards Dinant. Just before Foy-Notre-Dame, near the farm of Mahenne, a British Firefly Sherman of the 3rd Royal Tank Regiment lay in wait. The Firefly had the longer and far more powerful 17-pounder or 76.2mm high-velocity gun. Sergeant Probert, the commander, hearing the unmistakable noise of tracked vehicles approaching, woke his crew. The first round missed the leading vehicle but hit a munitions truck, causing an explosion which must have shaken the whole German column. After rapidly reloading, Probert's crew got off another round which destroyed a Mark IV panzer. Then, following the Royal Armoured Corps slogan of 'shoot and scoot', they reversed out rapidly before the Panthers in the column targeted their position. They reported back to Major Watts at Sorinnes. Major von Böhm, unsure after the ambush how strong the Allies were in the area, and because his vehicles were almost out of fuel, decided to halt at the small village of Foy-Notre-Dame. His crews concealed their vehicles in farmyards, and packed into the houses to warm up and find food.

During that night of 23–24 December, the thermometer dropped to minus 17 Centigrade, and the moon shone on the frozen, snowbound landscape. The Baron de Villenfagne, with his friend Lieutenant Philippe le Hardy de Beaulieu, both dressed in white, managed to identify several of the main German positions. They came across a group of amphibious vehicles concealed under trees at Sanzinnes, which was subsequently shelled by American artillery. The two men returned to the Château de Sorinnes at 04.00 hours and woke Major Watts. Lieutenant Colonel Alan Brown, the commanding officer of the 3rd Royal Tank Regiment, arrived soon afterwards and they briefed them on the German dispositions and the location of Cochenhausen's command post. The vital target was the Ferme de Mahenne, because if that were neutralized the Kampfgruppe Böhm would be separated from Cochenhausen's force. The baron then went to see the 29th Brigade's artillery commander, begging him to spare the great church at Foy-Notre-Dame, which the gunners managed to do when shelling the village taken over by Böhm's Kampfgruppe.

Hitler was exultant when he heard that the forward elements of the 2nd Panzer-Division were now only seven kilometres from Dinant. He passed on his warmest congratulations to Lüttwitz and Lauchert, the divisional commander. Both men must have winced, knowing how precarious their position was, with little chance of supplies getting through. Lüttwitz, who had commanded the 2nd Panzer in the doomed Avranches counter-attack in August, recommended to Manteuffel that they should start to withdraw the division from the tip of the whole German salient. But he knew that Hitler would never contemplate such a move.

On the left flank of the 2nd Panzer, Bayerlein's Panzer Lehr had advanced from Saint-Hubert north to Rochefort, with General von Manteuffel accompanying them. Their artillery shelled the town in the afternoon. A patrol entered the edge of Rochefort and reported back that it was empty, but they had not looked carefully enough. A battalion from the 84th Infantry Division and a platoon of tank destroyers were concealed and waiting. The road into Rochefort ran along the L'Homme river in a rocky gorge, which made the German attack a risky enterprise. As night fell, Bayerlein gave a characteristic order: 'Right, let's go! Shut your eyes and in you go.'

Led by the 902nd Panzergrenadiers, commanded by Oberstleutnant Joachim Ritter von Poschinger, the charge was brought to a sudden halt under a massive fusillade at a major barricade in Rochefort. The fighting was ferocious and lasted through the night. The panzergrenadiers lost many men and a heavy Jagdpanzer was knocked out near the central square. The American defenders, heavily outnumbered, were eventually forced back. The survivors escaped north next day, to join up with the 2nd Armored Division.

Most of the townsfolk sought shelter in caves at the base of the cliffs surrounding Rochefort. They were to stay there for some time, since Rochefort now became a target for American artillery. During the worst of the shelling, Jeanne Ory and her younger sister asked their mother: 'Mummy, are we going to die?' She replied: 'Say your prayers, my children.' And everyone around would recite the rosary together. One man found a friend dead in the frozen street face down with a cat sitting serenely on his back, profiting from the last of the body's heat. The Trappist monks from the Abbaye de Saint-Remy took on the task of removing bodies.

That evening, President Roosevelt in Washington wrote to Josef Stalin. 'I wish to direct General Eisenhower to send to Moscow a fully qualified officer of his staff to discuss with you Eisenhower's situation on the Western Front and its relation to the Eastern Front, in order that all of us may have information essential to our coordination of effort . . . The situation in Belgium is not bad but it is time to talk of the next plan. In view of the emergency an early reply to this proposal is requested.' Stalin replied two days later to agree. The very mention of 'emergency' in the last sentence must have suggested to him that the Allies had their backs against the wall. Air Chief Marshal Tedder and General Bull were designated to confer with Stalin. They prepared to fly from France to Cairo and then on to Moscow, but because of long delays they would not see Stalin until 15 January, well after the crisis was over.

17

Sunday 24 December

Sunday 24 December again produced bright sun and blue skies. Captain Mudgett, the 12th Army Group meteorologist in Luxembourg, was 'almost hysterical with his continued success in the weather. He looks proudly out over the blue sky that stretches way into Germany over the stone ramparts and the three spires of the cathedral.'

Bradley's Eagle Tac headquarters now had few fears about the defence of Bastogne, with the men of the 101st Airborne 'clinging stubbornly to their position like a wagon train in the pioneer days of the west'. But staff officers were well aware of the plight of the wounded in the town. McAuliffe had asked for four surgical teams to be dropped by parachute. Plans went ahead for them to be brought in by glider instead.

While Patton's III Corps with the 4th Armored Division was struggling to break through to Bastogne from the south against much heavier resistance than expected, Hansen was amused by a bizarre report. 'Today a quartermaster soldier asked for the road to Luxembourg while passing through Arlon. He got on the wrong road, [and] drove up the road to Bastogne. When someone fired on him, he only got more frightened, pressed his accelerator and finally drove into the area of the 101st – the first person to make contact with them, and in a purely accidental manner.'

Confirmation of the tough fighting on the southern side of the perimeter came from a signals intercept. The 5th Fallschirmjäger-Division was clamouring for more Panzerfausts and anti-tank guns to help in its battle against the 4th Armored Division. The Third Army commander appeared to have no doubts about the outcome. 'General Patton was in several times today,' Hansen noted. 'He is boisterous and noisy, feeling good in the middle of a fight.' But in fact Patton was concealing his embarrassment that the 4th Armored's advance was not going nearly as rapidly as he had predicted and was meeting tough opposition. The division had also found that VIII Corps engineers in the retreat to Bastogne 'blew everything in sight', so their progress 'was impeded not by the enemy but by demolitions and blown bridges caused by friendly engineers'.

The Luxembourgers were more confident. They were reassured by the endless convoys of Third Army troops streaming through the city, and believed that the Germans would not be coming back. Strangely, 12th Army Group intelligence suddenly increased their estimate of German tank and assault-gun strength from 345 to 905, which was rather more than the earlier estimated panzer total for the whole of the western front.

Despite the terrible cold which made men shiver uncontrollably in their foxholes, morale was high within the Bastogne perimeter. Although the paratroopers and 10th Armored looked forward to relief by Patton's forces, they rejected any idea that they needed to be saved. With another brilliant day of flying weather, they watched the sky fill with Allied planes of every description. They listened to bombs exploding and the clatter of machine guns, as fighters strafed the German columns. Dogfights against the few Focke-Wulfs and Messerschmitts provoked ferocious cheers and roars as if it were a deadly boxing match, and bitter cries broke out if an Allied transport dropping supplies was hit by ground fire.

Allied fighter-bombers during this period proved very effective in breaking up German attacks as they were assembling. They were directed on to targets by air controllers in Bastogne. A warning of the threat, with co-ordinates coming from a regimental command post or an artillery liaison plane, meant that 'it was usually only a matter of minutes until planes were striking the enemy forces'.

With priority on artillery ammunition in the airdrops, the food situation for troops barely improved. Many depended on the generosity of Belgian families sharing what they had. Both in Bastogne and on the northern shoulder, 'rations were frequently supplemented with beef, venison and rabbit when these animals set off the mines by running into the trip-wires'. Snipers shot hare and even boar, but the longing for wild pork was greatly reduced after hogs had been sighted eating the intestines of battle casualties.

The intense cold and deep snow caused more than discomfort. They greatly affected fighting performance. Those who did not keep a spare set of dry socks in their helmet–liner and change them frequently were the first to suffer from trench foot or frostbite. The newly arrived 11th Armored Division on the Meuse followed, perhaps unknowingly, the old practice of Russian armies for avoiding frostbite, by providing blanket strips to make foot bandages. Tank crewmen standing on metal in such conditions for hours on end, not moving their feet sufficiently, were particularly vulnerable. But at least those in armoured vehicles and truck drivers could dry out their footwear on engine exhausts.

Condoms were fitted over the sights of anti-tank guns, and also on radio and telephone mouthpieces, because breath condensation soon froze them up. The traverse mechanism on tanks and tank destroyers needed to be thawed out. Snow would get into weapons and ammunition clips and freeze solid. Machine guns were the most likely to jam. The heavy .50 machine gun was essential for shooting enemy marksmen out of trees and other hiding places. American soldiers soon discovered that German snipers waited for artillery or anti-aircraft fire before they pulled the trigger, so that their shot would not be heard.

Lessons learned in one sector were rapidly passed to other formations through 'combat observer' reports. German patrols would cut cables at night and run one of the severed ends into an ambush position, so that they could seize any linesman sent out to repair it. German soldiers sometimes fired a bullet through their own helmet in advance, so that if they were overrun they could play dead and then shoot one of their attackers in the back. They often mined or booby-trapped their own trenches just before withdrawing.

American patrols were advised that when encountering the enemy at night, 'fire at random, throw yourself into cover, then yell like mad as if you were going into the attack, and they will start firing', which would reveal their position. In defence, they should place dummies well to the front of their foxholes to prompt Germans to open fire prematurely. They should provide cover for the enemy in front, but bury mines under it; construct fake defences between strongpoints. Just before going into the attack, it helped to make digging noises to mislead the enemy. And when inside a house, they should never fire from the window, but keep it open and shoot from well back in the room.

The most respected and vital members of a company were the aid men. They were trusted with grain alcohol to prevent the water freezing in their canteens which they would offer to the wounded. 'The stimulating effect of the alcohol does no harm either,' the report added. Chaplains were also sent to the aid stations with alcohol to make a hot toddy for wounded men coming in. Countless men later acknowledged that they owed their lives to the dedication, courage and sometimes inventiveness of aid men. PFC Floyd Maquart, with the 101st, saved one soldier severely wounded in the face and neck by cutting open his throat with a parachute knife and inserting the hollow part of a fountain pen into his windpipe.

Conditions for more than 700 patients in the riding school and the chapel of the seminary in Bastogne continued to deteriorate, since the German capture of the field hospital meant that there was only one surgeon. The doctor from the 10th Armored was assisted by two trained Belgian nurses: Augusta Chiwy, a fearless young woman from the Congo, and Renée Lemaire, the fiancée of a Jew arrested in Brussels by the Gestapo earlier in the year. Those with serious head and stomach wounds were least likely to survive, and the piles of frozen corpses grew, stacked like cordwood under tarpaulins outside. A number of patients suffered from gas gangrene which gave off an appalling stench, and the stock of hydrogen peroxide to clean such wounds was almost all gone. The dwindling supply of plasma froze solid, and bags had to be thawed by being placed in somebody's armpit. For some operations, a slug of cognac had to replace anaesthetics. Sedatives were also in very short supply to deal with the increasing number of combat-fatigue casualties, who would sit up and suddenly start screaming. Men who had demonstrated great bravery in Normandy and in Holland had finally succumbed to stress and exhaustion. Cold and lack of proper food had accelerated the process.

As well as the setpiece assaults, which Generalmajor Kokott had been forced to launch, there were many more German attacks at night, often with four tanks and a hundred infantry. Their soldiers in snow suits were well camouflaged out in the snowfields, but when they were against a dark background of trees or buildings they stood out. Realizing this they took off the jacket, but the white legs still gave them away.

'Knocking out tanks is a matter of team-work, mutual confidence and guts,' an VIII Corps report stated. 'The infantry stay in their foxholes and take care of the hostile infantry and the tank destroyers take care of the tanks.' Providing both elements did their job, the Germans were usually repulsed. Some paratroopers, however, clearly got a thrill out of stalking panzers with bazookas. The 101st claimed that altogether between 19 and 30 December it knocked out 151 tanks and assault guns and 25 half-tracks. These figures were almost certainly exaggerated, rather like the victories claimed by fighter pilots. Many targets were shared with the Sherman tanks of the 10th Armored and the Hellcats of Colonel Templeton's 705th Tank Destroyer Battalion.

The continuing fight against the 901st Panzergrenadiers around Marvie had become increasingly confused in the early hours of the morning. An American machine-gunner shot two glider infantrymen who appeared over a crest. The Americans were forced back from the village, but managed to hold the hill to the west. McAuliffe's headquarters in Bastogne re-examined their defences. The push into the town from Marvie had only just been stopped, but they were also vulnerable on the western side of the perimeter. It was decided to pull back from the Flamierge and Mande-Saint-Etienne salient, and withdraw from Senonchamps. Reducing the overall frontage would strengthen their lines, but they also reorganized their forces by attaching tanks and tank destroyers permanently to each regiment.

Generalmajor Kokott, meanwhile, was left in no doubt from both his corps commander Lüttwitz and Manteuffel that Bastogne must be crushed next day, before the 4th Armored Division broke through from the south. Kokott, while waiting for the 15th Panzergrenadier-Division to deploy on the north-western sector, became increasingly concerned about the 5th Fallschirmjäger's defence line to the south. He thought it prudent to set up a southern security screen of 'emergency platoons' from his own supply personnel with a few anti-tank guns. The anti-aircraft battalion near Hompré was also told to be ready to switch to a ground role to take on American tanks. It was a comfort to know that at least the main road south to Arlon was covered by the 901st Panzergrenadier-Regiment from the Panzer Lehr.

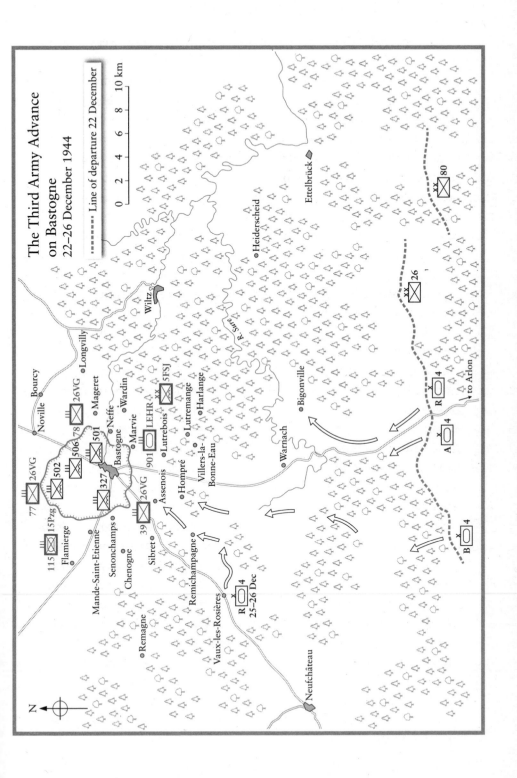

The Third Army Advance
on Bastogne
22–26 December 1944

- - - - Line of departure 22 December

0 2 4 6 8 10 km

N

Noville
Bourcy
Longville
26VG
Mageret
78
506
501
Neffe
Bastogne
Marvie
Wardin
LEHR
5FSJ
Lutrebois
Lutremange
Harlange
Villers-la-
Bonne-Eau
Hompré
Warnach
Bigonville
Heiderscheid
Ettelbrück
80
26
R 4
A 4
to Arlon
B 4
R-Sûre
Wiltz
26VG
77
502
15Pzg
115
Flamierge
Mande-Saint-Etienne
Senonchamps
Chenogne
327
26VG
39
Assenois
Sibret
Remichampagne
Remagne
Vaux-les-Rosières
Neufchâteau
901
R 4
25–26 Dec

The 5th Fallschirmjäger-Division certainly appeared ill equipped for its task of defending the southern flank of the Fifth Panzer Army. Its much disliked commander Generalmajor Ludwig Heilmann despised his Luftwaffe staff, claiming to have discovered 'corruption and profiteering' when he took over command. 'So far these people had been employed only in France and Holland,' he said later, 'and had vegetated on plundered loot and were all accomplices together.' He claimed that the older Unteroffizieren said quite openly that they 'would not dream of risking their life now at the end of the war'. The young soldiers, on the other hand, almost all of them under twenty and some just sixteen, 'made a better impression', even though they had received little training. Heilmann was being constantly questioned by his superiors on the exact positions of his regiments, but the reports he had received were so few and imprecise that he decided to go forward himself, if only to escape the 'harassing demands' from corps headquarters.

Yet despite the 5th Fallschirmjäger's apparent deficiencies, its mostly teenage soldiers were fighting with formidable resilience, as the 4th Armored Division was finding to its cost. That morning at dawn, the 53rd Armored Infantry Battalion and the 37th Tank Battalion attacked the village of Bigonville, more than twenty kilometres south of Kokott's command post. They were led by Lieutenant Colonel Creighton W. Abrams (later the commander of US forces in Vietnam), and took the place and the high ground behind in less than three hours. But then 'the enemy managed to infiltrate back into the town and more fighting was required to clear it'. To make matters worse, the American force was then bombed and strafed by P-47 Thunderbolts, which turned away only after coloured smoke grenades had been set off and snow brushed off identification panels. Securing Bigonville a second time took another three hours, and this village came at a heavy cost. Tank commanders, with their heads out of the turret, attracted the fire of German snipers, who 'accounted for nine in the 37th Tank Battalion, including the C Company commander'.

The 4th Armored Division was also suffering from the extreme weather. 'Our company commander was evacuated with pneumonia,' wrote a soldier with the 51st Armored Infantry Battalion, 'and we lost our platoon sergeant because his feet froze.' By the next day there was only one officer left in the company. Patton's hope of relieving Bastogne by Christmas was fading fast.

Kokott's forces like most German formations in the Ardennes were running short of ammunition, especially mortar rounds. Allied airstrikes on marshalling yards and forward supply lines were already having an effect. That afternoon, the Americans noticed that the German guns had fallen silent. The defenders guessed that they were conserving their ammunition for a major attack on Christmas morning.

Some fifty kilometres to the north, the remnants of Kampfgruppe Peiper in La Gleize had prepared the destruction of their vehicles, prior to a breakout on foot across the River Amblève. At 03.00 on 24 December, the main group of some 800 men crossed the river and trudged up through the thick woods on the south side towards the ridge line. Peiper, just behind the point detachment, took Major McCown with him. Two hours later they heard explosions behind them and, down in the valley, the ruined village was lit by the flames from burning vehicles.

Peiper, unsure where the German lines lay, led them south parallel with the River Salm. McCown recounted later that they had nothing to eat but four dried biscuits and two gulps of cognac. An hour after dark they bumped into an American outpost, where a sentry opened fire. The panzergrenadiers were exhausted, especially the two dozen walking wounded. They blundered about in the dark, wading streams to avoid roads and villages. In the early hours of Christmas morning they ran into another American position north of Bergeval, triggering a formidable response with mortars and machine guns firing tracer. McCown escaped during the confusion, and rejoined the American lines where he identified himself to paratroopers of the 82nd Airborne. He was taken to General Jim Gavin's command post.

Peiper and his men withdrew down into the Salm valley and swam across the freezing river. The I SS Panzer Corps reported his arrival, apparently wounded, later on Christmas morning. This was at about the same time as the 30th Infantry Division crushed the other pocket of his men, trapped near Stavelot. Their resistance was fanatical, probably out of a belief that their opponents would not be taking prisoners. 'Attacking waves literally waded knee-deep through their own dead in their desperate assaults,' the after-action report stated. The divisional artillery commander estimated that there were more than a thousand German dead piled at one point, and the woods around Stavelot and La

Gleize were strewn with corpses. The Americans estimated that 2,500 members of the Kampfgruppe had been killed and ninety-two tanks and assault guns destroyed.

Now that the only breakthrough by the Sixth Panzer Army had been thoroughly destroyed, the eyes of Hitler and the OKW were firmly on Manteuffel's panzer divisions to the west. The build-up against the northern shoulder line appeared overwhelming. After the 2nd SS Panzer-Division *Das Reich* had crushed the force at Baraque-de-Fraiture, it was reinforced by the advance guard of the 9th Panzer-Division. The *Führer Begleit* Brigade was on its way to attack Hotton, and the 18th and 62nd Volksgrenadier-Divisions, supported by the 9th SS Panzer-Division *Hohenstaufen*, were attacking the 82nd Airborne on the Vielsalm sector, where General Ridgway insisted on holding a right-angled wedge.

General Bradley was outraged to hear that Montgomery had deployed Collins's VII Corps along the shoulder line rather than hold it back for a major counter-attack. (In fact it was Collins himself who had committed his divisions because there was no choice.) Once again it demonstrated how completely Bradley failed to understand what was really happening. With four panzer divisions attacking north and north-west, a defence line had to be secured before a counter-attack took place. First Army headquarters, which was considering a major withdrawal on the VII Corps front, even recorded that evening: 'Despite the air's magnificent performance today things tonight look, if anything, worse than before.' Concern about a breakthrough by the panzer divisions to the west even prompted First Army to consider pulling back all the heavy equipment of V Corps in case of a sudden retreat.

Ridgway was livid when Montgomery overruled him once more, on this occasion by ordering Gavin's 82nd Airborne to withdraw from Vielsalm to the base of the triangle from Trois-Ponts to Manhay. The 82nd was coming under heavy pressure from the 9th SS Panzer-Division *Hohenstaufen*, the rest of the 1st SS Panzer-Division and the 18th and 62nd Volksgrenadier-Divisions. Yet Ridgway felt insulted by the idea that the United States Army should be ordered to give ground in this way. He attributed the move to Montgomery's obsession with 'tidying-up the battlefield', and protested vehemently to General Hodges, 'but apparently received little sympathy there', as Hansen later acknowledged. Bradley became obsessed with Montgomery's decision and harped on about it for some time to come.

Gavin, however, saw the point of the redeployment, and Montgomery was almost certainly right. The 82nd was already overstretched even before the next wave of German formations was due to arrive. Reducing their front from twenty-seven kilometres to sixteen meant a much stronger defence line. The withdrawal began that night, and 'morale in the 82nd was not materially affected'. Gavin's paratroopers soon had plenty of frozen German corpses to use as sandbags in their new positions, and they refused to allow Graves Registration personnel to take them away.

Task Force Kane and a regiment of the newly arrived 17th Airborne were positioned to defend the Manhay crossroads, against what First Army headquarters still believed to be an attempt to capture American supply bases in Liège. The untried 75th Infantry Division was on its way to support Rose's 3rd Armored Division as it attempted to extricate Task Force Hogan, surrounded at Marcouray.

The defenders at Manhay expected a fearsome attack by the *Das Reich*, but it advanced cautiously through the forests either side of the highway and occupied Odeigne. This was partly due to continuing fuel-supply problems, but mainly to avoid moving in the open on another day of brilliant sunshine. An armoured column in daylight would become easy prey for the fighter-bombers overhead, scouring the snow-bound landscape for targets.

Brigadeführer Heinz Lammerding, the commander of the *Das Reich* responsible for the massacres of Tulle and Oradour-sur-Glane on their advance north to Normandy in June, was tall and arrogant with a pitted face. He was famous for his ruthlessness, like most of his officers. They even thought it funny that the *Das Reich* had murdered the inhabitants of the wrong Oradour. 'An SS-Führer told me with a laugh', Heydte was secretly recorded later as saying, 'that it had been the wrong village. "It was just too bad for them," [he said]. It turned out afterwards that there weren't any partisans in that village.'

As soon as dark fell and the Thunderbolt and Lightning fighter-bombers had departed, the tanks and half-tracks of the SS *Das Reich* emerged from the woods and drove north towards Manhay. The Germans employed their usual trick of placing a captured Sherman at the head of the column. The Americans held their fire, in case it was a task force from the 3rd Armored Division. But then the SS fired flares to blind the American tank gunners. Two panzergrenadier regiments attacked abreast at 21.00. By midnight, they had taken Manhay. The combat command of the 7th Armored lost nineteen tanks in the night battle, and its exhausted tank crews had to escape on foot. The *Das Reich* panzer regiment lost none.

Waldenburg's 116th Panzer-Division, having been sent round to the west of the River Ourthe, received orders to break through between Marche-en-Famenne and Hotton, then to swing west towards Ciney to protect the right flank of the 2nd Panzer-Division. But Bolling's 84th Infantry Division held a strong line south of the main Marche–Hotton road. The 116th managed to break through around the village of Verdenne, but the success did not last. This was just the start of what Waldenburg called 'bitter and ever-changing' battles. Houses and positions changed hands many times.

Marche itself was threatened. The twenty-one-year-old Henry Kissinger with the 84th's intelligence branch volunteered to stay behind under cover despite the added risk of being Jewish. But Bolling's men held firm and his artillery eventually inflicted terrible losses on Waldenburg's men. Field artillery battalions used the new Pozit fuse at high elevation, if necessary by digging down the trails, so as to achieve air bursts over the German positions. The American infantry watched the effect with savage glee, and reported back '*beaucoup* dead'.

Allied fighter-bombers also wheeled back and forth, dropping bombs and strafing. 'Of the German Luftwaffe nothing was to be seen or heard,' Waldenburg commented angrily. The closest his panzergrenadiers came to Marche was the treeline north-west of Champlon-Famenne overlooking the town, where they were constantly bombarded by American artillery. To this day the local landowner cannot sell timber from the forest because of the shards of metal buried deep in the massive conifers.

At the furthest tip of the German salient, the 2nd Panzer-Division had now lost three tanks in its clashes with the 3rd Royal Tank Regiment. Lieutenant Colonel Brown, concerned that the Germans were now so close to the bridge at Dinant, reinforced the approaches in case panzer-grenadiers tried to slip through on foot. He had learned that the German fuel situation had become desperate. British artillery began to bombard 2nd Panzer positions around Celles, and plans were made to attack from Sorinnes the next day to crush Böhm's reconnaissance battalion in Foy-Notre-Dame. Brown did not yet know that the British 53rd Division was starting to cross the Meuse, so he would have strong support.

Major General Harmon, instantly recognizable from his barrel-chest, military moustache and gravelly voice, could scarcely control his impatience to be at the enemy. He had received orders from General Collins to hold back until the moment was ripe for a counter-attack, but Collins could not be reached as he was preoccupied with the dangerous situation on his east flank. Montgomery had even issued an instruction that, because of the threat from the 2nd Panzer and Panzer Lehr in the west, Collins's corps could, 'if forced', swing back to a line between Hotton and Andenne, some thirty kilometres north of Marche as the crow flies. This would have constituted a major retreat and, unlike the withdrawal of Gavin's 82nd Airborne, a huge mistake. But fortunately Montgomery had left Collins with the authority to take his own decisions.

Harmon suspected that there was a large panzer force around Celles, but had no confirmation until two P-51 Mustangs reported flak firing from near by. (No contact had yet been established with the British at Sorinnes.) Amid considerable confusion between First Army headquarters and VII Corps during Collins's absence, Harmon refused to wait any longer. He ordered his Combat Command B to join Combat Command A at Ciney, and sent forward two battalions of self-propelled artillery. When finally Collins spoke to Harmon by telephone that evening and gave him leave to attack next morning, Harmon apparently roared: 'The bastards are in the bag!' Montgomery backed Collins's decision to deploy the 2nd Armored Division, even though it now meant that his plan to hold back the VII Corps for a counter-attack had unravelled.

The Cochenhausen Kampfgruppe had taken up all-round defence in two pockets between Celles and Conneux, while awaiting promised reinforcements from the 9th Panzer-Division. But the 9th Panzer was in turn delayed, waiting to refuel. The 2nd Panzer's forward elements were also clamouring for ammunition and fuel, but the extended supply line was far from secure. This was made worse by renewed American attacks on the high ground south-west of Marche and the increasing numbers of Allied fighter-bombers overhead. Staff in the 2nd Panzer-Division headquarters south of Marche burned with frustration that this should happen when they were so close to their objective. An instruction from Generalfeldmarschall Model went out to Foy-Notre-Dame: 'If necessary, elements of the reconnaissance battalion were to capture the Dinant bridge on foot, in a coup de main,' just as Colonel Brown had imagined. But Böhm's Kampfgruppe was the hardest pressed of all, as British artillery ranged in on it.

Frustration soon turned to alarm in the 2nd Panzer-Division head-quarters 'since both pockets reported that their supply of ammunition and fuel would not allow them to continue the battle much longer', Oberstleutnant Rüdiger Weiz recorded. 'And since the fuel available at the front was not sufficient for the withdrawal of the forces, the nearly unsolvable question arose how to bring help to the elements fighting in the front line.'

Lauchert decided to pull out the Kampfgruppe commanded by Major Friedrich Holtmeyer screening Marche. He ordered it to move west via Rochefort, and thrust towards Conneux to relieve the encircled forces there. This operation could be carried out only at night because of American air supremacy. Lüttwitz agreed with the plan, but permission first had to be obtained from Fifth Panzer Army headquarters. Lauchert received authorization that afternoon, but the reconnaissance battalion was no longer responding on the radio. Holtmeyer's force set out that evening, but this difficult manoeuvre in the dark was further hindered by American groups attacking as they withdrew.

Ten kilometres south-east of Marche, the village of Bande stands on a hill above the N4 highway from Marche to Bastogne. As mentioned earlier, German SS troops had burned thirty-five houses along the N4 highway near the village during their retreat from the region in September as a reprisal for attacks by the Belgian Resistance. On 22 December, leading elements of the 2nd Panzer-Division had passed by, and on the following day some of their troops were billeted in the village. They behaved well. On Christmas Eve, a very different group, some thirty strong, appeared wearing grey SS uniforms. They had the badge of the

Sicherheitsdienst – an SD in a lozenge – on the left sleeve. The majority of this Sondereinheitkommando 8 were not German, but French, Belgian and Dutch fascists led by a Swiss and attached to the Gestapo.

They stayed apart from the panzergrenadiers, and took over some wooden buildings near the main road. Christmas Eve happened to be a Sunday, so almost the whole village was at mass. As the doors opened afterwards and the congregation came out, every man of military age was seized, supposedly for an examination of identity papers. Altogether some seventy men were rounded up. Just under half – those aged between seventeen and thirty-one – were taken under guard down to a sawmill near the main road where they were locked up. Many of them were refugees from elsewhere, but they too were interrogated brutally about the attacks in the area on retreating German forces three and a half months before. One by one, they were taken out and shot.

There was just a single survivor, Léon Praile, a powerful and athletic twenty-one-year-old. He had tried to persuade others to join him in rushing their guards, but could find no volunteers. When his turn came – by then night was falling fast – he suddenly punched his escort hard in the face and took off, leaping a low stone wall and sprinting towards the stream. Shots were fired in his direction, but he escaped.

When the village was eventually liberated in January by British paratroopers from the 6th Airborne Division, the Abbé Musty and Léon Praile took them to where the thirty-four bodies, by now frozen stiff, had been concealed. 'After the deed was done,' stated the British report, 'the Germans half covered the bodies with earth and planks. Finally they wrote on a wall of the house "Revenging the honour of our German heroes, killed by the Belgians" . . . [the victims] show signs of having been beaten before being shot through the back of the head.'

The massacre seemed inexplicable to the villagers, and the shock produced a false rumour that Praile could have escaped death only by betraying his comrades. Over the years this idea became a fixation. Praile decided never to return to the region.

Generaloberst Guderian, the army chief of staff responsible for the eastern front, drove from Zossen, south of Berlin, to see Hitler at the Adlerhorst. It was quite clear to him that the Ardennes offensive had failed to achieve its goals and was not worth continuing. The point of maximum danger lay to the east, where the Red Army was preparing its great winter offensive. In his briefcase he had a rather more accurate assessment than usual from Generalmajor Reinhard Gehlen, the head of Fremde Heere Ost, the army intelligence department dealing with the eastern front. Gehlen had been wrong many times in the past, which did not help his arguments, but Guderian was convinced that his warnings were correct. Gehlen's department estimated that the Red Army had a superiority of eleven to one in infantry, seven to one in tanks and twenty to one in artillery. Soviet aviation also enjoyed almost total air supremacy, which prevented the Germans from carrying out photo-reconnaissance.

In the conference room, Guderian found himself facing Heinrich Himmler, the Reichsführer-SS, Generalfeldmarschall Keitel and Generaloberst Jodl. As he presented the intelligence estimates, Hitler stopped him. He declared that such estimates of Soviet strength were preposterous. Red Army tank corps had hardly any tanks and their rifle divisions were reduced to little more than 7,000 men each. 'It's the greatest imposture since Genghis Khan,' he shouted. 'Who is responsible for producing all this rubbish?'

Guderian's attempts to defend Gehlen's figures were treated with contempt, and Jodl, to his horror, argued that attacks in the west should continue. At dinner Himmler, a military ignoramus who had just been made commander-in-chief Army Group Upper Rhine, confidently told Guderian that the Soviet build-up was an enormous bluff. Guderian had no option but to return in despair to Zossen.

On the extreme right of Patton's two army corps, the 5th Infantry Division had begun to advance north-west from behind the 4th Infantry Division. Hemingway, recovered from flu and drinking his own urine, watched and joked on a hilltop with friends from his adopted division as the soldiers below proceeded in extended order wearing their bedsheet camouflage and firing aimlessly in front of them. There did not seem to be any Germans shooting back. On Christmas Eve he went to the 22nd Infantry's headquarters at Rodenbourg not knowing that the new commander, Colonel Ruggles, had also invited Hemingway's estranged wife. Ruggles had sent a Jeep to Luxembourg to fetch Martha Gellhorn, hoping it would be a pleasant surprise for both of them. The disengaged couple found themselves having to share a room.

The night before Christmas carried a special significance for soldiers on both sides. In Bastogne, the less seriously wounded received rations of brandy and listened to the endlessly repeated song 'White Christmas' on a salvaged civilian radio. North-east of the town in Foy, German soldiers packed into houses and farms to get warm. A young German soldier quietly told the Belgian family in whose house he was billeted that he intended to go home alive: three of his brothers had already been killed. On other parts of the perimeter American soldiers listened to their enemies singing 'Stille Nacht, Heilige Nacht'. They could only talk about Christmas at home, imagining their families in front of warm fires. Some of their luckier comrades to the rear attended a midnight mass, such as the one in the chapel of the Château de Rolley, packed with refugees and the family of the owners. In most cases, they also sang 'Silent Night', thinking of home. In Bastogne, about a hundred soldiers assembled for mass in front of an improvised altar lit by candles set in empty ration tins. The chaplain in his address to them offered simple advice. 'Do not plan, for God's plan will prevail.'

At Boisseilles, between Celles and Foy-Notre-Dame, German soldiers also joined the civilians sheltering in the chateau there. One panzergrenadier from the 2nd Panzer, perhaps inflamed by alcohol, declared that 'Tomorrow we will cross the Meuse!' Another, in a more realistic frame of mind, sighed, 'Poor Christmas.'

The advanced units of the 2nd Panzer were famished, if not starving. In Celles an Alsatian soldier knocked at a door and, when the family opened it cautiously, went down on his knees to beg for a little food. The condition of many of them was so pitiable that locals felt compelled to give their occupiers something to eat out of Christian charity. There were impressively few cases of 2nd Panzer soldiers seizing food at gunpoint, although some might order a farmer's wife to make them soup, or a pie from her store of preserved fruits in jars, as a Christmas gesture. Others forced local women to wash their socks or underclothes.

German soldiers, despite their intense hunger, were even more desperate to find drink to drown their sorrows on Christmas Eve. In Rochefort, a fourteen-year-old girl, Liliane Delhomme, saw a *Landser* smash the glass door of the Café Grégoire with his fist, cutting himself badly in the process, to get himself a bottle. Homesickness is worse at Christmas. Many soldiers gazed at photographs of their family and wept silently.

Infantrymen on both sides spent the night in their foxholes. The Americans had only frozen C-Rations to celebrate with, which was at any rate more than most Germans. One paratrooper described how he cut out chunks of frozen hash one by one to thaw them out in his mouth before being able to eat them. On the most northerly shoulder at Höfen, a soldier in the 99th Infantry Division wrote in his diary: 'The fellows are calling up and down the line wishing each other a Merry Christmas. It is a very pretty night with the ground covered with snow.' The fortunate ones were visited by an officer passing round a bottle.

Command posts and higher headquarters had Christmas trees, usually decorated with the strips of aluminium foil for radar-jamming. The higher the headquarters, the greater the opportunity for a proper celebration. The city of Luxembourg, still untouched by the war, now felt secure. And as snowflakes fell gently on the night of Christmas Eve, US Army chaplain Frederick A. McDonald was about to conduct the service in a candle-lit church. He had been warned that General Patton would be attending communion that night. The church was packed, but McDonald had no trouble recognizing 'this General of stern expression' standing alone and erect at the back. He went to welcome him and mentioned that, in the First World War, Kaiser Wilhelm II had come to services in this church. McDonald, no doubt aware of this general's desire to commune with history, asked: 'Would you, sir, like to sit in the Kaiser's pew?' Patton smiled. 'Lead me to it,' he said.

18

Christmas Day

The short-lived silence of Christmas night in Bastogne was broken by a Luftwaffe bomber flying over the town dropping magnesium flares, followed by waves of Junkers 88. The Americans had come to regard the Luftwaffe as a spent force, and the effect was far more devastating than even the most intense artillery bombardment. The shock was still worse for the refugees and Bastognards packed into the cellars, when buildings collapsed above them.

McAuliffe's headquarters were hit. Walls vibrated as in an earthquake, and everyone was terrified they would be crushed by falling masonry. In the packed cellars of the Institut de Notre-Dame, people prayed or screamed in panic as clouds of dust descended. Several became completely crazed.

Captain Prior, the doctor with the 10th Armored aid station, had been sharing a Christmas bottle of champagne with several of his colleagues, including Augusta Chiwy, the Congolese nurse. They were all thrown to the ground by the force of a blast, and Prior suddenly feared that the aid post itself had been hit. Coated in dust, they struggled out into the street. The three-storey building had collapsed on top of their wounded patients and the ruins were on fire. Chiwy's fellow nurse Renée Lemaire was killed along with some twenty-five of the seriously wounded, burned to death in their beds. Soldiers rushed up to pull away debris to create an exit, but attempts to put out the fire with buckets of water were fruitless and soon abandoned. Some of the wounded, surrounded by flames, begged to be shot. The low-flying bombers machine-gunned the streets, prompting paratroopers to fire back with rifles. Bastogne had no anti-aircraft defences because the quadruple .50 half-tracks were all deployed to bolster the perimeter defences.

This attack, which was renewed several hours later, was clearly the opening salvo of the Germans' Christmas Day onslaught. The *Arko*, or senior artillery commander of the Fifth Panzer Army, had come on Manteuffel's instructions to supervise fire control. Kokott had moved his command post to Givry opposite the north-west flank. This sector had fewer woods and villages, which the Americans had used so effectively as strongpoints, and the open terrain presented obstacles no greater than small gullies covered with snow. Even so, most of his volks-grenadiers dreaded the battle to come, and were not convinced by the exhortations and promises of their officers that this time they had over-whelming strength.

The double offensive from the north-west and the south-east was planned to break into Bastogne itself within five hours, but Kokott was dismayed to find that the 15th Panzergrenadier-Division was much weaker than he had expected. It had little more than a Kampfgruppe commanded by Oberstleutnant Wolfgang Maucke, with three battalions of panzergrenadiers, twenty tanks and assault guns, and two battalions of self-propelled artillery. A smaller force from the division had yet to catch up and would not be there until a day later.

The first assault was directed against the sector just in front of the village of Champs. At 05.00, Kokott's 77th Grenadier-Regiment stole up on American foxholes without a preparatory bombardment. Only then did German artillery begin firing against American gun positions. The village of Champs was 'taken, lost and re-taken' in furious fighting, Kokott observed. A company of paratroopers and two tank destroyers inflicted heavy casualties on his men. Their intensive training to 'strip and repair weapons under fire and in the dark' had certainly paid off. Stoppages on a jammed machine gun were cleared in moments, and the firing recommenced. Corporal Willis Fowler manning a machine gun on the west side of Champs managed to destroy a whole company of grenadiers while four German panzers hung back on the ridgeline behind them. American artillery was also extremely effective in break-ing up attacks, and at 09.00 the warning cry of 'Jabos!' was heard in German ranks as American fighter-bombers dived in.

Kampfgruppe Maucke, meanwhile, had steamrollered the positions of the 401st Glider Infantry south-west of Champs and reached the hamlet of Hemroulle, less than three kilometres beyond. A group split off north to attack Champs, and a savage battle took place around the 502nd Parachute Infantry Regiment's command post and aid station. They were based in the Château de Rolley, an imposing eighteenth-century building next to a massive round tower which remained from the original medieval castle. A bridge leading to Rolley had been mined, but the extreme frost meant that the firing mechanism failed as the German panzers crossed. On that morning of plunging temperatures, when the wind whipped particles of snow off the frozen crust like sea-spray, paratroopers resorted to urinating on their machine guns to unfreeze the mechanism.

Every signaller, driver and cook in the chateau grabbed a rifle or bazooka to form a defence platoon. The doctor caring for the wounded on stretchers even had to hand a rifle to one of his patients, who became agitated at the thought of being caught unarmed. People shouted at the doctor to burn the book recording the dog-tag numbers of their dead, so that the enemy would not know how many paratroopers they had killed.

One member of the improvised defence group, Sergeant 'Sky' Jackson, managed to knock out several tanks. Another bazooka man was so carried away by excitement that he forgot to arm his round, so when it hit the tank there was just a loud clang. A Hellcat tank destroyer knocked out one more Panther. 'The Germans piled out of the tanks and they were mowed down,' another soldier recorded. 'It was just red blood on the snow.' Screams could be heard from inside one of the panzers.

A company of the 502nd Parachute Infantry Regiment sighted around 150 German infantry and four Mark IV panzers, which opened fire. The paratroop lieutenant pulled his men back to the line of a wood. He ordered his machine-gunners to keep the infantry down and the tanks 'buttoned up' by constant fire, while he and another bazooka team stalked them from around their flanks. They knocked out three tanks with their bazookas, and the neighbouring company got the fourth. The paratroopers had little to eat that day. Most had no more than half a cup of soup with white 'navy', or haricot, beans to keep them going.

In this all-out effort, Kampfgruppe Kunkel attacked again in the south-west near Senonchamps up towards Hemroulle. And on the far side of the perimeter, 'success seemed very close' by 10.00 as the 901st Panzergrenadiers fought their way in from the south-east. An assault group reached the road-fork at the entrance to Bastogne, and a German breakthrough appeared almost inevitable. In McAuliffe's makeshift headquarters staff officers prepared their weapons, and supply personnel collected any spare bazookas for a last-ditch defence.

'The Germans attacked our positions with tanks,' Corporal Jackson of the 502nd Parachute Infantry Regiment recorded. 'I was back at the C[ommand] P[ost] and we received word that more bazookas and bazooka ammunition were needed up front. I took a bazooka and all the ammunition I could carry. When I got to the front, I saw one tank retreating and one Mark IV, with nine men riding on it, out in a field. When the tank was about 40 yards away and broadside on, I jumped out and fired, hitting the tank in the side, just above the track. The rocket killed or stunned four of the men riding on the tank, and the tank immediately stopped and started to burn.' The crew and the remaining infantry were shot down as they tried to escape.

Even the snub-barrelled howitzers of a parachute field artillery battalion took on the panzers over open sights. Most destructive of all were the P-47 Thunderbolt fighter-bombers, dropping napalm 'blaze bombs' or strafing with their .50 machine guns. Local farms and their inhabitants were not spared in what American commanders saw as a fight to the finish.

The fire of Shermans, Hellcat tank destroyers and bazookas in the fighting around Champs, Rolley and Hemroulle inflicted heavy losses. By the afternoon, the 15th Panzergrenadier-Division reported that it hardly had a battle-worthy tank left. Another desperate assault was launched after dark, supported by the remaining Jagdpanzer tank destroyers from the reconnaissance battalion. Bazooka teams from the 502nd Parachute Infantry stalked and knocked out half of them at close range, including the commander's vehicle.

In the south-east, the assault group from the Panzer Lehr's 901st Panzergrenadiers were 'cut off and annihilated'. The regiment had no reserves left to reinforce or extricate them. Almost every man available had already been thrown into the battle. Kokott called off any further attacks. The 15th Panzergrenadier-Division was practically wiped out, and his own division had suffered more than 800 casualties. Most companies now mustered fewer than twenty men, and a whole battalion in the 78th Grenadier-Regiment was reduced to forty. The worst losses were among the experienced officers and Unteroffizieren. 'We were 900 metres from the edge of Bastogne,' an officer in the 26th Volksgrenadier-Division complained bitterly, 'and couldn't get into the town.'

Kokott reported to corps headquarters that his forces were so reduced that any further attacks on Bastogne would be 'irresponsible and unfeasible'. Lüttwitz agreed that the encircling forces should simply hold their present positions until the arrival of Remer's *Führer Begleit* Brigade in the next forty-eight hours. But Kokott also heard that the 5th Fallschirmjäger was failing to hold the increasing attacks by Patton's forces coming from the south. All his volksgrenadiers could do was to lay minefields and prepare more anti-tank positions on the approach routes. The Ardennes offensive had failed, Kokott concluded. He wrote that the great operation had turned into a 'bloody, dubious and costly struggle for what was, in the final analysis, an unimportant village'. Evidently Führer headquarters was not prepared to accept the facts of the situation.

While the battle raged north and south-east of Bastogne, the pilot of a light observation plane, braving the flak, flew in a surgeon with supplies of penicillin. A P-38 Lightning also dropped maps, which were still in short supply, and a set of photo-reconnaissance prints of the whole area. That was all the defenders received that day, for bad visibility in England had prevented another major airdrop. To make matters worse, Patton's promised Christmas present of a breakthrough to Bastogne had not materialized. McAuliffe made his feelings clear by telephone to General Middleton, the VIII Corps commander. 'We have been let down,' he said.

Patton's III Corps was close. Around Lutrebois, just six kilometres south of the centre of Bastogne, the 134th Infantry Regiment of the 35th Division was closely supported by artillery and tank destroyers. German tanks had been spotted in the woods ahead, so the field artillery opened fire. Some Shermans, attracted by the firing, came up and joined in. Bazooka men had 'to lie in wait or sneak up just like stalking a moose'. They had been told to aim for the tracks on a Panther, as rounds simply bounced off its armour. In the end, out of twenty-seven German tanks, only three escaped.

The 4th Armored Division was battering the 5th Fallschirmjäger units south of Bastogne between the roads to Arlon and Neufchâteau. As the village of Assenois shook from the relentless explosions of shells, civilians could do little but hope and pray. 'We feel like we are in God's hand,' a woman wrote, 'and we surrender ourselves to it.' The Walloons were largely Catholic and deeply religious. Committing themselves to the hands of the Almighty was undoubtedly a comfort, when they had so little control over their own fate. Reciting the rosary together helped dull the pain of individual fear, and calm the nerves.

During the battle for Hemroulle, Model and Manteuffel had visited Lüttwitz's corps headquarters at the Château de Roumont near the highway to Marche. Lüttwitz was even more concerned about his old division stranded round Celles, and again urged that the 2nd Panzer must be saved by permitting its rapid withdrawal. Model and Manteuffel 'showed understanding', but they 'obviously were not authorized to decide the withdrawal of the 2nd Panzer-Division'. That order could come only from Hitler, and he was certainly not prepared to admit defeat.

Lüttwitz's worst fears for the Böhm and Cochenhausen Kampfgruppen were being realized as they spoke. The Allied counter-attack had begun before dawn. The artillery with the 29th Armoured Brigade began to bombard Böhm's reconnaissance battalion in Foy-Notre-Dame, and fulfilled their promise of avoiding the seventeenth-century church. American artillery batteries took up position in the fields around the villages of Haid and Chevetogne. When they had reached Haid the evening before they celebrated with the locals, who made galettes and hot chocolate: with milk from their own cows and melted Hershey bars. Afterwards, the American soldiers accompanied their new friends to midnight mass in the church. Only a couple of days before a sixteen-year-old Alsatian, who had been dragooned into the Wehrmacht, had broken down in tears, telling a farmer's wife about the horrors they had been through.

In Chevetogne, an officer went round the houses warning people to leave their windows open, or the blast from the guns would shatter them. Villagers watched an artillery spotter plane, which they called 'Petit Jules', circle over German positions. A little later, twin-tailed P-38 Lightning fighter-bombers appeared in force.

Combat Command A of Harmon's 2nd Armored Division advanced

south to Buissonville a dozen kilometres to the east of the Cochenhausen Kampfgruppe, and clashed with a force from the Panzer Lehr
which had advanced from Rochefort. They tracked one of the German
columns to the farm of La Happe where fighting began. Most civilians
in the area immediately took to their cellars, but a few climbed up to
attics to watch the deadly firework display of a tank battle. Some twenty-
nine Germans were killed and many more seriously wounded. The
latter were carried to a barn and laid on the straw.

Combat Command B, meanwhile, coming from Ciney, split into two,
with one task force heading for Conjoux and the other for Celles to surround the main Cochenhausen Kampfgruppe spread between the two
villages. The Germans round Celles were sitting targets: they did not
even have enough fuel for the *Feldlazarett*'s ambulance. In Celles itself,
most of the inhabitants sheltered in the crypt of the church with the
nuns and the priest. The straw laid during the September fighting was
still there. Some farmworkers brought down a pail of milk for the children when there was a lull in the firing, and cooked a chicken which had
been killed by an explosion. The rest crouched in cellars as the shells
flew overhead. The Americans were using phosphorus shells, and naturally the locals feared for their farms.

The Shermans of the 3rd Royal Tank Regiment, supported by the
American 82nd Reconnaissance Battalion and with P-38 Lightning fighters overhead, advanced from Sorinnes on Foy-Notre-Dame. It was
retaken that afternoon, along with Major von Böhm and 148 of his men.
Only a few managed to escape through the deep snow. Some families
stayed hidden after the village had been liberated because they still heard
firing, but this was due to a blazing half-track in a farmyard on which the
ammunition continued to explode for a long time. For most, the first thing
to do was to cut squares of cardboard as an emergency repair to their
smashed windows. It was a great relief that this battle of the 'Tommies'
and 'Sammies' against 'les gris' – the 'greys', or Germans – had finally
come to an end.

A small girl among those being evacuated to Sorinnes had lost her
shoes, so an American soldier from the 82nd Reconnaissance Battalion
forced a German prisoner at gunpoint to take off his boots and give
them to her. They were much too large, but she was just able to walk,
while the German soldier faced frostbitten feet.

After American and British artillery had hammered the German positions round the farm of Mahenne between Foy-Notre-Dame and Celles, a local story grew up that SS officers had set fire to the place; but no SS were in the area and the destruction was entirely caused by shelling. Once again the black overalls and death's-head badge of the panzer arm appear to have been mistaken for the Waffen-SS.

Combat Command B of the 2nd Armored Division also entered Celles that afternoon. The famished and exhausted panzer troops, short of ammunition and out of fuel, could not resist for long. Mopping up continued for another two days. Some 2,500 Germans were killed or wounded and another 1,200 captured. In addition, eighty-two armoured fighting vehicles and eighty-two artillery pieces were taken or destroyed, as well as countless vehicles, many of which had been booty taken from American forces earlier. Most were out of fuel and ammunition.

Major von Cochenhausen, with some 600 of his men, managed to escape on foot across country after splitting up. Many were only too willing to give up. Around Celles, hidden Germans begged locals to find the Americans and tell them that they were ready to surrender. They were worried that if they appeared suddenly, even with their hands up, they might be shot. Some were afraid that, because they wore so many items of American uniform, they might be mistaken for members of the Skorzeny Kampfgruppe. In a few cases as a sign of goodwill they handed over their pistol to a Belgian civilian, who would then hand it over to the American soldiers. The locals did not realize until it was too late that they could have made a lot of money selling them instead. 'The Americans were mad to get their hands on one,' a farmer said. Many civilians were also afraid of holding on to items of German equipment in case the enemy returned yet again and found them in their houses.

Apart from the 2nd SS *Das Reich*, which still caused great concern to First Army in the fighting round Manhay and Grandménil, the other panzer divisions fared little better on the north-western flank of the Bulge. The 116th Panzer was still ordered to break through east of Marche, but as Generalmajor von Waldenburg recorded, the 'divisional units which fought in this battle were nearly completely wiped out', and Kampfgruppe Beyer of the 60th Panzergrenadiers was cut off. Only a few men and vehicles managed to escape.

That night Generalfeldmarschall von Rundstedt informed Hitler that the offensive had failed. He recommended a withdrawal from the salient before the bulk of Army Group B was trapped. Hitler rejected his advice angrily and insisted on more attacks against Bastogne, unaware that even more Allied reinforcements were arriving. The 17th Airborne Division was moving into position, although an VIII Corps staff officer thought that its paratroopers had 'a lot to learn'. The newly arrived 11th Armored Division also lacked experience, especially the drivers of their Shermans. 'Their tanks left a trail of uprooted trees and torn wire lines,' a report commented.

'A clear cold Christmas,' Patton wrote in his diary that day, 'lovely weather for killing Germans, which seems a bit queer, seeing Whose birthday it is.' Patton had moved his headquarters into the Industrial School in Luxembourg. He proudly showed off his lights, with the bulbs hanging in captured German helmets acting as lampshades.

But the festival brought little joy to the Belgian population of the Ardennes. In a village close to Elsenborn, where the fighting had died down, the Gronsfeld family decided to come out of their cellar to celebrate Christmas Day. The light was blinding with the sun reflecting off the snow as they sat at the kitchen table, father, mother and their young daughter, Elfriede. Suddenly, a German shell exploded near by, sending a sliver of shrapnel through the window. 'It cut deep into Elfriede Gronsfeld's neck. American medics came to her aid, but there was nothing they could do. The girl was buried on December 29. She was five years old. "What can one say to the mother?" one of the village's women mourned in her diary. "She cries and cannot understand."'

An American soldier on the Elsenborn ridge wrote to his wife that day: 'The bombers have fine, feathery white streams of vapor streaked across the sky and the fighters scrawl wavy designs as they try to murder each other.' They would keep their eye on Piper Cub artillery spotters, often half dozen or more in the sky at once. When the aircraft suddenly kicked their tails straight up and dived towards the ground, 'we knew it was time to look for cover'. In another letter he wrote, 'We're getting strafed once or twice a day by our own planes.'

Profiting from clear skies again, American fighter-bombers 'like a swarm of wasps' roamed over St Vith as well. 'We prefer to walk instead of using a car on the main highway,' a German officer wrote in his diary.

'The American Jabos keep on attacking everything which moves on the roads . . . We walk across the fields from hedgerow to hedgerow.' But soon a much heavier droning sound of aircraft engines could be heard. Formations with seventy-six B-26 bombers had arrived and proceeded to flatten the remains of St Vith. The tactic was cynically known as 'putting the city in the street', that is to say filling the roads with rubble so that German supply convoys could not get through this key crossroads.

General Bradley, who had withdrawn into himself due to the shame of losing the bulk of his 12th Army Group to Montgomery, had barely involved himself in the advance of Patton's two corps. But on Christmas Day, at Montgomery's invitation, he flew to St Trond near 21st Army Group headquarters at Zonhoven accompanied by a fighter escort. He was determined to push Montgomery into launching an immediate counter-offensive. 'Monty was always expecting everybody to come to him,' Bradley complained later with justification. 'Ike insisted on my going up to see him. I don't know why in the hell I should.' Although Montgomery's headquarters looked 'very festive', with the walls covered in Christmas cards, Bradley claimed that he had only an apple for lunch.

Bradley's version of their encounter was so suffused with resentment that it is hard to take it literally. One can certainly imagine that Montgomery showed his habitual lack of tact and displayed an arrogant self-regard to the point of humiliating Bradley. He even harped on again about the single command of ground forces which should be given to him, and repeated his exasperating mantra that all their setbacks could have been avoided if only his strategy had been followed. But Bradley's accusation that 'Monty has dissipated the VII Corps' by putting it into the line rather than holding it back for a counter-attack again demonstrated his ignorance of events in the north-west. He even claimed to Patton on his return to Luxembourg that Montgomery had said that 'the First Army cannot attack for three months'. This is very hard to believe.

On the other hand, there is no doubt that Montgomery was influenced by intelligence reports which said that the Germans intended to make another reinforced lunge for the Meuse. He therefore wanted to hold back until they had spent their strength. But his instruction the day before to Hodges's headquarters that Collins's VII Corps should be prepared to fall back in the west as far north as Andenne on the Meuse was an astonishing mistake which Collins had been absolutely right to disregard. So while Bradley had underestimated the German threat between Dinant and Marche, Montgomery had exaggerated it. Unlike American commanders, he did not sense that Christmas Day had marked the moment of maximum German effort.

Bradley had convinced himself that the field marshal was exploiting the situation for his own ends and was frightening SHAEF deliberately with his reports. He told Hansen later: 'I am sure [it was] Montgomery's alarms that were being reflected in Paris. Whether we realized it or not Paris was just hysterical.'* He then added: 'I am sure [the] Press in the US got all their information and panic from Versailles.' He felt that they should have a press section at 12th Army Group to counter the wrong impressions. British newspapers seemed to revel in stories of disaster, with headlines such as 'Months Added to War?' The next morning after his return, Bradley contacted SHAEF to demand that the First and Ninth Armies should be returned to his command, and he proposed to move his forward headquarters to Namur, close to the action on the northern flank. The war within the Allied camp was approaching a climax, and Montgomery had no inkling that he was playing a losing hand very badly indeed.

* SHAEF was hardly being duped by Montgomery. General Bedell Smith admitted later that the alarmist tone in cables back to Washington was a deliberate tactic. 'You know, we exploited the Ardennes crisis for all it was worth' to get resources and replacements which were otherwise going to the Pacific. 'We were short of men, so we yelled loud. We asked for everything we could get.'

19

Tuesday 26 December

On Tuesday 26 December, Patton famously boasted to Bradley: 'The Kraut has stuck his head in the meat grinder and I've got the handle.' But this bravado concealed his lingering embarrassment that the advance to Bastogne had not gone as he had claimed it would. He was acutely aware of Eisenhower's disappointment and frustration.

After the brilliant redeployment of his formations between 19 and 22 December, Patton knew that his subsequent handling of the operation had not been his best. He had underestimated the weather, the terrain and the determined resistance of the German Seventh Army formations defending the southern flank of the salient. American intelligence had failed to identify the presence of the *Führer Grenadier* Brigade, another offshoot of the *Grossdeutschland* Division. And the 352nd Volksgrenadier-Division, based on the formation which had inflicted such heavy losses on Omaha beach, deployed next to the 5th Fallschirmjäger. At the same time, Patton had overestimated the capacity of his own troops, many of them replacements, especially in the weakened 26th Infantry Division in the centre. His favourite formation, the 4th Armored Division, was also handicapped by battle-weary tanks. The roads were so icy that the metal-tracked Shermans slid off them or crashed into each other, and the terrain, with woods and steep little valleys, was not good tank-country.

Patton's impatience had made things worse by demanding head-on attacks, which resulted in many casualties. On 24 December, he acknowledged in his diary: 'This has been a very bad Christmas Eve. All along our line we have received violent counter-attacks, one of which forced the

4th Armored back some miles with the loss of ten tanks. This was probably my fault, because I had been insisting on day and night attacks.' His men were weak from lack of rest. Things looked little better on the morning of 26 December. 'Today has been rather trying in spite of our efforts,' he wrote. 'We have failed to make contact with the defenders of Bastogne.'

The defenders could hear the battle going on a few kilometres to the south, but having been let down before, they did not expect Patton's forces to break through. In any case, they were fully occupied in other ways. Another attack on the north-west sector reached Hemroulle. It was fought off by the exhausted paratroopers supported by the fire of field artillery battalions, but the American guns were now down literally to their last few rounds. At least the clear, freezing weather continued so the fighter-bombers could act as flying artillery. In the town, fires still raged from the bombing. The Institut de Notre-Dame was ablaze. American engineers tried to blast firebreaks, and human chains of refugees, soldiers and nuns passed buckets of water to keep the flames at bay.

The clear skies also permitted the arrival of sorely needed medical assistance. Escorted by four P-47 Thunderbolts, a C-47 transport appeared towing a Waco glider, loaded with five surgeons, four surgical assistants and 600 pounds of equipment, instruments and dressings. The glider 'cut loose at 300 feet' as if for a perfect landing, but it overshot and skidded over the frozen snow towards the German front line. 'The medical personnel barreled out and ran back to American lines while the doughboys charged forward to rescue the glider which carried medical supplies.' Another ten gliders followed bringing urgently needed fuel, then more waves of C-47 transports appeared to drop parachute bundles with 320 tons of ammunition, rations and even cigarettes.

The surgeons wasted no time. They went straight to the improvised hospital in the barracks and began operating on the 150 most seriously wounded out of more than 700 patients. They operated all through the night and until noon on 27 December, on wounds that in some cases had gone for eight days without surgical attention. As a result they had to perform 'many amputations'. In the circumstances, it was a testament to their skill that there were only three post-operative deaths.

Generalmajor Kokott became increasingly concerned during the artillery battle on the southern side about the weight of guns supporting the

4th Armored Division. He heard alarming rumours about what was happening, but could obtain no details from the 5th Fallschirmjäger-Division. He knew that there had been heavy fighting round Remichampagne, then in the afternoon he heard that an American task force had taken Hompré. Assenois was now threatened, so Kokott had to start transferring his own forces south.

At 14.00, Patton received a call from the III Corps commander, who proposed a risky venture. Instead of attacking Sibret to widen the salient, he suggested a charge straight through Assenois north into Bastogne. Patton instantly gave the plan his blessing. Lieutenant Colonel Creighton Abrams, who commanded the 37th Tank Battalion from a Sherman named 'Thunderbolt', was told to go all the way. Abrams asked Captain William A. Dwight to lead a column of five Shermans and a half-track with infantry straight up the road. The corps artillery shelled Assenois and fighter-bombers dropped napalm, just before the Shermans in tight formation charged into the village firing every gun they had. The Germans who scattered on both sides of the road risked hitting each other if they fired back. Beyond Assenois, some volksgrenadiers hurriedly pushed some Teller mines on to the road. One blew up the half-track, but Dwight leaped down from his tank and threw the other mines aside to clear a path.

When Kokott heard from the commander of his 39th Regiment that American tanks had entered Assenois, he immediately knew that 'it was all over'. He gave orders for the road to be blocked, but, as he feared, they were too late. With the lead Sherman firing forward, and the others firing outwards, Dwight's little column blasted any resistance from the woods on either side of the road. At 16.45, soon after dusk, the lead Shermans of Abrams's tank battalion made contact with the 326th Airborne Engineers manning that sector. Troops and tanks from the rest of the 4th Armored Division rushed in to secure the slim corridor and protect a convoy of trucks with provisions, which raced in during the night. Major General Maxwell D. Taylor, the commander of the 101st Airborne, who had been in the United States, came in soon afterwards to take over from Brigadier General McAuliffe. The siege of Bastogne was over, but many feared that the main battle was about to begin.

The 5th Fallschirmjäger had been badly mauled. Major Frank, a battalion commander in the 13th Fallschirmjäger-Regiment who was captured that day and interrogated, was intensely proud of the way his youngsters had fought. Some of them were only fifteen. 'But what spirit!' he exclaimed later in prison camp. 'After we had been taken prisoner, when I was alone, had been beaten and was being led out, there were two of them standing there with their heads to the wall, just in their socks: "Heil Hitler, Herr Major!" [they said]. It makes your heart swell.'

Lüttwitz heard that the *Führer Begleit* Brigade was coming to help cut the corridor, but he and his staff did not believe it would arrive in time for an attack planned for the next morning. He then heard that they had run out of fuel. Lüttwitz observed acidly that 'the *Führer Begleit* Brigade under the command of Oberst Remer always had gasoline trouble'.

News of the 4th Armored's breakthrough spread rapidly and prompted exuberant rejoicing in American headquarters. The correspondents Martha Gellhorn and Leland Stowe stopped by Bradley's headquarters that evening to obtain more information, as they wanted to cover the relief of Bastogne. So did almost every journalist on the continent. The story was on almost every front page in the western hemisphere. The 101st Airborne found itself famous, but press accounts overlooked the vital roles of Combat Command B of the 10th Armored Division, the 705th Tank Destroyer Battalion and the artillery battalions.

Around Celles and Conneux mopping up continued all day, with some fierce engagements. But since the Panthers and Mark IVs were out of fuel and armour-piercing rounds, the fight was certainly one sided. The forward air controller with the 3rd Royal Tank Regiment called in a 'cab-rank' of rocket-firing Typhoons. The target was indicated with red smoke canisters, but the Germans rapidly fired similar-coloured smoke canisters into American positions east of Celles. 'Fortunately the RAF were not deceived by this,' Colonel Brown recorded, 'and made their attack on the correct target.' The 29th Armoured Brigade, still in the area, heard that it was to be reinforced by the 6th Airborne Division.

The Kampfgruppe Holtmeyer, on its way from Rochefort in a vain attempt to help its comrades at Celles and Conneux, had been blocked at Grande Trussogne, a few kilometres short of its objective. It picked up exhausted men who had escaped the night before from the reconnaissance battalion overrun at Foy-Notre-Dame. At Grande Trussogne, these troops were attacked by an infantry battalion of the 2nd Armored

Division supported by Shermans. An American Piper Cub spotter plane then called in British Typhoons whose rockets smashed the column mercilessly, killing Major Holtmeyer.

Manteuffel instructed the Kampfgruppe to withdraw to the bridge-head at Rochefort held by the Panzer Lehr. Lüttwitz's headquarters passed on the message immediately by radio. Holtmeyer's replacement gave the order to blow up the remaining vehicles. Next day, he and most of his men made their way on foot back towards Rochefort, concealed by falling snow. 'Luckily,' wrote Oberstleutnant Rüdiger Weiz, 'the enemy was slow in following up and did not attack the route of retreat in any way worth mentioning.' But American artillery did catch up and shell the bridge in Rochefort over the River L'Homme, causing a number of casualties. That night and the following day, some 600 men in small groups managed to rejoin the division.

Between Celles and Conneux, several Germans were captured in American uniform. They were not part of the Skorzeny Kampfgruppe, but were shot on the spot anyway. These unfortunates, suffering from the cold and on the edge of starvation, had stripped the clothes from dead Americans. In their desperation to live they pleaded with their captors, showing their wedding rings and, producing photographs from home, talked desperately of their wives and children. Most Alsatians and Luxembourgers from the 2nd Panzer-Division wanted to surrender at the first opportunity, and even some Austrians had lost their enthusiasm for the fight. One of them murmured to an inhabitant of Rochefort: 'Moi, pas Allemand! Autrichien.' And he raised his hands in the air to show that he wanted to surrender.

American soldiers in Celles, believing that Germans were hiding in the Ferme de la Cour just by the church, attacked it with flamethrowers. There were no Germans, only livestock which burned to death. It was the second time this farm had been burned down during the war. The first was in 1940 during the previous German charge to the Meuse.

At Buissonville, between Celles and Marche, American medical personnel set up their first-aid post in the church. The local priest and the American Catholic chaplain communicated in Latin as they worked together. In the same village, a less Christian attitude was adopted when American soldiers in a half-track took two German prisoners into the woods and shot them. They explained to Belgians who had witnessed the scene that they had killed them in revenge for the American prisoners who perished near Malmédy.

Some American officers became rather carried away by the victory over the 2nd Panzer-Division. 'It was estimated that the division's strength just before this four-day period was approximately 8,000 men and 100 tanks,' claimed a senior officer at VII Corps. 'Of the personnel, 1,050 were captured and an estimated 2,000–2,500 killed. Materiel captured or destroyed included 55 tanks, 18 artillery pieces, 8 anti-tank guns, 5 assault guns, and 190 vehicles . . . The meeting of the US 2nd Armored Division and the German 2nd Panzer-Division was a fitting comparison of Allied and German might.' But this triumphalism rather overlooked the fact that the 2nd Panzer was out of fuel and low on ammunition, and the men were half starved.

After the battle, according to the Baron de Villenfagne, the countryside around Celles was 'a vast cemetery of vehicles, destroyed or abandoned, and of equipment half buried in the snow'. Teenagers, obsessed by the war, explored burned-out panzers and examined the carbonized bodies inside. A number indulged in dangerous war games. Some collected hand grenades, then threw them to blow up in abandoned half-tracks. A boy in Foy-Notre-Dame died after playing with a Panzerfaust which exploded.

The setback before Dinant only seemed to increase German bitterness. When a woman in Jemelle had the courage to ask a German officer why his men had nearly destroyed their village, he retorted: 'We want to do in Belgium what was done to Aachen.'

West of Hotton, most of the 116th Panzer-Division's attempts to relieve its surrounded Kampfgruppe were crushed by American artillery fire. But eventually a feint attack to distract the Americans enabled the survivors to break out clinging to armoured vehicles, and throwing grenades as they crashed through American lines.

During the battle, the *Führer Begleit* Brigade had received orders to disengage and head to Bastogne to assist Kokott's attempts to close the corridor. Oberst Remer protested twice at the casualties that this would cost, but was overruled each time. Remer also complained that 'motor fuel was so scarce that almost half of the vehicles had to be towed', so it is hard to tell whether Lüttwitz's suspicions were justified.

East of Hotton, Rose's 3rd Armored Division faced attacks from the

560th Volksgrenadiers consisting mainly of 'four or five tanks with an infantry company or about twenty tanks with an infantry battalion'. These were supported by self-propelled assault guns and artillery. But the arrival of the 75th Infantry Division to strengthen Rose's task forces meant that the sector had a stronger defence, even though its untried units suffered badly in their counter-attacks to secure the Soy–Hotton road. The icy conditions were proving particularly difficult for Sherman tank crews, because the metal tracks were so narrow and had little grip. Urgent efforts were made to add track extensions and spike-like studs to cope with the problem.

Lammerding, the commander of the *Das Reich*, was still trying to turn his division west from Manhay and Grandménil to open the road to Hotton and attack the 3rd Armored Division from behind; but the 9th SS Panzer-Division *Hohenstaufen* had still not come up to protect his right flank. With thirteen American field artillery battalions on a ten-kilometre frontage to the north, such a manoeuvre was doubly dangerous; and the *Das Reich* was fast running out of ammunition and fuel. Local farmers were forced at gunpoint to take their horses and carts to the rear to fetch tank and artillery shells from German dumps.

On the morning of 26 December, the 3rd SS Panzergrenadier-Regiment *Deutschland* from the *Das Reich* Division again attacked west from Grandménil. But American artillery firing shells with Pozit fuses decimated its ranks, then a reinforced task force from the 3rd Armored Division attacked the village. One German battalion commander was killed and another badly wounded. The II Battalion was trapped in Grandménil, and the rest of the regiment was forced to withdraw towards Manhay. American tanks and artillery harried it all the way back.

General Hodges and Major General Ridgway, still mistakenly fearing an attack north towards Liège, had been furious at the loss of Manhay. They left Brigadier General Hasbrouck of the battered and exhausted 7th Armored under no doubt that he had to retake it at whatever cost. The division's assault on Christmas Day had been dogged by heavy losses, largely because of the number of trees which it had blasted down across the road in its retreat. But preceded by a fresh battalion of the 517th Parachute Infantry, Hasbrouck's force entered Manhay that night.

Fifty wounded from the II Battalion of the 3rd SS Panzergrenadier-Regiment could not be extricated from Grandménil. The Germans claimed that when they sent in ambulances well marked with the Red Cross, American tank crews shot them up. The regiment then attempted to send out an officer and an interpreter under a white flag of truce, and a doctor with a flag and armband, to see whether they could evacuate their wounded from Grandménil. But according to the German account, 'the enemy opened fire on the parliamentaries, so this attempt had to be abandoned'. The Germans did not seem to understand that after the Malmédy massacre the SS were unlikely to be accorded any honours of war. So, leaving a medical orderly with their wounded, the remnants of the battalion slipped back to a defence line with the *Der Führer* Regiment near Odeigne, which was shelled all day by American artillery.

German activity around the Elsenborn ridge had almost ceased, so patrols from the 99th Infantry Division went forward to destroy ten enemy tanks from the 3rd Panzergrenadiers which had been abandoned after being stuck in the mud. This was to forestall German recovery teams, which were tireless and often ingenious in their attempts to retrieve and repair armoured vehicles.

American salvage parties, often manned by those showing signs of combat fatigue to give them a bit of a break, were sent off to collect weapons and ammunition thrown away earlier in the battle. American commanders were appalled by the tendency of their men to discard equipment and expect the military cornucopia to replace them at will. 'If the soldier does not need it right then, he will get rid of it,' one report stated. 'A bazooka man must not have a rifle. He must be given a pistol instead for personal protection. Otherwise, he will discard the bazooka and its shells because they are cumbersome and heavy.' Winter clothing, on the other hand, was jealously guarded. In most battalions a man at the aid station was told to take the padded 'arctic' coats from wounded men so that these vital items of clothing would not be lost to the unit.

St Vith had suffered badly on Christmas Day. Civilians had stayed in their cellars thinking that the worst must now be over, but in the afternoon of 26 December the 'heavies' of RAF Bomber Command arrived overhead. Nearly 300 Lancasters and Halifaxes dropped 1,140 tons of high explosive and incendiary bombs.

The blast effect created shockwaves which could be felt in villages several kilometres away, and terrorized the townsfolk sheltering underground as buildings collapsed above them. According to one account, 'people were struggling against the asphyxiating smoke and soot when another bomb blew a hole in the cellar wall that made them catch their breaths again. Before long, however, burning phosphorus was seeping into the cellar. The malicious substance released poisonous fumes and in the larger rooms set mattresses on fire. With the help of German soldiers, the panic-stricken civilians clawed their way through the hole and into the pulverised street.'

In the St Josef Kloster the chapel collapsed, with blocks of stone and beams smashing through the floor and crushing those below. The incendiaries set fire to anything remotely combustible. They also turned the convent itself into a raging blaze, consuming the old and incapacitated trapped on the upper floors. 'Most of them were burned alive. Like a more liquid form of lava, hissing phosphorus poured into the cellars that remained standing. People with horrible burns, broken bones, and blown minds were pulled out through the few unobstructed air shafts. Among the last to leave the inferno were the convent's sisters, blankets tightly drawn over their heads and shoulders.'

'Saint-Vith is still burning,' a German officer outside the town recorded. 'The bomb carpets come close to our village. I have never seen anything like that in all my life. The whole countryside is covered by one big cloud of smoke and fire.' He returned to St Vith in the evening. 'All streets are burning ... Cattle are howling, ammunition exploding, tires burst. There is a strong smell of burnt rubber.' Delayed-action bombs continued to detonate from time to time.

In purely military terms, the raid was effective. St Vith was no more than 'a giant heap of rubble'. All roads were blocked for three days at least and some for over a week, while German engineers were forced to create bypasses round the town. But the cost in civilian lives and suffering was untold. Nobody knew exactly how many had taken shelter in St Vith, but some 250 are estimated to have died. The survivors fled to neighbouring villages where they were cared for and fed.

That same night and the next, medium bombers of the Ninth US Air Force attacked La Roche-en-Ardenne. Since La Roche was situated along a river in a narrow defile, it provided a much easier target and only 150 tons of bombs were needed to block the route.

'Things continued to look better all day today,' the First Army diarist recorded after a meeting between Montgomery and Hodges. Prisoner interviews suggested that the Germans were facing real supply problems. 'Although it is yet too early to be optimistic the picture tonight is certainly far rosier than on any other day since the counteroffensive began.' Bradley, however, was still obsessed with what he regarded as the premature deployment of Collins's VII Corps. He wrote to Hodges to complain of the 'stagnating conservatism of tactics there where Monty has dissipated his reserve'. Patton, heavily influenced by Bradley's view of the field marshal, wrote in his diary: 'Monty is a tired little fart. War requires the taking of risks and he won't take them.'

After a telephone call from Manteuffel, General Jodl summoned up the courage to tell Hitler, who had not moved from the Adlerhorst at Ziegenberg: '*Mein Führer*, we must face facts. We cannot force the Meuse.' Reichsmarschall Göring arrived at Ziegenberg the same evening and declared, 'The war is lost!' He suggested that they must seek a truce. Hitler, trembling with rage, warned him against trying to negotiate behind his back. 'If you go against my orders, I will have you shot!' Hitler made no further mention of Antwerp. Instead no effort was to be spared to take Bastogne. Just as he had focused on Stalingrad in September 1942, when victory in the Caucasus eluded him, the recapture of Bastogne now became his ersatz symbol of victory.

But while Hitler refused to face reality in public, in rare moments he acknowledged the hopelessness of their position. Late in the evening in the bunker at Ziegenberg, he spoke to his Luftwaffe adjutant, Oberst Nicolaus von Below, about taking his own life. He still blamed setbacks on the Luftwaffe and the 'traitors' in the German army. 'I know the war is lost,' he told Below. 'The enemy superiority is too great. I have been betrayed. After 20 July everything came out, things I had considered impossible. It was precisely those circles against me who had profited most from National Socialism. I pampered and decorated them, and that was all the thanks I got. My best course now is to put a bullet in my head. I lacked hard fighters . . . We will not capitulate, ever. We may go down, but we will take the world with us.'

20

Preparing the Allied Counter-Offensive

Even though the 4th Armored Division had broken through to Bastogne, the airdrop planned for 27 December still went ahead. This time, however, the Germans were better prepared. General McAuliffe's warning that the aircraft should approach by a different route never got through. The curtain of flak and machine-gun fire was formidable, but the C-47 transports towing the gliders held their course. Eighteen gliders out of fifty were shot down and many others were riddled with bullets. One glider exploded in a fireball as a direct hit from flak set off the ammunition it was carrying. Gasoline cans were also hit and began to leak, but miraculously none caught fire.

Altogether some 900 aircraft – both transport and escort fighters – took part in the operation, and twenty-three were shot down. Paratroopers on the ground rushed from their foxholes to rescue those who had baled out and gave them slugs of brandy, to dull the pain from burns and twisted limbs. The pilot of one heavily hit C-47 managed a belly landing in the snow, although it clipped a truck on the road and spun it round, to the terror of the driver who had not seen it coming in.

The forty trucks that had brought in supplies during the night turned south again, loaded with the less seriously wounded, some of the German prisoners of war and glider pilots. Together with seventy ambulances carrying the 150 most serious cases, they trundled south escorted by light tanks through the narrow corridor. Intensive fighting began around

Bastogne's southern flank as the Americans tried to widen the gap, and the Germans did all they could to seal it.

On 28 December, General Bradley wrote a memo for Eisenhower, urging him to put pressure on Montgomery. 'With the enemy attack losing its momentum in the Ardennes,' he wrote, 'it is important that strong counter-attacks be launched while his stocks of supplies are depleted, his troops tired and before he has had time thoroughly to dig in and consolidate his gains. The object of the counter-attack would be to trap the maximum enemy troops in the salient and to put our forces in a favorable position for further offensive action . . . The counter-attack must be launched immediately. Reports have been received that the enemy is digging in along the shoulders of his salient.'* Bradley was wrong to think that 'further delay will permit the enemy to bring more troops into the salient'. That very day First Army noted that 'high intelligence channels [a euphemism for Ultra] report that German concerns over the Soviet advance in Hungary might prompt the transfer of troops from the Ardennes to the Balkan front'. And in fact the opposite to what Bradley feared was soon to happen as the Red Army prepared its major winter offensive.

That evening Bradley was at least able to divert himself when Leland Stowe and Martha Gellhorn, who had not managed to get to Bastogne, came to dinner at the Hôtel Alfa in Luxembourg. Bradley appeared to be 'much smitten with "Marty" Gellhorn', Hansen recorded. 'She's a reddish blonde woman with a cover girl figure, a bouncing manner and a brilliant studied wit where each comment seems to come out perfectly tailored and smartly cut to fit the occasion, yet losing none of the spontaneity that makes it good.' Hansen added that General Patton, also present, 'grew flirtatious in his own inimitable manner with Marty'.

While Bradley twitched with impatience, Eisenhower was keen to discuss the situation with the field marshal. To a certain degree, he shared Montgomery's concern that the Allies had not yet assembled

---

* It is worth noting that Generalmajor von Waldenburg of the 116th Panzer argued later that the Allied 'counter-attack started too early' and that this was what saved the German forces 'from total annihilation'.

strong enough forces to crush the German salient. The slowness of Patton's advance from the south did not bode well, rather as Montgomery had predicted five days before. But at the same time Eisenhower was all too aware of Montgomery's ingrained reluctance to move until he had overwhelming force. The crushing of the 2nd Panzer-Division had greatly encouraged him.

Montgomery, who had been overinfluenced by his impression that 'the Americans have taken the most awful "bloody nose"', correspondingly underestimated the damage inflicted on their attackers. He refused to believe that First Army had recovered sufficiently to mount such an ambitious operation. And he certainly did not think that Patton in the south was capable of achieving what he so belligerently claimed. Montgomery also feared that the Germans, once surrounded, would fight with even more desperation, and inflict far more casualties on the Allies. He was convinced that, using their massive airpower and artillery, the Allies could cause greater damage from defensive positions than by advancing into a battle of attrition.

On 26 December, Bradley wrote to General Hodges, arguing that the Germans had suffered badly and that he did not view the situation 'in as grave a light as Marshal Montgomery'. He urged Hodges to consider pushing the enemy back 'as soon as the situation seems to warrant'. Hodges does not appear to have seen that moment coming as quickly as Bradley. In fact right up to the afternoon of Christmas Day Hodges and his chief of staff had been begging for reinforcements just to hold the line. And 'General Hodges', as his headquarters diarist noted, 'has had enough of exposed flanks for the last two weeks.'

In stark contrast Patton wanted to advance north from Luxembourg, with his earlier idea of cutting the German salient off at the base. This was ruled out by First Army because the road network south-east of the Elsenborn ridge would not support the massive armoured advance necessary. 'Lightning Joe' Collins accordingly prepared three plans of attack, and took them to First Army headquarters on 27 December. His preferred one was for his VII Corps to advance from Malmédy south-east to St Vith to join up with Patton's Third Army and cut the Germans off there. Hodges, however, clearly preferred 'the most conservative of the three plans'.

Montgomery also insisted on the shallower thrust, just heading for

Houffalize. In his forthright way, Collins told Montgomery: 'You're going to push the Germans out of the bag, just like you did at Falaise.' But as far as Montgomery was concerned, this was not Normandy in the summer. A major encirclement in such terrain and in such weather was far too ambitious. He had a point. It would be fine for the Red Army, equipped for warfare in deepest winter. The broad tracks of its T-34 tanks could cope with the ice and snow, but Shermans had already shown how vulnerable they were in such conditions.

Eisenhower's planned meeting with Montgomery in Brussels had to be postponed until 28 December because the Luftwaffe destroyed his train in a bombing raid. Just before leaving, he heard that Montgomery was at last contemplating a general offensive. 'Praise God from Whom all blessings flow!' he exclaimed. To his exasperation, the Counter Intelligence Corps remained obsessed with his personal security, and because of fog and ice the meeting had to be switched to Hasselt, close to Montgomery's headquarters. 'The roads are a sheet of ice, following last night's snow and ice storm,' General Simpson of Ninth Army noted that day.

Just before his meeting with the Supreme Commander, Montgomery had called a conference at Zonhoven on 28 December at 09.45 with the northern army commanders – Hodges, Simpson, Dempsey and General Harry Crerar of the First Canadian Army. Montgomery reaffirmed his plan. His own intelligence chief, the G-2 at First Army and Major General Strong at SHAEF all pointed to a renewed German attack. He therefore proposed to let the Germans first exhaust themselves and their resources, battering against the northern line, while fighter-bombers dealt with their rear. He also expected 'some sort of engagement on the British or Ninth Army fronts, as a demonstration'. In fact, Hitler had already cancelled the Fifteenth Army offensive planned to the north.*

Montgomery would move the British XXX Corps in to take over the defence from Hotton to Dinant, so that Collins's VII Corps could reform ready to lead a counter-strike down to Houffalize. During the

---

* Even Bradley's 12th Army Group headquarters seemed to believe in a renewed attack northwards towards Liège with 'from four to five panzer divisions', according to Hansen. Three days later Hansen made the unexpected remark: 'Americans are very poor on intelligence; we have to depend upon the British for almost everything we have.'

final phase of crushing the German salient, he intended to launch Operation Veritable, the planned Canadian army offensive down the west bank of the lower Rhine.

That afternoon at 14.30, Eisenhower and Montgomery met in Hasselt station. This was their first encounter since the battle had begun, and Montgomery was irritated that the Supreme Commander had not replied to his daily signals outlining the course of events. Closeted under guard at Versailles, Eisenhower had not ventured out since the Verdun conference. And during the unfortunate meeting on Christmas Day, Bradley had been forced to admit that he had no idea what Eisenhower's plans were. Montgomery was scornful of what he saw as Eisenhower's total inaction.

Eisenhower agreed to Montgomery's plan to advance on Houffalize, rather than St Vith as Bradley wanted. But once again Montgomery could not contain himself. He said that Bradley had made a mess of the situation, and that if he, Montgomery, did not have full operational command of all the armies north of the Moselle, then the advance to the Rhine would fail. For form's sake he offered to serve under Bradley, but this was hardly sincere after what he had said about him.

Montgomery assumed that his bullying had worked and that Eisenhower had agreed to all his proposals. Back in London, however, Field Marshal Sir Alan Brooke was disturbed when he heard Montgomery's account of the meeting. 'It looks to me as if Monty with his usual lack of tact has been rubbing into Ike the results of not having listened to Monty's advice!! Too much "I told you so".'

Eisenhower's staff at SHAEF, including the British, were furious at what they heard of the meeting, but Montgomery was about to make things much worse. Afraid that Eisenhower might back off from what he thought had been agreed, the field marshal wrote a letter on 29 December, again insisting on a single field command and again claiming that the Allies would fail if his advice was not followed. Major General de Guingand, his chief of staff now back in Belgium, delivered it to Eisenhower next day. For Eisenhower, Montgomery's letter was the final straw. The field marshal even had the temerity to dictate what Eisenhower's order should say when giving him 'full operational direction, control and co-ordination' over Bradley's 12th Army Group in the attack on the Ruhr.

The arrival of Montgomery's letter happened to coincide with a cable from General Marshall in Washington. He had been shown articles in the British press claiming that Montgomery had saved the Americans in the Ardennes and that he should be appointed overall ground force commander. Marshall made his feelings very clear to Eisenhower. 'Under no circumstances make any concessions of any kind whatsoever. You not only have our complete confidence but there would be a terrific resentment in this country following such an action. I am not assuming that you had in mind such a concession. I just wish you to be certain of our attitude on this side. You are doing a grand job and go on and give them hell.'

Eisenhower replied to Montgomery in reasoned tones, but with an unmistakable ultimatum. 'In your latest letter you disturb me by predictions of "failure" unless your exact opinions in the matter of giving you command over Bradley are met in detail. I assure you that in this matter I can go no further . . . For my part I would deplore the development of such an unbridgeable gulf of convictions between us that we would have to present our differences to the CC/S [Combined Chiefs of Staff].' There was no doubt whom the Combined Chiefs would back in a showdown.

De Guingand, hearing that Eisenhower was writing to Marshall, begged him to wait; and, although quite seriously ill, he immediately flew back to Zonhoven and explained to Montgomery that he was heading straight for the rocks. At first Montgomery refused to believe that things could be so bad. In any case, who could replace him? Field Marshal Sir Harold Alexander, came the reply. Montgomery was shaken to the core when the truth finally sank in. He had confidently told Eisenhower on an earlier occasion that 'the British public would not stand for a change'. From what de Guingand was telling him, that no longer counted. The Americans were now definitely in charge. 'What shall I do, Freddie?' an utterly deflated Montgomery asked.

De Guingand produced from the pocket of his battledress the draft of a letter. 'Dear Ike,' it read. 'Have seen Freddie and understand you are greatly worried by many considerations in these difficult days. I have given you my frank views because I have felt you like this . . . Whatever your decision may be you can rely on me one hundred percent to make it work and I know Brad will do the same. Very distressed that my letter may have upset you and I would ask you to tear it up. Your very devoted subordinate, Monty.' He signed, and it was encyphered and transmitted by cable without delay. The estimable Freddie de Guingand had once again saved his chief from his insufferable self. He then went to 21st Army Group's rear headquarters in Brussels to speak to journalists. He emphasized that Montgomery's command over the two American armies was temporary, and that in the interests of Allied solidarity the clamour for him to be made ground commander and the veiled criticism of Eisenhower must stop. They promised to consult their editors. De Guingand then rang Bedell Smith in Versailles to assure him that the field marshal had backed down completely.

All that needed to be settled was the date of the northern offensive. Eisenhower had convinced himself that it would be New Year's Day. Montgomery had at first favoured 4 January, but now brought it forward by twenty-four hours to 3 January. But a groundswell of hostile opinion lingered on. Many American senior officers regretted later that Eisenhower had not seized the opportunity to get rid of the field marshal. They wanted a strategic victory in the Ardennes, utterly destroying all German forces in the Bulge. Montgomery believed that this was impracticable, and felt that they just wanted to wipe out the embarrassment of having been caught napping. He was impatient to get on with Operation Veritable to clear the Reichswald before crossing the Rhine north of the Ruhr. Bradley and Patton, on the other hand, had no intention of waiting until 3 January. They planned to launch their counter-offensive from Bastogne on 31 December.

On the southern side of Bastogne, the 35th Infantry Division, which had been greatly weakened during the battles in Lorraine, arrived to fill the gap between the 4th Armored Division and the 26th Infantry Division. The 35th was to attack north-east towards Marvie and the Longvilly–Bastogne road while the rest of the 4th Armored helped clear the villages east of the Arlon road. The infantry, with sodden boots from fording streams, were suffering as many cases of frostbite and trench foot as battle casualties. 'It was so cold . . . that the water in our canteens froze right on our bodies,' an officer in the 51st Armored Infantry wrote in his diary. 'We ate snow or melted it down to drink or make coffee.' His battalion, which had been 600 strong, suffered 461 battle and non-battle casualties in three weeks.

To the west, the 9th Armored Division's Combat Command A advanced up the road from Neufchâteau which ran close to Sibret, an important American objective. German reinforcements also began to arrive as the fighting for Bastogne intensified. On Thursday 28 December the *Führer*

Begleit took over the Sibret sector on the south-west side. Oberst Remer claimed that, on the way down from the northern front, their medical company was shot up during 'a fighter-bomber attack lasting 35 minutes, although all vehicles were painted white and bore the red cross'. Manteuffel believed that Remer's formation would make all the difference, and its Panthers and Mark IVs went straight into action against the 9th Armored's tanks, setting a number of them on fire.

Remer was angry and mortified to learn that he was now under the orders of the greatly reduced 3rd Panzergrenadier-Division. The *Führer Begleit*, despite being less than half the size of a standard division, was heavily armed at a time when the 5th Fallschirmjäger-Division was left with little artillery support, and the 26th Volksgrenadier had no more armour-piercing shells. Remer, who had a battery of 105mm anti-aircraft guns, transferred them to Chenogne ready to take on Patton's tanks. His 88mm batteries were deployed five kilometres further north round Flamierge where they claimed to have shot down 'ten cargo-carrying gliders'. But the *Führer Begleit* was too late to save the key village of Sibret. After a heavy artillery bombardment, the Americans forced the Germans out that night. A shot-down glider pilot had been captured by the Germans near by. He hid in a potato bin when they withdrew, and found himself a free man again.

The loss of Sibret dismayed Manteuffel as well as Lüttwitz, for now their chances of re-establishing the encirclement of Bastogne were greatly reduced. Lüttwitz ordered Remer to recapture Sibret the next morning with help from a Kampfgruppe from the 3rd Panzergrenadier-Division. 'If this attack failed,' Lüttwitz wrote, 'the Corps believed that it would be necessary to begin the immediate withdrawal of the front salient.' But Hitler, refusing yet again to accept reality, announced the creation of a so-called 'Army Group Lüttwitz' to crush Bastogne. In theory, it included the 2nd Panzer-Division, the Panzer Lehr, the 9th Panzer-Division, the 3rd and the 15th Panzergrenadier-Divisions, the 1st SS Panzer-Division *Leibstandarte Adolf Hitler*, the 5th Fallschirmjäger-Division and the *Führer Begleit* Brigade. But, despite its typically Hitlerian appellation, most of the formations designated were little more than remnants.

During the early hours of Friday 29 December, the *Führer Begleit* Brigade assembled on the southern edge of the woods near Chenogne for its counter-attack against Sibret. But as soon as Remer's troops emerged from the trees they were greeted by a massive concentration of fire from the field artillery battalions brought up to crush this expected riposte. Flanking fire from Villeroux to the east, which the Americans had taken after a fierce fight on 28 December, also caused many casualties. The woods south-east of Chenogne changed hands several times. One of Remer's 105mm anti-aircraft guns knocked out several American tanks during the fighting, but eventually its crew, despite defending their gun as infantrymen in close-combat fighting, were overwhelmed. A Sherman tank crushed their gun under its tracks. That evening Remer reported that the *Führer Begleit* was now too weak to attempt another attack against Sibret.

Luftwaffe bombers raided Bastogne on the night of Friday 29 December just as the weather turned, with snow and mist now coming down from Scandinavia. But at least the corridor was secure, so hundreds of trucks ferried in large quantities of supplies for the defenders of Bastogne as well as 400 replacements for the 101st Airborne. General Taylor visited his troops in the front line of the perimeter to congratulate them. Some found his manner irritating. 'His instructions before leaving us', recorded Major Dick Winters of the 506th, 'were "Watch those woods in front of you!" What the hell did he think we had been doing while he was in Washington?'

The paratroopers were dejected to find that, despite their heroic treatment in the press, they were not to be replaced and returned to Mourmelon-le-Grand. At least they had received their mail and Christmas packages from home. The contents were shared with other platoon members or Belgian civilians. And finally they had enough to eat, with their preferred 'ten-in-one' ration packs. Some paratroopers also managed to 'liberate' the store of spirits which VIII Corps headquarters had left behind: it had been revealed when one of the Luftwaffe bombs had blown down the wall of a building. But the bitter cold and the routine of deadly skirmishes and dangerous patrols at night continued. Their commanders still wanted intelligence on the enemy units opposite, so snatch squads had to go out to seize a 'tongue' for interrogation. (German officers had confiscated their men's paybooks because they revealed too much information about their unit.) But moving silently at night was impossible, since every step made a noise as each foot crunched through the hard crust on top of the snow. And their white capes, frozen stiff, crackled as they moved. Experiments with bleached fatigue suits for camouflage were not very successful. Paratroopers envied the Germans' reversible jacket with a white lining, which was far better.

Since it was common practice to set up dummies out in front of defensive positions to prompt an enemy patrol to open fire prematurely, paratroopers resorted to using frozen German corpses propped up in the snow. One was called 'Oscar' after the unit's puppet-like mascot, which parachuted with them. It also served as a directional marker for fire orders in the event of a surprise attack. Paratroopers had been surprised to find that the faces of men who died in that extreme cold did not have the usual grey tinge, but went a burgundy colour as the blood capillaries froze rapidly under the skin.

As well as trench foot and frostbite many paratroopers, already filthy and bearded, were suffering from dysentery, largely due to the impossibility of cleaning mess kits properly. Temperatures as low as minus 20 Centigrade could make the cooling jackets of their heavy machine guns burst. These weapons could be seen by their muzzle flash from a great distance, while its German equivalent could not be spotted at over a hundred metres. Paratroopers were not alone in preferring to use captured German MG-42 machine guns. New replacements needed to learn to avoid firing too long a burst which gave away their position.

Many soldiers liked to debate the best way to throw a grenade: whether like a baseball, a shot-put or an overarm lob. The baseball throw was rejected by many as it was liable to wrench the arm and shoulder. To prevent the Germans catching it and throwing it back, experienced soldiers would pull the pin, count to two or three and then throw. Grenades were often carried with the lever hooked into buttonholes. Officers despaired, knowing that they would fall off and be lost when men lay down. Clueless replacements were also found attaching them to their equipment by the rings, which was a quick way of blowing yourself up. A spare canteen cover usually proved the best carrier.

On 30 December, General Patton entered Bastogne wearing his famous pearl-handled revolvers. He congratulated officers and men in his curiously high-pitched voice, presented medals, had his photograph taken in many places, examined burned-out German tanks and visited the main battle sites. They included the Château de Rolley, where he slept for a few hours before continuing his tour. An artillery observation officer with the 327th Glider Infantry, already under fire on a ridge from German tanks, was infuriated to see a group walking up quite openly from behind to join him. He swore at them to get down only to find an imperturbable General Patton who had come to watch. Having ranged in with a single gun, the captain ordered 'fire for effect' from his field battalion on the panzers. One lucky round scored a direct hit on the turret, setting off the ammunition inside and blasting the tank to pieces. 'Now by God that is good firing!' a triumphant Patton exclaimed. It had clearly made his day.

While the *Führer Begleit* and the 3rd Panzergrenadiers attacked from the west, a Kampfgruppe from the 1st SS Panzer-Division together with the 14th Fallschirmjäger-Regiment and the 167th Volksgrenadier-Division, newly arrived from Hungary, attacked from the east around Lutrebois. A battalion of the American 35th Infantry Division in Villers-la-Bonne-Eau was taken by surprise in the fog before dawn. Two companies were wiped out, but the field artillery once again played a major role in saving the situation. With divisional and corps guns firing shells with the new Pozit fuses, the 167th Volksgrenadiers were 'cut to pieces', in the words of their commander.

When Shermans and tank destroyers from the 4th Armored, drawn by the sound of battle, joined in this chaotic battle, the infantry passed on their sightings of German tanks in the woods. The 134th Infantry Regiment claimed that twenty-seven tanks had been knocked out and the estimates of other units brought the total to over fifty, but this was a gross exaggeration. Even so the *Leibstandarte Adolf Hitler* had suffered heavy losses, and blamed its failure on the 5th Fallschirmjäger-Division. According to its commander, Generalmajor Heilmann, 'The SS spread the rumor that [my] paratroopers sat down in peace with Americans in the cellar of a house in Villers-la-Bonne-Eau and made a toast to brotherhood.' The *Leibstandarte* commander Brigadeführer Wilhelm Mohnke wanted to court-martial the officers of the 14th Fallschirmjäger-Regiment for cowardice, and apparently said that a 'National Socialist leadership officer* should be set at the throat of the Fallschirmjäger division'.

---

* The role of Nazionalsozialistischen Führungsoffizier, or National Socialist leadership officer, was instituted on Hitler's orders in imitation of the Soviet commissar, or political officer, to watch over the loyalty and determination of army officers.

The mutual dislike between the Waffen-SS and other Wehrmacht formations reached new depths. The SS Panzer formations demanded priority on every route, causing chaos. 'These road conditions reached their peak when SS formations arrived in the Bastogne combat sector,' wrote Generalmajor Kokott. 'These units – unduly boastful and arrogant anyway – with their total lack of discipline so typical of them, with their well-known ruthlessness combined with considerable lack of logic, had a downright devastating effect and in all cases proved a handicap for any systematic conduct of fighting.' This hatred of the SS did not exist solely at senior officer level. Feldwebel Rösner in Kokott's division described how the SS 'broke into houses in Luxembourg and out of vandalism destroyed everything'. They had also destroyed holy pictures in the German Eifel, because the region was very Catholic.

The most encouraging event for Patton's III Corps was the arrival of forward elements of the 6th Armored Division to take over from the exhausted 4th Armored. This formation was both at full strength and experienced, a rare combination at that time. Some of their Shermans had the new 76mm gun – based on the British 17-pounder – which could finally take on a Mark VI Tiger with confidence. Although one combat command was delayed on its approach by having to share the same road as the 11th Armored, the other one moved into position on the south-east of the perimeter near Neffe ready to attack Wardin the next day.

Not all mistaken attacks on American troops came from Thunderbolt and Lightning fighter-bombers. On 31 December Third Army reported that 'bombers from the Eighth Air Force unfortunately bombed the headquarters of 4th Armored Division, the town of Wecker, and that part of the 4th Infantry Division at Echternach'. An urgent meeting was called with the air force generals Doolittle and Spaatz to discuss accidental bombing of 'our own forces' and 'inversely the firing upon our own airplanes by our own anti-aircraft guns'. The 'accidental bombing' was hushed up in order 'not to shake the faith of the troops'. Faults lay on both sides, but after several incidents many American troops reverted to the slogan from Normandy 'If it flies, it dies', and they frequently opened fire at any aircraft approaching whether in or out of range. The army was also openly sceptical about the air force's inflated estimates of the number of panzers it had destroyed. 'It is obvious that Air Corps claims must be exaggerated,' 12th Army Group observed, 'otherwise the Germans would be without tanks whereas our recon indicates plenty of them.'

The Luftwaffe still made night bombing raids on Bastogne. On 1 January, German prisoners of war under guard were clearing debris near Bastogne's central square when one of them stepped on a 'Butterfly' bomblet dropped in the previous night's raid. It exploded upward into his groin. He fell to the ground screaming. The scene was witnessed by soldiers from the 52nd Armored Infantry of the 9th Armored Division. One of their officers wrote later: 'You could hear laughter coming from the throats of our GIs in the trucks.'

On the First Army front to the north, Montgomery had now moved in the 53rd Welsh Division and the American 83rd Infantry Division to relieve the 2nd Armored in the west and the 84th Infantry Division round Marche. The 51st Highland Division became a First Army reserve. As more of Horrocks's XXX Corps arrived, the rest of Collins's VII Corps could pull back to redeploy ready for the counter-attack on 3 January.* The British 6th Airborne Division which moved in east of Celles tried to dig defensive positions, but the ground was frozen so hard that the men's spades were useless. They resorted instead to hammering hollow camouflet rods into the ground, and then filled them with explosive to blast holes. They soon found that dealing with Teller mines buried under the snow was a dangerous task.

All around the area of maximum German advance, starving and frozen stragglers were being rounded up. A farmer's son went to look after the horses near Ychippe. When he returned a German soldier, whom he had seen limping towards their house, knocked at the door. Pointing to his feet, he said: 'Kaput!' He had been sleeping in a barn. He sat down by their stove, put down his pistol and removed his boots. An American patrol arrived, and took the German prisoner before he had a chance to seize his pistol. Other German soldiers had been hiding in neighbouring houses and farm buildings. One of them refused to come out of a

---

* Montgomery had in fact just sent his favourite corps commander home on enforced medical leave. He feared that his judgement had become impaired through exhaustion. Horrocks had suddenly advocated that they should let the Germans cross the Meuse then defeat them on the battlefield of Waterloo just south of Brussels.

barn when they were surrounded. He was wearing American uniform and feared being shot. Eventually he was persuaded to come out when the Americans threatened to burn the barn down. They forced him to strip off the items of American uniform and then took him away in a Jeep. The villagers had no idea what happened to him.

In a number of places, such as Conjoux, villagers watched with sadness as American tank drivers smashed down their little orchards and hedgerows. They were less anxious when they saw American infantry approaching with columns of men on both sides of the road in Indian file. The parsimonious existence of farming folk in the region meant that nothing could be wasted. They took whatever they could from abandoned German vehicles, since this was likely to be the only compensation they could hope for in exchange for the damage to their fields, barns and houses, as well as the loss of fodder, horses and carts seized by the Germans. A caterpillar-tracked motorcycle constituted a great prize. They siphoned fuel from abandoned vehicles and took tool kits, tinned rations, tyres and wheels, and stripped almost anything else which could be disassembled. A few took away grenades in the hope of some productive fishing in the summer.

Several farmers tried removing the wheels from field guns, hoping to make a cart, but they found that they were too heavy for a horse to pull. In a far more successful improvisation, a mechanically expert farmer managed to build his own tractor entirely from parts taken from a range of German armoured vehicles. The engine came from a half-track. One household even removed the front seats from a *Kübelwagen*, the Wehrmacht equivalent of a Jeep, and used them in their parlour for almost thirty years. At Ychippe, a dead German officer was left for many days slumped back in the front seat of another *Kübelwagen*. Seventeen-year-old Theóphile Solot was fascinated by the fact that his beard continued to grow after death.

Women were desperately anxious about the fate of sons and husbands. Those who had escaped across the Meuse were indeed fortunate, because the Germans had rounded up large numbers of the men and boys who had remained. They were made to clear snow from roads and haul supplies. Many did not have the right clothes for the snow and ice. Barely fed, certainly not enough for hard work, they were also ill equipped. Few had gloves or even spades. They were treated as prisoners, and locked in barns at night. In some cases, their guards fixed grenades to doors and windows so that they could not escape. Many were marched all the way back to Germany to work there and were not liberated until the closing stages of the war. A number were killed by Allied aircraft because the pilots could not distinguish between groups of German soldiers and Belgian civilians. They all looked like little black figures against the snow.

In the last days of December, the British XXX Corps extended its new positions between the Meuse and Hotton. An English civil affairs officer took a rather romantic view of their surroundings. 'The Ardennes has a pronounced Ruritanian atmosphere,' he wrote, 'as one imagines in the story of the Prisoner of Zenda. The chateaus give the added effect, together with the larger woods of fir trees, laden with snow.'

Once the weather closed in, air reconnaissance had become impossible. When the 53rd Welsh Division replaced the Americans at Marche-en-Famenne, the Allies needed to know how the Panzer Lehr and the remnants of the 2nd Panzer were redeploying after their withdrawal from Rochefort. The British 61st Reconnaissance Regiment attached to the 6th Airborne Division, as well as Belgian and French SAS forces, some 350 strong, was sent into the large area of forest and bog south of Rochefort and Marche to find out.

The French squadron headed for Saint-Hubert, and on 31 December a Belgian squadron from the 5th SAS Regiment located part of the Panzer Lehr at Bure ten kilometres south of Rochefort. In their Jeeps, armed only with twin Vickers machine guns, they could do little more than harass the panzergrenadiers. Three of their best men were killed straight off by a German 88mm gun. The Germans were holding on desperately in this area because almost all the remnants from the 2nd and 9th Panzer-Divisions, as well as the Panzer Lehr, had been extricating themselves from Rochefort along this route. After most of the inhabitants had sought shelter in the cellars of the religious college, the Germans seized all their sheets for camouflage. And while the villagers sheltering underground had nothing to eat but potatoes, the panzergrenadiers killed and ate their chickens.

German artillery now shelled Rochefort, and the townsfolk remained in the surrounding caves. Only a few ventured out during lulls to fetch food. All were deeply grateful to Frère Jacques, 'with his beret and big black rubber gloves', who collected corpses to give them a Christian burial.

The Germans also continued to bombard Liège with V-1 bombs. On New Year's Eve, Lance-Sergeant Walker in the Middlesex Regiment, a veteran of North Africa, Sicily and Normandy, was on his way to attend mass in a church at Sur-le-Mont just south of the city. A V-1 flying bomb was passing overhead, and as he looked up, he saw it turn over and start to dive. 'A Belgian child was standing a few yards from him oblivious of the danger,' the citation for his medal stated. 'Lance-Sergeant Walker leaped to the child, pulled him down on the ground and shielded him with his own body. The bomb exploded a few yards from where they lay and severely wounded Lance-Sergeant Walker. The child was unhurt.' The Royal Army Medical Corps gave up on Walker because his wounds were so severe, but he survived because the Americans scooped him up and conducted pioneering flesh-graft surgery on him which was filmed and sent to other field surgical hospitals for instructional purposes.

American headquarters all organized their own parties for New Year's Eve. At Simpson's Ninth Army, they celebrated with highballs and turkey. At Hodges's First Army, dinners were always formal. 'In his mess every night,' one of his officers recorded, 'we dressed for dinner: jacket, necktie, combat boots.' Hodges usually had a bourbon and Dubonnet on the rocks with a dash of bitters, but that night he ordered that the case of champagne which Collins had given him after the capture of Cherbourg should be opened to toast the New Year. At midnight there was a panic when soldiers began 'indiscriminately firing their rifles. Hasty investigation showed that no attack was going on but that simple exuberance [was] having its day.'

Bradley's 12th Army Group headquarters also had a party. According to Hansen, Martha Gellhorn 'talked passionately half the evening of the war in Spain . . . she is the original newspaperwoman who believes in the goodness of man, having seen so much of his worst, having seen it abased in the battlefronts of the entire world'. It seems the party atmosphere was slightly spoiled by nervousness that there might be an official inquiry into the intelligence failure to foresee the German offensive. General William Donovan, the founder of the Office of

Strategic Services, had just arrived from Washington, and mentioned that there was 'talk of a congressional investigation to determine why we were lax'. Bradley was extremely nervous and defensive over his 'calculated risk' before the German attack, leaving only four divisions to defend the Ardennes.

In Berlin, the diarist Ursula von Kardorff, who was connected to the July plotters, entertained a few friends on New Year's Eve. 'At midnight all was still. We stood there with raised glasses, hardly daring to clink them together. A single bell tinkled in the distance for the passing of the year, and we heard shots, and heavy boots crunching on the splintered glass [in the street from broken windows]. It was eerie, as though a shadow were passing over us and touching us with its dark wings.' In the Ardennes, Germans, and also Belgians, braced themselves for the Allied counter-offensive and the fighting still to come. 'My prayer on the threshold of the new year', wrote a young Volksgrenadier officer near St Vith, 'is with the Führer's and our strength to end this war victoriously.' In the next few hours, the Germans struck again, both in the air and in Alsace.

21

The Double Surprise

On New Year's Eve at midnight, American artillery all around the Ardennes fired salvoes to tell the Wehrmacht that the year of its final defeat had begun. But the Germans had New Year messages of their own. A few minutes before the old year was out, Army Group Upper Rhine commanded by Reichsführer-SS Heinrich Himmler launched an offensive called Operation *Nordwind* against the left flank of General Devers's 6th Army Group.

The day after Christmas, Seventh Army intelligence had warned that the Germans might attack in northern Alsace during the first few days of January. General Devers had flown to Versailles to see General Eisenhower. Their relationship had not improved since Eisenhower rebuffed his plan to seize a bridgehead across the Rhine. And because the struggle in the Ardennes was approaching its climax, SHAEF simply wanted the American and French divisions in the south to go on the defensive. With most of Patton's Third Army deployed on the southern side of the salient, Devers's forces, stripped to the bone to strengthen the Ardennes, had been forced to extend their frontage to more than 300 kilometres.

Eisenhower wanted to shorten the line in Alsace by withdrawing to the Vosges mountains, and probably giving up Strasbourg in the process. Tedder warned him strongly against such a move. (Ironically, it was now the British who opposed giving up territory.) This was to lead to a major confrontation with the French, for whom Strasbourg had powerful significance.

The other attack was much more unexpected. Reichsmarschall

Hermann Göring, stung by the bitter criticism of his Luftwaffe, had decided on his own lightning strike. His plan for a major surprise against the Allied air forces had first been mentioned on 6 November, when Generalmajor Christian told Hitler that 'The Reichsmarschall has ordered that all these new groups now standing by should be deployed in a single day – a day when the weather doesn't pose a problem – all together, in one strike.'

Hitler was dubious. 'I am just afraid that, when this day comes, the groups won't co-ordinate and that they won't find the enemy . . . The hope of decimating the enemy with a mass deployment is not realistic.' He was also very sceptical of Luftwaffe claims and figures of aircraft ratios, and was exasperated that his pilots had shot down so few Allied planes. He exclaimed: 'There are still tons of [Luftwaffe aircraft] being produced. They're only eating up labor and material.'

The Luftwaffe faced many problems, but also created its own. Few veteran pilots remained because of the wasteful system of failing to give them sufficient breaks from front-line duty, and of not using them to pass on their expertise to trainees. 'They are all young pilots now with no experience,' a Messerschmitt 109 pilot said. 'All the experienced ones have gone.' 'What sort of training have the newcomers had to-day?' said another. 'It's pitiful, appalling.' Mainly because of fuel shortages, they arrived at operational units after only a few hours of flying solo. No wonder American fighter pilots said that they would far prefer to take on four new pilots than one veteran.

Morale was bad. One captured officer detailed the number of excuses pilots used to avoid flying or engaging in combat. They included 'engine trouble', and 'undercarriage not retracting'. One pilot who went up, flew around and shot at nothing was arrested when he landed. More senior officers 'used to fly', said another veteran pilot, 'but all that is over now. They don't do a thing. They don't fancy a hero's death any longer, those days are past.' A profound cynicism spread to all ranks. 'In our Staffel [squadron] you were looked at in amazement if you hadn't got venereal disease,' a Feldwebel reported. 'At least 70% had gonorrhoea.'

The greatest cynicism was reserved for their commander-in-chief, the Reichsmarschall. He 'seems to have run the Luftwaffe with much the same methods as those used by the Queen of Hearts in *Alice in Wonderland*', a senior officer with the Oberkommando Luftwaffe remarked, 'and with much the same effectiveness ... For him the Luftwaffe was just another toy.' One of the few senior officers who took part in the great New Year's Day attack recalled asking a superior, 'Well, what's our Reichsmarschall doing now, Herr General?' The general replied: 'The Reichsmarschall is dealing in diamonds at the moment. He hasn't any time for us.' On the other hand, General der Flieger Karl Koller, the chief of staff, blamed Hitler more than anyone. 'He had no understanding of the needs of the Luftwaffe, remaining an infantryman in outlook throughout his life.'

In any case, Göring felt that he had no option but to go all out. He 'practically cried' about the state of the Luftwaffe, according to an Oberstleutnant, and said that 'unless we gained mastery in the air quickly, then we have lost the war'. Göring's final gamble, a shadow of Hitler's whole Ardennes offensive, was to be called *Unternehmen Bodenplatte* – Operation Baseplate. Practically every fighter that could fly would take off to attack Allied airfields and shoot up their aircraft on the ground.

Although Luftwaffe officers had known of the plan for several weeks, the operational order caused astonishment and horror when they were called for briefing on the afternoon of New Year's Eve. Pilots were forbidden to drink any alcohol that evening or stay up to celebrate the New Year. Many dreaded the prospect of the morrow, and what looked like a suicidal Japanese *banzai* charge. Flying personnel were at least allocated 'take-off' rations, with extra butter, eggs and white bread. They were promised that on return from the operation they would receive a slab of chocolate, real coffee and a full 'operations' meal.

Almost 1,000 German aircraft on thirty-eight airfields started their engines soon after dawn. Oberstleutnant Johann Kogler, due to lead Jagdgeschwader 6 against Volkel airfield in Holland, sat in the cockpit of his Focke-Wulf 190. Kogler had few illusions. General der Flieger Adolf Galland had 'poured out his troubles to me; it was pretty grim'. Kogler's chief was the useless General der Flieger Beppo Schmidt, who had so misled Göring as his intelligence chief in 1940 that Generaloberst Franz Halder remarked that Göring was 'the worst-informed officer in the whole Luftwaffe'. Schmidt, appalled by the loss of fighter commanders, had tried to keep them on the ground. Kogler objected to such an idea on principle. 'Herr General, if we must fly to give the enemy some fun, so that they have something to shoot at; and if we are just being put into the air for the sake of doing something, then I do request that I should be allowed to accompany [my pilots] every time.'

The commander of a Focke-Wulf 190 Staffel, in Jagdgeschwader 26, found the choice of their targets bitterly ironic. 'We had been stationed on these airfields ourselves. I had to take my own Staffel to shoot up the very airfield where I used to be based.' Far more depressing was Göring's order. 'Whoever [returns after failing] to attack the airfield properly, or fails to find it, must immediately take off again afterwards and attack it again.' This was to prove a disastrous idea. Each group was to be accompanied by an Me 262 jet whose pilot's role was to identify anyone who showed a lack of determination in the attack.

Some pilots at least seemed to revel in their mission, reminiscing about their exploits earlier in the war. 'What a smashing we gave them at the beginning!' remembered one who was due to attack the airfield near Ghent. 'Sixty aircraft took off in each Gruppe.' He was clearly exultant even at this stage at the impression of power which *Bodenplatte* gave. 'Now in our sortie on the 1st [January] – Oh my goodness! What there was up in the air. I myself was amazed. I no longer knew which Geschwader I belonged to. They flew about all over the place. The civilians stared at us. Afterwards we flew over the front [and] the soldiers stood and gazed. We all flew low.'

This very optimistic impression omitted another aspect of the chaos. Following Hitler's security precautions before the Ardennes offensive, Göring had refused to allow German flak defences to be warned of Operation *Bodenplatte* in advance. As a result the flak batteries assumed that these large formations, which they suddenly saw overhead, must be enemy. They opened fire. Apparently sixteen of their own aircraft fell victim to friendly fire on the way to their objectives.

Their simultaneous attacks at 09.20 hours had targeted twelve British airfields in Belgium and southern Holland, and four American bases in France. But due mainly to navigational errors, they hit thirteen British bases and only three American. The Germans achieved surprise, but not in every case. The Geschwader attacking the Sint-Denijs-Westrem airfield at Ghent bounced a Polish squadron of Spitfires just as it was landing, and very short of fuel. The attackers destroyed nine of them and another six on the ground. But they in turn were caught by the other two Polish squadrons of 131 Wing, which shot down eighteen of them and damaged another five for the loss of only one Spitfire. Among the captured Focke-Wulf pilots was the one who had rejoiced at the number of German aircraft in the air.

The Americans fared better than the British, because one group of attackers became totally lost and failed to find their target, and a patrol of P-47 Thunderbolts dived into the force aiming for Metz; but the Germans still managed to destroy twenty out of forty fighter-bombers on the ground there. The heaviest British losses were at Eindhoven, where the Germans were lucky enough to hit the first squadron of Typhoons just as they were taking off. The crashed aircraft blocked the runway, trapping the other squadrons behind. 'One frustrated Typhoon pilot stood on his brakes and applied power to lift his aircraft's tail, so he could shoot at the low-flying attackers from the ground.'

At Evere a Spitfire squadron was also caught taxiing to the runway and destroyed, but one pilot managed to get airborne. He shot up one of the 'bandits', but was brought down himself. The Americans became convinced that the aircraft of the British 2nd Tactical Air Force had all been caught out 'closely parked in formation'. This was true only at Eindhoven, a photo-reconnaissance base, where Spitfires were lined up on an old Luftwaffe runway because there was nowhere else to put them. Bases were certainly over-full because many squadrons had had to concentrate on the airfields with hard runways, which could be cleared of snow more easily. The news that Field Marshal Montgomery's personal aircraft had also been destroyed on the ground prompted a distinct atmosphere of schadenfreude in American circles. 'They caught the British with their pants down so badly', wrote the First Army diarist the next day, 'that General Montgomery's G-2 [intelligence chief] sent a pair of suspenders [braces] as [a] present to the G-2 of their Tac[tical] Air Force.' Eisenhower, with great generosity, immediately gave Montgomery his own aircraft.

Staff officers at Ninth Army headquarters went out to watch the air battles. 'Mid-morning saw many dogfights in the Maastricht area, with ack-ack shooting wildly at unseen planes in the low hanging clouds.' Altogether the Allies lost 150 combat aircraft destroyed and 111 damaged, as well as 17 non-combat aircraft. Pilot losses were mercifully light, but more than a hundred ground personnel were killed.

Many German fighters were brought down by anti-aircraft fire, including Oberstleutnant Kogler who was captured. Near Brussels, bizarrely, one low-flying German pilot in a Focke-Wulf was brought down by a partridge 'which tore a large hole in his radiator so the coolant drained out stopping the engine'. But as Ninth Army headquarters recognized, 'Jerry made one big error in this surprise attack, which proved very costly. He stayed too long. Enjoying the fun of shooting the place up, he delayed so long that our fighters from rear bases had time to get into the air and caught him as he turned for home. He suffered extremely heavy losses as a result.'

Those pilots who, under Göring's order, were made to refuel, rearm and attack again, flew back to find Allied squadrons in overwhelming strength, determined to wipe them from the skies. Worst of all, German air defences were still kept in total ignorance, even after the attack. 'A catastrophe overtook the Luftwaffe's great operation on 1 January,' Hitler's adjutant Nicolaus von Below noted. 'On their return our aircraft flew into heavy and accurate fire from our own flak defences, which had never been informed of the operation on security grounds. Our formations suffered heavy losses which could never be made good. This was the last major effort of the Luftwaffe.'

It was not even a partial victory. The Luftwaffe lost 271 fighters destroyed and 65 damaged. Their air-crew casualties were disastrous. Altogether 143 pilots were dead or missing, another 70 were taken prisoner and a further 21 were wounded. The losses included three Kommodore, five Gruppenkommodore, or wing commanders, and fourteen Staffelkapitäne, or squadron leaders. They would be very hard to replace.

Germans could do little about their fate, so they just plodded on, stumbling through ruins after Allied bombing raids had knocked out tram and rail tracks, on their way to factories and offices, usually without windows or electricity. Hitler did not mention the Ardennes offensive in his New Year speech that day. As he rambled on, most of his audience realized that he had nothing new to offer.

Hitler also made no mention of *Unternehmen Nordwind* – Operation North Wind. He had thought up the idea of *Nordwind* on 21 December and gave the operation its name on Christmas Day. Although the official intent was to destroy the American VI Corps in northern Alsace by linking up with the Nineteenth Army holding the Colmar pocket, his real intentions were to upset Patton's advance in the Ardennes and to give

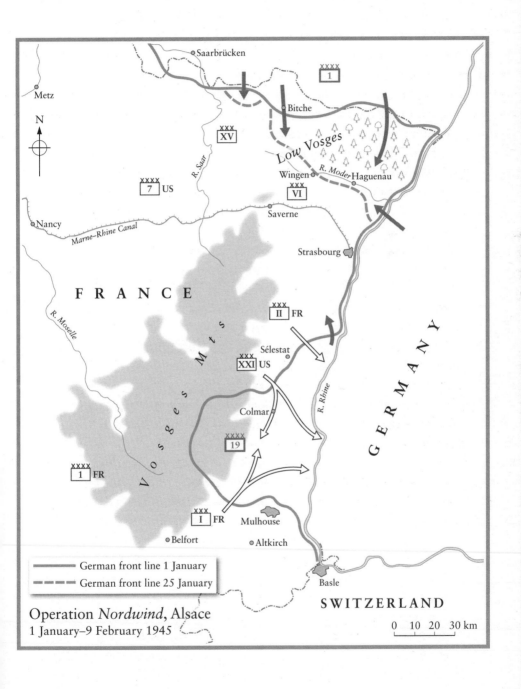

Saarbrücken

Metz

XXXX
1

N

Bitche

XXX
XV

R. Saar

Low Vosges

XXXX
7 US

Wingen   R. Moder   Haguenau

XXX
VI

Saverne

Nancy

Marne–Rhine Canal

Strasbourg

F R A N C E

R. Moselle

XXX
II FR

Sélestat

V o s g e s   M t s

XXX
XXI US

Colmar

R. Rhine

G E R M A N Y

XXXX
19

XXXX
1 FR

XXX
I FR   Mulhouse

Belfort   Altkirch

———— German front line 1 January
– – – – German front line 25 January

Basle

SWITZERLAND

Operation *Nordwind*, Alsace
1 January–9 February 1945

0   10 20 30 km

the impression that he still retained the initiative. On 28 December, Hitler had summoned the divisional commanders to the Adlerhorst so that he could address them personally, as he had done before the Ardennes offensive.

When Devers had returned to his headquarters after meeting Eisenhower in Versailles on 26 December, he had ordered fall-back lines to be studied in northern Alsace. After the German attack started on 1 January either side of Bitche, Eisenhower ordered Devers to leave covering forces, but pull back his main forces to the Vosges, leaving Strasbourg undefended. It was a serious blow to morale in the 6th Army Group. 'Spirits have reached a new low today,' a colonel wrote. Through a loudspeaker across the Rhine, the Germans warned the people of Strasbourg that they would be back. But American artillery, aiming by sound, managed to knock out the loudspeaker with impressive rapidity.

Not surprisingly, panic spread when word got around that the Americans might be withdrawing. The population of the city was 200,000, and many feared German reprisals. An American correspondent there estimated that 10,000 fled. 'They left mostly by train . . . women pushing baby carriages, wagons piled high with furniture.' The numbers of those who left by road over the next two days varied from 2,000 according to the Americans to 15,000 according to French sources.

In Paris, the French provisional government was up in arms. De Gaulle immediately sent his own order to General de Lattre de Tassigny, commanding the First French Army south of the city. 'It is self-evident that the French army can never agree to abandoning Strasbourg. In the eventuality of Allied forces withdrawing from their present positions to the north of the First French Army, I order you to take responsibility and ensure the defence of Strasbourg.' He then declared his position to Eisenhower and appealed to Churchill and Roosevelt to prevent an Allied withdrawal. SHAEF was warned that 100,000 people would have to be evacuated from the city, and another 300,000 more Alsatians risked German reprisals.

Next day General Alphonse Juin went to see Bedell Smith on de Gaulle's instruction, to say that the head of the provisional government would be coming to Versailles to see Eisenhower next day. Juin and Bedell Smith had fallen out before, and this was their stormiest meeting of all. Tensions had already arisen after General de Lattre had complained about the lack of equipment and supplies his First French Army had received, while the Americans had questioned the effectiveness of its attacks on the Colmar pocket. The French had suffered heavy casualties among their junior officers, and their replacements had trouble pushing their men forward.

Juin said that General de Gaulle would withdraw French troops from SHAEF command if American forces pulled back to the Vosges. According to Bedell Smith, he was extremely rude about Eisenhower's handling of the war. 'Juin said things to me', he told Eisenhower after the meeting, '[for] which, if he had been an American, I would have socked him in the jaw.'

On the morning of 3 January, before de Gaulle's visit, Eisenhower discussed the evacuation of Strasbourg with his staff. That afternoon, de Gaulle appeared with Juin. Winston Churchill, who was already on a visit to France, also appeared following de Gaulle's message. Eisenhower briefed the two heads of government on the dangerous position they faced. Then, in response to the French ultimatum of withdrawing their forces from SHAEF command, Eisenhower reminded de Gaulle that 'the French Army would get no ammunition, supplies, or food unless it obeyed my orders, and [I] pointedly told him that if the French Army had eliminated the Colmar Pocket this situation would not have arisen'. De Gaulle became extremely heated at this point.

'If we were involved in war games,' de Gaulle said, eventually controlling himself, 'I would agree with you. But I am forced to consider the affair from another point of view. The withdrawal in Alsace will hand French territory over to the enemy. On a strategic level, it would just be a manoeuvre. But for France it would be a national disaster, because Alsace is sacred to us. In any case, the Germans pretend that this province belongs to them, and so they will not miss the opportunity to take vengeance on the patriotism which its inhabitants have demonstrated.'

With Churchill's tacit support, de Gaulle won Eisenhower round. The Supreme Commander agreed to ring General Devers basically telling him to halt the withdrawal. 'This modification pleased de Gaulle very much,' Eisenhower wrote, 'and he left in a good humour.' He no longer had his offended expression, which Churchill once described as resembling a female llama surprised in her bath. After de Gaulle's departure, Churchill murmured to Eisenhower, 'I think we've done the wise and proper thing.'

De Gaulle was so exultant that he returned to dictate a communiqué to his *chef de cabinet* Gaston Palewski. Before issuing it, Palewski took it round to Duff Cooper, the British ambassador. It was so vainglorious that Cooper warned Palewski that it would hardly help matters. 'It suggested', wrote Cooper in his diary, 'that de Gaulle had summoned a military conference which the P[rime] M[inister] and Eisenhower had been allowed to attend.' In any case, Eisenhower justified his change of mind to President Roosevelt, whose opinion of the French leader had still not improved, on the grounds that if the provisional government collapsed, Allied armies might well face chaos in their rear areas.

The US VI Corps was 'in high spirits' when 'the order to withdraw to a line just east of the Vosges mountains was rescinded', wrote Colonel Heffner. 'It would have been a terrible blow to American prestige. We could never have lived it down. To be driven back is one thing and to give up without a fight is something else.'

French forces remained under SHAEF command as a result of Eisenhower's compromise, but headaches in dealing with the French authorities persisted. Eisenhower subsequently complained that the French 'next to the weather . . . have caused me more trouble in this war than any other single factor'. SHAEF decided to stop passing 'signal intelligence to First French Army' since it was 'not sufficiently secure'. On 7 January Devers warned General Patch, the commander of the Seventh Army in Alsace, that its telephone wires may be tapped. 'This presents a serious threat to Ultra security if reference should be made to Ultra intelligence by message or by disguised reference to a special form of intelligence. A few such references if pieced together by the enemy might be dangerously revealing.'

The German First Army's attack south was more or less held west of Bitche, where it was led by the 17th SS Panzergrenadier-Division *Götz von Berlichingen*, the 101st Airborne's opponent at Carentan in Normandy. The XV Corps had good positions and was supported by Leclerc's 2nd Armored Division, which once again showed its mettle. (According to the staff of 6th Army Group, Leclerc 'simply refused to fight under de Lattre', because Lattre had served in Pétain's Army of the Armistice.) But from Bitche to the Rhine two German army corps, attacking without an artillery bombardment and in heavy fog, managed to infiltrate past American positions in the forested areas. Advancing down towards the Saverne Gap, the German divisions forced back the overstretched American VI Corps spread across the Low Vosges and Rhine plain.

General Patch's Seventh Army was heavily outnumbered, and it fought well, with just a few exceptions due to panic in the rear or laziness at the front. Divisional commanders were angry to hear of troops 'surprised, captured or surrounded while bivouacked in or defending a town or village'. This was nearly always due to a lack of all-round security, or alertness. In Bannstein 'a unit was completely surprised. The men were sleeping and the Germans walked into the town unopposed and captured our troops, arms and a considerable number of vehicles.' In three other places, similar incidents took place, but most of the men were released when US troops came to their rescue.

Fighting conditions were made far worse by heavy snow and the twisting, ice-bound roads of the Low Vosges. By 5 January, the 6th SS Mountain Division, brought down from Scandinavia, had reached Wingen-sur-Moder twenty kilometres short of Saverne. Resisted strongly by the 45th Infantry Division, that was as far as they advanced on the western side. For the moment, the other three American infantry divisions held the line of the River Rothbach. But Himmler had obtained further divisions, including the 10th SS Panzer-Division *Frundsberg*, and prepared a fresh attack.

General Eisenhower may have rated the French as his biggest problem next to the weather, but he had also mentioned to General de Gaulle that Field Marshal Montgomery was not easy to deal with. He did not, however, foresee that the greatest crisis in Anglo-American relations was about to explode. On 5 January, Eisenhower heard that news in the States of Montgomery taking command of the Ninth and First US Armies had just broken, despite the fact that SHAEF had unwisely tried to suppress it. All of Air Chief Marshal Tedder's fears about the British press were realized. General de Guingand's plea to correspondents had failed: their newspapers again demanded that Montgomery should now be confirmed as ground forces commander in western Europe. The American press, not surprisingly, did not like the idea that a Briton, and especially Montgomery, should be in charge of two whole American armies. SHAEF was nevertheless forced to issue its own communiqué confirming the arrangement. Correspondents, both American and British, had become enraged by the inept and complacent treatment of the press by the military authorities at Versailles.

Bradley, already rattled by the prospect of a congressional investigation into why the US Army had been so unprepared for the Ardennes offensive, also feared how the news of Montgomery taking over two of his armies would be construed back home. And he deeply resented the fact that, in a poll for *Time* magazine's Man of the Year, Patton had been voted second to Eisenhower, while he had never even been considered. Deeply upset, he immediately suspected Montgomery of leaking the story about the change in command and regarded it as a deliberate 'attempt to discredit the Americans'. He rang Eisenhower to complain, but Eisenhower assured him that the story had broken in the States and had not been leaked from 21st Army Group headquarters.

According to Hansen, Bradley believed that 'the public clamor for this appointment is obviously officially inspired'. He remained convinced that Winston Churchill was scheming to have Montgomery named as overall ground forces commander. Clearly he still believed this to be a possibility, for he declared to Eisenhower that he 'wouldn't serve one day under Montgomery's command . . . General Patton has likewise indicated that he will not serve a single day under Montgomery. I intend to tell Montgomery this.' Eisenhower said that he would pass on his concerns to Churchill, but neither Churchill nor even Brooke was pushing for such a promotion. They were well aware of American views, and were privately appalled by the storm brewing. Churchill wrote to President Roosevelt, emphasizing British confidence in Eisenhower's leadership and praising the bravery of American divisions during the battle.

Bradley feared that the story would 'repudiate the efficacy of his Army Group command, undermine the confidence of his subordinate commanders and eventually [affect] the morale and confidence of the troops. Second, there is the equally evident picture that it may undermine public confidence in the States in his [Bradley's] command and indicate to our people there that it was necessary for us to resort in an emergency to British command in an effort to retrieve our "chestnuts from the fire".'

The British campaign to have Montgomery made field commander of the whole western front, Hansen wrote, implied that 'the German breakthrough would not have happened had Montgomery been in command to prevent it. The current inference of all news stories now is that the German attack succeeded because of the negligence of the American commander – namely Bradley . . . The effect has been a cataclysmic Roman holiday in the British press which has exulted over the announcement, and hailed it as an increase in the Montgomery command.' He went on: 'The troops are referred to as "Monty's troops" in a palavering gibberish that indicates a slavish hero devotion on the part of the British press . . . He is the symbol of success, the highly overrated and normally distorted picture of the British effort on our front.'

Bradley, wound up by his entourage, felt he was fighting for his career and reputation. He had just written to General Marshall, giving his view of the situation and justifying his 'calculated risk' in leaving the Ardennes front so weakly defended up to 16 December. 'At the same time,' he added, 'I don't want to apologize for what has happened.'

Montgomery telephoned Churchill to tell him that he planned to give a press conference to make a strong call for Allied unity and support for Eisenhower. Churchill replied that he thought it would be 'invaluable'. Field Marshal Brooke, on the other hand, was not so sure. He knew too well Montgomery's inability to control his bragging. So did several of Montgomery's senior staff officers.

Monty appeared at the press conference on 7 Janaury wearing a new airborne maroon beret with double badge, having just been appointed colonel commandant of the Parachute Regiment. His chief of intelligence, the brilliant academic Brigadier Bill Williams, had read the draft of his speech and dreaded how it would be received, even though the text as it stood was relatively innocuous. The only provocative part was when he said: 'The battle has been most interesting – I think possibly one of the most interesting and tricky battles I have ever handled, with great issues at stake.' The rest of the text was a tribute to the American soldier and a declaration of loyalty to Eisenhower, and a plea for Allied solidarity from the press.

But then, having reached the end of his prepared statement, Montgomery proceeded to speak off the cuff. He gave a brief lecture on his 'military philosophy'. 'If he [the enemy] puts in a hard bang I have to be ready for him. That is terrifically important in the battle fighting. I learned it in Africa. You learn all these things by hard experience. When

Rundstedt put in his hard blow and parted the American Army, it was automatic that the battle area must be untidy. Therefore the first thing I did when I was brought in and told to take over was to busy myself in getting the battle area tidy – getting it sorted out.' Montgomery also greatly exaggerated the British contribution to the battle, almost making it sound as if the whole thing had been an Anglo-American operation.

In London the Cabinet Office commented later that 'although this statement, read in its entirety, was a handsome tribute to the American Army, its general tone and a certain smugness of delivery undoubtedly gave deep offence to many American officers at SHAEF and 12th Army Group'.

Many journalists present fumed or cringed, depending on their nationality, yet both the British and the American press concentrated on the positive aspects of what he had said. The next morning, however, a German radio station put out a fake broadcast on a BBC wavelength, with a commentary which deliberately set out to stir American anger, implying that Montgomery had sorted out a First US Army disaster. 'The Battle of the Ardennes', it concluded, 'can now be written off thanks to Field Marshal Montgomery.' This fake broadcast was taken as genuine by American troops and the wire services. And for some time afterwards, even when it had been revealed that it was a Nazi propaganda trick, many aggrieved Americans still believed the British were just trying to bolster their role because their international standing was failing fast.

Even before the Nazi broadcast, Bradley was so angry that he rang Eisenhower to complain about Montgomery's statement, and expressed his fear that the Ninth Army would be left under British command. He begged Eisenhower to 'return it to me if it's only for twenty-four hours for the prestige of the American command'. He explained to Hansen that 'I wanted it back for prestige reasons, because the British had made so much of it.' Bradley still went on that day about Montgomery's order to the 82nd Airborne to withdraw.

Without warning Eisenhower, Bradley called his own press conference on 9 January. He wanted to justify the weakness of the American forces on the Ardennes front on 16 December and defend himself against accusations of being caught flat-footed; but also to emphasize that Montgomery's command of US forces was purely temporary. This prompted the *Daily Mail* to bang Montgomery's drum in the most provocative way, once more demanding that he be made land forces commander. The transatlantic press war began all over again with renewed ferocity.

Churchill was appalled. 'I fear great offence has been given to the American generals,' he wrote to his chief military assistant General Ismay on 10 January, 'not so much by Montgomery's speech as by the manner in which some of our papers seem to appropriate the whole credit for saving the battle to him. Personally I thought his speech most unfortunate. It had a patronising tone and completely overlooked the fact that the United States have lost perhaps 80,000 men and we but 2,000 or 3,000 . . . Eisenhower told me that the anger of his generals was such that he would hardly dare to order any of them to serve under Montgomery.' Eisenhower later claimed that the whole episode caused him more distress and worry than any other during the war.

While Eisenhower's emissaries, Air Chief Marshal Tedder and General Bull, were still struggling to get to Moscow, Churchill had been corresponding with Stalin about plans for the Red Army's great winter offensive. On 6 January he had written to the Soviet leader, making clear that the German offensive in the Ardennes had been halted and the Allies were masters of the situation. This did not stop Stalin (and Russian historians subsequently) from trying to claim that Churchill had been begging for help. Roosevelt's communication of 23 December, talking of an 'emergency', might have been seen in that light with rather more justification, but Stalin liked to take every opportunity to make the western Allies feel guilty or beholden to him. And he would play the same card again at the Yalta conference in February.

Stalin pretended that the major offensives westwards from the Vistula on 12 January and north into East Prussia the next day had been planned for 20 January, but that he had brought them forward to help the Allies in the Ardennes. The real reason was that meteorological reports had warned that a thaw would set in later in the month, and the Red Army needed the ground hard for its tanks. All of Guderian's fears about the German 'house of cards' collapsing in Poland and Silesia were to be proved justified. Hitler's Ardennes adventure had left the eastern front utterly vulnerable.

22

Counter-Attack

Patton's impatience to start the advance from round Bastogne was soon frustrated. Remer proclaimed the efforts of the *Führer Begleit* 'a defensive success on 31 December and estimated that they had destroyed thirty American tanks'. The Germans were left unmolested that night. This allowed them to form a new line of defence, which 'astonished us eastern front warriors very greatly'. Yet Remer acknowledged that the inexperienced American 87th Infantry Division had fought well. 'They were excellent fighters and had a number of commandos who spoke German and came behind our lines where they were able to knife many of our guards.' There is, however, little confirmation of such irregular tactics from American sources. But since Remer's tanks and assault guns were down to less than twenty kilometres' worth of fuel, he 'radioed Corps [headquarters] that we were fighting our last battle, and that they should send help'.

On the eastern flank, the 6th Armored Division passed through Bastogne on the morning of 1 January to attack Bizôry, Neffe and Mageret, where so many battles had been fought in the early days of the encirclement. The equally inexperienced 11th Armored Division, working with the 87th Infantry Division on the south-west side of Bastogne as part of Middleton's VIII Corps, was to advance towards Mande-Saint-Etienne, but came off badly in a clash with the 3rd Panzergrenadiers and the *Führer Begleit*. 'The 11th Armored is very green and took unnecessary casualties to no effect,' Patton recorded. The division was shaken by the shock of battle. Even its commander was thought to be close to cracking

33. A bazooka team from Cota's 28th Infantry Division withdraw after three days of fighting in Wiltz. This helped delay the Germans and allow the 101st Airborne just enough time to establish a defensive perimeter around Bastogne.

34. A young SS trooper taken prisoner near Malmédy, fortunate not to have been shot out of hand after the massacre nearby at Baugnez.

35. Civilians murdered by Kampfgruppe Peiper at Stavelot.

36. Vapour trails over Bastogne. On 23 December, the skies suddenly cleared to Allied relief and German anxiety. This allowed the Allied air forces to deploy the overwhelming strength of their air forces.

37. The change in the weather at last allowed the US Air Force to send in its C-47 Dakota transport aircraft to drop supplies into the Bastogne perimeter.

38. Unable to evacuate their wounded from Bastogne, the American command had to leave their casualties in cellars in the town, where they lay on straw awaiting the arrival of surgical teams dropped in by glider.

39. Paratroopers of the 101st Airborne sing carols on Christmas Eve just a few hours before the all-out German attack on the perimeter.

40. The end of the German thrust to the Meuse. Remnants of the Kampfgruppe Böhm from the 2nd Panzer-Division in a farmyard in Foy-Notre-Dame.

41. General Patton (*right*) reaches Bastogne on 30 December and decorates both Brigadier General Anthony McAuliffe (*left*) and Lieutenant Colonel Steve Chappuis (*centre*), the commander of the 502nd Parachute Infantry, with the Distinguished Service Cross.

42. American reinforcements advancing in steeply wooded Ardennes terrain.

43. A patrol from the British XXX Corps in the Ardennes wearing snowsuits made out of villagers' bedsheets.

44. The Allied counter-offensive in January 1945. Soldiers from the 26th Infantry Regiment of the 1st Division finally advance from Bütgenbach, which they had defended since 17 December.

45. La Roche-en-Ardenne was so badly destroyed that when swallows returned to rebuild their nests in the spring, they became disorientated.

46. Investigators start the work of identifying the American soldiers massacred at Baugnez near Malmédy.

47. After the massacre of American soldiers near Malmédy, their comrades, with the encouragement of senior commanders, shot most Waffen-SS soldiers who surrendered. Yet many had been forced into SS uniform against their will, or were pathetically young, like this boy.

48. Joachim Peiper on trial for war crimes including the massacre near Malmédy. Although the death sentence was commuted, members of the French Resistance killed him later.

up under the strain, and officers seemed unable to control their men. After bitter fighting to take the ruins of Chenogne on 1 January, about sixty German prisoners were shot. 'There were some unfortunate incidents in the shooting of prisoners,' Patton wrote in his diary. 'I hope we can conceal this.' It would indeed have been embarrassing after all the American fulminations over the Malmédy–Baugnez massacre.

Tuesday 2 January was 'a bitter cold morning', with bright clear skies, but meteorologists warned that bad weather was on the way. Manteuffel appealed to Model to accept that Bastogne could no longer be taken. They had to withdraw, but Model knew that Hitler would never agree. Lüttwitz also wanted to pull back east of the River Ourthe, as he recognized that the remnants of the 2nd Panzer-Division and the Panzer Lehr were dangerously exposed at Saint-Hubert and east of Rochefort. In the *Führer Begleit*, battalions were down to less than 150 men and their commanders were all casualties. Remer claimed that there was not even enough fuel to tow away the damaged tanks. The answer from the Adlerhorst was predictable. Hitler insisted on another attempt on 4 January, promising the 12th SS *Hitler Jugend* and a fresh Volksgrenadier division. He now justified his obstinacy on the grounds that, although his armies had failed to reach the Meuse, they had stopped Eisenhower from launching an offensive against the Ruhr.

The First Army and the British XXX Corps began the counter-offensive on 3 January as planned. Collins's VII Corps, led by the 2nd and 3rd Armored Divisions, attacked between Hotton and Manhay, with Ridgway's XVIII Airborne Corps on its eastern flank. But the advance was very slow. The weather conditions had worsened with snow, ice and now fog again. Shermans kept sliding off roads. No fighter-bombers could support the advance in the bad visibility. And the German divisions, although greatly reduced, fought back fiercely.

Although the 116th Panzer-Division was forced back from Hotton, German artillery, even while withdrawing, 'continued to pour destruction' on the town. The theatre, the school, the church, the sawmill, the Fanfare Royale café, the small shops on the main street, the houses and finally the Hôtel de la Paix were smashed. The only structure undamaged in Hotton was the bandstand on an island in the Ourthe river, and its roof was riddled by shell fragments.

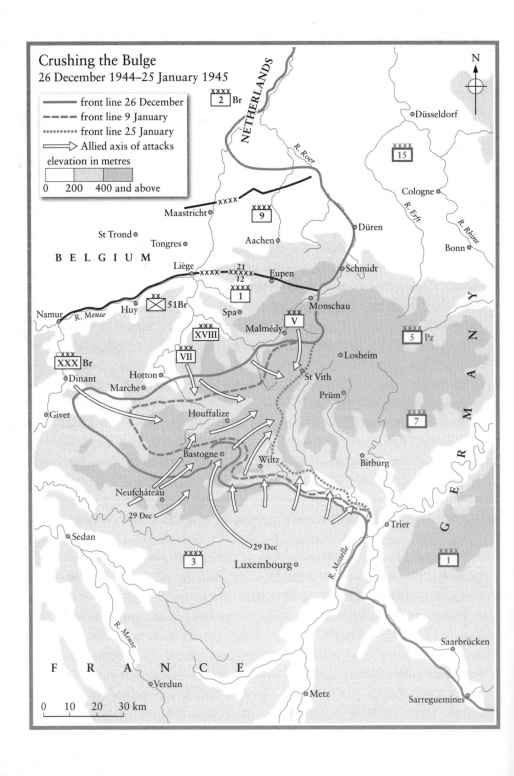

Crushing the Bulge
26 December 1944–25 January 1945

front line 26 December
front line 9 January
front line 25 January
Allied axis of attacks

elevation in metres

0   200   400 and above

N

NETHERLANDS

Düsseldorf

R. Roer

XXXX
2 Br

XXXX
15

Cologne

R. Erft

R. Rhine

XXXX
9

Maastricht

Düren

Bonn

St Trond
Tongres

Aachen

BELGIUM

Liège

21
XXXXX
12

Eupen

Schmidt

XXXX
1

Spa

Monschau

Namur
R. Meuse
Huy

XX
51Br

XXX
XVIII

Malmédy

XXX
V

R. Moselle

GERMANY

XXXX
5 Pz

Losheim

XXX
VII

St Vith

Prüm

XXXX
7

XXX
XXX Br

Dinant

Hotton

Marche

Houffalize

Givet

Bastogne

Wiltz

Bitburg

Neufchâteau

29 Dec

Sedan

29 Dec

Trier

XXXX
1

XXXX
3

Luxembourg

R. Moselle

Saarbrücken

R. Meuse

FRANCE

Verdun

Metz

Sarreguemines

0   10   20   30 km

On 4 January, Manteuffel launched a renewed assault on Bastogne as ordered, but this time his troops came in from the north and north-east led by the 9th SS *Hohenstaufen* and the SS *Hitler Jugend* supported by two Volksgrenadier divisions. In the north near Longchamps the 502nd Parachute Infantry, which had just fought a protracted battle, received a lucky break. A German panzergrenadier from the SS *Hohenstaufen* became lost in the snow-bound landscape. Seeing a soldier standing in a foxhole with his back to him, he assumed he was German, went up and tapped him on the shoulder to find out where he was. The paratrooper, although taken by surprise, managed to knock him down and overpower him. During interrogation, it transpired that the German prisoner was a company runner, carrying all the details of the attack planned for the following morning. He even volunteered the exact position of the assembly areas for 04.00 hours. Since the information seemed too good to be true, the regimental interrogator suspected that he must be planting disinformation, but then began to realize that it might well be genuine. The 101st Airborne headquarters was informed, and every available field artillery battalion and mortar platoon stood ready.

The attack of the SS *Hohenstaufen* against the 502nd Parachute Infantry was severely disrupted in the north. But the offensive against the Bastogne pocket, as it was now termed, hit the 327th Glider Infantry round Champs, the scene of the battle on Christmas Day, and was especially ferocious in the south-west. The 6th Armored Division, attacked by the *Hitler Jugend*, was close to breaking point; and after one battalion collapsed, a general withdrawal took place, losing Mageret and Wardin. A complete collapse was prevented by massive artillery concentrations.

Even the experienced 6th Armored had lessons to learn. A lot of the fog of war on the American side came from the simple failure of commanders at all levels to report their position accurately. 'Units frequently make errors of several thousand yards in reporting the location of their troops,' a staff officer at the division's headquarters observed. And on a more general perspective he wrote that American divisions were 'too sensitive to their flanks . . . they often do not move unless someone else is protecting their flanks when they are quite capable of furnishing the necessary protection themselves'. 'If you enter a village and you see no civilians,' another 6th Armored officer advised, 'be very very cautious.

It means that they have gone to ground in their cellars expecting a battle, because they know German soldiers are around.'

Many soldiers closed their minds to the suffering of the Belgians as they focused on the priority of killing the enemy. Those who did care were marked for life by the horrors that they witnessed. Villages, the principal targets for artillery, were totally destroyed. Farms and barns blazed. Women and children, forced out into the snow by the Germans, were in many cases maimed or killed by mines or artillery from both sides, or simply gunned down by fighter-bombers because dark figures against the snow were frequently mistaken for the enemy. GIs found wounded livestock bellowing in pain, and starving dogs chewing at the flesh of lacerated cows and horses even before they were dead. Water sources were poisoned by white phosphorus. The Americans did what they could to evacuate civilians to safety, but all too often it was impossible in the middle of a battle.

West of Bastogne, the 17th Airborne Division took over from the 11th Armored Division on 3 January. The 11th Armored had advanced just ten kilometres in four days, at the cost of 661 battle casualties and fifty-four tanks. The newly arrived paratroopers appeared to fare little better in their first action. 'The 17th Airborne, which attacked this morning,' Patton wrote in his diary on 4 January, 'got a very bloody nose and reported the loss of 40% in some of its battalions. This is, of course, hysterical.'

The 17th Airborne, fighting towards Flamierge and Flamizoulle on the western edge of the Bastogne perimeter, was up against the far more experienced *Führer Begleit* and the 3rd Panzergrenadier-Division. 'We have had replacements who would flop down with the first burst of enemy fire and would not shoot even to protect others advancing,' an officer complained.

American advice came thick and fast. 'The German follows a fixed form. He sends over a barrage followed by tanks, followed by infantry. Never run, if you do you will surely get killed. Stick in your hole and let the barrage go over. Stick in your hole and let the tanks go by, then cut loose and mow the German infantry down.' 'Don't go to a white flag. Make the Germans come to you. Keep the Krauts covered.' Officers also found that their men must be trained what to do when shot in different parts of the body, so that they could look after themselves until a medic arrived. 'Each man takes care of himself until the medical men arrive. *No one* stops the fight to help another.' Yet badly wounded men left in the snow without help were unlikely to survive more than half an hour.

The 17th Airborne Division had a tank battalion manned entirely by African-American soldiers attached to it. 'Our men had great confidence in them,' a colonel reported. 'We used the tanks to protect our infantry moving forward. The tanks would come first with the doughboys riding on them and following in squad columns [behind them]. Selected men were in the last wave, tail end of the company, to knock off Jerries in snow capes. The Jerries in snow capes would let the tanks and bulk of the infantry pass, then rise up to shoot our infantry in the back, but our "tail enders" ended that.'

When they captured a position, they usually found that the ground was frozen so hard that it was impossible to dig in. The division decided that they needed to use their 155mm guns to blast shellholes on an objective or piece of ground to be occupied, so that foxholes could be prepared rapidly. With so much to learn against such hardened opponents, it was hardly surprising that the 17th Airborne had such a baptism of fire. 'The 17th has suffered a bloody nose,' 12th Army Group noted, 'and in its first action lacks the élan of its airborne companions.' But there were also examples of outstanding heroism. Sergeant Isidore Jachman, from a Berlin Jewish family who had emigrated to the United States, seized a bazooka from another soldier who had been killed, and saved his company by fighting off two tanks. He was killed in the process and was awarded a posthumous Congressional Medal of Honor.

The 87th Infantry Division to the west was not making any better progress, having come up against a Kampfgruppe from the Panzer Lehr. There were constant complaints about soldiers being far too trigger-happy and wasting ammunition. A sergeant in the 87th Division described how he 'saw a rifleman shoot a German and then empty his gun and another clip into him although it was obvious that the first shot had done the job. A 57mm gun fired about forty rounds into a house suspected of having some Germans in it. Practically all were A[rmor] P[iercing] shells and fired into the upper floors. The Germans were in the basement and lower floor and stayed there until we attacked.'

The 87th Division, despite Remer's compliments on their fighting prowess, suffered all the usual faults of green troops. Men froze under mortar attack instead of running forward to escape it. And when soldiers were wounded, several would rush over to help them instead of leaving them to the aid men following on behind. Unused to winter warfare, the 87th and the 17th Airborne suffered many casualties from frostbite. Men were told to obtain footwear which was two sizes too big and then put on at least two pairs of socks, but it was a bit late for that once they were already in action.

Middleton was utterly dejected by the performance of the inexperienced divisions. Patton was furious: his reputation was at stake. He was even more convinced that the counter-attack should have been aimed at the eighty-kilometre base of the salient along the German frontier. He blamed Montgomery, but also Bradley who was 'all for putting new divisions in the Bastogne fight'. He was so disheartened that he wrote: 'We can still lose this war . . . the Germans are colder and hungrier than we are, but they fight better. I can never get over the stupidity of our green troops.' Patton refused to recognize that the lack of a good road network at the base of the salient, together with the terrain and the atrocious winter weather which frustrated Allied airpower, meant that his preferred option would probably have stood even less chance of rapid success.

The advance of the counter-offensive in the north fared only slightly better, even with the bulk of the German divisions switched to the Bastogne sector. There was nearly a metre of snow in the region and temperatures had dropped to minus 20 Centigrade. 'Roads were icy and tanks, despite the fact that gravel was laid, slipped off into the sides, destroying communication set-ups and slowing traffic.' The metal studs welded to the tracks for grip wore off in a very short time. In the freezing fog, artillery-spotting Cub planes could operate for only part of the day, and the fighter-bombers were grounded. The 2nd Armored Division found itself in an 'extremely heavy fight' with the remnants of the 2nd Panzer-Division. 'A lucky tree burst from an 88-mm shell knocked out between fifty and sixty of our armored infantry, the largest known number of casualties' from a single shell. But 'Trois Ponts was cleared as was Reharmont and by nightfall the line Hierlot–Amcomont–Dairmont–Bergeval was reached,' First Army noted. The 82nd Airborne Division took 500 prisoners.

Field Marshal Montgomery, who visited Hodges at 14.00, was 'greatly pleased with the progress made and kept remarking "Good show. Good show"'. He informed Hodges that two brigades of the British 53rd Division would attack at first light the next morning in the extreme west, to maintain contact with the flanks of the 2nd Armored Division. Yet the counter-attack was not proving nearly as easy as Bradley had assumed. Even 'the 2nd Armored Division of Bulldog Ernie Harmon is running into the same kind of resistance', wrote Hansen, 'finding it difficult to get an impetus in this difficult country with stern opposition'.

South of Rochefort, part of the British 6th Airborne Division advanced on Bure, which the Belgian SAS had reconnoitred four days before. The 13th (Lancashire) Battalion of the Parachute Regiment went into the attack at 13.00 hours. Heavy mortar fire from the Lehr's panzergrenadiers caused a number of casualties, but A Company made it into the village despite fire from six assault guns and automatic weapons. Panzergrenadiers supported by a Mark VI Tiger launched a counter-attack. Shermans from the Fife and Forfar Yeomanry arrived to help, but these tanks also had no control on the icy roads. The Germans were beaten off after dark, but during the night they attacked again and again, while tracer bullets set barns and farmhouses on fire.

The following day the paratroopers, under intense shellfire, managed to hold the village against another five attacks. The lone Tiger tank remained in the centre of the village, impervious to the anti-tank rounds fired by PIATs, the much less effective British counterpart to the American bazooka. Along with the German artillery, the Tiger accounted for sixteen Shermans from the Fife and Forfar. Houses shook and windows shattered every time the monster fired its 88mm main armament. Because the Tiger could control the main street with its machine guns, the wounded could not be evacuated. The firing was so intense that the only way the medical aid post was able to send more field dressings to paratroopers on the other side of the street was to tape them to rifle magazines and throw them across the road from one house to another through smashed windows. A company from the 2nd Battalion of the Oxfordshire and Buckinghamshire Light Infantry arrived to reinforce the paratroopers after so many losses. But late that evening another attack supported by two Tiger tanks forced the Ox and Bucks back from their section of the village.

On 5 January, in house-to-house combat with grenades and bayonets, the paratroopers began to clear the large village systematically. Belgians, sheltering in cellars and afraid of grenades being thrown down the stairs, cried out that they were civilians. Many villagers had sought shelter in the religious college, the Alumnat, where conditions became horrific from dysentery and people driven mad by the shelling. During the day the Panzer Lehr made more counter-attacks supported this time by four Tigers, but soon after nightfall the last German positions were eliminated. The battalion was ordered into reserve, having lost seven officers and 182 men. The 5th Battalion of the Parachute Regiment took its place and the 23rd Hussars replaced the Fife and Forfar.

The inhabitants had been forced to remain in their dark cellars while the battle raged overhead. Yvonne Louviaux, then fourteen years old, remembered her mother telling her children to squeeze up close to each other so that if they were killed, they would all die together. After three days, with only apples to eat, they were finally able to climb back to the ground floor. They found their sofa covered in blood from one of the wounded soldiers. The village itself was 70 per cent destroyed or seriously damaged, and most of the livestock killed. Telephone poles were smashed and wires and electric cables dangled dangerously on the blackened snow. Severed limbs from bodies blown apart in the fighting lay around. With a slightly sinister symmetry, two babies were born during the battle while two villagers were killed. Others died later from stepping on mines left from the battle.

One family returned to their house and found what at first sight seemed like a naked human corpse strung from the ceiling of their living room. On closer inspection they saw it was the carcass of their pig, which the Germans had started to butcher, but then evidently they had been interrupted by the arrival of the Allies. They were luckier than the majority, who had lost all their livestock, hams and preserves to German hunger, as well as their draught horses and forage to the Wehrmacht. There was so little food available that a large bull, which had survived, was butchered to feed the village. Everyone, including small children, gathered to watch.

*

Impatient optimism still seemed to get the better of 12th Army Group headquarters, perhaps because General Bradley could not wait for the moment when First Army and Third Army met up. This would mark the moment when the First Army would be returned to his command. But Hodges's diary keeper noted on 6 January that 'this headquarters thought laughable the suggestion made by General Siebert, G-2 of the 12th Army Group, that we should be on the alert for any "imminent German collapse"'. Even 'Lightning Joe' Collins thought the suggestion 'fairly ridiculous'. The very next day, Bradley called Patton to claim that the Germans were pulling all their armour and troops back from the Bastogne pocket. But according to Patton's staff the intelligence officers of all divisions and corps 'declare there's no evidence of this and in fact 6th Armored Division was fighting the strongest counterattack launched against them during the present campaign'.*

The advance of the British gave the Germans the excuse to begin their fighting withdrawal from round Jemelle. Sergeant G. O. Sanford of the Parachute Regiment was captured at the village of On next to Jemelle. Two panzergrenadiers led him off into a wood and shot him dead. At Forrières, when surrendering Germans emerged from a wood with their hands on their head, two British armoured cars positioned by the station opened fire and mowed them down. As a local observed: 'Undoubtedly the hard fighting in Bure had led these English to act in such a way.' Belgians expected British soldiers to be better behaved than those of other nations, and were shocked to witness lapses. One woman, on seeing a British paratrooper take a watch from the wrist of a dead German, remarked: 'they certainly did not seem to have that renowned English composure'.

In Jemelle on Monday 8 January, Sister Alexia Bruyère wrote in her diary: 'At 09.30 we saw the Germans leave, keeping close to the walls, packs on their backs, heading towards the bridge at the railway station. The last ones were wearing white trousers (it is snowing), a bedsheet

* This idea at 12th Army Group must have been based on speculation, since the first hint of withdrawal through Ultra intercepts did not come until late on 8 January when the 9th Panzer-Division revealed that it had pulled back to a line east of Rochefort and Marche, while the first indication of retreat around the Bastogne pocket came on 9 January.

like a burnous and a cloth like a turban. One would have thought they were real Arabs.'

Refugees began to return with their remaining possessions piled on handcarts. One family entered their house in Rochefort and, on hearing little noises behind some heavy furniture, assumed that rats or mice had started a nest in their absence. But, on moving the furniture, they found a German soldier, hunched up in a ball and trembling with fear. He begged them not to give him up. He was an Austrian deserter. They reassured him that his unit had left, and he now could surrender to the Allies.

On the night of 5–6 January, ninety RAF Lancasters of Bomber Command flattened the town of Houffalize to block the key crossroads for German supply columns and the escape route for German forces. The place was impassable for three days.*

Partly due to the bombing of Houffalize, the 116th Panzer-Division found that the roads became more and more congested during the gradual retreat, which at first averaged less than two kilometres a day. Most movements had to take place in daylight, but with the weather generally overcast until 10 January, there were few fighter-bomber attacks.

'Resistance never let up,' wrote an officer with the 83rd Infantry Division east of Manhay, 'and the brutality for which SS troops were notorious was brought home to us. A platoon of infantrymen from the 331st's 2nd Battalion became pinned down in an open field in drifting, waist-deep snow. With a hail of intense fire directed at them, they could only burrow deeper into the snow. Some were killed, and others were wounded. When the firing finally stopped, the platoon sergeant raised his head and saw two Germans approaching. They kicked each of the prostrate infantrymen, and if one groaned, he was shot in the head. After rifling the pockets of their victims, the Germans left. When darkness

---

* General Patton, who unfortunately was drawn to writing verse, penned the following lines:

O little town of Houffalize,	Yet in thy dark streets shineth
How still we see thee lie;	Not any Goddamned light;
Above thy steep and battered streets	The hopes and fears of all thy years
The aeroplanes sail by.	Were blown to hell last night.

fell, the sergeant staggered back to safety, half frozen and half shocked out of his mind. Of 27 men in the platoon, he was the only one to come out alive. When kicked, he had played dead.'

German soldiers fought on even though many longed to be taken prisoner. 'Everyone thinks: "If only the time would come",' a German soldier called Friedl remarked, 'and then comes the officer, and you just carry out orders. That's what's tragic about the situation.' As American interrogators found from prisoners, German morale was suffering badly as the half-starved soldiers struggled to push vehicles and guns in freezing conditions, with the knowledge that the great offensive had failed. Nazi attempts to bludgeon their men into further efforts were based on orders which had been standard in Waffen-SS divisions since Normandy. 'Anyone taken prisoner without being wounded loses his honour and his dependants get no support.'

Waffen-SS prisoners were conspicuous by their rarity, either because of their determination to go down fighting, or from being shot on sight by their captors. One SS officer, however, attempted to justify his presence with unconvincing logic. He told his interrogator in a First Army cage: 'Do not get the impression that I am a coward because I have let myself become a prisoner of war. I would gladly have died a hero's death, but I thought it only fair and just to share the misfortune of my men.'

American divisions in the Third Army felt that prisoners should be treated differently according to circumstances. 'When the Germans are having success along a front,' the 6th Armored Division observed, 'prisoners taken are apt to be cocky and feel that though they were taken prisoner they just had an unlucky break. In the treatment of such PWs, they should not be fed, allowed to smoke, or given anything bordering on soft treatment until they have been questioned. On the other hand, prisoners taken when the Germans are suffering general reverses along the line are generally discouraged and disgusted with conditions in their lines and with their superiors. Many of these prisoners have voluntarily surrendered and are willing and eager to talk if well treated. If they are put at ease, allowed to sit down and smoke during questioning these men will unburden themselves, often volunteering information that has not been asked for.' This was true of both officers and ordinary soldiers.

In the case of captured SS, all depended on whether they saw themselves as Aryan supermen or whether they had been forced into the SS against their will, as was often the case with Poles and Alsatians. The latter could be treated as ordinary prisoners. 'The true "superman" requires stern treatment; it is all he has given anyone else and is what he expects. He has been in the habit of threatening physical violence and then carrying out his threat. For this reason he seems to be particularly susceptible to the threat of physical violence. It is not necessary to beat him up, but if he thinks he had better talk or else – he talks! To put it bluntly, we have found the best system is: for the humble and whipped prisoner, "A full stomach and an empty bladder"; for the arrogant and cocky, "A full bladder and an empty stomach".' The 35th Infantry Division, on the other hand, reported that the prisoners it had captured from the 1st SS Panzer-Division 'were more meek [than the volksgrenadiers], probably in anticipation of retribution', and they complained that their 'officers had withdrawn in time of danger, leaving them to hold their positions'.

The soldiers of the 28th Division did not believe in a dual approach. They objected to seeing rear-area troops giving German prisoners candy and cigarettes. Their own prisoners were all made to march back rather than ride in a truck, and they received only water until after they had been interrogated. 'Too good treatment of prisoners has a bad effect on our men. The way we handle them, our men distinctly have the idea that being a prisoner of war is not so good.' Another division was even tougher in its views. 'We have never been benefited by treating prisoners well . . . We are here to Kill Germans, not to baby them.' Some soldiers in the 30th Division exacted their own revenge when they captured Germans wearing American combat boots taken from the dead. They forced them at gunpoint to remove them and walk barefoot along the icy roads.

The US First Army noted that 'prisoners were beginning to complain of the lack of food and many told stories of long marches with heavy equipment owing to the lack of transportation'. On both the north and south sides of the salient, prisoner-of-war interrogations confirmed that German troops dreaded the air bursts from the new Pozit fuses on American artillery shells. 'The results of these new shells on German bodies and minds are very effective,' a First Army report on prisoner-of-war interrogations stated.

Around the Bastogne pocket, the fighting slackened a little after the battles of 3 and 4 January. The 5th Fallschirmjäger-Division now came under General der Panzertruppe Krüger's LVIII Panzer Corps. But when the paratroopers' commander Generalmajor Heilmann argued that it was futile to waste more lives in doomed attacks, Krüger retorted: 'If we want to win the war the 5th Fallschirmjäger-Division has to take part in it too!'

On 6 January, Heilmann had received a secret order from Himmler which read: 'If there is any suspicion that a soldier has absented himself from his unit with a view to deserting and thus impairing the fighting strength of his unit one member of the soldier's family (wife) will be shot.' Presumably this had been prompted by a report from Brigadeführer Mohnke of the *Leibstandarte* to the SS-Reichsführer. Heilmann was sacked a few days later. Even in the more reliable 26th Volksgrenadier-Division men began to desert. 'Ten or twelve of the remnants of our company dressed in civilian clothes and hid,' a Feldwebel acknowledged in captivity.

As in all armies, it was not so much the fear of death as the fear of mutilation which preyed on minds. A German field hospital, or *Feld-lazarett*, was little more than an amputation line. American doctors were horrified by the German army's tendency to cut off limbs without a moment's thought. A wounded American prisoner from the 401st Glider Infantry was appalled when taken into the operating room. 'I nearly gagged,' he wrote. 'There were half a dozen tables surrounded by doctors in white rubber aprons splattered with blood. All the tables were occupied with German wounded or men with frozen limbs. Buckets on the floor held toes, fingers and other appendages. The men on the tables had been given a local anesthetic, but were still screaming and groaning as the doctors worked.' When the buckets were left or emptied outside, local dogs soon helped themselves, as Belgians noted. The corpses of those who died under the knife were stacked outside, frozen solid, some with a coating of ice over their faces as if in a glass sarcophagus. Even those lucky enough to be evacuated to Germany had no idea of their destination or fate. 'The wounded are sent to wherever the hospital train happens to go,' a German doctor said. 'Nobody at the front knows the destination.'

American field hospitals could also be a grisly spectacle. A senior nurse with the Third Army described a ward known as the 'Chamber of Horrors', which stank of 'gore and sweat and human excretions'. She recounted a night shift, tending two soldiers who 'had been dying all day yesterday, and they were dying all night now . . . One, a private in the infantry, had lost both legs and one hand: he had a deep chest wound and his bowels were perforated by a shell fragment . . . The other patient was a corporal in a tank outfit. His spinal cord was severed and he was paralyzed from the waist down. His belly was open, and so was his chest.' Both boys were in a coma, breathing noisily. 'It's a good thing their mothers can't see them when they die,' she said.

Non-battle casualties were also mounting. In November and December losses to cold amounted to 23,000 men. Almost all were combat infantrymen, and since a division usually had 4,000 of them, this amounted to the equivalent of at least five and a half divisions. Neuropsychiatric cases, termed combat exhaustion, rose to nearly a quarter of all hospital admissions. The German army, which refused to recognize the condition, apparently suffered far fewer cases.

Combat exhaustion produced recognizable symptoms: 'nausea, crying, extreme nervousness and gastric conditions'. Some commanders felt that officer patients were returned to their unit too rapidly, because they often broke down again. The effect could also be infectious. 'When one man cracks, others will soon follow.' Yet isolation was the main problem. It was vital to get men out of their foxholes and mix with the others when not under shellfire. 'Tank fatigue' was due more to 'prolonged periods of continuous combat action'. It differed from the infantry version, even though symptoms were similar with 'upset stomach, nausea, dysentery, limpness and men crying in some cases in almost a state of hysteria'. The 2nd Armored Division blamed unhealthy eating, 'long hours of exposure' in extreme cold, as well as physical exhaustion. 'Cold C and K rations do not materially increase vitality and resistance, and in some cases cause upset stomachs.' Attempts to use captured German blowtorches to heat cans of food failed to resolve the problem. American doctors did not of course know then what the Germans had discovered after the battle of Stalingrad. The combination of stress, exhaustion, cold and malnourishment upsets the metabolism, and gravely reduces the body's capacity to absorb calories and vitamins.

'Even with hard and experienced troops, a soldier is only good for so long,' an officer with the 5th Infantry Division on Patton's right flank observed. 'I have seen some marvellous things done by some of my men and I have seen some of these men crack finally . . . Tired troops cannot do a job well. They'll go, but they lack smack. When you lack smack you start losing battles.'

On 8 January, the remnants of the 2nd and 9th Panzer-Divisions received the order to withdraw the next day. 'It is the coldest weather I've ever experienced,' a British civil affairs officer noted in his diary. 'The wind was just like a knife to the face . . . The roads are full of ditched vehicles with freezing drivers alongside them, waiting for whatever help can come.' Some people, however, thought it slightly ironic that the atrocious driving conditions greatly reduced the number of traffic accidents and deaths because the drivers were forced to proceed so carefully.

On 10 January, Generalfeldmarschall Model passed on an instruction from Hitler at the Adlerhorst. 'The Führer has ordered that I and II Panzer Corps, with the 1st, 2nd, 9th and 12th SS Panzer-Divisions, with immediate effect, are to assemble for rapid refitting behind Army Group B and placed at the disposal of Commander-in-Chief West in such a way that they no longer become involved in combat.' Army formations would once again feel angry that they would be expected to hold the line while Waffen-SS divisions were withdrawn to be rested and re-equipped.

The bitterness of defeat in the Ardennes was reflected among some German generals held prisoner in England. Having exulted in their material superiority earlier in the war, they now seemed to regard such advantages as unfair. Generalmajor Hans Bruhn, a divisional commander captured by the French in Alsace, was secretly recorded saying to his companions: 'It's the greatest mockery in the history of the world and at the same time the saddest part of it, that the flower of our manhood is being mowed down by the aircraft and the massed tanks of an army which has no real soldiers and which doesn't really want to fight.'

On Thursday 11 January, there were unmistakable signs that the Germans were pulling back. In the Houffalize–Bastogne area, their corridor was only thirteen kilometres wide and under heavy American artillery fire. The 30th Infantry Division told Ninth Army headquarters that bad visibility was allowing the Germans to escape. 'The Germans are pulling all their armor and heavy stuff entirely out of the Bulge in an orderly and leisurely withdrawal.' Also that day, the BBC announced that the broadcast on Montgomery's comments had been the product of German propaganda. The news did little to soften Bradley's feelings about his *bête noire*.

The next morning 12th Army Group received authorization to stockpile gas munitions in case the Germans resorted to chemical weapons in desperation, or on Hitler's orders. This had been prompted by a report from SHAEF to General Marshall's intelligence chief in Washington five days earlier. Major General Strong and his staff had been perturbed by five references to 'gas' found in Ultra decrypts.*

Friday 12 January was eventful in other ways. Göring, apparently forgiven for the disaster of Operation *Bodenplatte*, was summoned to the Führer's presence at the Adlerhorst to receive Hitler's congratulations on his fifty-second birthday. It was hardly an auspicious occasion. The date was far more important for other reasons. At 05.00 Moscow time, Marshal Ivan Konev's First Ukrainian Front attacked out of the Sandomierz bridgehead west of the River Vistula following a massive bombardment, which a panzergrenadier officer said was 'like the heavens falling down on earth'. Soviet tank armies advanced with slogans painted on their tank turrets declaring: 'Forward into the fascist lair!' and 'Revenge and death to the German occupiers!' The next day Marshal Georgy Zhukov's First Belorussian Front attacked from south of Warsaw, while two other Fronts assaulted East Prussia.

General Guderian had not exaggerated, but, like Cassandra's, his warnings had been ignored. The Red Army had deployed 6.7 million men along the whole of the eastern front. He was almost speechless when he heard that Dietrich's Sixth Panzer Army, which was being withdrawn from the Ardennes, was to be transferred not to the Vistula or East Prussia but to Hungary to save the oilfields.

---

* 'We are aware of your views on this question but again wish to emphasize that this offensive is an all-out effort in which Hitler will employ any weapon. It has always been appreciated by you that Germany might initiate gas warfare to obtain a decisive result. The battle having gone badly, Hitler may regard this as the moment. We should not overlook the chaos which would result among the civilian population in NW Europe on the possible employment of a gas warhead in V-1 and V-2 [missiles] . . . Would you please re-examine the matter in light of this further information and inform us of your views urgently.'

As soon as news of the great Soviet offensive reached 12th Army Group, Bradley immediately wanted to spread the impression that his forces' imminent victory in the Ardennes 'had enabled the Russian to attack with far greater numbers and more spectacular success than would otherwise have been possible'. He was right. There can be little doubt that the commitment and then grinding down of German forces in the Ardennes, especially the panzer divisions, had mortally weakened the Wehrmacht's capacity to defend the eastern front. But as another general in British captivity observed: 'The fear of Russia will keep Germany fighting to the bitter end.'

23

Flattening the Bulge

Just as the final battle in the Ardennes commenced, the Germans threw more divisions into Operation *Nordwind*. On 5 January, after the initial attack had failed in its objectives, Himmler's Army Group *Oberrhein* finally began its supporting thrusts against the southern flank of the American VI Corps. The XIV SS Corps launched an attack across the Rhine north of Strasbourg, and two days later the Nineteenth Army advanced north from the Colmar pocket either side of the Rhône–Rhine Canal. The very survival of General Patch's VI Corps was threatened.

Devers, receiving no sympathy from Eisenhower, handed responsibility for the defence of Strasbourg to Lattre de Tassigny's First French Army, which now had to extend its front from the city to the Belfort Gap, a distance of 120 kilometres. But the point of greatest danger was round Gambsheim and Herrlisheim, where the XIV SS Corps had created a bridgehead south-east of Haguenau.

On 7 January, the 25th Panzergrenadier and the 21st Panzer-Division went into the attack. They reached the Haguenau Forest thirty kilometres north of Strasbourg, but were halted by the 14th Armored Division, Devers's last reserve. To the north in the Low Vosges, the 45th Infantry Division managed to hold back the 6th SS Mountain Division. One of the 45th Division's battalions was surrounded, and fought on for almost a week. Only two men escaped.

Hitler was still obsessed with Frederick the Great's dictum that he who throws in his last battalions wins the war. On 16 January, he sent in his final reserves, the 7th Fallschirmjäger-Division and the 10th SS

Panzer-Division *Frundsberg*. Their attack along the Rhine as they tried to reach the Gambsheim bridgehead battered the inexperienced 12th Armored Division at Herrlisheim. This development provided the main subject for discussion at Eisenhower's morning briefing on 20 January. 'What gets me, Honest to God,' the Supreme Commander exclaimed, 'is that when two of their divisions are loose, we sit around and get scared.' Air Marshal Sir James Robb noted in his diary: 'The discussion which follows reveals a growing wonderment at the failure of our forces, whether divisions or corps, to achieve any real results compared to the immediate success of comparatively small German attacks.'

Faced with this unexpected advance, Devers was forced to retreat to a new line along the Rothbach, Moder and Zorn rivers. This withdrawal was well executed, and the new defensive positions held. The German offensive petered out around 25 January after General de Lattre's First Army, aided by the US XXI Corps on the northern side, began to crush the Colmar pocket, or what the Germans called Bridgehead Alsace. The American 3rd Infantry Division was supported by Cota's 28th Division, which one would have thought had suffered enough after the Hürtgen Forest and being crushed east of Bastogne. Fighting in the snow-covered forest of Riedwihr, the 3rd Infantry Division found itself under heavy counter-attacks, and Lieutenant Audie Murphy's astonishing bravery won him a Congressional Medal of Honor and a future career as a movie star in Hollywood. Once again, the Germans fought so doggedly in retreat, despite Allied superiority in aircraft and artillery, that more units from the Ardennes were diverted south. The Colmar pocket was not finally crushed until 9 February.

The 101st Airborne Division was one of the formations allocated to finish the fighting in Alsace, so its men were relieved to find that this time they were too late to take part. Ten days before, on hearing that the 101st was to move to Alsace, Major Dick Winters had thought: 'My God, don't they have anybody else in this army to plug these gaps?' The division certainly needed a rest. During its last days at the northern end of the Bastogne pocket, Easy Company of the 506th Parachute Infantry had first been sent in to capture Foy. 'Every replacement that came into the platoon got killed in that town,' said a veteran of the company, 'and I don't know why.' The attack had started as a disaster, until the company commander was rapidly replaced. Then on 14 January, as temperatures dropped to minus 23 Centigrade and the snow deepened, the 506th advanced across open snowfields towards Noville where many of their comrades had died with Team Desobry at the very start of the battle.

Once Noville had been taken they were given another objective, the village of Rachamps just east of the route to Houffalize. Sergeant Earl Hale and Private Joseph Liebgott cornered six SS officers in a barn. They lined them up and warned them that they would shoot if they tried anything. A shell exploded outside, wounding Hale by the door, and instantly an SS officer whipped out a knife from his boot and slashed Hale's throat. Liebgott shot him dead, and then gunned down the others. A medic patched up Hale's throat. He was lucky – the oesophagus had been cut, but not the windpipe. Hale was evacuated by Jeep to Bastogne.*

Sergeant Robert Rader noticed an ordinary German soldier taken at Rachamps who looked as if he were grinning. An infuriated Rader raised his rifle to shoot him, but another paratrooper grabbed the barrel, shouting, 'Sarge, he has no lips or eyelids!' The German had lost them through frostbite on the eastern front. Rachamps was Easy Company's very last action in the battle for Bastogne. On 17 January, the 101st was relieved by the 17th Airborne. Packed into open trucks once again instead of aircraft, they were off to Alsace.

Resistance did not lessen in the salient, as the Fifth Panzer Army started to withdraw on 14 January towards Houffalize, which was still being bombed by the Allied air forces. The 2nd Panzer-Division and the Panzer Lehr covered the retreat in the usual German way of using assault guns and tanks with infantry to cover the withdrawal of their artillery regiments. Whenever American howitzers fired white phosphorus shells, it brought a 'violent enemy artillery reaction'.

Just as on the southern front, artillery pounded villages, setting houses and farms on fire. Often the shelling was so intense that German soldiers would seek shelter in the cellars, forcing the civilians aside.

* Hale recovered, but with a crooked oesophagus. The doctor gave him a medical chit excusing him from wearing a tie. Hale was later confronted by an obsessive General Patton demanding to know why he was improperly dressed. The sergeant was able to produce his authorization, which apparently left Patton speechless.

Pigs, horses and cows trapped in burning barns and byres stood little chance. In one village eleven people died from a single shell, which hit a stable in which twenty civilians were sheltering. Sometimes the old men, women and children could not stand the relentless shelling any longer, and would try to escape out into the snow. Mistaken for combatants, several were shot down. If those wounded were lucky, American ambulances or trucks would evacuate them to hospitals in the rear. Little, however, could be done for all those suffering from dysentery, pneumonia, diphtheria and a host of other serious ailments brought on by the filthy and freezing conditions of the last few weeks.

Moved by the fate of the luckless Belgians, American troops handed out rations, cigarettes, candy and chocolate. Only a few, brutalized by the war, went about looting and molesting women. To tell the compassionate from the brutal by outward appearances was impossible. Troops of all three nations by that stage looked like brigands, filthy, dishevelled and bearded. Villagers who had benefited earlier from American largesse were struck by the comparative poverty of British troops, who still shared what little they had. The Belgians did not much like the taste of either bully beef or British army-issue cigarettes, but were too polite to say so.

'Having visited villages recently cleared of the German Offensive,' a British civil affairs officer noted, 'it's good to see the joy of the people and their expressions of relief.' But in some places both British and American troops appalled their hosts by smashing up furniture for firewood. An officer in the 53rd Welsh Division noted that to escape the terrible cold, 'the troops have been over-enthusiastic in building up a roaring blaze in the old stone hearth, and consequently the chimney overheated, setting fire to part of the roof'. Almost every house occupied by Allied soldiers was left a squalid mess, with substantial damage. The British 6th Airborne Division appears to have provoked the greatest number of complaints.

The British XXX Corps pursued the Germans from the direction of La Roche-en-Ardenne, on the southern flank of Collins's VII Corps. 'The right wing of the 2nd Panzer-Division in the area of Nisramont had to face west,' wrote Generalmajor Lauchert. 'During this redeployment, a gap opened into which a British battalion advanced as far as Engreux. The British attack behind the back of the defence line could only be halted by a feint attack. The divisional command post had to pull out back to Mont.' Like the American infantry, the British struggled badly in the deep snow. They were not helped by their sodden ammunition boots freezing rock hard. German jackboots were known to be more weather-resistant. The commanding officer of the 1st Gordons in the 51st Highland Division came across one of his sergeants in a wood, where he had strung up the corpse of a German soldier from a branch and had lit a fire under him. 'He was trying to thaw him out,' he wrote, 'in order to take off his boots.'

A Kampfgruppe of the 2nd Panzer-Division, with engineers, infantry, assault guns and tanks, set up a defence line in front of Houffalize. Hidden by the dark, its Panthers were able to take on American tanks at a range of 400–500 metres as they emerged from the woods because they showed up so clearly against the snow. 'Very soon an American tank burst into flames and provided such brightness that the American tanks were well lit and were easy to shoot. After a fire-fight lasting at most fifteen minutes, twenty-four American tanks went up in flames and a further ten were captured undamaged. The Germans lost only two tanks destroyed out of twenty-four.' As with most of these encounters, this account was probably both optimistic and boastful, but there can be little doubt that the Germans inflicted a number of bloody noses in the final stages of the battle.

On 15 January, the 30th Infantry Division attacking the village of Thirimont found that 'brick houses had been turned into veritable pill boxes, and heavy machineguns and other automatic weapons emplaced in them'. It required two battalions from the 120th Infantry Regiment, a tank battalion and a tank-destroyer battalion, as well as 'over 11,000 rounds of 105mm and 155mm ammunition', to take the place. The regiment suffered more than 450 casualties at the hands of the 3rd Fallschirmjäger-Division. Because of the deep snow and ice, 'ambulances couldn't get anywhere near the wounded', so the medical battalion borrowed horses and sledges from farmers to bring them back. Most of the Germans taken prisoner were suffering from frostbitten feet and could hardly walk.

Patton drove out in his Jeep to see the troops attacking Houffalize. 'At one point', he wrote, 'we came across a German machinegunner who had been killed and apparently instantly frozen as he was in a half-sitting position with his arms extended, holding a loaded belt of ammunition. I saw a lot of black objects sticking out of the snow and, on investigating, found that they were the toes of dead men.' He too was struck by the way the faces of men frozen rapidly on death turned 'a sort of claret color'. Patton regretted not having his camera with him to record this.

On 15 January, Hitler returned by train to Berlin, as Zhukov's and Konev's tank armies raced towards the line of the rivers Oder and Neisse. The industrial region of Silesia was about to be overrun. Apart from one sortie to an army headquarters on the Oder front, the Führer would never leave the capital again.

By nightfall on 15 January, both combat commands of the 2nd Armored Division had advanced to within a kilometre or so of Houffalize and consolidated for the night. Patrols were sent into the ruins of the town to discover enemy dispositions. They entered the town at 01.00 on 16 January but found little sign of the enemy. Patrols were also sent east to the River Ourthe where enemy positions had also been abandoned. 'Contact was established with Third Army patrols at 09.30 that day, marking the juncture of the First and Third Armies in the Ardennes offensive.'

The Ardennes offensive was almost at an end. A British regiment discovered that the Wehrmacht had run out of decorations for valour. Signed photographs of Generalfeldmarschall von Rundstedt were being offered in lieu. But a captured German communication to a corps headquarters stated: 'The Division does not consider that this type of reward has any effect in encouraging the infantry to fight.'

As Eisenhower had decided, the US First Army reverted to the control of Bradley's 12th Army Group after the First and Third Armies had joined hands. This became official at midnight on 17 January. 'The situation is now restored,' Hansen recorded triumphantly. But Montgomery was not finished yet. Determined to retain control of the Ninth Army, he came up with a plan to give it priority over the proud First Army.

'At 10.30', General Simpson's diarist recorded on 15 January, 'the Field Marshal Monty [sic] arrived at our office for a conference with the C[ommanding] G[eneral] re the Ninth's taking over an additional sector. The FM tossed a bombshell. He requested the CG to prepare plans for the Ninth Army, of four Corps and 16 Divisions, to advance on Cologne and the Rhine river at the earliest practicable date . . . This would mean that the Ninth was to carry the ball for the western front drive – be the main effort, while the First Army would assume a holding mission on our south and, after the breakthru, protect the Ninth's south flank . . . 21st Army Group is now apparently considering such an operation quite seriously, and will submit our plan to SHAEF for approval.'

This was clearly a ploy by Montgomery, going behind the back of Bradley. But getting the Ninth Army to formulate its plans first was a clever move, especially since Simpson and his officers were thrilled with the idea of being given priority over the First Army, which would be forced into a subordinate role. 'That "protect the Ninth's flank" would be the greatest and most satisfying crack at the Grand Old Armie possible!' Simpson's diary recorded. 'How all here would love to see that in print!'

Montgomery believed that SHAEF had agreed with his plan, which he had shown only to Whiteley, the British deputy chief of operations. He did not know that Eisenhower considered Bradley stood a better chance of breaking through to the south, because the Germans would transfer their best formations to the north to protect the Ruhr. Above all, there was the general opposition among all American commanders, and voiced most passionately by Bradley on Tuesday 16 January, when he flew to Paris. Bradley landed at Villacoublay aerodrome, and drove to Versailles. The tensions of the last two weeks, and no doubt sleepless nights, had made him tired, but the flame of righteous indignation kept him going. Eisenhower was made to see that, after the recent row, there would be a storm of protest if Montgomery was allowed to command the main offensive with American forces under his command. It was Montgomery's own fault that political considerations and rivalries now dictated Allied strategy.

On 18 January, determined to repair fences, Churchill made a speech in the House of Commons to emphasize that 'the United States troops have done almost all the fighting and have suffered almost all the losses . . . Care must be taken in telling our proud tale not to claim for the British Army an undue share of what is undoubtedly the greatest American battle of the war and will, I believe, be regarded as an ever famous American victory.'

The same afternoon, Simpson rang Montgomery. 'I have just finished talking to Brad. He asked if it would be convenient for you to meet him here at my place [Maastricht] at 10.30 tomorrow morning.'

'I will be delighted,' Montgomery said. 'Where is Brad now?'

'He is with Courtney [Hodges].'

Simpson then rang Bradley straight away. Bradley said that he intended to get to Maastricht early so that he could talk to Simpson before Montgomery arrived. The purpose of the visit was to have a conference on 'future inter-group plans'. This presumably meant that he wanted to thwart Montgomery's arguments, which were based on the premise that 'First and Third US Armies in their present condition' would be incapable of continuing the counter-offensive in the Ardennes, which aimed to break through the Siegfried Line towards Prüm and Bonn. What Bradley said to Simpson drastically changed his previously positive attitude both to Montgomery and to his plan.

'Any future moves of the Ninth,' Simpson then wrote, 'in the light of present British publicity policy, will be [to] the greater glory of the FM himself, since he sees fit to assume all the glory and scarcely permits the mention of an Army Commander's name. Bitterness and real resentment is creeping in because of both the FM's and the British press's attitude in presenting British military accomplishments won with American blood, broadcast throughout Europe by the BBC.'

Bradley was finally getting his revenge for the way the field marshal had humiliated him on Christmas Day and afterwards. Montgomery was the one who would be sidelined once the Allied armies were across the Rhine. Bradley had said at the beginning of December that 'His forces are now relegated to a very minor and virtually unimportant role in this campaign where they are used simply to protect the flank of our giant steamroller.' Although not true then, it was about to become true now.

Montgomery was not 12th Army Group's only *bête noire*. Relations with SHAEF had continued to deteriorate. This was partly because Bradley could not forgive Eisenhower for having transferred First Army to Montgomery, and partly because Bedell Smith did not conceal his rather low opinion of Bradley's headquarters and Hodges. On 24 January, Bradley held a conference in his office after lunch, with Hodges, Patton and seven other generals. During this meeting Major General

Whiteley called from SHAEF to say that several divisions would be withdrawn from his forthcoming offensive to create a strategic reserve and to strengthen Devers in Alsace.*

Bradley lost his temper and said for everyone in the room to hear: 'The reputation and the good will of the American soldiers and the American Army and its commanders are at stake. If you feel that way about it, then as far as I am concerned, you can take any goddam division and/ or corps in the 12th Army Group, do with them as you see fit, and those of us that you leave back will sit on our ass until hell freezes over. I trust you do not think I am angry, but I want to impress upon you that I am goddam well incensed.' At this every officer in the room stood and clapped. Patton said in a voice loud enough to be heard: 'Tell them to go to hell and all three of us [Bradley, Patton and Hodges] will resign. I will lead the procession.'

On 20 January, as the Americans approached St Vith, a German artillery officer wrote in his diary: 'The town is in ruins, but we will defend the ruins.' Attacking would not be easy with waist-deep snowdrifts. The next day he wrote: 'The noise of battle comes closer to the town . . . I'm sending back all my personal belongings. One never knows.' On 23 January, Combat Command B of the 7th Armored Division was given the honour of retaking the town which it had so bravely defended.

The fighters and fighter-bombers of the XIX Tactical Air Command and the Typhoons of 2nd Tactical Air Force continued to attack the retreating German vehicles. On 22 January XIX TAC claimed more than 1,100 motor vehicles destroyed and another 536 damaged. But such estimates were not confirmed by research later. 'The three tactical air forces claimed the destruction of a total of 413 enemy armoured vehicles,' the British official report stated. 'From a subsequent ground check carried out it appears that this figure is at least ten times too large.' The real contribution of Allied aircraft, it stated, came from 'the strafing and bombing of the supply-routes which prevented essential supplies from reaching the front'. German sources supported this conclusion. The Allied air forces 'did not play a decisive tactical part' in

* The call from SHAEF in this account was said to be from Bedell Smith, but his biographer is certain that it was Major General Whiteley.

fighting at the front, Generalmajor von Waldenburg said later. 'The effect on the rear areas was stronger.'

On 23 January the 7th Armored Division secured St Vith. All survivors had fled, and the town was as silent as the grave. The only building of note left standing was the Büchel Tower. By 29 January the front line had been more or less restored to that of 15 December: it had taken a month and two weeks. Hansen wrote in his diary: 'The Third Army today regarded the battle of the salient as officially ended and started new attacks toward German objectives.'

In that last week of January, Bradley moved his Eagle Tac command post from Luxembourg to the provincial capital of Namur. Patton called on him to say goodbye. 'He is a good officer,' Patton wrote in his diary, 'but utterly lacks "it". Too bad.' The provincial governor was made to move out of the magnificent Palais de Namur, and Bradley established himself in vice-regal style. Simpson, visiting on 30 January, described it as 'a tremendous palace, replete with satin wall covers, velvet drapes, too many full-sized oils of the royal family, thick carpets and polished marble floors. The bedrooms, used as offices, are immense – as large as the ground floor of a good sized private home.'

For his private residence, Bradley took over the Château de Namur. It was in rather a forlorn state, so German prisoners of war were sent in to clean it up. Bradley's staff felt 'compelled to ransack the houses of collaborationists' for furniture. Even Hansen acknowledged that Eagle Tac was now being known as 'Eagle Took'. The chateau too had marble fireplaces and floors, according to Simpson, as well as large gardens and a magnificent view over the Meuse valley. Bradley insisted on having an ice-cream machine installed.

On Sunday 4 February, Montgomery was invited for a meeting and lunch. He arrived in his Rolls-Royce flying the Union Jack and escorted by outriders. According to Hansen, he made 'his customary slow, dramatic, deliberate hawk-like entrance'. Apparently he received a very cool reception from all the American officers. 'His ego, however, remained impervious to it and he joked, talked and gesticulated. He prevailed consistently and talked too loudly throughout the meal.'

In what appears to have been a deliberate snub, Bradley and Eisenhower simply left Montgomery at the table. They drove off through the rain to Bastogne to meet Patton. Soon after they had crossed the Meuse, they 'passed scarred and blackened hulks of enemy tanks as well as Shermans. There appeared remains of crashed C-47s and a lot of other abandoned impedimenta of war. Patton met us at the rear echelon headquarters of the VIII Corps in Bastogne. He consulted with Ike and Bradley in a small coal-stove room where the 101st Airborne sheltered its troops during the historic siege of the city.' The three generals then had their photographs taken together in the bombed centre of the town, climbed back into their vehicles and drove north up to Houffalize. They 'passed [numerous] Sherman tanks with scars of enemy artillery plainly imprinted on their armor'. From there, they carried on to meet General Hodges, who had moved his headquarters back to the town of Spa. It was a symbolic lap of honour which excluded the field marshal.

Belgium faced a crisis, to which SHAEF reacted slowly. Food shortages led to strikes in the mines, which in turn produced crippling coal shortages during that harsh winter. Government attempts to control rocketing prices were easily circumvented and the black market spread. In the countryside people reverted even more to barter, with much of the trade consisting of American and British troops exchanging tins of rations for fresh eggs.

An estimated 2,500 civilians had been killed in Belgium as a result of the Ardennes offensive, with another 500 non-combatants dead in the Grand Duchy of Luxembourg. It is thought that about a third had been killed by Allied air raids. If one adds in those who perished in V-weapon bombardments from at least 5,000 missiles during the whole winter from October to March, civilian casualties increase to more than 8,000 dead and missing and 23,584 wounded.

The destruction had been massive. Buildings, churches, farms, roads and railways had suffered terrible damage. So had sewers, water-pipes, telephone wires and electricity cables. Some 88,000 people were homeless. Those families returning with their few possessions on a handcart found that even houses which had not been hit by shells or bombs had no doors. Both Germans and Allies had ripped them out to provide overhead covering for foxholes and trenches. Bedding had also been seized in an attempt to provide a little warmth or camouflage. There was also a great shortage of warm clothing. A British civil affairs officer noted that a 'tremendous number of Belgian women are wearing coats made from Army blankets, and ski-suits from battledress, having just dyed them to black or brown and removed the pockets'.

In the Belgian provinces of Luxembourg and Namur, eighteen churches had been ruined and sixty-nine others badly damaged. In many cases, the shelling had also ploughed up graveyards, hurling ancient bones around. In La Roche, which had been bombarded by both sides, 114 civilians had died and only four houses out of 639 remained habitable. The town was a mass of rubble. American bulldozers had to be called in to clear paths down the main streets. The following spring, locals noticed that swallows returning to nest became completely disorientated.

The Ardennes, which depended almost entirely on farming and forestry, had been dealt a body-blow. Few chickens were left, and some 50,000 farm animals had been killed in the fighting or taken by the Germans. The shelling had also filled trees with shards of shrapnel, reducing the value of timber and causing problems in sawmills for a long time afterwards. Only a small amount of the livestock slaughtered in the battle could be butchered for consumption. The vast majority had to be buried. Many of the surviving livestock died after drinking water from shellholes, or other sources contaminated by rotting bodies or white phosphorus. There was also a food crisis in the Grand Duchy of Luxembourg from war-damage and because the Germans had stripped the north of the country.

One of the worst problems was how to deal with well over 100,000 mines buried by both sides, as well as booby-traps, unexploded shells and explosives abandoned all over the place. Some forty Belgians died in and around the former Bastogne perimeter after the fighting was over. In one incident ten British soldiers were maimed or badly wounded when one of their comrades stepped on a mine. The minefield must have been densely sown in a real 'devil's garden', because one after another fell victim trying to rescue the others.

Children were sent away to safe areas when the thaw came so that they would not step on a mine. But a number were hurt playing with munitions, especially when they emptied live shells to make their own fireworks. Allied troops did what they could in the short time before they were redeployed, but the main task fell upon the Belgian army, as well as volunteers and later conscripts brought in as *démineurs*. The squads dealing with unexploded shells and mines had to explode them in place. In villages and towns, they would warn the local inhabitants before the blast to open their windows, but some houses were so old that they could not be opened.

The rains which brought a rapid thaw in late January meant that carcasses and corpses, hidden by the snow, began to decompose rapidly. The stench was terrible, but the threat of disease, which might affect their own troops, prompted the American military authorities to send in army engineers with bulldozers. Moving German corpses was always dangerous as they might have been booby-trapped, so a rope had to be attached round the legs or hands, then the body towed a distance to make sure that a grenade had not been placed underneath. The Allied dead received individual graves, many of which were decorated with flowers by the local people. German bodies were simply dumped in mass pits like plague victims. Some corpses were so carbonized by phosphorus that their nationality was impossible to distinguish. Whether German or Allied, people hoped that death had come quickly for them.

24

Conclusions

The fatal crossroads at Baugnez–Malmédy had been retaken on 13 January. The next morning teams of engineers with mine detectors began to check whether SS panzergrenadiers had booby-trapped the bodies of those they had massacred. Then the Graves Registration teams and doctors began their work. The task was extremely difficult, for all the bodies were covered with at least half a metre of snow and frozen hard.

Most had multiple wounds, with bullet holes in foreheads, temples and the back of the head, presumably from when officers and panzergrenadiers went around delivering *coups de grâce*. Some were without eyes, which had probably been pecked out by crows. The empty sockets were filled with snow. A number of the dead still had their hands above their heads. The bodies were taken back to Malmédy to be defrosted in a railway building. Razors and knives had to be used to cut out pockets to retrieve personal items.

Evidence was assembled for a war crimes trial, and eventually the US Military Tribunal at Dachau sentenced seventy-three former members of the Kampfgruppe Peiper: forty-three of them to death; twenty-two to lifelong imprisonment; and eight to prison terms ranging from ten to twenty years. Another eleven were tried by a Belgian court in Liège in July 1948, where ten of them received sentences of between ten and fifteen years' hard labour. In the post-Nuremberg period of the nascent Cold War, all the death sentences handed out at Dachau were commuted, and the prisoners went home in the 1950s. Peiper was the last to be released. After serving eleven and a half years he went to live in obscurity in Traves, in the French department of Haute-Saône. Former members of the French Resistance killed him there on 13 July 1976. Peiper knew they were coming for him. Shortly before his death, he said that his former comrades would be waiting for him in Valhalla.

Fighting in the Ardennes had reached a degree of savagery unprecedented on the western front. The shooting of prisoners of war has always been a far more common practice than military historians in the past have been prepared to acknowledge, especially when writing of their own countrymen. The Kampfgruppe Peiper's cold-blooded slaughter of prisoners in the Baugnez–Malmédy massacre was of course chilling, and its indiscriminate killing of civilians even more so. That American soldiers took revenge was hardly surprising, but it is surely shocking that a number of generals, from Bradley downwards, openly approved of the shooting of prisoners in retaliation. There are few details in the archives or in American accounts of the Chenogne massacre, where the ill-trained and badly bruised 11th Armored Division took out its rage on some sixty prisoners. Their vengeance was different from the cold-blooded executions perpetrated by the Waffen-SS at Baugnez–Malmédy, but it still reflects badly on their officers.

There were a few incidents of American soldiers killing Belgian or Luxembourg civilians, either by mistake or from suspicion that they might be fifth-columnists in an area where some of the German-speaking population still harboured sympathies for the Nazi regime. But on the whole American soldiers demonstrated great sympathy for civilians trapped in the battle, and US Army medical services did whatever they could to treat civilian casualties. The Waffen-SS and some Wehrmacht units, on the other hand, took out their anger at losing the war on innocent people. The worst, of course, were those obsessed with taking revenge on the Belgian Resistance for its activities during the German retreat to the Siegfried Line in September. And one must not of course forget the other massacres of civilians at Noville and Bande, mainly by Sondereinheitkommando 8.

Historians, however, have often overlooked the terrible irony of twentieth-century warfare. After the bloodbath of the First World War, army commanders from western democracies were under great pressure at home to reduce their own casualties, so they relied on a massive use of artillery shells and bombs. As a result far more civilians died. White phosphorus especially was a weapon of terrible indiscrimination.

On 20 July 1945, a year to the day after the explosion of Stauffenberg's bomb at the Wolfsschanze, Generalfeldmarschall Keitel and General-oberst Jodl were interrogated about the Ardennes offensive. Both the bombastic Keitel and the cold, calculating Jodl were fatalistic in their replies. They knew that they too would soon be facing a war crimes tribunal.

'The criticism', they said in a joint statement, 'whether it would have been better to have employed our available reserves in the East rather than in the West, we submit to the judgement of history. Whether it was a "crime" to prolong the war by this attack, we leave to the Allied courts. Our own judgement is unchanged and independent of them.' But they did acknowledge that 'with the Fifth and Sixth Panzer Armies commit-ted in the Ardennes, the way was paved for the Russian offensive which was launched on 12 January from the Vistula bridgeheads'. Despite the reluctance of Russian historians to accept the fact, there can be no doubt that the success of the Red Army's advance from the Vistula to the Oder was in large part due to Hitler's offensive in the Ardennes.

It is impossible to assess how much Bradley's 'calculated risk' in leaving the Ardennes front so weakly defended aided the German breakthrough. In any case his deployment reflected Allied thinking at the time that the Germans were incapable of launching a strategic offen-sive. German misconceptions were much more serious. Not only Hitler and the OKW but most generals believed that the Americans would fall back in disorder to the Meuse and defend from there. They had not foreseen the resolute defence of the northern and southern shoulders, which cramped their movements and supply lines so disastrously on an inadequate road network in such bad weather. Also, as already men-tioned, Hitler was convinced that Eisenhower would not be able to take quick decisions, because of the complications of coalition warfare.

'The promptness with which the Allies reacted did perhaps exceed our expectations,' Jodl acknowledged later. 'But above all it was the speed of our own movements which lagged far behind expectations.' Bradley had boasted with justification on Christmas Eve that 'no other army in the world could possibly have shifted forces as expertly and quickly as we have'. On the second day of the offensive, First Army moved 60,000 troops into the Ardennes in just twenty-four hours. The despised Com Z of General Lee had achieved miracles. It also managed to transport 85 per cent of ordnance stocks out of German reach. Between 17 and 26 December, 50,000 trucks and 248,000 men from quartermaster units shifted 2.8 million gallons of gasoline so that panzer spearheads could not refuel from captured dumps.

Although Hitler refused to face reality until it was far too late, German generals realized that the great offensive was doomed by the end of the first week. They may have achieved surprise, but they had failed to cause the collapse in American morale that they needed. It was German morale which began to suffer. 'Officers and men began to show more and more their loss of confidence in the German High Command,' wrote Generalmajor von Gersdorff. 'It was only the realization of the immediate danger of the homeland and its frontiers, which spurred the troops to increase their effort against an unmerciful enemy.'

Bayerlein of the Panzer Lehr despaired of the obstinacy of Hitler and the OKW after it had become obvious that German forces could not reach the Meuse. 'Every day that the troops waited and continued to hold the salient meant further losses in men and materiel which were disproportionate to the operational significance of the bulge for the German command.' He argued that the greatest mistake in the planning was to give the Sixth Panzer Army the main strength, when it was bound to face the strongest resistance. The only chance of reaching the Meuse lay with Manteuffel's Fifth Panzer Army, but even then the idea of reaching Antwerp was impossible given the balance of forces on the western front. Bayerlein described the Ardennes offensive as 'the last gasp of the collapsing Wehrmacht and the supreme command before its end'.

While undoubtedly an American triumph, the Ardennes campaign produced a political defeat for the British. Monty's disastrous press conference and the ill-considered clamour of the London press had stoked a rampant Anglophobia in the United States and especially among senior American officers in Europe. The row thwarted Churchill's hope that Field Marshal Alexander could replace Air Chief Marshal Tedder as deputy to Eisenhower. General Marshall firmly vetoed the idea because it might indicate that the British had won 'a major point in getting control of ground operations'. And as Churchill recognized, there was a much graver consequence. Montgomery would find himself sidelined once across the Rhine on the advance into Germany, and all British advice would be ignored. The country's influence in Allied councils was at an end. In fact, one cannot entirely rule out the possibility that President Eisenhower's anger at British perfidy during the Suez crisis just over eleven years later was partly conditioned by his experiences in January 1945.*

German and Allied casualties in the Ardennes fighting from 16 December 1944 to 29 January 1945 were fairly equal. Total German losses were around 80,000 dead, wounded and missing. The Americans suffered 75,482 casualties, with 8,407 killed. The British lost 1,408, of whom 200 were killed. The unfortunate 106th Infantry Division lost the most men, 8,568, but many of them were prisoners of war. The 101st Airborne suffered the highest death rate with 535 killed in action.

In the Ardennes, front-line units manned entirely by African-American soldiers served for the first time in considerable numbers. Despite the fears and prejudices of many senior American officers they fought well, as the 17th Airborne testified. No fewer than nine of the field artillery battalions in VIII Corps had been black, as were four of the seven corps artillery units supporting the 106th Division. Two of them moved to Bastogne and played an important part in the defence of the perimeter. The 969th Field Artillery received the first Distinguished Unit Citation given to a black combat unit in the Second World War. There were also three tank-destroyer battalions and the 761st Tank Battalion, all with black soldiers, fighting in the Ardennes. Captain John Long, the officer commanding Company B of the 761st Tank Battalion, declared that he was fighting 'Not for God and country, but for me and my people'.

The unsung American victims of the Ardennes offensive were those captured by the enemy and condemned to spend the last months of the

---

* The rancour lasted for the rest of his life. When Cornelius Ryan asked about Montgomery some years after Suez and long after the war, Eisenhower exploded. 'He's a psychopath, don't forget that. He is such an egocentric . . . He has never made a mistake in his life.' Montgomery was trying 'to make sure that the Americans, and me in particular, had no credit, had nothing to do with this war. I just stopped communicating with him.'

war in grim Stalag prison camps. Their journey to Germany was a series of long cold marches, interminable rail journeys packed into boxcars, being bombed and strafed by Allied aircraft and dogged by the debilitating squalor of dysentery.

Sergeant John Kline from the 106th Division described his ordeal in a diary. On 20 December, he and his fellow prisoners were made to march all day without food and with no water to drink. They resorted to handfuls of snow. At a little village 'the Germans made us take off our overshoes and give them to the civilians'. They saw German soldiers sitting in captured Jeeps eating what was supposed to have been their Christmas dinner. On 25 December, after German civilians threw stones at the column of prisoners of war, he wrote, 'No Christmas, except in our hearts.' Two days later they reached Koblenz in the afternoon, and were given some soup and bread from a portable kitchen. As they were marched on in groups of 500, a man in a business suit lunged into the street and hit him over the head with his briefcase. The German guard told him that the man must have been upset over the recent bombings.

As the fighting approached its end in April 1945, the Australian war correspondent Godfrey Blunden came across a group of young, half-starved American prisoners of war, presumably also from the 106th Infantry Division. He described them as having 'xylophone ribs', sunken cheeks, thin necks and 'gangling arms'. They were 'a little hysterical' in their joy at encountering fellow Anglo-Saxons. 'Some American prisoners whom I met this morning seemed to me to be the most pitiful of all I have seen,' Blunden wrote. 'They had arrived in Europe only last December, gone immediately into the front line and had received the full brunt of the German counter-offensive in the Ardennes that month. Since their capture they had been moved almost constantly from one place to another and they told stories of comrades clubbed to death by German guards merely for breaking line to grab sugar beets from fields. They were more pitiful because they were only boys drafted from nice homes in a nice country knowing nothing about Europe, not tough like Australians, or shrewd like the French or irreducibly stubborn like the English. They just didn't know what it was all about.' They at least were alive. A good number of their comrades had lacked the will to survive their imprisonment, like the original for Kurt

Vonnegut's Billy Pilgrim, who acquired the '5,000 mile stare'. Reduced to blank apathy, they would not move or eat and died silently of starvation.

The surprise and ruthlessness of Hitler's Ardennes offensive had brought the terrifying brutality of the eastern front to the west. But, as with the Japanese invasion of China in 1937 and the Nazi invasion of the Soviet Union in 1941, the shock of total warfare did not achieve the universal panic and collapse expected. It provoked instead a critical mass of desperate resistance, a bloody-minded determination to fight on even when surrounded. When German formations attacked, screaming and whistling, isolated companies defended key villages against overwhelming odds. Their sacrifice bought the time needed to bring in reinforcements, and this was their vital contribution to the destruction of Hitler's dream. Perhaps the German leadership's greatest mistake in the Ardennes offensive was to have misjudged the soldiers of an army they had affected to despise.

Order of Battle, Ardennes Offensive

ALLIED

12th Army Group
Lieutenant General Omar N. Bradley

US First Army
Lieutenant General Courtney H. Hodges

V Corps
Major General Leonard T. Gerow

102nd Cavalry Group; 38th and 102nd Cavalry Reconnaissance Squadrons (attached)

613th Tank Destroyer Battalion

186th, 196th, 200th and 955th Field Artillery Battalions

187th Field Artillery Group (751st and 997th Field Artillery Battalions)

190th Field Artillery Group (62nd, 190th, 272nd and 268th Field Artillery Battalions)

406th Field Artillery Group (76th, 941st, 953rd and 987th Field Artillery Battalions)

1111th Engineer Combat Group (51st, 202nd, 291st and 296th Engineer Combat Battalions)

1121st Engineer Combat Group (146th and 254th Engineer Combat Battalions)

1195th Engineer Combat Group

134th, 387th, 445th, 460th, 461st, 531st, 602nd, 639th and 863rd Anti-Aircraft Artillery Battalions

1st Infantry Division 'Big Red One'
Brigadier General Clift Andrus
16th, 18th and 26th Infantry Regiments
5th, 7th, 32nd and 33rd Field Artillery Battalions
745th Tank Battalion; 634th and 703rd Tank Destroyer Battalions
1st Engineer Combat Battalion; 103rd Anti-Aircraft Artillery Battalion

2nd Infantry Division 'Indianhead'
Major General Walter M. Robertson
9th, 23rd and 38th Infantry Regiments
12th, 15th, 37th and 38th Field Artillery Battalions
741st Tank Battalion; 612th and 644th Tank Destroyer Battalions
2nd Engineer Combat Battalion; 462nd Anti-Aircraft Artillery Battalion

9th Infantry Division 'Old Reliables'
Major General Louis A. Craig
39th, 47th and 60th Infantry Regiments
26th, 34th, 60th and 84th Field Artillery Battalions
15th Engineer Combat Battalion; 38th Cavalry Reconnaissance Squadron
746th Tank Battalion; 376th and 413th Anti-Aircraft Artillery Battalions

78th Infantry Division 'Lightning'
Major General Edwin P. Parker Jr
309th, 310th and 311th Infantry Regiments
307th, 308th, 309th and 903rd Field Artillery Battalions
709th Tank Battalion; 628th and 893rd Tank Destroyer Battalions
303rd Engineer Combat Battalion; 552nd Anti-Aircraft Artillery Battalion
Combat Command R, 5th Armored Division (attached); 2nd Ranger Battalion
(attached)

99th Infantry Division 'Checkerboard'
Major General Walter E. Lauer
393rd, 394th and 395th Infantry Regiments
370th, 371st, 372nd and 924th Field Artillery Battalions
324th Engineer Combat Battalion; 801st Tank Destroyer Battalion
535th Anti-Aircraft Artillery Battalion

VII Corps

Major General Joseph Lawton Collins

4th Cavalry Group, Mechanized; 29th Infantry Regiment; 740th Tank Battalion

509th Parachute Infantry Battalion; 298th Engineer Combat Battalion

18th Field Artillery Group (188th, 666th and 981st Field Artillery Battalions)

142nd Field Artillery Group (195th and 266th Field Artillery Battalions)

188th Field Artillery Group (172nd, 951st and 980th Field Artillery Battalions)

18th, 83rd, 87th, 183rd, 193rd, 957th and 991st Field Artillery Battalions

Two French Light Infantry Battalions

2nd Armored Division 'Hell on Wheels'

Major General Ernest N. Harmon

CCA, CCB and CCR; 41st Armored Infantry Regiment; 66th and 67th Armored
  Regiments

14th, 78th and 92nd Armored Field Artillery Battalions

17th Armored Engineer Battalion; 82nd Armored Reconnaissance Battalion

702nd Tank Destroyer Battalion; 195th Anti-Aircraft Artillery Battalion

Elements of 738th Tank Battalion (special – mine clearing) attached

3rd Armored Division 'Spearhead'

Major General Maurice Rose

CCA, CCB and CCR; 36th Armored Infantry Regiment; 32nd and 33rd Armored
  Regiments

54th, 67th and 391st Armored Field Artillery Battalions

23rd Armored Engineer Battalion; 83rd Reconnaissance Squadron

643rd and 703rd Tank Destroyer Battalions; 486th Anti-Aircraft Artillery Battalion

83rd Infantry Division 'Ohio'

Major General Robert C. Macon

329th, 330th and 331st Infantry Regiments

322nd, 323rd, 324th and 908th Field Artillery Battalions

308th Engineer Combat Battalion; 453rd Anti-Aircraft Artillery Battalion

774th Tank Battalion; 772nd Tank Destroyer Battalion

84th Infantry Division 'Railsplitters'

Brigadier General Alexander R. Bolling

333rd, 334th and 335th Infantry Regiments

325th, 326th, 327th and 909th Field Artillery Battalions
309th Engineer Combat Battalion
701st Tank Battalion, replaced by 771st Tank Battalion on 20 December
638th Tank Destroyer Battalion; 557th Anti-Aircraft Artillery Battalion

XVIII Airborne Corps

Major General Matthew B. Ridgway
14th Cavalry Group, Mechanized
254th, 275th, 400th and 460th Field Artillery Battalions
79th Field Artillery Group (153rd, 551st and 552nd Field Artillery Battalions)
179th Field Artillery Group (259th and 965th Field Artillery Battalions)
211th Field Artillery Group (240th and 264th Field Artillery Battalions)
401st Field Artillery Group (187th and 809th Field Artillery Battalions)

7th Armored Division 'Lucky Seventh'

Brigadier General Robert W. Hasbrouck
CCA, CCB and CCR; 23rd, 38th and 48th Armored Infantry Battalions
17th, 31st and 40th Tank Battalions; 87th Reconnaissance Squadron
434th, 440th and 489th Armored Field Artillery Battalions
33rd Armored Engineer Battalion; 814th Tank Destroyer Battalion
203rd Anti-Aircraft Artillery Battalion
820th Tank Destroyer Battalion (25–30 December)

30th Infantry Division 'Old Hickory'

Major General Leland S. Hobbs
117th, 119th and 120th Infantry Regiments
113th, 118th, 197th and 230th Field Artillery Battalions
517th Parachute Infantry Regiment attached; 105th Engineer Combat Battalion
743rd Tank Battalion; 823rd Tank Destroyer Battalion
110th, 431st and 448th Anti-Aircraft Artillery Battalions

75th Infantry Division

Major General Fay B. Prickett
289th, 290th and 291st Infantry Regiments
730th, 897th, 898th and 899th Field Artillery Battalions
275th Engineer Combat Battalion; 440th Anti-Aircraft Artillery Battalion
750th Tank Battalion; 629th and 772nd Tank Destroyer Battalions

82nd Airborne Division 'All American'

Major General James M. Gavin

504th, 505th, 507th and 508th Parachute Infantry Regiments

325th Glider Infantry Regiment; 307th Airborne Engineer Battalion

319th and 320th Glider Field Artillery Battalions

376th and 456th Parachute Field Artillery Battalions; 80th Anti-Aircraft Artillery Battalion

551st Parachute Infantry Battalion; 628th Tank Destroyer Battalion (2–11 January)

740th Tank Battalion (30 December–11 January)

643rd Tank Destroyer Battalion (4–5 January)

106th Infantry Division 'Golden Lions'

Major General Alan W. Jones

422nd, 423rd and 424th Infantry Regiments

589th, 590th, 591st and 592nd Field Artillery Battalions

81st Engineer Combat Battalion; 820th Tank Destroyer Battalion

634th Anti-Aircraft Artillery Battalion (8–18 December)

440th Anti-Aircraft Artillery Battalion (8 December–4 January)

563rd Anti-Aircraft Artillery Battalion (9–18 December)

101st Airborne Division 'Screaming Eagles'

Brigadier General Anthony C. McAuliffe (Major General Maxwell D. Taylor)

501st, 502nd and 506th Parachute Infantry Regiments

327th Glider Infantry Regiment; 1st Battalion, 401st Glider Infantry

321st and 907th Glider Field Artillery Battalions

377th and 463rd Parachute Field Artillery Battalion

326th Airborne Engineer Battalion; 705th Tank Destroyer Battalion

81st Airborne Anti-Aircraft Artillery Battalion

US Third Army

Lieutenant General George S. Patton Jr

109th, 115th, 217th and 777th Anti-Aircraft Gun Battalions

456th, 465th, 550th and 565th Anti-Aircraft Artillery Battalions

280th Engineer Combat Battalion (later assigned to Ninth Army)

III Corps

Major General John Millikin

6th Cavalry Group, Mechanized; 179th, 274th, 776th and 777th Field Artillery Battalions

193rd Field Artillery Group (177th, 253rd, 696th, 776th and 949th Field Artillery Battalions)

203rd Field Artillery Group (278th, 742nd, 762nd Field Artillery Battalions)

1137th Engineer Combat Group (145th, 188th and 249th Engineer Combat Battalions)

183rd and 243rd Engineer Combat Battalions; 467th and 468th Anti-Aircraft Artillery Battalions

4th Armored Division
Major General Hugh J. Gaffey
CCA, CCB and CCR; 8th, 35th and 37th Tank Battalions
10th, 51st and 53rd Armored Infantry Battalions
22nd, 66th and 94th Armored Field Artillery Battalions
24th Armored Engineer Battalion; 25th Cavalry Reconnaissance Squadron
489th Anti-Aircraft Artillery Battalion; 704th Tank Destroyer Battalion

6th Armored Division 'Super Sixth'
Major General Robert W. Grow
CCA, CCB and CCR; 15th, 68th and 69th Tank Battalions
9th, 44th and 50th Armored Infantry Battalions
128th, 212th and 231st Armored Field Artillery Battalions
25th Armored Engineer Battalion; 86th Cavalry Reconnaissance Squadron
691st Tank Destroyer Battalion; 777th Anti-Aircraft Artillery Battalion

26th Infantry Division 'Yankee'
Major General Willard S. Paul
101st, 104th and 328th Infantry Regiments
101st, 102nd, 180th and 263rd Field Artillery Battalions
101st Engineer Combat Battalion; 735th Tank Battalion
818th Tank Destroyer Battalion; 390th Anti-Aircraft Artillery Battalion

35th Infantry Division 'Santa Fe'
Major General Paul W. Baade
134th, 137th and 320th Infantry Regiments

127th, 161st, 216th and 219th Field Artillery Battalions
60th Engineer Combat Battalion; 654th Tank Destroyer Battalion
448th Anti-Aircraft Artillery Battalion

90th Infantry Division 'Tough 'Ombres'
Major General James A. Van Fleet
357th, 358th and 359th Infantry Regiments
343rd, 344th, 345th and 915th Field Artillery Battalions
315th Engineer Combat Battalion; 773rd Tank Destroyer Battalion
774th Tank Destroyer Battalion (21 December–6 January)
537th Anti-Aircraft Artillery Battalion

VIII Corps

Major General Troy H. Middleton
174th Field Artillery Group (965th, 969th and 700th Field Artillery Battalions)
333rd Field Artillery Group (333rd and 771st Field Artillery Battalions)
402nd Field Artillery Group (559th, 561st and 740th Field Artillery Battalions)
422nd Field Artillery Group (81st and 174th Field Artillery Battalions)
687th Field Artillery Battalion; 178th and 249th Engineer Combat Battalions
1102nd Engineer Group (341st Engineer General Service Regiment)
1107th Engineer Combat Group (159th and 168th Engineer Combat Battalions)
1128th Engineer Combat Group (35th, 44th and 202nd Engineer Combat Battalions)
French Light Infantry (six Light Infantry Battalions from Metz region)
467th, 635th and 778th Anti-Aircraft Artillery Battalions

9th Armored Division 'Phantom'
Major General John W. Leonard
CCA, CCB and CCR; 27th, 52nd and 60th Armored Infantry Battalions
2nd, 14th and 19th Tank Battalions; 3rd, 16th and 73rd Armored Field Artillery Battalions
9th Armored Engineer Battalion; 89th Cavalry Squadron
811th Tank Destroyer Battalion; 482nd Anti-Aircraft Artillery Battalion

11th Armored Division 'Thunderbolt'
Brigadier General Charles S. Kilburn

CCA, CCB and CCR; 21st, 55th and 63rd Armored Infantry Battalions

22nd, 41st and 42nd Tank Battalions

490th, 491st and 492nd Armored Field Artillery Battalions

56th Armored Engineer Battalion; 602nd Tank Destroyer Battalion

41st Cavalry Squadron; 575th Anti-Aircraft Artillery Battalion

17th Airborne Division 'Golden Talons'

Major General William M. Miley

507th and 513th Parachute Infantry Regiments; 193rd and 194th Glider Infantry Regiments

680th and 681st Glider Field Artillery Battalions; 466th Parachute Field Artillery Battalion

139th Airborne Engineer Battalion; 155th Airborne Anti-Aircraft Artillery Battalion

28th Infantry Division 'Keystone'

Major General Norman D. Cota

109th, 110th and 112th Infantry Regiments

107th, 108th, 109th and 229th Field Artillery Battalions

103rd Engineer Combat Battalion; 447th Anti-Aircraft Artillery Battalion

707th Tank Battalion; 602nd and 630th Tank Destroyer Battalions

87th Infantry Division 'Golden Acorn'

Brigadier General Frank L. Culin Jr

345th, 346th and 347th Infantry Regiments

334th, 335th, 336th and 912th Field Artillery Battalions; 312th Engineer Combat Battalion

761st Tank Battalion; 549th Anti-Aircraft Artillery Battalion

610th Tank Destroyer Battalion (14–22 December)

691st Tank Destroyer Battalion (22–24 December and 8–26 January)

704th Tank Destroyer Battalion (17–19 December)

XII Corps

Major General Manton S. Eddy

2nd Cavalry Group, Mechanized

161st, 244th, 277th, 334th, 336th and 736th Field Artillery Battalions

177th Field Artillery Group (215th, 255th and 775th Field Artillery Battalions)

182nd Field Artillery Group (802nd, 945th and 974th Field Artillery Battalions)

183rd Field Artillery Group (695th and 776th Field Artillery Battalions)

404th Field Artillery Group (273rd, 512th and 752nd Field Artillery Battalions)

4th Infantry Division 'Ivy'

Major General Raymond O. Barton

8th, 12th and 22nd Infantry Regiments; 20th, 29th, 42nd and 44th Field Artillery
Battalions

4th Engineer Combat Battalion; 70th Tank Battalion

802nd and 803rd Tank Destroyer Battalions; 377th Anti-Aircraft Artillery Battalion

5th Infantry Division 'Red Diamond'

Major General Stafford L. Irwin

2nd, 10th and 11th Infantry Regiments; 19th, 21st, 46th and 50th Field Artillery
Battalions

7th Engineer Combat Battalion; 737th Tank Battalion; 449th Anti-Aircraft Artillery Battalion

654th Tank Destroyer Battalion (22–25 December); 803rd Tank Destroyer Battalion
(from 25 December)

807th Tank Destroyer Battalion (17–21 December); 818th Tank Destroyer Battalion
(13 July–20 December)

10th Armored Division 'Tiger'

Major General William H. H. Morris Jr

CCA, CCB and CCR; 20th, 54th and 61st Armored Infantry Battalions

3rd, 11th and 21st Tank Battalions; 609th Tank Destroyer Battalion

419th, 420th and 423rd Armored Field Artillery Battalions

55th Armored Engineer Battalion; 90th Cavalry Reconnaissance Squadron

796th Anti-Aircraft Artillery Battalion

80th Infantry Division 'Blue Ridge'

Major General Horace L. McBride

317th, 318th and 319th Infantry Regiments

313th, 314th, 315th and 905th Field Artillery Battalions; 702nd Tank Battalion

305th Engineer Combat Battalion; 633rd Anti-Aircraft Artillery Battalion

610th Tank Destroyer Battalion (23 November–6 December and 21 December–28
January)

808th Tank Destroyer Battalion (25 September–21 December)

XXX Corps

Lieutenant General Sir Brian Horrocks

2nd Household Cavalry Regiment; 11th Hussars

4th and 5th Regiments, Royal Horse Artillery; 27th Light Anti-Aircraft Regiment, Royal Artillery

7th, 64th and 84th Medium Regiments, Royal Artillery

6th Airborne Division

Major General Eric Bols

6th Airborne Armoured Reconnaissance Regiment, Royal Armoured Corps

249th Airborne Field Company, Royal Engineers; 3rd and 591st Parachute Squadrons, Royal Engineers; 3rd and 9th Airborne Squadrons, Royal Engineers; 53rd Light Regiment, Royal Artillery; 3rd and 4th Airlanding Anti-Tank Batteries, Royal Artillery

22nd Independent Parachute Company

3rd Parachute Brigade (8th Parachute Battalion; 9th Parachute Battalion; 1st Canadian Parachute Battalion)

5th Parachute Brigade (7th Parachute Battalion; 12th Parachute Battalion; 13th Parachute Battalion)

6th Airlanding Brigade (12th Battalion, Devonshire Regiment; 2nd Battalion, Oxfordshire and Buckinghamshire Light Infantry; 1st Battalion, Royal Ulster Rifles)

51st (Highland) Infantry Division

Major General G. T. G. Rennie

2nd Derbyshire Yeomanry

126th, 127th and 128th Field Regiments, Royal Artillery; 61st Anti-Tank Regiment, Royal Artillery; 40th Light Anti-Aircraft Regiment, Royal Artillery

274th, 275th and 276th Field Companies, Royal Engineers

1/7 Machine-Gun Battalion, Middlesex Regiment

152nd Infantry Brigade (2nd Battalion, Seaforth Highlanders; 5th Battalion, Seaforth Highlanders; 5th Battalion, Queen's Own Cameron Highlanders)

153rd Infantry Brigade (5th Battalion, Black Watch; 1st Battalion, Gordon Highlanders; 5/7th Battalion, Gordon Highlanders)

154th Infantry Brigade (1st Battalion, Black Watch; 7th Battalion, Black Watch; 7th Battalion, Argyll and Sutherland Highlanders)

53rd (Welsh) Infantry Division

Major General R. K. Ross

81st, 83rd and 133rd Field Regiments, Royal Artillery

53rd Reconnaissance Regiment, Royal Armoured Corps

71st Anti-Tank Regiment, Royal Artillery; 25th Light Anti-Aircraft Regiment, Royal Artillery

244th, 282nd and 555th Field Companies, Royal Engineers

71st Infantry Brigade (1st Battalion, Oxford and Buckinghamshire Light Infantry; 1st Battalion, Highland Light Infantry; 4th Battalion, Royal Welch Fusiliers)

158th Infantry Brigade (7th Battalion, Royal Welch Fusiliers; 1/5th Battalion, Welch Regiment; 1st Battalion, The East Lancashire Regiment)

160th Infantry Brigade (2nd Battalion, Monmouthshire Regiment; 1/5th Battalion, Welch Regiment; 6th Battalion, Royal Welch Fusiliers)

29th Armoured Brigade

Brigadier C. B. Harvey

23rd Hussars; 3rd Royal Tank Regiment; 2nd Fife and Forfar Yeomanry; 8th Battalion, Rifle Brigade

33rd Armoured Brigade

Brigadier H. B. Scott

144th Regiment, Royal Armoured Corps; 1st Northamptonshire Yeomanry; 1st East Riding Yeomanry

34th Army Tank Brigade

Brigadier W. S. Clarke

9th Royal Tank Regiment; 107th Regiment, Royal Armoured Corps; 147th Regiment, Royal Armoured Corps

Corps Reserve

Guards Armoured Division

50th (Northumbrian) Infantry Division

WEHRMACHT

Army Group B
Generalfeldmarschall Walter Model

Fifth Panzer Army
General der Panzertruppe Hasso von Manteuffel
19th Flak-Brigade; 207th and 600th Engineer Battalions
653rd Heavy Panzerjäger Battalion; 669th Ost (East) Battalion
638th, 1094th and 1095th Heavy Artillery Batteries
25th/975th Fortress Artillery Battery; 1099th, 1119th and 1121st Heavy Mortar
   Batteries

XLVII Panzer Corps
General der Panzertruppe Heinrich Freiherr von Lüttwitz
766th Volksartillerie Corps; 15th Volkswerfer-Brigade; 182nd Flak-Regiment

2nd Panzer-Division
Oberst Meinrad von Lauchert
3rd Panzer-Regiment; 2nd and 304th Panzergrenadier-Regiments
74th Artillery Regiment; 2nd Reconnaissance Battalion
38th Anti-Tank Battalion; 38th Engineer Battalion; 273rd Flak Battalion

9th Panzer-Division
Generalmajor Harald Freiherr von Elverfeldt
33rd Panzer-Regiment; 10th and 11th Panzergrenadier-Regiments
102nd Artillery Regiment; 9th Reconnaissance Battalion
50th Anti-Tank Battalion; 86th Engineer Battalion; 287th Flak Battalion
301st Heavy Panzer Battalion (attached)

Panzer Lehr Division
Generalleutnant Fritz Bayerlein
130th Panzer-Regiment; 901st and 902nd Panzergrenadier-Regiments
130th Artillery Regiment; 130th Reconnaissance Battalion
130th Anti-Tank Battalion; 130th Engineer Battalion; 311th Flak Battalion
559th Anti-Tank Battalion (attached); 243rd Assault Gun Brigade (attached)

26th Volksgrenadier-Division
Generalmajor Heinz Kokott
39th Fusilier Regiment; 77th and 78th Volksgrenadier-Regiments; 26th Artillery
Regiment;
26th Reconnaissance Battalion; 26th Anti-Tank Battalion; 26th Engineer Battalion

Führer Begleit Brigade
Oberst Otto Remer
102nd Panzer Battalion; 100th Panzergrenadier-Regiment; 120th Artillery Regiment
120th Reconnaissance Battalion; 120th Anti-Tank Battalion; 120th Engineer Battalion
828th Grenadier Battalion; 673rd Flak-Regiment

LXVI Corps
General der Artillerie Walter Lucht
16th Volkswerfer-Brigade (86th and 87th Werfer-Regiments)
244th Assault Gun Brigade; 460th Heavy Artillery Battalion

18th Volksgrenadier-Division
Oberst Günther Hoffmann-Schönborn
293rd, 294th and 295th Volksgrenadier-Regiments; 1818th Artillery Regiment
1818th Anti-Tank Battalion; 1818th Engineer Battalion

62nd Volksgrenadier-Division
Oberst Friedrich Kittel
164th, 190th and 193rd Volksgrenadier-Regiments; 162nd Artillery Regiment
162nd Anti-Tank Battalion; 162nd Engineer Battalion

LVIII Panzer Corps
General der Panzertruppe Walter Krüger
401st Volksartillerie Corps; 7th Volkswerfer-Brigade (84th and 85th Werfer-Regiments)
1st Flak-Regiment

116th Panzer-Division
Generalmajor Siegfried von Waldenburg
16th Panzer-Regiment; 60th and 156th Panzergrenadier-Regiments
146th Artillery Regiment; 146th Reconnaissance Battalion; 226th Anti-Tank Battalion
675th Engineer Battalion; 281st Flak Battalion

560th Volksgrenadier-Division

Oberst Rudolf Langhauser

1128th, 1129th and 1130th Volksgrenadier-Regiments; 1560th Artillery Regiment
1560th Anti-Tank Battalion; 1560th Engineer Battalion

XXXIX Panzer Corps

Generalleutnant Karl Decker

167th Volksgrenadier-Division

Generalleutnant Hans-Kurt Höcker

331st, 339th and 387th Volksgrenadier-Regiments; 167th Artillery Regiment
167th Anti-Tank Battalion; 167th Engineer Battalion

Sixth Panzer Army

SS-Oberstgruppenführer Josef Dietrich

506th Heavy Panzer Battalion; 683rd Heavy Anti-Tank Battalion
217th Assault Panzer Battalion; 394th, 667th and 902nd Assault Gun Battalions
741st Anti-Tank Battalion; 1098th, 1110th and 1120th Heavy Howitzer Batteries
428th Heavy Mortar Battery; 2nd Flak-Division (41st and 43rd Regiments)
Kampfgruppe Heydte

I SS Panzer Corps

SS-Gruppenführer Hermann Priess

14th, 51st, 53rd and 54th Werfer-Regiments; 501st SS Artillery Battalion
388th Volksartillerie Corps; 402nd Volksartillerie Corps

1st SS Panzer-Division Leibstandarte Adolf Hitler

SS-Brigadeführer Wilhelm Mohnke

1st SS Panzer-Regiment; 1st and 2nd SS Panzergrenadier-Regiments
1st SS Artillery Regiment; 1st SS Reconnaissance Battalion; 1st SS Anti-Tank Battalion
1st SS Engineer Battalion; 1st SS Flak Battalion; 501st SS Heavy Panzer Battalion
   (attached); 84th Luftwaffe Flak Battalion (attached)

3rd Fallschirmjäger-Division

Generalmajor Walther Wadehn

5th, 8th and 9th Fallschirmjäger-Regiments; 3rd Artillery Regiment;
3rd Reconnaissance Battalion; 3rd Anti-Tank Battalion; 3rd Engineer Battalion

12th SS Panzer-Division Hitler Jugend
SS-Standartenführer Hugo Kraas
12th SS Panzer-Regiment; 25th and 26th SS Panzergrenadier-Regiments
12th SS Artillery Regiment; 12th SS Reconnaissance Battalion
12th SS Anti-Tank Battalion; 12th SS Engineer Battalion; 12th SS Flak Battalion
560th Heavy Anti-Tank Battalion (attached)

12th Volksgrenadier-Division
Generalmajor Gerhard Engel
27th Fusilier Regiment; 48th and 89th Volksgrenadier-Regiments; 12th Fusilier Battalion
12th Artillery Regiment; 12th Anti-Tank Battalion; 12th Engineer Battalion

277th Volksgrenadier-Division
Oberst Wilhelm Viebig
289th, 990th and 991st Volksgrenadier-Regiments; 277th Artillery Regiment
277th Anti-Tank Battalion; 277th Engineer Battalion

150th Panzer-Brigade
SS-Obersturmbannführer Otto Skorzeny
Two Panzer companies; two Panzergrenadier companies; two anti-tank companies
A heavy mortar battalion (two batteries); 600th SS Parachute Battalion Kampfgruppe 200

II SS Panzer Corps
SS-Obergruppenführer Willi Bittrich
410th Volksartillerie Corps; 502nd SS Heavy Artillery Battalion

2nd SS Panzer-Division Das Reich
SS-Brigadeführer Heinz Lammerding
2nd SS Panzer-Regiment; 3rd and 4th SS Panzergrenadier-Regiments; 2nd SS Artillery Regiment; 2nd SS Reconnaissance Battalion; 2nd SS Engineer Battalion; 2nd SS Flak Battalion

9th SS Panzer-Division Hohenstaufen
SS-Oberführer Sylvester Stadler
9th SS Panzer-Regiment; 19th and 20th SS Panzergrenadier-Regiments

9th SS Artillery Regiment; 9th SS Reconnaissance Battalion; 9th SS Anti-Tank Battalion

9th SS Engineer Battalion; 9th SS Flak Battalion; 519th Heavy Anti-Tank Battalion (attached)

LXVII Corps

Generalleutnant Otto Hitzfeld

17th Volkswerfer-Brigade (88th and 89th Werfer-Regiments)

405th Volksartillerie Corps; 1001st Heavy Assault Gun Company

3rd Panzergrenadier-Division

Generalmajor Walter Denkert

8th and 29th Panzergrenadier-Regiments; 103rd Panzer Battalion; 3rd Artillery Regiment

103rd Reconnaissance Battalion; 3rd Anti-Tank Battalion; 3rd Engineer Battalion

3rd Flak Battalion

246th Volksgrenadier-Division

Oberst Peter Körte

352nd, 404th and 689th Volksgrenadier-Regiments; 246th Artillery Regiment

246th Anti-Tank Battalion; 246th Engineer Battalion

272nd Volksgrenadier-Division

Generalmajor Eugen König

980th, 981st and 982nd Volksgrenadier-Regiments; 272nd Artillery Regiment

272nd Anti-Tank Battalion; 272nd Engineer Battalion

326th Volksgrenadier-Division

751st, 752nd and 753rd Volksgrenadier-Regiments; 326th Artillery Regiment

326th Anti-Tank Battalion; 326th Engineer Battalion

Seventh Army

General der Panzertruppe Erich Brandenberger

657th and 668th Heavy Anti-Tank Battalions; 501st Fortress Anti-Tank Battalion

47th Engineer Battalion; 1092nd, 1093rd, 1124th and 1125th Heavy Howitzer Batteries

660th Heavy Artillery Battery; 1029th, 1039th and 1122nd Heavy Mortar Batteries

999th Penal Battalion; 44th Machine-Gun Battalion; 15th Flak-Regiment

LIII Corps
General der Kavallerie Edwin von Rothkirch

9th Volksgrenadier-Division
Oberst Werner Kolb
36th, 57th and 116th Volksgrenadier-Regiments; 9th Artillery Regiment
9th Anti-Tank Battalion; 9th Engineer Battalion

15th Panzergrenadier-Division
Oberst Hans Joachim Deckert
104th and 115th Panzergrenadier-Regiments; 115th Panzer Battalion; 115th Artillery Regiment
115th Reconnaissance Battalion; 33rd Anti-Tank Battalion; 33rd Engineer Battalion
33rd Flak Battalion

Führer Grenadier Brigade
Oberst Hans-Joachim Kahler
99th Panzergrenadier-Regiment; 101st Panzer Battalion; 911th Assault Gun Brigade
124th Anti-Tank Battalion; 124th Engineer Battalion; 124th Flak Battalion
124th Artillery Regiment

LXXX Corps
General der Infanterie Franz Beyer
408th Volksartillerie Corps; 8th Volkswerfer-Brigade; 2nd and *Lehr* Werfer-Regiments

212th Volksgrenadier-Division
Generalmajor Franz Sensfuss
316th, 320th and 423rd Volksgrenadier-Regiments; 212th Artillery Regiment
212th Anti-Tank Battalion; 212th Engineer Battalion

276th Volksgrenadier-Division
Generalmajor Kurt Möhring (later Oberst Hugo Dempwolff)
986th, 987th and 988th Volksgrenadier-Regiments; 276th Artillery Regiment;
276th Anti-Tank Battalion; 276th Engineer Battalion

340th Volksgrenadier-Division
Oberst Theodor Tolsdorff

694th, 695th and 696th Volksgrenadier-Regiments; 340th Artillery Regiment 340th Anti-Tank Battalion; 340th Engineer Battalion

LXXXV Corps
General der Infanterie Baptist Kniess
406th Volksartillerie Corps; 18th Volkswerfer-Brigade (21st and 22nd Werfer-Regiments)

5th Fallschirmjäger-Division
Generalmajor Ludwig Heilmann
13th, 14th and 15th Fallschirmjäger-Regiments; 5th Artillery Regiment; 5th Reconnaissance Battalion; 5th Engineer Battalion; 5th Flak Battalion; 11th Assault Gun Brigade

352nd Volksgrenadier-Division
Oberst Erich-Otto Schmidt
914th, 915th and 916th Volksgrenadier-Regiments; 352nd Artillery Regiment; 352nd Anti-Tank Battalion; 352nd Engineer Battalion

79th Volksgrenadier-Division
Oberst Alois Weber
208th, 212th and 226th Volksgrenadier-Regiments; 179th Artillery Regiment; 179th Anti-Tank Battalion; 179th Engineer Battalion

Notes

ABBREVIATIONS

BA-MA   Bundesarchiv-Militärarchiv, Freiburg-im-Breisgau

BfZ-SS   Bibliothek für Zeitgeschichte, Sammlung Sterz, Stuttgart

CARL   Combined Arms Research Library, Fort Leavenworth, KS

CBHD   Chester B. Hansen Diaries, Chester B. Hansen Collection, Box 5, USAMHI

CBMP   Charles B. MacDonald Papers, USAMHI

CEOH   US Army Corps of Engineers, Office of History, Fort Belvoir, VA

CMH   Center of Military History, Fort McNair, Washington, DC

CMH *Ardennes*   Center of Military History, Hugh M. Cole, *United States Army in World War II: The European Theater of Operations: The Ardennes: Battle of the Bulge*, Washington, DC, 1988

CMH *Medical*   Center of Military History, Graham A. Cosmas and Albert E. Cowdrey, *United States Army in World War II: The European Theater of Operations: Medical Service in the European Theater of Operations*, Washington, DC, 1992

CMH *SC*   Center of Military History, Forrest C. Pogue, *United States Army in World War II: The European Theater of Operations: The Supreme Command*, Washington, DC, 1954

CSDIC   Combined Services Detailed Interrogation Centre

CSI   Combat Studies Institute, Fort Leavenworth, KS

DCD   Duff Cooper Diaries (private collection)

DDE Lib   Dwight D. Eisenhower Library, Abilene, KS

DRZW   *Das Deutsche Reich und der Zweiten Weltkrieg*, vols. 6–10, Munich, 2004–8

ETHINT   European Theater Historical Interrogations, 1945, OCMH, USAMHI

FCP *SC*   Forrest C. Pogue, background interviews for *The Supreme Command*, USAMHI

FDRL MR   Franklin Delano Roosevelt Library, Hyde Park, NY, Map Room documents

FMS   Foreign Military Studies, USAMHI

GBP   Godfrey Blunden Papers (private collection)

HLB   *Hitlers Lagebesprechungen: Die Protokollfragmente seiner militärischen Konferenzen 1942–1945*, Munich, 1984 (Helmut Heiber and David M. Glantz (eds.), *Hitler and his Generals: Military Conferences, 1942–1945*, London, 2002)

IWM   Documents Collection, Imperial War Museum, London

LHC-DP   Liddell Hart Centre – Dempsey Papers

LHCMA   Liddell Hart Centre of Military Archives, King's College London

MFF   MFF Armed Forces Oral Histories, LHCMA

NARA   National Archives and Records Administration, College Park, MD

OCMH   Office of the Chief of Military History, USAMHI

PDDE   *The Papers of Dwight David Eisenhower*, ed. Alfred D. Chandler, 21 vols., Baltimore, MA, 1970–2001

PP   *The Patton Papers*, ed. Martin Blumenson, New York, 1974

PWS   Papers of William Sylvan, OCMH, USAMHI

RWHP   Robert W. Hasbrouck Papers, USAMHI

SHD-DAT   Service Historique de la Défense, Département de l'Armée de Terre, Vincennes

SOOHP   Senior Officers Oral History Program, US Army War College, USAMHI

TBJG   *Die Tagebücher von Joseph Goebbels*, ed. Elke Fröhlich, 29 vols., Munich, 1992–2005

TNA   The National Archives, Kew

USAMHI   The United States Army Military History Institute at US Army Heritage and Education Center, Carlisle, PA

I VICTORY FEVER

p. 1 'It's Sunday', Omar N. Bradley, *A Soldier's Story*, New York, 1964, 389–90; also Dwight D. Eisenhower, *Crusade in Europe*, New York, 1948, 325

'informal visit', NARA 407/427/24235

Gerow and Leclerc; 'continue on present mission', SHD-DAT 11 P 218; also NARA 407/427/24235

p. 2 'a field of rubble', BA-MA RH19 IX/7 40, quoted Joachim Ludewig, *Rückzug: The German Retreat from France, 1944*, Lexington, KY, 2012, 133

'Pire que les boches', Forrest C. Pogue, *Pogue's War: Diaries of a WWII Combat Historian*, Lexington, KY, 2001, 214

p. 3 'a show of force', 'to establish . . .', Eisenhower, *Crusade in Europe*, 326; and Bradley, 391

'From what I heard at SHAEF . . .', Arthur Tedder, *With Prejudice*, London, 1966, 586

28th Division in Paris, see Uzal W. Ent (ed.), *The First Century: A History of the 28th Infantry Division*, Harrisburg, PA, 1979, 165

p. 4 'Une armée de mécanos', Jean Galtier-Boissière, *Mon journal pendant l'Occupation*, Paris, 1944, 288

'It was one of the most . . .', 1.2.45, CBHD

p. 5 'The August battles . . .', CMH *SC*, 245

'The West Front is finished . . .',

diary Oberstleutnant Fritz Fullriede, *Hermann Göring* Division, 2 September 1944, quoted Robert Kershaw, *It Never Snows in September*, London, 2008, 63

'We want peace . . .', prisoner-of-war interview, CSDIC, TNA WO 208/3616

Wehrmacht losses, Rüdiger Overmans, *Deutsche militärische Verluste im Zweiten Weltkrieg*, Munich, 2000, 238 and 278

p. 6 For the German retreat from France see: Ludewig, 108/ff.; and David Wingeate Pike, 'Oberbefehl West: Armeegruppe G: Les Armées allemandes dans le Midi de la France', *Guerres Mondiales et Conflits Contemporains*, Nos. 152, 164, 174, 181

'You are fish', Generaloberst Student, CSDIC, TNA WO 208/4177

'a club of intellectuals', Generaloberst Halder, CSDIC, TNA WO 208/4366 GRGG 332

'Now I know why . . .', Albert Speer, *Inside the Third Reich*, London, 1971, 525

'There will be moments . . .', *HLB*, 466 and 468

'It is certain that the political conflicts . . .', CMH *SC*, 249

p. 7 'In the evening . . .', Kreipe diary, 31.8.44, FMS P-069

'By now a huge . . .', Traudl Junge, *Until the Final Hour: Hitler's Last Secretary*, London, 2002, 146

'an air landing . . .', 'unusual array', Generalmajor Otto Ernst Remer, *Führer Begleit* Brigade, FMS B-592 'typing out whole reams . . .', Junge, 144

p. 9 For German civilian morale, see Richard J. Evans, *The Third Reich at War*, London, 2008, 650–3

'a military statesman . . .', Chester Wilmot, *The Struggle for Europe*, London, 1952, 496

p. 10 'Ike said that Monty . . .', 'Ike did not thank . . .', *PP*, 533, 537

'what with champagne . . .', Brian Horrocks, *Corps Commander*, London, 1977, 79

p. 11 'The captives sat on the straw . . .', Caroline Moorehead, *Martha Gellhorn*, London, 2003, 269

'You had barely crossed . . .', interrogation, General der Artillerie Walter Warlimont, Deputy Chief of the Wehrmachtführungsstab, CSDIC, TNA WO 208/3151

'We would let . . .', VII Corps, NARA RG 498 290/56/2/3, Box 1459

'with practically no maintenance', ibid.

'We employed . . .', VII Corps, ibid.

p. 12 'The pace of the retreat . . .', Maurice Delvenne, 1.9.44, cited Jean-Michel Delvaux, *La Bataille des Ardennes autour de Rochefort*, 2 vols., Hubaille, 2004–5, ii, 159–60

'Their looks are hard . . .', ibid.

p. 13 'a sad platoon of Dutch . . .', Fullriede diary, 13 September 1944, quoted Kershaw, *It Never Snows in September*, 38

'a picture that is unworthy . . .',

BA-MA RH24-89/10, quoted Ludewig, 191

'the world situation . . .', 'OKW Feldjäger' etc., Obergefreiter Gogl, Abt. V, Feldjäger Regiment (mot.) 3., OKW Streifendienst, TNA WO 208/3610

p. 14 'malingerers and cowardly shirkers . . .', BA-MA RW4/vol. 494

'the only reinforcements . . .', NARA RG 498 290/56/2/3, Box 1466

'as much use to us . . .', Stephen Roskill, *Churchill and the Admirals*, London, 1977, 245, quoted Rick Atkinson, *The Guns at Last Light*, New York, 2013, 233

'Napoleon, no doubt . . .', Horrocks, 81

p. 15 'Newspapers reported . . .', Pogue, *Pogue's War*, 208

2   ANTWERP AND THE GERMAN FRONTIER

p. 16–17 Montgomery and Rhine crossing at expense of Scheldt estuary, LHCMA, Alanbrooke 6/2/31

p. 17 Montgomery to Brooke, 3.9.44; IWM LMD 62/12, Montgomery diary, 3.9.44; see John Buckley, *Monty's Men: The British Army and the Liberation of Europe*, London, 2013, 206

'In order to attack', *PP*, 538

'with [the] compliments . . .', Forrest C. Pogue, *Pogue's War: Diaries of a WWII Combat Historian*, Lexington, KY, 2001, 215–16

50,000 cases of champagne, Patton letter, *PP*, 549

p. 18 'Even if all our allies ...', Uffz. Alfred Lehmann, 11.9.44, BA-MA RH13/49, 5

Cancelled airborne operations, Head-quarters Allied Airborne Army, NARA RG 498 290/56/2/3, Box 1466

'The damn airborne ...', *PP*, 540

p. 20 Versailles and Paris, Com Z, see Rick Atkinson, *The Guns at Last Light*, New York, 2013, 236

p. 21 Letter of 21 September, CMH *SC*, 293

'The whole point ...', CSDIC, TNA WO 208/4177

'narrow front', 'single knife-like drive ...', CMH *SC*, 292

'dagger-thrust ...', Patton diary, *PP*, 550

'The problem was ...', Buckley, 203

p. 23 'overwhelming egotism', Forrest C. Pogue, *George C. Marshall: Organizer of Victory*, New York, 1973, 475, quoted Atkinson, 304

'If you, as the ...', 'You will hear ...', *PDDE*, iii, 2224

p. 24 'We took enough prisoners', XX Corps, NARA RG 498 290/56/2/3, Box 1465

'kept breaking down ...', Ober-sturmbannführer Loenholdt, 17 SS PzGr-Div, CSDIC, TNA WO 208/4140 SRM 1254

'Relations between officers and men ...', First Army report to the OKW, 1.10.44, BA-MA RH13/49, 9

p. 25 'The war has reached ...', O.Gefr. Ankenbeil, 22.9.44, BA-MA RH13/49, 10

'He doesn't attack ...', O.Gefr. M. Kriebel, 18.9.44, BA-MA RH13/49, 11

'The American infantryman ...', O.Gefr. Hans Büscher, 20.9.44, BA-MA RH13/49, 11

'Whoever has air ...', O.Gefr. G. Riegler, 21.9.44, BA-MA RH13/49, 11

'Why sacrifice more and more ...', O.Gefr. Hans Hoes, 15.9.44, BA-MA RH13/49, 12

'Führer interrupts Jodl ...', diary of General der Flieger Kreipe, FMS P-069

p. 26 'OKH [Army High Command] has serious doubts ...', 18.9.44, ibid.

Rundstedt's drinking, CSDIC, TNA WO 208/4364 GRGG 208

'The [Nazi Party] Kreisleiter of Reutlingen ...', Hauptmann Delica, II Battalion, 19th Fallschirmjäger-Regiment, CSDIC, TNA WO 208/4140 SRM 1227

p. 26–7 'We have been lied to ...', CSDIC, TNA WO 208/4139 SRM 968

3 THE BATTLE FOR AACHEN

p. 28 'As we pass a pillbox ...', PFC Richard Lowe Ballou, 117th Infantry, 30th Infantry Division, MFF-7, C1-97 (3)

'The wounded come out ...', V Corps, NARA RG 498 290/56/2/3, Box 1455

p. 29 'When the doors . . .', MFF-7, C1-97(2)

'After a second charge of TNT . . .', ibid.

p. 30 'The Führer wanted to defend . . .', Reichsmarschall Hermann Göring, ETHINT 30

'The sight of the Luftwaffe . . .', Generalmajor Rudolf Freiherr von Gersdorff, ETHINT 53

'We were reduced . . .', Gardner Botsford, *A Life of Privilege, Mostly*, New York, 2003, 47

p. 31 Rumours of bacteriological weapons, CSDIC, TNA WO 208/4140 SRM 1245

'You should have seen . . .', CSDIC, TNA WO 208/4139 SRM 983

'And when the houses . . .', ibid.

Fear of foreign workers, CSDIC, TNA WO 208/4139 SRM 1103

'The Allied Forces serving . . .', CMH *SC*, 357

p. 33 'American officers [are] using . . .', TNA WO 208/3654 PWIS H/LDC/631

'the troops were indignant . . .', ibid.

'former proud regiment . . .', letter of 26.9.44 to Hauptmann Knapp, NARA RG 498 290/56/5/3, Box 1463

p. 34 'I had the most excellent . . .', CSDIC, TNA WO 208/4139 SRM 982

'a job that should have . . .', 'To make sure . . .', NARA RG 498 290/56/2/3, Box 1459

'resulted in a quick . . .', NARA RG 407 270/65/7/2 ML 248

p. 35 'When attacked in this way . . .', V Corps, NARA RG 498 290/56/2/3, Box 1455

'The few assault guns . . .', CSDIC, TNA WO 208/4139 SRM 982

'no close-in bombing . . .', 'the flattened condition of the buildings . . .', NARA RG 498 290/56/2/3, Box 1459

'The operation was not unduly . . .', ibid.

p. 36 'Numerous times we have had . . .', NARA RG 498 290/56/2, Box 1456

'the direct fire of the 155mm . . .', VII Corps, NARA RG 498 290/56/2/3, Box 1459

'Civilians must be . . .', Lt Col. Shaffer F. Jarrell, VII Corps, ibid.

'they held up all . . .', CSDIC, TNA WO 208/4156

'Eisenhower is attacking . . .', Victor Klemperer, *To the Bitter End: The Diaries of Victor Klemperer, 1942–45*, London, 2000, 462

'Every German homestead . . .', CSDIC, TNA WO 208/4140 SRM 1211

p. 37 'Even the Führer's adjutant . . .', Wilck, CSDIC, TNA WO 208/4364 GRGG 216

'The civilian population . . .', Unterfeldwebel Kunz, 104th Infanterie-Regt, CSDIC, TNA WO 208/4164 SRX 2050

'the time gained at Aachen . . .', NARA RG 407 270/65/7/2, Box 19105 ML 258

p. 38n 'he would have been given . . .', CSDIC, TNA WO 208/5542 SIR 1548

p. 38 'he has to watch . . .', FMS P-069

'Before the Generals or anyone . . .', CSDIC, TNA WO 208/4134 SRA 5610

'Fears in East Prussia . . .', FMS P-069

'Gumbinnen is on fire . . .', ibid.

4 INTO THE WINTER OF WAR

p. 40 'The soldiers' behaviour today . . .', Stabartz Köllensperger, 8th Regiment, 3rd Fallschirmjäger-Division, TNA WO 311/54

'German propaganda urging . . .', CSDIC, TNA WO 208/3165

p. 41 'You've no idea . . .', Luftwaffe Obergefreiter Hlavac, KG 51, TNA WO 208/4164 SRX 2117

'They called us prolongers . . .', Obergefreiter Marke, 16th Fallschirmjäger-Regiment, ibid.

'The mood there is shit . . .', CSDIC, TNA WO 208/4164 SRX 2084

'Versager-1', Nicholas Stargardt, *Witnesses of War: Children's Lives under the Nazis*, London, 2005, 262

'into a country . . .', quoted Martin Gilbert, *The Second World War*, London, 1989, 592

'every American soldier . . .', NARA RG 407 270/65/7/2, Box 19105 ML 258

'Well, it probably won't be . . .', 2.12.44, CBHD

'The German people must realize . . .', CMH *SC*, 342

'The power of Germany . . .', NARA RG 407 270/65/7/2, Box 19105 ML 258

p. 42 'generally expected', ibid.

'Tommy and his Yankee pal . . .', 'while Americans . . .', TNA WO 171/4184

'German civilians don't know . . .', 24.11.44, NARA RG 407 270/65/7/2, Box 19105 ML 285

Nazi Party corruption, CSDIC, TNA WO 208/4139 SRM 902

'armed with a few . . .', 'suspicious civilians', 'intelligence missions of their own', NARA RG 407 270/65/7/2, Box 19105 ML 285

'Don't kick them around . . .', ibid.

p. 43 Cologne and 'Edelweiss Pirates', CSDIC, TNA WO 208/4164 SRX 2074

'A Leutnant of ours . . .', Luftwaffe Unteroffizier Bock 3/JG 27, CSDIC, TNA WO 208/4164 SRX 2126

'What is cowardice?', 4.5.44, Victor Klemperer, *To the Bitter End: The Diaries of Victor Klemperer, 1942–45*, London, 2000, 383

'I am so accustomed now . . .', Marie 'Missie' Vassiltchikov, *The Berlin Diaries, 1940–1945*, London, 1987, 240

p. 44 'Skin diseases . . .', CSDIC, TNA WO 208/3165 SIR 1573

Deserters in Berlin, CSDIC, TNA WO 208/4135 SRA 5727 13/1/45

'War is just like . . .', TNA WO 171/4184

10,000 executions, *DRZW*, 9/1 (Echternkamp), 48–50

'During the night of . . .', VI Corps, NARA RG 498 290/56/5/3, Box 1463

Black market in Berlin, CSDIC, TNA WO 208/4164 SRX 2074

p. 45 Black-market coffee from Holland, CSDIC, TNA WO 208/4140 SRM 1189

'Greiser boasted . . .', TNA WO 311/54, 32

'Main meal without meat' ('Hauptgerichte einmal ohne Fleisch'), Branden-burgische Landeshauptarchiv, Pr. Br. Rep. 61A/11

'The prices rise . . .', NARA RG 407 270/65/7/2 ML 2279

p. 46 'the over-heated soul . . .', Louis Simpson, *Selected Prose*, New York, 1989, 98

p. 46n 'according to his VD . . .', CMH *Medical*, 541

p. 46 'Avenue de Salute', Forrest C. Pogue, *Pogue's War: Diaries of a WWII Combat Historian*, Lexington, KY, 2001, 230

p. 47 'ardent and often . . .', NARA 711.51/3-945

Reaction of young woman, Antony Beevor and Artemis Cooper, *Paris after the Liberation, 1944–1949*, London, 1994, 129

'The French, cynical before . . .', Simpson, 143

US Army soldiers in black market, Allan B. Ecker, 'GI Racketeers in the Paris Black Market', *Yank*, 4.5.45

p. 48 'extremely frigid . . .', 24.10.44, DCD

'there is absolutely no one . . .', NARA 851.00/9-745

p. 49 'ardent admirers', Carlos Baker, *Ernest Hemingway: A Life Story*, New York, 1969, 564

p. 50 For the political situation in Belgium, see CMH *SC*, 329–31

p. 51 'We're still a . . .', V Corps, NARA RG 498 290/56/2/3, Box 1455

p. 52 'Each morning . . .', Arthur S. Couch, 'An American Infantry Soldier in World War II Europe', unpublished memoir, private collection

'We couldn't get the new untrained . . .', NARA RG 498 290/56/2/3, Box 1465

p. 53 'Sergeant Postalozzi . . .', Martha Gellhorn, *Point of No Return*, New York, 1989, 30

p. 53n Hemingway, *Across the River and into the Trees*, New York, 1950, 255

p. 53 'His chances seem at their . . .', Ralph Ingersoll, *Top Secret*, London, 1946, 185–6

'I was lucky . . .', Couch, 'An American Infantry Soldier in World War II Europe'

'The quality of replacements . . .', NARA RG 498 290/56/2/3, Box 1459

p. 54 'Replacements have 13 weeks . . .', Tech. Sgt. Edward L. Brule, NARA RG 498 290/56/5/2, Box 3

'enemy weapons could . . .', 358th Infantry, NARA RG 498 290/56/2/3, Box 1465

'The worst fault I have . . .', V Corps, NARA RG 498 290/56/2/3, Box 1455

'Jerry puts mortar fire . . .', V Corps, ibid.

'We actually had . . .', NARA RG 498 290/56/5/2, Box 3

p. 55 'My first contact . . .', 358th Infantry, 90th Division, XX Corps, NARA RG 498 290/56/2/3, Box 1465

'one group of officer . . .', NARA RG 498 290/56/2/3, Box 1459

'Before entering combat . . .', Lt Col. J. E. Kelly, 3rd Battalion, 378th Infantry, NARA RG 498 290/56/2/3, Box 1465

5 THE HÜRTGEN FOREST

p. 58 'In general it was believed . . .', Generalleutnant Hans Schmidt, 275th Infanterie-Division, FMS B-810

'This consisted . . .', Major Gen. Kenneth Strong, 02/14/2 3/25 – Intelligence Notes No. 33, IWM Documents 11656

'absolutely unfit . . .', Generalleutnant Hans Schmidt, 275th Infanterie-Division, FMS B-810

'almost the entire company . . .', ibid.
'the greatest demands . . .', ibid.
'cold rations at irregular intervals', ibid.

p. 59 'It was like a drop of water . . .', ibid.

'without counting the great number . . .', ibid.

'The commitment of the old paterfamilias . . .', ibid.

p. 61 'the German soldier shows . . .', 14.10.44, GBP

'I am returning . . .', VII Corps, NARA RG 498 290/56/2/3, Box 1459

'In dense woods . . .', ibid.

p. 62 'One man kicked . . .', Charles B. MacDonald, *The Mighty Endeavour: The American War in Europe*, New York, 1992, 385

'Schu, Riegel, Teller . . .', NARA RG 498 290/56/2/3, Box 1459

'When mines are . . .', 5.11.44, V Corps, NARA RG 498 290/56/2/3, Box 1455

297th Engineer Combat Battalion, VII Corps, NARA RG 498 290/56/2/3, Box 1459

'The Germans are burying . . .', 22nd Infantry, 4th Inf. Div., ibid.

p. 63 'The effective range . . .', VII Corps, ibid.

'Men over thirty . . .', ibid.

p. 64 'It took guts . . .', Colonel Edwin M. Burnett, V Corps, NARA RG 498 290/56/2/3, Box 1455

'excellent', Rick Atkinson, *The Guns at Last Light*, New York, 2013, 317

'Certainly there will be . . .', Diary of General der Flieger Kreipe, FMS P-069, 43

p. 65 'one big, old country . . .', V Corps, NARA RG 498 290/56/2/3, Box 1455

'When the driver . . .', Edward G. Miller, *A Dark and Bloody Ground: The Hürtgen Forest and the Roer River Dams, 1944–1945*, College Station, TX, 2008, 64

p. 66 'after the effectiveness . . .', Generalmajor Rudolf Freiherr von Gersdorff, FMS A-892

p. 67 'to prevent American troops from . . .', Gersdorff, FMS A-891

Lack of bazooka ammunition in Schmidt, Col. Nelson 112th Infantry, NARA RG 498 290/56/2/3, Box 1463

'General Eisenhower, General Bradley . . .', 8.11.44, PWS

p. 68 'When the strength of an outfit . . .', Ralph Ingersoll, *Top Secret*, London, 1946, 185

'The surrounded American task force . . .', NARA RG 407 270/65/7/2, Box 19105 ML 258

p. 69 'There was a stream . . .', Arthur S. Couch, 'An American Infantry Soldier in World War II Europe', unpublished memoir, private collection

'then blast hell . . .', VII Corps, NARA RG 498 290/56/2/3, Box 1459

4.2-inch mortars, NARA RG 407 270/65/7/2 ML 248

p. 70 'The German artillery . . .', Couch, 'An American Infantry Soldier in World War II Europe'

'easier to defend . . .', Generalmajor Rudolf Freiherr von Gersdorff, ETHINT 53

'Just before dawn . . .', Couch, 'An American Infantry Soldier in World War II Europe'

p. 71 275th Infanterie-Division, Generalleutnant Hans Schmidt, FMS B-373

Colonel Luckett, V Corps, NARA RG 498 290/56/2/3, Box 1455

'twelve to twenty men . . .', NARA RG 498 290/56/2/3, Box 1465

'In the daytime . . .', NARA RG 498 290/56/2/3, Box 1464

p. 72 'One time we didn't . . .', quoted John Ellis, *The Sharp End: The Fighting Man in World War II*, London, 1990, 152

'booby-trapped stretch . . .', Robert Sterling Rush, *Hell in Hürtgen Forest: The Ordeal and Triumph of an American Infantry Regiment*, Lawrence, KS, 2001, 139

1st Division avoiding trails, 18th Infantry, 1st Division, NARA RG 498 290/56/2/3, Box 1459

p. 73 'A heavy snow . . .', Couch, 'An American Infantry Soldier in World War II Europe'

'Armistice Day and Georgie . . .', 11.11.44, CBHD

'The whole damn company . . .', Omar N. Bradley, *A Soldier's Story*, New York, 1964, 430–1

p. 74 'fight to the last round', Generalmajor Ullersperger, CSDIC, TNA WO 208/4364 GRGG 237

'I am surprised that Himmler . . .', Generalmajor Vaterrodt, CSDIC, TNA WO 208/4177

'I've lost my unit', etc., ibid.

p. 76 'Especially distressing . . .', Generalleutnant Straube, FMS A-891

'an open wound', FMS A-891

'death-mill', Gersdorff, FMS A-892

'Passchendaele with tree bursts', Ernest Hemingway, *Across the River and into the Trees*, New York, 1950, 249

'Old Ernie Hemorrhoid . . .', Carlos

Baker, *Ernest Hemingway: A Life Story*, New York, 1969, 552

'an unoccupied foxhole', J. D. Salinger, 'Contributors', *Story*, No. 25 (November–December 1944), 1

'After five days . . .', Charles Whiting, *The Battle of Hürtgen Forest*, Stroud, 2007, 71

'The young battalion commanders . . .', Ingersoll, 184–5

p. 77 'The men accept poor . . .', V Corps, NARA RG 498 290/56/2/3, Box 1455

'You drive by the surgical tents . . .', Ingersoll, 185

22nd Infantry casualties, Sterling Rush, 163

'keep control of . . .', FMS A-891

'Our men appear to have . . .', Sgt David Rothbart, 22nd Inf. Rgt, quoted Sterling Rush, 178

p. 78 'would get up . . .', quoted Paul Fussell, *The Boys' Crusade*, New York, 2003, 91

'tree bursts that sent . . .', etc., Captain H. O. Sweet, US 908th Field Artillery, Attached to 331st Infantry, 83rd Division, IWM Documents 3415 95/33/1

8,000 psychological casualties, Peter Schrijvers, *The Crash of Ruin: American Combat Soldiers in Europe during World War II*, New York, 1998, 8

p. 79 'There were few cases . . .', Generalarzt Schepukat, ETHINT 60

'In some cases . . .', Gersdorff, FMS A-892

'more than 5,000 battle . . .', 'The Ardennes', CSI Battlebook 10-A, May 1984

6 THE GERMANS PREPARE

p. 80 'with the rather melancholy . . .', Traudl Junge, *Until the Final Hour: Hitler's Last Secretary*, London, 2002, 147

'He knew very well . . .', ibid.

'the column of cars . . .', ibid., 148

p. 81 'Hitler had all day . . .', Generaloberst Alfred Jodl, ETHINT 50

'By remaining on the defensive . . .', ibid.

'another Dunkirk', CMH *Ardennes*, 18

p. 83 'whisked away', General der Kavallerie Siegfried Westphal, ETHINT 79

'German divisions were gradually . . .', Generalmajor Rudolf Freiherr von Gersdorff, FMS A-892

p. 84 'small solution' and conferences beginning November, CSDIC, TNA WO 208/4178 GRGG 330 (c)

'a snowplow effect', CMH *Ardennes*, 26

Hitler and American forces in front of Aachen, Generaloberst Alfred Jodl, ETHINT 50

Oberstleutnant Guderian, CSDIC, TNA WO 208/3653

'In our current . . .', *DRZW*, 6, 125

p. 85 Manteuffel's fuel requests, Manteuffel, Fifth Panzer Army, ETHINT 45 'on principle, otherwise . . .', Generaloberst Alfred Jodl, ETHINT 50

Preference for SS, General der Artillerie Walter Warlimont, CSDIC, TNA WO 208/3151

'There was a certain . . .', Generaloberst Alfred Jodl, ETHINT 51

'expressed his astonishment . . .', Jodl, TNA WO 231/30

'Not to be altered', 'to their subordinate . . .',CSDIC, TNA WO 208/4178 GRGG 330 (c)

p. 86 'last gamble', TNA WO 231/30, 4

'final objective . . .', CSDIC, TNA WO 208/4178 GRGG 330 (c)

'Surprise, when it succeeds . . .', CSDIC, TNA WO 208/4178 GRGG 322

Security measures, CSDIC, TNA WO 208/4178 GRGG 330 (c)

'full to bursting point', Hauptmann Gaum, 3rd Bn, *Führer Begleit* Brigade, CSDIC, TNA WO 208/3611

p. 87 Storch aircraft, TNA WO 231/30

Volksgrenadier divisions taking documents, CSDIC, TNA WO 208/4140 SRM 1140

'started a rumour . . .', Manteuffel, Fifth Panzer Army, ETHINT 46

'the political crisis in the . . .', Goebbels diaries, 1.12.44, *TBJG* II/14, 305

'We have all been . . .', SS Standartenführer Lingner, CSDIC, TNA WO 208/4140 SRM 1211

p. 88 'The only thing . . .', Generalleutnant Heim, CSDIC, TNA WO 208/4364 GRGG 220

'What a filthy trick!', CSDIC, TNA WO 208/4140 SRM 1210

'There were many comments . . .', Warlimont, CSDIC, TNA WO 208/3151

Dietrich refuses Kruse, CSDIC, TNA WO 208/4178 GRGG 330 (c)

'was not commanded as one formation . . .', CSDIC, TNA WO 208/4178 GRGG 330 (c)

'Objectives, objectives! . . .', TNA WO 231/30

'a people's general', ibid.

p. 89 Questionnaire after 20 July, CSDIC, TNA WO 208/4140 SRM 1199

'and then give the English . . .', CSDIC, TNA WO 208/5541 SIR 1425

'The Führer has ordered . . .', FMS B-823

'There was nothing but . . .', CSDIC, TNA WO 208/4140 SRM 1187

'Germany's last reserves . . .', ibid.

p. 90 'Only two pilots . . .', ibid.

'who was heavily . . .', 'Success or failure . . .', CSDIC, TNA WO 208/3662

'the entire offensive had not more . . .', Heydte, FMS B-823

'an old non-commissioned . . .', ibid.

p. 91 'All that was known . . .', ibid.

'We'll annihilate them,' CSDIC, TNA WO 208/4140 SRM 1167

'a highly overstrung . . .', CSDIC, TNA WO 208/5541 SIR 1425

p. 92 'Skorzeny, this next . . .', Skorzeny's account to his officers, NARA RG 407 ML 2279

'typical evil Nazi', Heydte to Leutnant von Trott zu Solz, CSDIC, TNA WO 208/4140 SRM 1182

'a real dirty dog . . .', CSDIC, TNA WO 208/4178 GRGG 301

'order from the Reichsführer', SS-Untersturmführer Schreiber, CSDIC, TNA WO 208/4140 SRM 1259

'Everything I know . . .', Mobile Field Interrogation Unit No. 1, NARA RG 407 ML 2279

'decisive effect on . . .', ibid.

Leutnant zur See Müntz, CSDIC, TNA WO 208/3619

p. 93 'with the fork . . .', Mobile Field Interrogation Unit No. 1, NARA RG 407 ML 2279

'emphasized that the . . .', ibid.

'conspicuous friendship', Schreiber, CSDIC, TNA WO 208/4140 SRM 1259

'he was our pirate captain', Hans Post, *One Man in his Time*, Sydney, 2002, 167

p. 94 'according to the German radio . . .', Leutnant Günther Schultz, captured Liège 19.12.44, Mobile Field Interrogation Unit No. 1, NARA RG 407 ML 2279

150th Panzer-Brigade, 'Ardennes Offensive', Obersturmbannführer Otto Skorzeny, ETHINT 12

Skorzeny and plans for Basle, CSDIC, TNA WO 208/5543 SIR 1673

SHAEF and plan to go through Switzerland, NARA RG 407 270/65/7/2, Box 19124 ML 754

Trains needed for Ardennes offensive, TNA WO 231/30

p. 95 'was already seeing in his mind's eye . . .', Nicolaus von Below, *Als Hitlers Adjutant, 1937–1945*, Mainz, 1980, 396

'Is your army ready?', SS-Obergruppenführer Sepp Dietrich, ETHINT 16

Hitler's speech, *HLB*, 535–40

p. 96 'the worst prepared . . .', Dietrich, ETHINT 16.

Divisions remove insignia, 116th Panzer-Division, CSDIC, TNA WO 208/3628

p. 97 Peiper's orders, 14.12.44, Obersturmbannführer Joachim Peiper, ETHINT 10

'In twelve or fourteen . . .', Gefreiter Unruh, CSDIC, TNA WO 208/3611 SIR 1408

'an extraordinary optimism . . .', SS-Brigadeführer Heinz Harmel, 10th SS Panzer-Division *Frundsberg*, FMS P-109f

'the fighting spirit . . .', 2nd Panzer-Division, FMS P-109e

7 INTELLIGENCE FAILURE

p. 99 'pathetically alone', etc., 6.12.44, CBHD, Box 5

'If we were fighting . . .', ibid.

'Victory or Siberia!', John S. D. Eisenhower, *The Bitter Woods*, New York, 1970, 200

p. 100 'sledgehammer blows . . .', 7.12.44, CBHD

'Field Marshal Montgomery . . .', 'Notes of Meeting at Maastricht on 7.12.1944', Sidney H. Negrotto Papers, Box 4, USAMHI

'all operations north . . .', ibid.

'I think only Attila . . .', *PP*, 576

p. 101 'This is General Patton . . .', James H. O'Neill, former Third Army chaplain, 'The True Story of the Patton Prayer', *Leadership*, No. 25

'Well, Padre . . .', ibid.

p. 102 Eberbach conversation, CSDIC, TNA WO 208/4364 GRGG 220

'the big offensive . . .', Leutnant von der Goltz (St./Gren-Rgt 1039), CSDIC, TNA WO 208/4139 SRM 1083

German deserter, CMH *SC*, 363

p. 103 'Germany's crippling shortage . . .', TNA CAB 106/1107

'the enemy's present practice . . .', CMH *SC*, 365

p. 104 'aware of the danger', Strong, letter of 31.8.51, quoted ibid.

'as a Christmas present for the Führer', CMH *SC*, 370

'Hitler's orders for setting up . . .', 'Indications of the German Offensive of December 1944', dated 28.12.44, 'C' to Victor Cavendish-Bentinck, TNA HW 13/45

p. 105 'as soon as replenishing . . .', BAY/XL 152, TNA HW 13/45

'The GAF [Luftwaffe] evidence shows . . .', etc., 'Indications of the German Offensive of December 1944', 28.12.44, 'C' to Victor Cavendish-Bentinck, TNA HW 13/45

'a little startling . . .', 'Ever since . . .', ibid.

p. 106 'quiet paradise . . .', 'The Ardennes', CSI Battlebook 10-A, May 1984

'The steady traffic . . .', Forrest C. Pogue, *Pogue's War: Diaries of a WWII Combat Historian*, Lexington, KY, 2001, 250

Evacuation of eastern cantons, Peter Schrijvers, *The Unknown Dead: Civilians in the Battle of the Bulge*, Lexington, KY, 2005, 12

p. 107 Elections and *Rucksackdeutsche*, ibid., 7–8

'The bloody Heinies!', Louis Simpson, *Selected Prose*, New York, 1989, 117

'La Dietrich was bitching', 8.12.44, CBHD

p. 108 'a good part of the afternoon', 13.12.44, PWS

'It is now certain that attrition . . .', TNA CAB 106/1107

12th Army Group short of 17,581 men, NARA RG 498 UD603, Box 3

'We think he is spread . . .', etc., 15.12.44, CBHD

'GI's in their zest . . .', Omar N. Bradley, *A Soldier's Story*, New York, 1964, 428

'German manpower . . .', John Buckley, *Monty's Men: The British Army and the Liberation of Europe*, London, 2013, 259

p. 109 'My men were amazed . . .', Charles B. MacDonald, *Company Commander*, New York, 2002, 78

'It has been very quiet . . .', Colonel R. Ernest Dupuy, *St. Vith: Lion in the Way: The 106th Infantry Division in World War II*, Washington, DC, 1949, 15–16

'Dear Ruth . . .', captured letter translated 19 December, headquarters 1st Infantry Division, CBMP, Box 2

8 SATURDAY 16 DECEMBER

p. 111 German artillery targeting houses, V Corps, NARA RG 498 290/56/2/3, Box 1455

p. 112 Manderfeld, Peter Schrijvers, *The Unknown Dead: Civilians in the Battle of the Bulge*, Lexington, KY, 2005, 14

'a World War I concept . . .', Manteuffel, Fifth Panzer Army, ETHINT 46

'a significant obstacle . . .', 'The Ardennes', CSI Battlebook 10-A, May 1984

'that surprise had been . . .', Generaloberst Alfred Jodl, ETHINT 51

'If in places . . .', Charles P. Roland, 99th Infantry Division, CBMP, Box 4

p. 114 'They might at least . . .', John S. D. Eisenhower, *The Bitter Woods*, New York, 1970, 229

Lanzerath engagement, letter from Lieutenant Colonel Robert L. Kriz, 394th Infantry; and letter from Lyle J. Bouck, 19 January 1983, CBMP, Box 4

p. 115 'Hold at all costs!', Eisenhower, *Bitter Woods*, 188

p. 116 'to push through rapidly . . .',

Obersturmbannführer Joachim Peiper, 1st SS Panzer-Regiment, ETHINT 10

'shouting that they were . . .', Adolf Schür, Lanzerath, CBMP, Box 6

'They might just as well . . .', Peiper, ETHINT 10

'We pulled our jeep . . .', FO, C Battery, 371st FA Bn, 99th Infantry Division, Richard H. Byers Papers, Box 1, USAMHI

p. 117 'There were fellows . . .', Standartenführer Lingner, 17th SS Pzg-Div, CSDIC, TNA WO 208/4140 SRM 1205

'At 06.00 the Germans . . .', 'Defense of Höfen', *Infantry School Quarterly*, July 1948, CBMP, Box 4

'On the K Company front . . .', CBMP, Box 4

p. 118 'We administered plasma . . .', Harry S. Arnold, E Company, 393rd Infantry, 99th Infantry Division, CBMP, Box 4

Nervous breakdown and self-inflicted injuries, Charles P. Roland, 99th Infantry Division, CBMP, Box 4

p. 120 'The American Army never retreats!', Sidney Salins, CBMP, Box 4

p. 121 Volksgrenadier divisions and artillery, General der Artillerie Kruse, CSDIC, TNA WO 208/4178 GRGG 330 (c)

'just a local diversion', NARA RG 407 270/65/7/2 ML 2280

'05.15: Asleep in . . .', etc., Matt F. C. Konop, diary, 2nd Infantry Division, CBMP, Box 2

p. 122 'local enemy action', ibid.

'They turned searchlights . . .', NARA RG 498 290/56/2/3, Box 1455

28th Infantry Division and artillery, NARA RG 498 290/56/2/3, Box 1463

p. 123 'Ten Germans will be reported . . .', 28th Infantry Division, ibid.

'on the morning of the . . .', 112th Infantry Regiment, NARA RG 498 290/56/5/2, Box 3

'nearly destroyed', Generalmajor Siegfried von Waldenburg, 116th Panzer-Division, FMS A-873

p. 125 'was the fact that . . .', Generalmajor Heinz Kokott, '26th Volksgrenadier Division in the Ardennes Offensive', FMS B-040

p. 126 'willing but inept', etc., Major Frank, battalion commander, III/13th Fallschirmjäger, CSDIC, TNA WO 208/4140 SRM 1148, and WO 208/5540 SIR 1375

'a very ambitious, reckless soldier . . .', Heydte, CSDIC, TNA WO 208/5541 SIR 1425

'der Schlächter von Cassino', CSDIC, TNA WO 208/3611

Crossing the Our, 'Ardennes Offensive of Seventh Army', FMS A-876

p. 127 'We are here!', 'The Ardennes', CSI Battlebook 10-A, May 1984

Lauterborn, ibid.

'It was the towns and road junctions . . .', ibid.

p. 129 'God, I just want to see . . .', 16.12.44, CBHD

'The room, with two . . .', ibid.

'Tell him that Ike . . .', Eisenhower, *Bitter Woods*, 266

p. 130 'That broke our hearts . . .', William R. Desobry Papers, USAMHI

'looks like the real thing', *PP*, 595

'It reminds me very much . . .', *PP*, 596

'Hodges [is] having a bit . . .', William H. Simpson Papers, Box 11, USAMHI

p. 131 'very conscientious . . .', CSDIC, TNA WO 208/5541 SIR 1444

'new and nervous', ibid.

'an utter failure', CSDIC, TNA WO 208/3628

'pitifully small . . .', CSDIC, TNA WO 208/5541 SIR 1444

'German People, be confident!', TNA WO 171/4184

'We will win . . .', ibid.

p. 132 'We heard a siren-like . . .', Arthur S. Couch, 'An American Infantry Soldier in World War II Europe', unpublished memoir, private collection

Order to 2nd Division, Major William F. Hancock, 1st Battalion, 9th Infantry, 2nd Infantry Division, CBMP, Box 2

'the decisive role . . .', Peiper, ETHINT 10

9 SUNDAY 17 DECEMBER

p. 134 'Say, Konop, I want you . . .', Matt F. C. Konop, diary, 2nd Infantry Division, CBMP, Box 2

p. **136** 'had had the hell knocked out . . .', Charles B. MacDonald, *Company Commander*, New York, 2002, 82–3

'The snow around . . .', ibid.

p. **137** 'Owing to the wretched condition . . .', General der Waffen-SS H. Priess, I SS Panzer Corps, FMS A-877

Peiper's Kampfgruppe in Honsfeld, Peter Schrijvers, *The Unknown Dead: Civilians in the Battle of the Bulge*, Lexington, KY, 2005, 35–6

Nazi civilian in Büllingen, ibid., 35

p. **138** Fifty American prisoners shot at Büllingen, CMH *Ardennes*, 261

254th Engineer Battalion, V Corps, NARA RG 498 290/56/2/3, Box 1455

p. **138** 26th Infantry, CBMP, Box 2

'I think the war . . .', Gefreiter W.P., 17.12.44, BfZ-SS

p. **139** 'I will never move backwards . . .', etc., 17.12.44, CBHD

'the last air-raid . . .', Ralph Ingersoll, *Top Secret*, London, 1946, 194

'whether 12th Army Group . . .', First Army diary, quoted D. K. R. Crosswell, *Beetle: The Life of General Walter Bedell Smith*, Lexington, KY, 2010, 810

'The Army Group commander called . . .', Gaffey Papers, USAMHI

'a diversion for a larger . . .', 'everything depends . . .', 17.12.44, GBP

p. **140** Kampfgruppe Heydte, Oberstleutnant von der Heydte, ETHINT 75

p. **141** 106th on 16–17 December, CMH *Ardennes*, 156–7

'great bear of a man', John S. D. Eisenhower, *The Bitter Woods*, New York, 1970, 280

p. **142n** 'One futile effort', Royce L. Thompson, 'Air Resupply to Isolated Units, Ardennes Campaign', OCMH, Feb. 1951, typescript, CMH 2-3.7 AE P

Devine's combat fatigue, 'Report of Investigation, Action of 14th Cavalry Group on Occasion of German Attack Commencing on 16 Dec. 1944', 29.1.45, First Army IG NARA RG 338 290/62/05/1–2

p. **143** 'When I told him . . .', General der Panzertruppe Horst Stumpff, ETHINT 61

'I expected the right-hand . . .', NARA RG 407 270/65/7/2 ML 2280

p. **143** 'It was a case of . . .', Major Donald P. Boyer, 38th Armored Infantry Battalion, RWHP, Box 1

'panic stricken soldiers . . .', AAR, 7th AD Artillery, RWHP, Box 1

p. **144** 'the continuous stream of . . .', RWHP, Box 1

'The build-up of a defensive . . .', ibid.

p. **147** 'herded together . . .', 'Immediate publicity . . .', 17.12.44, PWS

'took the breath away from . . .', 18.12.44, CBHD

p. **147n** 'What utter madness . . .', CSDIC, TNA WO 208/5516

p. **147** Werbomont reprisals in September, Schrijvers, *Unknown Dead*, 40

Kampfgruppe Peiper at Stavelot, Obersturmbannführer Joachim Peiper, 1st SS Panzer-Regiment, ETHINT 10

p. **148** Dogfight over Wahlerscheid, 3rd Battalion, 38th Infantry, CBMP, Box 2

p. **149** 'Against this demoralizing picture . . .', 1st Battalion, 9th Infantry, 2nd Infantry Division, CBMP, Box 2

'screaming among the enemy', ibid.

p. **150** 'In heavy and close combat . . .', 'The Ardennes', CSI Battlebook 10-A, May 1984

'One enemy soldier . . .', 3rd Battalion, 38th Infantry, CBMP, Box 2

'plunged through the thickly . . .', 'I felt like . . .', MacDonald, *Company Commander*, 97, 100

p. **151** 'The Germans had sent him . . .', 1st Battalion, 9th Infantry, 2nd Infantry Division, CBMP, Box 2

'the crews were picked off . . .', ibid.

'a mediocre division with no . . .', General der Infanterie Baptist Kniess, LXXXV Corps, ETHINT 40

'A group of men nearby . . .', 28th Infantry Division, NARA RG 498 290/56/2/3, Box 1463

p. **152** German infiltration of Clervaux, interview Joseph Maertz, Clervaux, 22.8.81, CBMP, Box 6

p. **153** 'sitting in his . . .', and defence of Clervaux, 'The Breakthrough to Bastogne', vol. ii, Clervaux, typescript, n.d., CMH, 8-3.1 AR

'If you're a Jewish . . .', Roger Cohen, 'The Lost Soldiers of Stalag IX-B', *New York Times Magazine*, 27.2.2005

Jean Servé, Clervaux, CBMP, Box 6

'rolled headlong . . .', 'The Ardennes', CSI Battlebook 10-A

p. **154** 'The G-2 estimate tonight', 17.12.44, PWS

XLVII Panzer Corps, Lüttwitz, XLVII Panzer Corps, ETHINT 41

'to advance as rapidly . . .', Kniess, ETHINT 40

'All I know of the situation . . .', NARA RG 407 270/65/8/2 ML 130

p. **155** 'most of them, to hear them tell it . . .', Louis Simpson, *Selected Prose*, New York, 1989, 134

p. **156** 'As we walked through . . .', Walter Bedell Smith, *Eisenhower's Six Great Decisions*, London, 1956, 103

'There's been a complete . . .', Stanley Weintraub, *Eleven Days in December*, New York, 2006, 54–5

10 MONDAY 18 DECEMBER

p. **157** 'yells, catcalls and many . . .', NARA RG 498, 290/56/5/2, Box 3

'cumbersome', etc., NARA RG 498 290/56/2/3, Box 1455

p. **158** 'tanks knocked out of action . . .', V Corps, NARA RG 498 290/56/2/3, Box 1455

'When the Battalion assembled . . .', CBMP, Box 2

'it was artillery . . .', 1st Battalion, 9th Infantry, 2nd Infantry Division, CBMP, Box 2

p. **159** Battalion commander relieved,

CO, 2nd Bn, 394th Inf., NARA RG 407, E 427-A (270/65/4/7)

'Trojan Horse trick', CBMP, Box 2

'A tank was observed . . .', V Corps, NARA RG 498 290/56/2/3, Box 1455

'The bayonet was . . .', 'gunners, drivers, assistant drivers . . .', ibid.

p. 160 'saw a soldier silhouetted . . .', Charles B. MacDonald, *Company Commander*, New York, 2002, 103

'observed a Mark VI . . .', V Corps, NARA RG 498 290/56/2/3, Box 1455

'man from another outfit', ibid.

p. 161 'None of them got away', 3rd Battalion, 38th Infantry, 2nd Division, CBMP, Box 2

'But I've a rendezvous . . .', FO, C Battery, 371st FA Bn, 99th Infantry Division, Richard Henry Byers, 'Battle of the Bulge', typescript, 1983

p. 162 'It is dangerous at any time . . .', V Corps, NARA RG 498 290/56/2/3, Box 1455

Attack on Stavelot, Peiper, 1st SS Panzer-Regiment, ETHINT 10

p. 163 Evacuation of fuel, CMH *Ardennes*, 667

'General, if you don't get out . . .', J. Lawton Collins, SOOHP, USAMHI

'The situation is rapidly deteriorating', 18.12.44, PWS

'He says that the situation . . .', William H. Simpson Papers, Box 11, USAMHI

'American flags, pictures of the President . . .', 21.12.44, PWS

p. 164 'Hell, when this fight's over . . .',

John S. D. Eisenhower, *The Bitter Woods*, New York, 1970, 303

p. 165 'it would have been a simple . . .', Peiper, ETHINT 10

p. 166 'in their winter clothing . . .', Louis Simpson, *Selected Prose*, New York, 1989, 134

p. 167 'How many teams . . .', NARA RG 407 270/65/8/2 ML 130

Tensions in XLVII Panzer Corps, Kokott, FMS B-040

'The long resistance of Hosingen . . .', Generalmajor Heinz Kokott, 26th Volksgrenadier-Division, FMS B-040

'arrived too late . . .', Generalleutnant Fritz Bayerlein, Panzer Lehr Division, FMS A-942

p. 169 The defence of Wiltz, 'The Breakthrough to Bastogne', typescript, n.d., CMH 8-3.1 AR

'Panzer Lehr, with their barrels . . .', Bayerlein, FMS A-942

p. 170 Twenty-three Sherman tanks, Bayerlein, FMS A-941

'Noville is two towns up . . .', NARA RG 407 270/65/8/2 ML 130

'We could hear gunfire . . .', etc., William R. Desobry Papers, USAMHI

p. 172 'There was a muffled explosion . . .', RWHP, Box 1

'*Führer Begleit* Brigade was involved . . .', 'pushing forward . . .', Hauptmann Gaum, 3rd Bn, CSDIC, TNA WO 208/3610

'declined to move in that . . .', Generalmajor Otto Remer, ETHINT 80 and FMS B-592

p. 173 'There's not the slightest . . .', 18.12.44, GBP

'I feel that you won't like . . .', *PP*, 596

'What the hell . . .', Omar N. Bradley, *A Soldier's Story*, New York, 1964, 469

'A very dangerous operation . . .', *PP*, 597

'the situation up there is . . .', ibid.

11 SKORZENY AND HEYDTE

p. 174 Leutnant Günther Schultz, Mobile Field Interrogation Unit No. 1, NARA RG 407 ML 2279

p. 175 'may have a captured German officer . . .', 21.12.44, CBHD

Bradley security precautions, 22.12.44, CBHD

'Question the driver because . . .', 344/1/A TNA WO 171/4184

p. 176 'What is Sinatra's first name?', 21.12.44, PWS

'Only a kraut would . . .', quoted Danny S. Parker (ed.), *Hitler's Ardennes Offensive: The German View of the Battle of the Bulge*, London, 1997, 172

'I haven't the faintest idea . . .', David Niven, *The Moon's a Balloon*, London, 1994, 258

'General, if I were you . . .', Lord Tryon, conversation with author, 6.2.2013

Gerhardt Unger and Gunther Wertheim, Ernest Unger, conversation with author, 13.12.2012

p. 177 'We were sentenced to death . . .', TNA WO 171/4184

Aywaille, NARA RG 407 E 427 (270/65/8-9/6-1) ML 7, Box 24201

Vichy Milice and the SS *Charlemagne* Division, TNA WO 171/4184

p. 178 'the women sang in clear strong . . .', etc., 25.12.44, CBHD

'visibility was almost nil', Brigadier A. W. Brown, IWM Documents 13781 73/18/1

'swept up the bridge', 25.12.44, CBHD

150th Panzer-Brigade, 'Ardennes Offensive', Obersturmbannführer Otto Skorzeny, ETHINT 12

p. 179 'hindering the operation of the corps . . .', SS-Oberstgruppenführer Sepp Dietrich, ETHINT 15

'amateurish, almost frivolous . . .', Heydte, FMS B-823

Kampfgruppe Heydte, CSDIC, TNA WO 208/5541 SIR 1444; also TNA WO 208/3628, TNA WO 208/3612

p. 180 wire across road, NARA RG 498 290/56/2, Box 1456

'ambushed, captured and . . .', V Corps, NARA RG 498 290/56/2/3, Box 1455

'taken off believing . . .', 18.12.44, GBP; and V Corps, NARA RG 498 290/56/2/3, Box 1455

Failure to report parachutes found, NARA RG 498 290/56/2/3, Box 1459

Heydte Kampfgruppe casualties, ibid.

12 TUESDAY 19 DECEMBER

p. 182 Peiper Kampfgruppe at Stoumont, Peiper, FMS C-004

p. 183 Saint-Edouard sanatorium, Peter Schrijvers, *The Unknown Dead: Civilians in the Battle of the Bulge*, Lexington, KY, 2005, 54–6

'From his place of concealment . . .', V Corps, NARA RG 498 290/56/2/3, Box 1455

p. 184 'Our battalion advanced . . .', TNA WO 311/54

'Some of them came along . . .', conversation with Obergefreiter Pompe of the 18th Volksgrenadier-Division, CSDIC, TNA WO 311/54

105th Engineer Battalion, NARA RG 407 290/56/5/1–3, Box 7

3rd Fallschirmjäger, Faymonville, Operations of the Sixth Panzer Army, FMS A-924

p. 186 'poor physical specimens', etc., Kurt Vonnegut, C-Span, New Orleans, 30.5.95

'showers, warm beds . . .', NARA RG 407 E 427-A (270/65/4/7)

'Do not flee . . .', CBMP, Box 4

'the largest surrender . . .', Kurt Vonnegut, C-Span, New Orleans, 30.5.95

p. 187 'inferred that the two . . .', Colonel Walter Stanton, deputy chief of staff VIII Corps, NARA RG 407 270/65/8/2 ML 299

'Endless columns of prisoners . . .',

Diary of Oberleutnant Behman, Maurice Delaval Collection, Box 7, USAMHI

'licking its wounds', RWHP, Box 1

'the only Jerries we found . . .', etc., ibid.

p. 188 'hysterical and a nervous wreck . . .', Hauptmann Gaum, 3rd Battalion *Führer Begleit* Brigade, CSDIC, TNA WO 208/3611

'lifted the man's head up . . .', Hans Post, *One Man in his Time*, Sydney, 2002, 170

p. 189 'an ugly professional . . .', Ralph Ingersoll, *Top Secret*, London, 1946, 162

'fabulous Jeep . . .', 20.12.44, CBHD

'The present situation . . .', etc., Charles B. MacDonald, *A Time for Trumpets: The Untold Story of the Battle of the Bulge*, New York, 1984, 420; Dwight D. Eisenhower, *Crusade in Europe*, London, 1948, 371

p. 190 'On the morning of December 21st . . .', D. K. R. Crosswell, *Beetle: The Life of General Walter Bedell Smith*, Lexington, KY, 2010, 812

p. 190n Patton and date of counterattack, *PP*, 599

p. 190 'Every time I get a new star . . .', *PP*, 600

p. 191 'fighting mad', 'I don't want to commit . . .', 19.12.44, CBHD

'Where are you going?', VIII Corps, NARA RG 407 270/65/8/2 ML 299

The fighting in Wiltz, 'The Breakthrough to Bastogne', typescript, n.d., CMH 8-3.1 AR

p. 192 Scenes in Bastogne, Lieutenant

Ed Shames, in Tim G. W. Holbert, 'Brothers at Bastogne – Easy Company's Toughest Task', *World War II Chronicles*, Winter 2004/5, 22–5

'a hod-carrying . . .', Louis Simpson, *Selected Prose*, New York, 1989, 121

'We have been wiped out', NARA RG 407 270/65/8/2 ML 130

p. 193 'The surprise was complete', Generalmajor Heinz Kokott, 26th Volksgrenadier-Division, FMS B-040

p. 194 'painful losses', ibid.

'The enemy had made . . .', ibid.

Panzer Lehr draining fuel tanks, Generalleutnant Fritz Bayerlein, FMS A-941

'day of surprises', ibid.

'not sufficiently coherent . . .', ibid.

'Ammunition and rations . . .', Kokott, FMS B-040

20th Armored Infantry at Noville, William R. Desobry Papers, USAMHI, and NARA RG 407 270/65/8/2 ML 130

p. 196 'to go through the whole daggone . . .', NARA RG 407 270/65/8/2 ML 130

'They spread out . . .', William R. Desobry Papers, USAMHI

p. 197 'You know those sound . . .', Holbert, 'Brothers at Bastogne – Easy Company's Toughest Task', 22–5

'Go on back . . .', quoted George E. Koskimaki, *The Battered Bastards of Bastogne: The 101st Airborne in the Battle of the Bulge*, New York, 2007, 113

Capture of 326th Field Hospital, CMH *Medical*, 409–14

p. 198 Desobry's fortunes, William R. Desobry Papers, USAMHI

'laid in rows . . .', CMH *Medical*, 414

'We arrive at First Army HQ . . .', Carol Mather, *When the Grass Stops Growing*, Barnsley, 1997, 284–7

p. 199 'got any bloody tanks . . .', ibid., 286

'oddly deserted countryside', 'He is considerably . . .', ibid., 287

'clearly alarmed', etc., ibid.

p. 200 'Limey bastards', Crosswell, 814

p. 201 'Certainly if Monty's were . . .', CMH *SC*, 378

'By God, Ike . . .', Kenneth Strong, *Intelligence at the Top*, London, 1970, 226

'absolutely livid . . . walked up and down . . .', Coningham, FCP *SC*

'Montgomery for a long time . . .', Bedell Smith, FCP *SC*

'as the personal inspiration . . .', Ingersoll, 205

'as a slam to me', Chester B. Hansen Collection, Box 42, S-25, USAMHI

13 WEDNESDAY 20 DECEMBER

p. 202 'extremely delicate', Carol Mather, *When the Grass Stops Growing*, Barnsley, 1997, 287

'completely out of touch', Sir Carol Mather docs., IWM, 11/28/1 5

'On the important question . . .', ibid.

p. 203 'Monty, we are in a bit . . .', Dempsey, FCP *SC*

'like Christ . . .', quoted Nigel Hamilton, *Monty: Master of the Battlefield 1942–1944*, London, 1984, 213

'What's the form?', 'It was a slight . . .', Mather, 288

p. 203n 'The General is now well located . . .', 23.12.44, PWS

p. 204 'the weakest commander . . .', Bedell Smith, FCP *SC*

'whether we can hold . . .', 21.12.44, PWS

'We sandwiched the thermite grenades . . .', Ralph Ingersoll, *Top Secret*, London, 1946, 200

'The best way to handle . . .', 'The Ardennes', CSI Battlebook 10-A, May 1984

p. 205 'four inside and eleven . . .', ibid.

'Schloss Hemingstein 1944', Carlos Baker, *Ernest Hemingway: A Life Story*, New York, 1969, 558

p. 206 'caused a considerable waste . . .', Generalmajor Siegfried von Waldenburg, 116th Panzer-Division, FMS A-873

Easy Company, Lieutenant Ed Shames, in Tim G. W. Holbert, 'Brothers at Bastogne – Easy Company's Toughest Task', *World War II Chronicles*, Winter 2004/5, 22–5

Retreat from Noville, Charles B. MacDonald, *A Time for Trumpets: The Untold Story of the Battle of the Bulge*, New York, 1984, 499–500

'the fog up front . . .', 'Dead were lying . . .', quoted Peter Schrijvers, *Those Who Hold Bastogne*, New Haven, CN, 2014, 63

p. 207 'The 2nd Panzer . . .', etc., Generalmajor Heinz Kokott, 26th Volksgrenadier-Division, FMS B-040

p. 207n 'considered Bastogne . . .', Generalleutnant Fritz Bayerlein, Panzer Lehr Division, FMS A-941

p. 207 'Is Bastogne to be . . .', Kokott, FMS B-040.

p. 208 'The Division dutifully . . .', ibid.

'the deep rumble . . .', ibid.

'with devastating . . .', ibid.

p. 210 'seated negligently . . .', Louis Simpson, *Selected Prose*, New York, 1989, 137–8

p. 211 Action at Cheneux, Charles B. MacDonald, *The Battle of the Bulge*, London, 1984, 448–9

'still very bad', etc., RWHP, Box 1

p. 212 'We stressed to every . . .', Maj. Donald P. Boyer Jr, S-3, 'Narrative Account of Action of 38th Armored Infantry Battalion', n.d., RWHP, Box 1

Führer Begleit Brigade, Generalmajor Otto Remer, ETHINT 80

'neck-deep', etc., Mack Morriss, 'The Defense of Stavelot', *Yank*, 9.2.45

p. 213 SS atrocities in Stavelot, NARA RG 407 290/56/5/1–3, Box 7

Fighting in Stavelot on 20 December, ibid.

p. 214 'for the most part impassable . . .', Operations of the Sixth Panzer Army, FMS A-924

'under almost continuous . . .', V Corps, NARA RG 498 290/56/2/3, Box 1455

p. 215 Items taken from Camp Elsenborn,

Richard H. Byers, 'The Battle of the Bulge', Richard H. Byers Papers, Box 1, USAMHI

'Sherman Ecke', 'The concentrated ...', 3rd Panzergrenadier-Division, FMS A-978

p. 216 'Farmers learned to take ...', Peter Schrijvers, *The Unknown Dead: Civilians in the Battle of the Bulge*, Lexington, KY, 2005, 30

'a ring of steel', MacDonald, *A Time for Trumpets*, 406

'Soon I noticed that ...', Arthur S. Couch, 'An American Infantry Soldier in World War II Europe', unpublished memoir, private collection

p. 217 German casualties, MacDonald, *A Time for Trumpets*, 407

'That is precisely ...', Martin Lindsay, *So Few Got Through*, Barnsley, 2000, 161

Movement order to XXX Corps, TNA WO 231/30

'bombed-up, tanked up ...', J. W. Cunningham, IWM Documents 15439 06/126/1

'a small but steady ...', Brigadier A. W. Brown, IWM Documents 13781 73/18/1

p. 218 'I felt that we were all right ...', Bedell Smith, FCP *SC*

'clamped down ...', *Time*, 1.1.45

'Personally I would like to shoot ...', 21.12.44, Hobart Gay Papers, USAMHI

'disastrous results ...', Memo, R. H. C. Drummond-Wolff, chief, Liberated Territories Desk, PWD, 21.12.44, C. D. Jackson Papers, Box 3, DDE Lib

p. 219 'The wholly unexpected ...', Fritz Hockenjos, Kriegstagebuch, BA-MA, MsG2 4038

'You cannot imagine ...', LHC-DP, No. 217, II, 5, quoted Ian Kershaw, *The End: Hitler's Germany 1944–45*, London, 2011, 156

'Be practical ...', Antony Beevor, *Berlin: The Downfall 1945*, London, 2002, 1

'Just rumble forward ...', CSDIC, TNA WO 208/4364 GRGG 235/6

p. 220 'The old principle of tank warfare: "forward, forward, forward!" ...', ibid.

'This offensive is terrific!', ibid.

'That man will never ...', ibid.

'It's Wednesday ...', ibid.

14 THURSDAY 21 DECEMBER

p. 221 'pocketed without adequate supplies', Peiper, FMS C-004

Detilleux, Wanne and Refat, Peter Schrijvers, *The Unknown Dead: Civilians in the Battle of the Bulge*, Lexington, KY, 2005, 57–8

'duck shooting', NARA RG 407 290/56/5/1–3, Box 7

'After we saw ...', Mack Morriss, 'The Defense of Stavelot', *Yank*, 9.2.45

p. 222 'The prisoner bag is thus far small ...', 21.12.44, PWS

'Prisoners from the 12th SS?', 24.12.44, CBHD

'caked in mud', 'The GIs looked . . .', 21.12.44, CBHD

'General Collins is full . . .', 21.12.44, PWS

p. 223 'Monty would come . . .', J. Lawton Collins, SOOHP, Box 1, USAMHI

Hasbrouck and Clarke on Ridgway, Jonathan M. Soffer, *General Matthew B. Ridgway*, Westport, CN, 1998, 71

'dread Panzerfaust', etc., Major Donald P. Boyer Jr, RWHP, Box 1

'would prove to be . . .', ibid.

'Huge gashes . . .', etc., ibid.

p. 224 'Reform. Save what vehicles . . .', RWHP, Box 1

p. 225 St Vith and the St Josef Kloster; 'He took a chalice . . .', Schrijvers, *Unknown Dead*, 169

I&R Platoon, 423rd Infantry, 106th Division, Richard D. Sparks, 'A Walk through the Woods', 2003, http://www.ryansdom.com/theryans/sparks/adobe/walk2.pdf

p. 226 'a God-sent gift', etc., Generalmajor Siegfried von Waldenburg, 116th Panzer-Division, FMS A-873

'It was known . . .', 4th SS Panzergrenadier-Regiment *Der Führer*, FMS P-109b

'The troops began slowly . . .', Waldenburg, FMS A-873

p. 227 Tenneville, NARA RG 407 270/65/8/2 ML 130

'Ike and [Major General] Bull . . .', *PP*, 603

p. 228 Kokott and stragglers, NARA RG 407 270/65/8/2 ML 130

'It was like a tremendous . . .', Robert Harwick, 'Christmas for Real!', *The Magazine of the Gulf Companies*, November–December 1945, 70–1

p. 229 'Two prisoners came back', ibid.

'One, terrified . . .', ibid.

p. 230 The decision to send a negotiator to Bastogne, General der Panzertruppe Heinrich von Lüttwitz, XLVII Panzer Corps, FMS A-939

'After he was finished . . .', George E. Koskimaki, *The Battered Bastards of Bastogne: The 101st Airborne in the Battle of the Bulge*, New York, 2007, 148

15 FRIDAY 22 DECEMBER

p. 232 'Your orders are . . .', Maurice Delaval Collection, Box 7, USAMHI

p. 233 'We crawled wearily . . .', etc., I&R Platoon, 423rd Infantry, 106th Division, Richard D. Sparks, 'A Walk through the Woods', 2003, http://www.ryansdom.com/theryans/sparks/adobe/walk2.pdf

'As we crossed . . .', Sam Bordelon, ibid.

p. 234 'I am throwing in . . .', 22.12.44, RWHP, Box 1

'You have accomplished . . .', Misc'l AG Records, NARA RG 407 E 427 2280, Box 2425

p. 235 'The line troops vowed . . .', Sparks, 'A Walk through the Woods'

'broke the base plates . . .', Misc'l AG

Records, NARA RG 407 E 427 2280, Box 2425

p. 236 Withdrawal across the Salm, ibid.

'What the hell are you . . .', Maurice Delaval Collection, Box 7, USAMHI

Civilians in Bütgenbach, Peter Schrijvers, *The Unknown Dead: Civilians in the Battle of the Bulge*, Lexington, KY, 2005, 26–7

p. 237 Stoumont and SS wounded, NARA RG 407 290/56/5/1–3, Box 7

'very grave', 'conspicuously marked', Peiper, ETHINT 10

'a single infantry division', Generalmajor Heinz Kokott, 26th Volksgrenadier-Division, FMS B-040

p. 238 'In the course of . . .', ibid.

p. 239 Two German soldiers in Mande-Saint-Etienne, André Meurisse, quoted George E. Koskimaki, *The Battered Bastards of Bastogne: The 101st Airborne in the Battle of the Bulge*, New York, 2007, 221–2

p. 240 'I was never worried . . .', Bedell Smith interview, FCP *SC*

'The fog was sitting . . .', J. Lawton Collins, SOOHP, Box 1, USAMHI

'engaged in a fight . . .', John S. D. Eisenhower, *The Bitter Woods*, New York, 1970, 453

Advance on Marche, General der Panzertruppe Heinrich von Lüttwitz, XLVII Panzer Corps, FMS A-939

23rd Hussars report, William H. Simpson Papers, Box 11, USAMHI

p. 241 High ground south-west of Marche, Oberstleutnant Rüdiger Weiz,

2nd Panzer-Division, FMS B-456

p. 242 Change of route for 116th Panzer-Division, Generalmajor Siegfried von Waldenburg, FMS A-873

p. 243 'a veritable postcard scene . . .', 22.12.44, CBHD

'acutely worried over . . .', ibid.

'The enemy is making . . .', Eisenhower, *Bitter Woods*, 422

'kept his head magnificently . . .', CMH *SC*, 381

p. 244 'We learned that the . . .', Ralph Ingersoll, *Top Secret*, London, 1946, 201–4

16 SATURDAY 23 DECEMBER

p. 245 'visibility unlimited', CMH *Ardennes*, 468

'God damn! . . .', John S. D. Eisenhower, *The Bitter Woods*, New York, 1970, 424

'As soon as the enemy . . .', Generalleutnant Karl Thoholte, 'Army Group B Artillery in the Ardennes', FMS B-311

p. 245–6 Jemelle repeater station, ETO Historical Division, NARA RG 498 290/57/17/6

p. 246 Airdrops to Task Force Hogan, Royce L. Thompson, 'Air Resupply to Isolated Units, Ardennes Campaign', OCMH, Feb. 1951, typescript, CMH 2-3.7 AE P

p. 248 'Position considerably worsened . . .', General der Waffen-SS H. Priess, I SS Panzer Corps, FMS A-877

p. 249 'American troops are now refusing . . .', William H. Simpson Papers, Box 11, USAMHI

Civilians in Faymonville, Peter Schrijvers, *The Unknown Dead: Civilians in the Battle of the Bulge*, Lexington, KY, 2005, 27–8

p. 250 'Manteuffel's report that he could not . . .', Major Herbert Büchs, ETHINT 34

'up to ten men . . .', Generalmajor Heinz Kokott, 26th Volksgrenadier-Division, FMS B-040

p. 251 'The first enemy . . .', 'Towards noon . . .', ibid.

'Houses caught fire . . .', ibid.

p. 252 '*Achtung!* Strong enemy . . .', ibid.

Pathfinders and drop, Thompson, 'Air Resupply to Isolated Units, Ardennes Campaign'

'The first thing you saw . . .', Martin Wolfe, *Green Light!*, Philadelphia, PA, 1989, 348

'cheering them wildly . . .', George E. Koskimaki, *The Battered Bastards of Bastogne: The 101st Airborne in the Battle of the Bulge*, New York, 2007, 257

p. 253 'Watching those bundles . . .', ibid.

'but the bottles . . .', CMH *Medical*, 420

'Not a single German aircraft . . .', Kokott, FMS B-040

p. 254 'From then on', Koskimaki, 147

'in this cold . . .', Louis Simpson, *Selected Prose*, New York, 1989, 138

'I peer down the slope . . .', ibid., 139

p. 255 Allocation of air assets on 23.12.44, NARA RG 498 290/56/2/3, Box 1455

Friendly fire and 'Rules for Firing', V Corps, ibid.

'chipper and confident as usual', 22.12.44, PWS

'The German push . . .', A. J. Cowdery, Civil Affairs, IWM Documents 17395 10/18/1

p. 257 'battle-weary Shermans', Derrick Jones, IWM Documents 4309

'That's not a pig . . .', Henry Dubois, cited Jean-Michel Delvaux, *La Bataille des Ardennes autour de Rochefort*, 2 vols., Hubaille, 2004–5, i, 333

p. 258 Chapois, Jean-Michel Delvaux, *La Bataille des Ardennes autour de Celles*, Hubaille, 2003, 38–9

'But the road is mined . . .', ibid., 81–2

p. 260 'Right, let's go! . . .', CMH *Ardennes*, 437

p. 261 Civilians in Rochefort, Delvaux, *Rochefort*, i, 238–9 and ii, 236

'I wish to direct . . .', 23.12.44, FDRL MR

17   SUNDAY 24 DECEMBER

p. 262 'almost hysterical with . . .', 24.12.44, CBHD

'clinging stubbornly . . .', ibid.

'Today a quartermaster soldier . . .', ibid.

p. 263 'General Patton was in . . .', ibid.

'blew everything in sight', 'The Intervention of the Third Army: III

Corps in the Attack', typescript, n.d., CMH 8-3.1 AR

'it was usually . . .', VIII Corps, Third Army, NARA RG 498 290/56/2/3, Box 1463

'rations were frequently . . .', VII Corps, NARA RG 498 290/56/2/3, Box 1459

p. 264 German snipers, NARA RG 498, 290/56/5/2, Box 3

Combat observer reports, VIII Corps, Third Army, NARA RG 498 290/56/2/3, Box 1463

p. 265 Aid men, ibid.

p. 266 'Knocking out tanks . . .', ibid.

p. 268 'corruption and profiteering', 'So far these people . . .', Generalmajor Ludwig Heilmann, 5th Fallschirmjäger-Division, FMS B-023

'the enemy managed . . .', Robert R. Summers et al., 'Armor at Bastogne', Armored School, Advanced Course, May 1949, CARL N-2146.71-2

'Our company commander . . .', 24.12.44, Diary of Robert Calvert Jr, Company C, 51st Armored Infantry Battalion, 4th Armored Division, *American Valor Quarterly*, Summer 2008, 22

p. 269 'Attacking waves . . .', NARA RG 407 290/56/5/1–3, Box 7

p. 270 'Despite the air's . . .', 24.12.44, PWS

'but apparently received little . . .', 8.1.45, CBHD

p. 271 'morale in the 82nd . . .', John S. D. Eisenhower, *The Bitter Woods*, New York, 1970, 449

82nd Airborne keeping German corpses, William A. Carter, typescript, 1983, CEOH, Box V, 14, XII, 22

'An SS-Führer told me . . .', CSDIC, TNA WO 208/4140 SRM 1150

p. 272 'bitter and ever-changing', Generalmajor Siegfried von Waldenburg, 116th Panzer-Division, FMS A-873

'*beaucoup* dead', VII Corps, NARA RG 498 290/56/2/3, Box 1459

'Of the German Luftwaffe . . .', Waldenburg, FMS A-873

p. 272–3 3rd Royal Tank Regiment at Sorinnes, Brigadier A. W. Brown, IWM Documents 13781 73/18/1

p. 273 'if forced', David W. Hogan Jr, *A Command Post at War: First Army Headquarters in Europe, 1943–1945*, Washington, DC, 2000, 223

'The bastards are in . . .', Eisenhower, *Bitter Woods*, 466

p. 274 'If necessary, elements . . .', Oberstleutnant Rüdiger Weiz, 2nd Panzer-Division, FMS B-456

'since both pockets . . .', ibid.

p. 274–5 Bande massacre and Léon Praile, see Jean-Michel Delvaux, *La Bataille des Ardennes autour de Rochefort*, 2 vols., Hubaille, 2004–5, i, 17–41

Sondereinheitkommando 8, A. J. Cowdery, Civil Affairs, IWM Documents 17395 10/18/1

p. 275 'After the deed was done . . .', TNA WO 171/4184

p. 276 'It's the greatest imposture . . .', Heinz Guderian, *Panzer Leader*, New York, 1996, 310–11

Hemingway and Gellhorn, Carlos Baker, *Ernest Hemingway: A Life Story*, New York, 1969, 558–9

p. 277 Wounded in Bastogne, CMH *Medical*, 418

'Do not plan . . .', Stanley Weintraub, *Eleven Days in December*, New York, 2006, 137

'Tomorrow we will cross . . .', Simone Hesbois, quoted Delvaux, *Rochefort*, i, 328–9

Liliane Delhomme, Rochefort, Delvaux, *Rochefort*, ii, 240

p. 278 Frozen C-Rations, Gerald Astor, *Battling Buzzards: The Odyssey of the 517th Parachute Regimental Combat Team 1943–1945*, New York, 1993, 300

'The fellows are calling . . .', PFC Warren Wilson, Coy I, 2nd Bn, 395th Inf., Weintraub, 125

'this General of stern expression . . .', Frederick A. McDonald, *Remembered Light: Glass Fragments from World War II*, San Francisco, 2007, 29

18   CHRISTMAS DAY

p. 279 The bombing of Bastogne, Peter Schrijvers, *Those Who Hold Bastogne*, New Haven, CN, 2014, 119–20

p. 280 'taken, lost and re-taken', Generalmajor Heinz Kokott, 26th Volksgrenadier-Division, FMS B-040

'strip and repair weapons . . .', 502nd Parachute Infantry Regiment, VIII Corps, NARA RG 498 290/56/2/3, Box 1463

p. 281 'The Germans piled out . . .', PFC Leonard Schwartz, George E. Koskimaki, *The Battered Bastards of Bastogne: The 101st Airborne in the Battle of the Bulge*, New York, 2007, 325

'buttoned up', 502nd Parachute Infantry Regiment, VIII Corps, NARA RG 498 290/56/2/3, Box 1463

p. 282 'success seemed very close', Kokott, FMS B-040

'The Germans attacked our . . .', Cpl Jackson of the 502nd Parachute Infantry Regiment, VIII Corps, NARA RG 498 290/56/5/2, Box 3

'cut off and annihilated', Kokott, FMS B-040

p. 283 'We were 900 metres . . .', TNA WO 311/54

'irresponsible and unfeasible', 'bloody, dubious and costly . . .', Kokott, FMS B-040

Airdrop on Christmas Day, Royce L. Thompson, 'Air Resupply to Isolated Units, Ardennes Campaign', OCMH, Feb. 1951, typescript, CMH 2-3.7 AE P

'We have been let down', NARA RG 407 270/65/8/2 ML 130

Lutrebois, 'to lie in wait . . .', NARA RG 498 290/56/5/2, Box 3

p. 284 'We feel like we . . .', Denyse de Coune, 'Souvenirs de guerre: Assenois 1944–5', p. 125, quoted Peter Schrijvers, *The Unknown Dead: Civilians in the Battle of the Bulge*, Lexington, KY, 2005, p. xiii

'showed understanding', General der

Panzertruppe Heinrich von Lüttwitz, XLVII Panzer Corps, FMS A-939

Haid, Jean-Michel Delvaux, *La Bataille des Ardennes autour de Rochefort*, 2 vols., Hubaille, 2004–5, i, 341

p. 285 Advance from Sorinnes, Brigadier A. W. Brown, IWM Documents 13781 73/18/1

p. 286 Armoured vehicles at Celles, TNA WO 231/30

'The Americans were mad . . .', Jean-Michel Delvaux, *La Bataille des Ardennes autour de Celles*, Hubaille, 2003, 103

'divisional units which . . .', Generalmajor Siegfried von Waldenburg, 116th Panzer-Division, FMS A-873

p. 287 'a lot to learn', VIII Corps, NARA RG 498 290/56/2/3, Box 1463

'Their tanks left . . .', VIII Corps, NARA RG 407 270/65/8/2 ML 299

'A clear cold Christmas . . .', *PP*, 606

'It cut deep . . .', Schrijvers, *Unknown Dead*, 31

'The bombers have fine . . .', Richard Henry Byers, 'Battle of the Bulge', typescript, 1983

'like a swarm of wasps', etc., Leutnant Martin Opitz, 295th Volksgrenadier-Division, NARA RG 407 290/56/5/1–3, Box 7

p. 288 'Monty was always expecting . . .', etc., Chester B. Hansen Collection, Box 42, S-7, USAMHI

'the First Army cannot attack . . .', *PP*, 606

p. 289 'I am sure . . .', Chester B. Hansen Collection, Box 42, S-7, USAMHI

p. 289n 'You know, we exploited . . .', Bedell Smith, FCP *SC*

p. 289 'Months Added to War?', *Daily Express*, Stanley Weintraub, *Eleven Days in December*, New York, 2006, 79

19 TUESDAY 26 DECEMBER

p. 290 'The Kraut has stuck . . .', 26.12.44, CBHD

'This has been a very bad . . .', *PP*, 605

p. 291 'Today has been rather . . .', *PP*, 607

The fires in Bastogne, Peter Schrijvers, *Those Who Hold Bastogne*, New Haven, CN, 2014, 130

'cut loose at 300 feet', Royce L. Thompson, 'Air Resupply to Isolated Units, Ardennes Campaign', OCMH, Feb. 1951, typescript, CMH 2-3.7 AE P

'The medical personnel . . .', 26.12.44, CBHD

'many amputations', CMH *Medical*, 422

p. 292 37th Tank Battalion, *American Valor Quarterly*, Summer 2008, 19

Assenois, NARA RG 407 270/65/8/2 ML 130

'it was all over', Generalmajor Rudolf Freiherr von Gersdorff and Generalmajor Heinz Kokott, ETHINT 44

p. 293 'But what spirit!', Major Frank, commander III/13th Fallschirmjäger, CSDIC, TNA WO 208/4140 SRM 1148 'the *Führer Begleit* Brigade . . .', General der Panzertruppe Heinrich von Lüttwitz, XLVII Panzer Corps, ETHINT 42

Martha Gellhorn and Leland Stowe, 26.12.44, CBHD

'Fortunately, the RAF were not . . .', Brigadier A. W. Brown, IWM Documents 13781 73/18/1

p. 294 Order to Kampfgruppe Holtmeyer to withdraw, General der Panzertruppe Heinrich von Lüttwitz, XLVII Panzer Corps, FMS A-939

'Luckily the enemy was . . .', Oberstleutnant Rüdiger Weiz, 2nd Panzer-Division, FMS B-456

'Moi, pas Allemand! . . .', Jean-Michel Delvaux, *La Bataille des Ardennes autour de Rochefort*, 2 vols., Hubaille, 2004–5, i, 218

Buissonville, ibid., 304 and 308

p. 295 'It was estimated that . . .', Colonel Shaffer F. Jarrell, VII Corps, NARA RG 498 290/56/2/3, Box 1459

'a vast cemetery . . .', Jean-Michel Delvaux, *La Bataille des Ardennes autour de Celles*, Hubaille, 2003, 94

'We want to do in Belgium . . .', diary of Sister Alexia Bruyère, 26.12.44, quoted Delvaux, *Rochefort*, i, 143

Surrounded Kampfgruppe of 116th Panzer-Division, Generalmajor Siegfried von Waldenburg, FMS A-873

'motor fuel was so scarce . . .', Generalmajor Otto Remer, ETHINT 80

p. 296 'four or five tanks with . . .', CCA

from 3rd Armored Division, TNA WO 231/30

3rd SS Panzergrenadier-Regiment and Grandménil, FMS P-109

p. 297 'the enemy opened fire . . .', Alfred Zerbel, 3rd SS Panzergrenadier-Regiment *Deutschland*, FMS P-109

'If the soldier does not need . . .', NARA RG 498 290/56/2/3, Box 1463

p. 298 'people were struggling . . .', Peter Schrijvers, *The Unknown Dead: Civilians in the Battle of the Bulge*, Lexington, KY, 2005, 183

'Most of them were burned . . .', ibid., 184

'Saint-Vith is still burning . . .', Leutnant Martin Opitz, 295th Volksgrenadier-Division, NARA RG 407 290/56/5/1–3, Box 7

'a giant heap . . .', ibid.

Bombing campaign, La Roche, TNA WO 231/30

p. 299 'Things continued to look . . .', 26.12.44, PWS

'stagnating conservatism . . .', 26.12.44, CBHD

'Monty is a tired . . .', 27.12.44, *PP*, 608

'*Mein Führer* . . .', etc., Samuel W. Mitcham Jr, *Panzers in Winter*, Mechanicsburg, PA, 2008, 153–4

'traitors', 'I know the war is lost . . .', Nicolaus von Below, *Als Hitlers Adjutant, 1937–1945*, Mainz, 1980, 398

20 PREPARING THE ALLIED COUNTER-OFFENSIVE

p. 300 Airdrop on Bastogne, 27 December, Royce L. Thompson, 'Air Resupply to Isolated Units, Ardennes Campaign', OCMH, Feb. 1951, typescript, CMH 2-3.7 AE P

Belly landing, George E. Koskimaki, *The Battered Bastards of Bastogne: The 101st Airborne in the Battle of the Bulge*, New York, 2007, 365–6

p. 301 'With the enemy attack losing . . .', 'further delay will . . .', 12th Army Group, NARA RG 407 270/65/7/2 ML 209

p. 301n 'counter-attack started too early . . .', 'from total . . .',Generalmajor Siegfried von Waldenburg, 116th Panzer-Division, FMS B-038

p. 301 'high intelligence channels . . .', 28.12.44, PWS

'much smitten with . . .', 28.12.44, CBHD

p. 302 'the Americans have taken . . .', Montgomery letter to Mountbatten, 25.12.44, Nigel Hamilton, *Monty: The Field Marshal 1944–1976*, London, 1986, 238

'in as grave a light . . .', CMH *Ardennes*, 610

'General Hodges has had enough . . .', 27.12.44, PWS

'the most conservative . . .', ibid.

p. 303 'You're going to push . . .',

J. Lawton Collins, SOOHP, USAMHI

'Praise God from . . .', CMH *Ardennes*, 612

'The roads are a sheet of ice . . .', William H. Simpson Papers, Box 11, USAMHI

Montgomery's plan outlined at Zonhoven, Crerar diary, TNA CAB 106/1064

p. 303n 'from four to five panzer divisions', 31.12.44, CBHD

'Americans are very poor . . .', 2.1.45, CBHD

p. 304 'It looks to me as if . . .', Alanbrooke Diary, 30.12.44, LHCMA

'full operational direction . . .', quoted Russell F. Weigley, *Eisenhower's Lieutenants*, Bloomington, IN, 1990, 542–3

p. 305 'Under no circumstances . . .', quoted Hamilton, *Monty: The Field Marshal*, 275

'In your latest letter . . .', DDE Lib, Box 83

'the British public . . .', Eisenhower at SHAEF meeting on 30.12.44, Air Chief Marshal Sir James Robb's notes, NARA RG 319 270/19/5-6/7-1, Boxes 215–16 2-3.7 CB 8

'What shall I do . . .', F. de Guingand, quoted Hamilton, *Monty: The Field Marshal*, 279

'Dear Ike . . .', DDE Lib, Box 83

p. 306 'It was so cold . . .', diary of Robert Calvert Jr, Company C, 51st Armored Infantry Battalion, 4th Armored Division, *American Valor Quarterly*, Summer 2008, 22

p. 307 'a fighter-bomber attack . . .', Generalmajor Otto Remer, ETHINT 80

'ten cargo-carrying . . .', ibid.

'If this attack failed . . .', General der Panzertruppe Heinrich von Lüttwitz, XLVII Panzer Corps, FMS A-939

p. 307–8 Fighting for Chenogne and Sibret, Remer, ETHINT 80

p. 308 'His instructions before . . .', Stephen E. Ambrose, *Band of Brothers*, New York, 2001, 194

p. 309 'Oscar', Koskimaki, 393

p. 310 'Now by God . . .', ibid., 391

35th Division, MFF-7, C1-107

'cut to pieces', CMH *Ardennes*, 626

Battle round Lutrebois, III Corps, NARA RG 498 290/56/5/2, Box 3

'The SS spread the rumor . . .', etc., Generalmajor Ludwig Heilmann, 5th Fallschirmjäger-Division, FMS B-023

p. 311 'These road conditions . . .', Generalmajor Heinz Kokott, 26th Volksgrenadier-Division, FMS B-040

'broke into houses . . .', TNA WO 311/54

'bombers from the Eighth Air Force . . .', Third Army daily log, 31.12.44, Gaffey Papers, USAMHI

'It is obvious that . . .', 30.12.44, CBHD

p. 312 'You could hear . . .', Letter, Eugene A. Watts, S-3, 52nd Armored

Infantry Bn, 9th AD, 28.2.85, CBMP, Box 1

p. 312n Horrocks on medical leave, Hamilton, *Monty: The Field Marshal*, 255–6

p. 312 6th Airborne, Edward Horrell, IWM Documents 17408 10/4/1

p. 313 Belgians and abandoned German equipment, Jean-Michel Delvaux, *La Bataille des Ardennes autour de Celles*, Hubaille, 2003, 40

Dead German officer, ibid., 36

p. 314 'The Ardennes has a pronounced . . .', A. J. Cowdery, Civil Affairs, IWM Documents 17395 10/18/1

p. 315 'with his beret and . . .', Liliane Delhomme, Jean-Michel Delvaux, *La Bataille des Ardennes autour de Rochefort*, 2 vols., Hubaille, 2004–5, ii, 241

Lance-Sergeant Walker, Letter to author from his son, Air Marshal Sir David Walker, 27.4.14

highballs and turkey, William H. Simpson Papers, Box 11, USAMHI

'In his mess every night . . .', G. Patrick Murray, 1973, SOOHP

'indiscriminately firing . . .', 31.12.44, PWS

'talked passionately . . .', etc., 31.12.44, CBHD

p. 316 'At midnight all was still . . .', Ursula von Kardorff, *Diary of a Nightmare: Berlin 1942–1945*, London, 1965, 161

'My prayer . . .', Leutnant Martin Opitz, 295th Volksgrenadier-Division, NARA RG 407 290/56/5/1–3, Box 7

21 THE DOUBLE SURPRISE

p. 318 'The Reichsmarschall has . . .', *HLB*, 514, 517

'They are all young . . .', Fähnrich Schmid, CSDIC, TNA WO 208/4134 SRA 5615

'What sort of training . . .', Oberleutnant Hartigs, 4/JG 26, CSDIC, TNA WO 208/4135 SRA 5767

'engine trouble', CSDIC, TNA WO 208/4134 SRA 5515

'used to fly . . .', Hartigs, CSDIC, TNA WO 208/4135 SRA 5764 20/1/45

'In our Staffel . . .', Feldwebel Halbritter, CSDIC, TNA WO 208/4134 SRA 5569

'seems to have run . . .', CSDIC, TNA WO 208/4135 SRA 5760 23/1/45

p. 319 'Well, what's our Reichsmarschall . . .', CSDIC, TNA WO 208/4177

'He had no understanding . . .', CSDIC, TNA WO 208/4292 USAFE/M.72

'practically cried', 'unless we . . .', CSDIC, TNA WO 208/4164 SRX 21091

'take-off' rations, ibid.

'poured out his troubles . . .', Oberstleutnant Johann Kogler, CSDIC, TNA WO 208/4177

'the worst-informed . . .', CSDIC, TNA WO 208/4178

'Herr General . . .', CSDIC, TNA WO 208/4177

p. 320 'We had been stationed . . .',

Oberleutnant Hartigs, FW 190 4/JG 26, CSDIC, TNA WO 208/4164 SRX 2086

'Whoever [returns after failing] to attack . . .', ibid.

'What a smashing . . .', CSDIC, TNA WO 208/4164 SRX 2086

p. 321 'One frustrated Typhoon pilot . . .', Sebastian Cox of the Air Historical Branch of the Ministry of Defence, e-mail to author, 18.8.14. I am most grateful for his corrections and precise figures for aircraft losses on both sides

'closely parked in formation', 1.1.45, PWS

'They caught the British . . .', 2.1.45, PWS

'Mid-morning saw . . .', William H. Simpson Papers, Box 11, USAMHI

p. 322 'which tore a large hole . . .', Sebastian Cox, e-mail to author, 18.8.14

'Jerry made one big error . . .', William H. Simpson Papers, Box 11, USAMHI

'A catastrophe overtook . . .', Nicolaus von Below, *Als Hitlers Adjutant, 1937–1945*, Mainz, 1980, 399

p. 324 'Spirits have reached a new low . . .', letter to Colonel Waine Archer from Colonel Pete T. Heffner Jr, 3.1.45, NARA RG 498 290/56/5/3, Box 1463

Panic in Strasbourg, NARA RG 331, SHAEF records (290/715/2) E-240P, Box 38

'It is self-evident . . .', Charles de Gaulle, *Mémoires de Guerre: Le Salut, 1944–1946*, Paris, 1959, 145

p. 325 'Juin said things . . .', James Robb diary, DDE Lib, Papers, Pre-Pres., Box 98

'the French Army would get . . .', Dwight D. Eisenhower, *Crusade in Europe*, London, 1948, 396

'If we were involved . . .', De Gaulle, *Mémoires de Guerre: Le Salut, 1944–1946*, 148

'This modification . . .', 'I think we've done . . .', Eisenhower, *Crusade in Europe*, 396

p. 326 'It suggested that . . .', 4.1.45, DCD

'in high spirits', letter to Colonel Waine Archer from Colonel Pete T. Heffner Jr, 5.1.45, NARA RG 498 290/56/5/3, Box 1463

'next to the weather . . .', *PDDE*, iv, 2491

'signal intelligence to . . .', 3.1.45, TNA HW 14/119

'This presents a serious . . .', ibid.

'simply refused . . .', Thomas E. Griess, 14.10.70, York County Heritage Trust, York, PA, Box 94

p. 327 'surprised, captured or surrounded . . .', VI Corps, NARA RG 498 290/56/5/3, Box 1463

p. 328 'attempt to discredit the Americans', Chester B. Hansen Collection, Box 42, S-28, USAMHI

'the public clamor . . .', 6.1.45, CBHD

'wouldn't serve one day . . .', 8.1.45, CBHD

'repudiate the efficacy . . .', ibid.

'the German breakthrough . . .', etc., 6.1.45, CBHD

p. 329 'At the same time . . .', 5.1.45, CBHD

'invaluable', TNA CAB 106/1107

'The battle has been most interesting . . .', etc., TNA CAB 106/1107

p. 330 'although this statement . . .', ibid.

'The Battle of the Ardennes . . .', ibid.

'return it to me . . .', 'I wanted it back . . .', 8.1.45, CBHD

p. 331 'I fear great offence . . .', TNA CAB 106/1107

22 COUNTER-ATTACK

p. 332 'a defensive success . . .', etc., Generalmajor Otto Remer, ETHINT 80

'The 11th Armored is . . .', 4.1.45, *PP*, 615

p. 333 'There were some unfortunate . . .', ibid.

'a bitter cold . . .', CBHD, Box 5

'continued to pour destruction', Ed Cunningham, 'The Cooks and Clerks', *Yank*, 16.3.45

p. 335 'Units frequently make errors . . .', Lt Col. Glavin, G-3 6th Armored Division, VII Corps, NARA RG 498 290/56/2/3, Box 1459

'If you enter a village . . .', 6th Armored Division, NARA RG 498 290/56/5/2, Box 3

p. 336 11th Armored Division, CMH *Ardennes*, 647

'The 17th Airborne, which attacked this . . .', 4.1.45, *PP*, 615

'We have had replacements . . .', 17th Airborne, NARA RG 498 290/56/5/2, Box 3

'The German follows a fixed form . . .', etc., ibid.

p. 337 'Our men had great confidence . . .', Colonel J. R. Pierce, NARA RG 498 290/56/5/2, Box 3

Using artillery to dig foxholes, VII Corps, NARA RG 498 290/56/2/3, Box 1459

'The 17th has suffered . . .', 8.1.45, CBHD

Sergeant Isidore Jachman, Congressional Medal of Honor Library, vol. i, 172–3, Peter Schrijvers, *Those Who Hold Bastogne*, New Haven, CN, 2014, 225

'saw a rifleman . . .', VIII Corps, NARA RG 498 290/56/2/3, Box 1463

p. 338 'all for putting . . .', etc., *PP*, 615

'Roads were icy . . .', etc., 3.1.45, PWS

'A lucky tree burst . . .', William H. Simpson Papers, Box 11, USAMHI

'Trois Ponts was cleared . . .', 3.1.45, PWS

p. 339 'greatly pleased with . . .', ibid.

'the 2nd Armored Division . . .', 4.1.45, CBHD

Fighting for Bure, War Diary, 13th Bn Parachute Regiment, TNA WO 171/1246

p. 340 Yvonne Louviaux, in Jean-Michel

Delvaux, *La Bataille des Ardennes autour de Rochefort*, 2 vols., Hubaille, 2004–5, ii, 123–4

p. 341 'this headquarters thought . . .', 6.1.45, PWS

'declare there's no evidence . . .', 7.1.45, Hobart Gay Papers, USAMHI

'Undoubtedly the hard fighting . . .', José Cugnon, quoted Delvaux, *Rochefort*, ii, 28

'they certainly did not seem . . .', ibid., i, 232

'At 09.30, we saw . . .', diary of Sister Alexia Bruyère, quoted ibid., i, 143

p. 342n 'O little town of Houffalize . . .', *PP*, 632

p. 342 'Resistance never let up . . .', Captain H. O. Sweet, IWM, 95/33/1

p. 343 'Everyone thinks . . .', NARA RG 165, Entry 178, Box 146353

'Anyone taken prisoner . . .', CSDIC, TNA WO 208/4157 SRN 4772 25/3/45

'Do not get the impression . . .', Major Gen. Kenneth Strong 02/14/2 3/25 – Intelligence Notes No. 33, IWM Documents 11656

'When the Germans are having . . .', etc., NARA RG 498 290/56/2/3, Box 1459

p. 344 'were more meek . . .', MFF-7, C1-107

'Too good treatment . . .', VIII Corps, NARA RG 498 290/56/2/3, Box 1463

'We have never been . . .', NARA RG 498 290/56/2/3, Box 1466

Forcing German prisoners to walk

barefoot, Gerald Astor, *A Blood-Dimmed Tide*, New York, 1992, 375

'prisoners were beginning . . .', TNA WO 231/30

Pozit fuses, V Corps, NARA RG 498 290/56/2/3, Box 1455

'The results of these . . .', VII Corps, NARA RG 498 290/56/2/3, Box 1459

p. 345 'If we want to win the war . . .', Generalmajor Ludwig Heilmann, 5th Fallschirmjäger-Division, FMS B-023

'If there is any suspicion . . .', CSDIC, TNA WO 208/3616 SIR 1548

'Ten or twelve . . .', Feldwebel Rösner, 7th Battery, 26th Volksgrenadier-Division, TNA WO 311/54

'I nearly gagged . . .', Robert M. Bowen, *Fighting with the Screaming Eagles: With the 101st Airborne from Normandy to Bastogne*, London 2001, 204–5

'The wounded . . .', Assistant Arzt Dammann, CSDIC, TNA WO 208/3616 SIR 1573

'Chamber of Horrors', etc., 'Shock Nurse', Ernest O. Hauser, *Saturday Evening Post*, 10.3.45

p. 346 Non-battle casualties, CMH *Medical*, 385–6

'nausea, crying . . .', VII Corps, NARA RG 498 290/56/2/3, Box 1459

'When one man cracks . . .', ibid.

'Tank fatigue', ibid.

'long hours of exposure', ibid.

'Even with hard and experienced . . .', 5th Infantry Division, XX Corps, NARA RG 498 290/56/2/3, Box 1465

p. 347 2nd and 9th Panzer-Divisions,

General der Panzertruppe Heinrich von Lüttwitz, XLVII Panzer Corps, FMS A-939

'It is the coldest weather . . .', 8.1.45, A. J. Cowdery, Civil Affairs, IWM Documents 17395 10/18/1

'The Führer has ordered . . .', *HLB*, 597

'It's the greatest mockery . . .', Generalmajor Hans Bruhn, 533rd Volksgrenadier-Division, CSDIC, TNA WO 208/4364 GRGG 240

'The Germans are pulling . . .', 11.1.45, William H. Simpson Papers, Box 11, USAMHI

p. 348n 'We are aware of your views . . .', to Major General Clayton Bissell, TNA WO 171/4184

p. 348 'like the heavens . . .', Colonel Liebisch, *Art of War Symposium*, US Army War College, Carlisle, PA, 1986, 617

'Forward into the fascist . . .', *Velikaya Otechestvennaya Voina*, Moscow, 1999, iii, 26

p. 349 'had enabled the Russian . . .', 15.1.45, CBHD

'The fear of Russia . . .', Generalleutnant von Heyking, 6th Fallschirmjäger-Division, TNA WO 171/4184

23 FLATTENING THE BULGE

p. 351 'What gets me . . .', quoted Air Marshal Sir James Robb, 'Higher

Direction of War', typescript, 11.46, provided by his daughter

'My God, don't they have . . .', Stephen E. Ambrose, *Band of Brothers*, New York, 2001, 229

'Every replacement . . .', Tim G. W. Holbert, 'Brothers at Bastogne – Easy Company's Toughest Task', *World War II Chronicles*, Winter 2004/5, 22–5

p. 352 2nd Battalion, 506th at Rachamps, Ambrose, *Band of Brothers*, 223–4

'violent enemy . . .', NARA RG 498 290/56/5/3, Box 1463

p. 353 'Having visited villages . . .', 14.1.45, A. J. Cowdery, Civil Affairs, IWM Documents 17395 10/18/1

'the troops have been over-enthusiastic . . .', A. Fieber, 1st Bn, Manchester Rgt, in 53rd (Welsh) Div., IWM Documents 4050 84/50/1

'The right wing . . .', 2nd Panzer-Division, FMS P-109e

p. 354 'He was trying to thaw him out . . .', Martin Lindsay, *So Few Got Through*, Barnsley, 2000, 160

'Very soon an American . . .', 2nd Panzer-Division, FMS P-109e

'brick houses . . .', etc., MFF-7, C1-100/101

'At one point . . .', Patton, quoted Gerald Astor, *A Blood-Dimmed Tide*, New York, 1992, 366

p. 355 'Contact was established . . .', Armored School, Fort Knox, General Instruction Dept, 16.4.48, CARL N-18000.127

'The Division does not . . .', quoted

H. Essame, *The Battle for Germany*, London, 1970, 117

'The situation is now restored', 17.1.45, CBHD

'At 10.30 the Field Marshal . . .', William H. Simpson Papers, Box 11, USAMHI

p. 356 'That "protect the Ninth's . . .', ibid.

'the United States troops . . .', TNA CAB 106/1107

p. 357 Telephone transcript, William H. Simpson Papers, Box 11, USAMHI

'First and Third US Armies in . . .', Montgomery to Brooke, 14.1.45, Nigel Hamilton, *Monty: The Field Marshal 1944–1976*, London, 1986, 325

'Any future moves . . .', William H. Simpson Papers, Box 11, USAMHI

'His forces are now relegated . . .', 2.12.44, CBHD

p. 358n Whiteley, not Bedell Smith, D. K. R. Crosswell, *Beetle: The Life of General Walter Bedell Smith*, Lexington, KY, 2010, 853

p. 358 'The reputation and the good will . . .', 24.1.45, Hobart Gay Papers, USAMHI

'The town is in ruins . . .', NARA RG 407 E 427 2280, Box 2425

XIX TAC claims, CMH *SC*, 395 n. 111

'The three tactical air forces . . .', Joint Report No. 1 by Operational Research Section 2nd Tactical Air Force and No. 2 Operational Research Section, 21st Army Group, TNA WO 231/30 'did not play a decisive . . .', General-major Siegfried von Waldenburg, 116th Panzer-Division, FMS B-038

p. 359 'The Third Army today . . .', 29.1.45, CBHD

'He is a good officer . . .', *PP*, 630

'a tremendous palace . . .', William H. Simpson Papers, Box 11, USAMHI

'compelled to ransack . . .', 'Eagle Took', 16.1.45, CBHD

'his customary slow . . .', 4.2.45, CBHD

p. 360 'passed scarred and . . .', ibid.

Belgian civilian casualties, CMH *SC*, 332

'tremendous number . . .', 25.1.45, A. J. Cowdery, Civil Affairs, IWM Documents 17395 10/18/1

p. 361 Damage in La Roche, Peter Schrijvers, *The Unknown Dead: Civilians in the Battle of the Bulge*, Lexington, KY, 2005, 325

24 CONCLUSIONS

p. 363 Trial of Kampfgruppe Peiper, FMS C-004

p. 365 'The criticism whether it . . .', Interrogation of Generalfeldmarschall Keitel and Generaloberst Jodl, 20.7.45, TNA WO 231/30

Falling back to the Meuse, Seventh Army, FMS A-876

'The promptness with which . . .', Generaloberst Alfred Jodl, FMS A-928

'no other army in the world . . .', 24.12.44, CBHD

p. 366 'Officers and men . . .', Generalmajor Rudolf Freiherr von Gersdorff, FMS A-933

'Every day that . . .', 'the last gasp . . .', Generalleutnant Fritz Bayerlein, Panzer Lehr Division, FMS A-941

'a major point . . .', quoted D. K. R. Crosswell, *Beetle: The Life of General Walter Bedell Smith*, Lexington, KY, 2010, 837

p. 366–7 Churchill recognizing the graver consequence, Churchill to Ismay, 10.1.45, TNA PREM 3 4 31/2

p. 367n 'He's a psychopath . . .', Cornelius J. Ryan Collection, Ohio University, Box 43, file 7, typescript, n.d.

p. 367 Allied casualties in the Ardennes, CMH *SC*, 396; and Royce L. Thompson, OCMH, typescript, 28.4.52, CMH 2-3.7 AE P-15

'Not for God and country . . .', Gerald K. Johnson, 'The Black Soldiers in the Ardennes', *Soldiers*, February 1981, 16ff.

p. 368 'the Germans made us take off . . .', etc., 'The Service Diary of German War Prisoner #315136', Sgt John P. Kline, Coy M, 3rd Battalion, 423rd Infantry Regiment, CBMP, Box 2

'xylophone ribs . . .', etc., 19.4.45, GBP

p. 369 '5,000 mile stare', Vonnegut on C-Span, New Orleans, 30.5.95

Select Bibliography

Ambrose, Stephen E., *Band of Brothers*, New York, 2001

Arend, Guy Franz, *Bastogne et la Bataille des Ardennes*, Bastogne, 1974

Astor, Gerald, *A Blood-Dimmed Tide*, New York, 1992

—— *Battling Buzzards: The Odyssey of the 517th Parachute Regimental Combat Team 1943–1945*, New York, 1993

Atkinson, Rick, *The Guns at Last Light*, New York, 2013

Baker, Carlos, *Ernest Hemingway: A Life Story*, New York, 1969

Bauer, Eddy, *L'Offensive des Ardennes*, Paris, 1983

Bedell Smith, Walter, *Eisenhower's Six Great Decisions*, London, 1956

Beevor, Antony, *Berlin: The Downfall 1945*, London, 2002

—— *The Second World War*, London, 2012

Beevor, Antony, and Cooper, Artemis, *Paris after the Liberation, 1944–1949*, London, 1994

Belchem, David, *All in the Day's March*, London, 1978

Below, Nicolaus von, *Als Hitlers Adjutant, 1937–1945*, Mainz, 1980

Bennet, Ralph, *Ultra in the West*, New York, 1980

Boberach, Heinz (ed.), *Meldungen aus dem Reich: Die geheimen Lageberichte des Sicherheitsdienstes der SS 1938–1945*, 17 vols., Herrsching, 1984

Botsford, Gardner, *A Life of Privilege, Mostly*, New York, 2003

Bowen, Robert M., *Fighting with the Screaming Eagles: With the 101st Airborne from Normandy to Bastogne*, London 2001

Bradley, Omar N., *A Soldier's Story*, New York, 1964

Buckley, John, *Monty's Men: The British Army and the Liberation of Europe*, London, 2013

Cole, Hugh M., *United States Army in World War II: The European Theater of Operations: The Ardennes: Battle of the Bulge*, Washington, DC, 1988
Connell, J. Mark, *Ardennes: The Battle of the Bulge*, London, 2003
Couch, Arthur S., 'An American Infantry Soldier in World War II Europe', unpublished memoir, private collection
Crosswell, D. K. R., *Beetle: The Life of General Walter Bedell Smith*, Lexington, KY, 2010

D'Este, Carlo, *Eisenhower: Allied Supreme Commander*, London, 2002
De Gaulle, Charles, *Mémoires de Guerre: Le Salut, 1944–1946*, Paris, 1959
Delvaux, Jean-Michel, *La Bataille des Ardennes autour de Celles*, Hubaille, 2003
—— *La Bataille des Ardennes autour de Rochefort*, 2 vols., Hubaille, 2004–5
Domarus, Max (ed.), *Reden und Proklamationen 1932–1945*, Wiesbaden, 1973
Doubler, Michael D., *Closing with the Enemy: How GIs fought the War in Europe, 1944–1945*, Lawrence, KS, 1994
Dupuy, Colonel R. Ernest, *St. Vith: Lion in the Way: The 106th Infantry Division in World War II*, Washington, DC, 1949

Eisenhower, Dwight D., *Crusade in Europe*, London, 1948
Eisenhower, John S. D., *The Bitter Woods*, New York, 1970
Ellis, John, *The Sharp End: The Fighting Man in World War II*, London, 1990
Elstob, P., *Bastogne: La Bataille des Ardennes*, Paris, 1968
Ent, Uzal W. (ed.), *The First Century: A History of the 28th Infantry Division*, Harrisburg, PA, 1979
Essame, H. *The Battle for Germany*, London, 1970
Evans, Richard J., *The Third Reich at War*, London, 2008

Ferguson, Niall, *The War of the World*, London, 2007
Forty, George, *The Reich's Last Gamble: The Ardennes Offensive, December 1944*, London, 2000
Friedrich, Jörg, *Der Brand: Deutschland im Bombenkrieg 1940–1945*, Berlin, 2002
Fussell, Paul, *The Boys' Crusade*, New York, 2003

Galtier-Boissière, Jean, *Mon journal pendant l'Occupation*, Paris, 1944

Gehlen, Reinhard, *The Gehlen Memoirs*, London, 1972

Gellhorn, Martha, *Point of No Return*, New York, 1989

Gilbert, Martin, *The Second World War*, London, 1989

Guderian, Heinz, *Panzer Leader*, New York, 1996

Hamilton, Nigel, *Monty: Master of the Battlefield 1942–1944*, London, 1984

—— *Monty: The Field Marshal 1944–1976*, London, 1986

Hastings, Max, *Armageddon: The Battle for Germany 1944–45*, London, 2004

—— *Finest Years: Churchill as Warlord, 1940–45*, London, 2009

Heiber, Helmut, and Glantz, David M. (eds.), *Hitler and his Generals: Military Conferences 1942–1945*, London, 2002; *Hitlers Lagebesprechungen: Die Protokollfragmente seiner militärischen Konferenzen 1942–1945*, Munich, 1984

Hemingway, Ernest, *Across the River and into the Trees*, New York, 1950

Henke, Klaus-Dietmar, *Die amerikanische Besetzung Deutschlands*, Munich, 1995

Hitchcock, William I., *Liberation: The Bitter Road to Freedom: Europe 1944–1945*, London, 2009

Hogan, David W., Jr, *A Command Post at War: First Army Headquarters in Europe, 1943–1945*, Washington, DC, 2000

Horrocks, Brian, *Corps Commander*, London, 1977

Hynes, Samuel, *The Soldiers' Tale: Bearing Witness to Modern War*, London, 1998

Ingersoll, Ralph, *Top Secret*, London, 1946

Isaacson, Walter, *Kissinger: A Biography*, London, 1992

Jordan, David, *The Battle of the Bulge: The First 24 Hours*, London, 2003

Jung, Hermann, *Die Ardennen-Offensive 1944/45: Ein Beispiel für die Kriegführung Hitlers*, Göttingen, 1971

Junge, Traudl, *Until the Final Hour: Hitler's Last Secretary*, London, 2002

Kardorff, Ursula von, *Diary of a Nightmare: Berlin 1942–1945*, London, 1965

Kershaw, Alex, *The Longest Winter*, New York, 2004

Kershaw, Ian, *Hitler 1936–1945: Nemesis*, London 2000

—— *The End: Hitler's Germany 1944–45*, London, 2011

Kershaw, Robert, *It Never Snows in September*, London, 2008

Klemperer, Victor, *To the Bitter End: The Diaries of Victor Klemperer, 1942–45*, London, 2000

Koskimaki, George E., *The Battered Bastards of Bastogne: The 101st Airborne in the Battle of the Bulge*, New York, 2007

Lacouture, Jean, *De Gaulle: Le Politique*, Paris, 1985
Lindsay, Martin, *So Few Got Through*, Barnsley, 2000
Ludewig, Joachim, *Rückzug: The German Retreat from France, 1944*, Lexington, KY, 2012

MacDonald, Charles B., *A Time for Trumpets: The Untold Story of the Battle of the Bulge*, New York, 1984; *The Battle of the Bulge*, London, 1984
—— *The Mighty Endeavour: The American War in Europe*, New York, 1992
—— *Company Commander*, New York, 2002
—— *The Battle of the Huertgen Forest*, Philadelphia, PA, 2003
McDonald, Frederick A., *Remembered Light: Glass Fragments from World War II*, San Francisco, 2007
Massu, Jacques, *Sept ans avec Leclerc*, Paris, 1974
Mather, Carol, *When the Grass Stops Growing*, Barnsley, 1997
Merriam, Robert E., *Dark December*, New York, 1947
—— *The Battle of the Bulge*, New York, 1991
Meyer, Hubert, *The 12th SS: The History of the Hitler Youth Panzer Division*, vol. ii, Mechanicsburg, PA, 2005
Miller, Edward G., *A Dark and Bloody Ground: The Hürtgen Forest and the Roer River Dams, 1944–1945*, College Station, TX, 2008
Mitcham, Samuel W., Jr, *Panzers in Winter*, Mechanicsburg, PA, 2008
Moorehead, Caroline, *Martha Gellhorn*, London, 2003
Mortimer Moore, William, *Free France's Lion: The Life of Philippe Leclerc*, Havertown, PA, 2011

Neillands, Robin, *The Battle for the Rhine 1944: Arnhem and the Ardennes*, London, 2006
Neitzel, Sönke, and Welzer, Harald, *Soldaten: On Fighting, Killing and Dying*, New York, 2012
Niven, David, *The Moon's a Balloon*, London, 1994
Nobécourt, Jacques, *Le Dernier Coup de dés de Hitler*, Paris, 1962

Overmans, Rüdiger, *Deutsche militärische Verluste im Zweiten Weltkrieg*, Munich, 2000

Parker, Danny S. (ed.), *Hitler's Ardennes Offensive: The German View of the Battle of the Bulge*, London, 1997

Pogue, Forrest C., *The Supreme Command*, Washington, DC, 1954

—— *George C. Marshall: Organizer of Victory*, New York, 1973

—— *Pogue's War: Diaries of a WWII Combat Historian*, Lexington, KY, 2001

Post, Hans, *One Man in his Time*, Sydney, 2002

Ritchie, Sebastian, *Arnhem: Myth and Reality: Airborne Warfare, Air Power and the Failure of Operation Market Garden*, London, 2011

Roberts, Andrew, *Masters and Commanders*, London, 2008

Roberts, Mary Louise, *Foreign Affairs: Sex, Power, and American G.I.s in France, 1944–1946*, Chicago, 2013

Schrijvers, Peter, *The Crash of Ruin: American Combat Soldiers in Europe during World War II*, New York, 1998

—— *The Unknown Dead: Civilians in the Battle of the Bulge*, Lexington, KY, 2005

—— *Liberators: The Allies and Belgian Society, 1944–1945*, Cambridge, 2009

—— *Those Who Hold Bastogne*, New Haven, CN, 2014

Sears, Stephen W., *The Battle of the Bulge*, New York, 2004

Simpson, Louis, *Selected Prose*, New York, 1989

Soffer, Jonathan M., *General Matthew B. Ridgway*, Westport, CN, 1998

Speer, Albert, *Inside the Third Reich*, London, 1971

Spoto, Donald, *Blue Angel: The Life of Marlene Dietrich*, New York, 1992

Stargardt, Nicholas, *Witnesses of War: Children's Lives under the Nazis*, London, 2005

Sterling Rush, Robert, *Hell in Hürtgen Forest: The Ordeal and Triumph of an American Infantry Regiment*, Lawrence, KS, 2001

Strawson, John, *The Battle for the Ardennes*, London, 1972

Strong, Kenneth, *Intelligence at the Top*, London, 1970

Tedder, Arthur, *With Prejudice*, London, 1966

Van Creveld, Martin L., *Fighting Power: German and U.S. Army Performance, 1939–1945*, Westport, CN, 1982

Vassiltchikov, Marie 'Missie', *The Berlin Diaries, 1940–1945*, London, 1987

Weigley, Russell F., *Eisenhower's Lieutenants*, Bloomington, IN, 1990

Weinberg, Gerhard L., *A World at Arms: A Global History of World War II*, Cambridge, 1994

Weintraub, Stanley, *Eleven Days in December*, New York, 2006

Welch, David, *Propaganda and the German Cinema 1933–1945*, Oxford, 1983

Whiting, Charles, *The Battle of Hürtgen Forest*, Stroud, 2007

Wijers, Hans J. (ed.), *The Battle of the Bulge: The Losheim Gap, Doorway to the Meuse*, Brummen, 2001

Wilmot, Chester, *The Struggle for Europe*, London, 1952

Wingeate Pike, David, 'Oberbefehl West: Armeegruppe G: Les Armées allemandes dans le Midi de la France', *Guerres Mondiales et conflits contemporains*, Nos. 152, 164, 174, 181

Winton, Harold R., *Corps Commanders of the Bulge: Six American Generals and Victory in the Ardennes*, Lawrence, KS, 2007

Wolfe, Martin, *Green Light!*, Philadelphia, PA, 1989

Zimmermann, John, *Pflicht zum Untergang: Die deutsche Kriegführung im Westen des Reiches, 1944/45*, Paderborn, 2009

Acknowledgements

A book like this could not have been researched without an enormous amount of help from friends and strangers. I am above all deeply grateful to Rick Atkinson, who generously passed me all his research notes on the period. These proved an excellent guide, saving me much time in the early stages in the archives when one is apt to flounder.

I also owe a great deal to many others who deserve my heartfelt thanks. Le comte Hadelin de Liedekerke Beaufort, on whose estates round Celles the German spearhead of the 2nd Panzer-Division was smashed, not only invited me to stay. He also put me in touch with M. Jean-Michel Delvaux, the historian of civilian experiences in the region of Celles and Rochefort during the war, and whose own impressive work was a huge help. HSH le duc d'Arenberg, on whose estate the 116th Panzer-Division fought, kindly arranged for his steward, M. Paul Gobiet, to drive me around to all the places of interest.

Sebastian Cox, the head of the Air Historical Branch at the Ministry of Defence, provided general advice on the use of airpower and was especially helpful on the details of Operation *Bodenplatte*. Orlando Figes put me in touch with his uncle Ernest Unger, who kindly related the story of Gerhardt Unger. Ron Schroer of the Australian War Memorial contacted Hans Post, who kindly provided his memoir and tapes of his interviews on his experiences in the SS during the campaign. Professor Tami Davis Biddle of the US Army War College, Sir Max Hastings, Dr Stefan Goebel and James Holland all helped with advice, material and books.

I am also indebted to Ronald Blunden, my publisher in France, for the papers of his father, Godfrey Blunden; Mrs Anne Induni, the daughter of Air Marshal Sir James Robb, the Deputy Chief of Staff (Air) at SHAEF, for her father's paper 'Higher Direction of War', written at Bentley Priory in November 1946; and Dr Arthur S. Couch for his unpublished memoir of the winter of 1944.

I naturally owe a great deal to the help and good advice of archivists, including William Spencer and his colleagues at The National Archives at Kew; Dr Conrad Crane, Dr Richard Sommers and all the staff at USAMHI, Carlisle, Pennsylvania; Dr Tim Nenninger and Richard Peuser at the NARA at College Park, Maryland; the staff at the Liddell Hart Centre for Military Archives at King's College London and the staff at the Imperial War Museum. Harland Evans helped me gather material at The National Archives, the IWM and the Liddell Hart Centre.

Finally I am forever grateful to my agent and friend Andrew Nurnberg, as well as Robin Straus in the United States, and also Eleo Gordon, my editor at Penguin in London, and Kathryn Court in New York. Peter James again proved to be the ideal copy-editor, but my greatest thanks as always go to my wife and editor of first resort, Artemis. The book is dedicated to our son Adam, who achieved a First in Modern History while I was writing some of the most complex chapters and thus spurred me on to greater effort.

Index

The Ardennes
Furthest point of German advance
25 December 1944

Liège

R. Meuse

Amay

Huy

Andenne

Namur

R. Ourthe

B E L G I U M

Soy

Gr

Dinant

Celles

Hotton

Marche-en-Famenne

R. Lesse

Jemelle

La Roche

Rochefort

Givet

Tennevill

Vonêche

Saint-Hubert

R. Meuse

Libramont

Neufchâteau

F R A N C E

Mézières

Sedan

R. Semois

0   5   10   15   20 km